ASSEGAIS, DRUMS
AND DRAGOONS

Without their history, cultures doom themselves to remain trapped
in the most illusionary tense of all, namely the present.
For, when trapped in the present, you become akin to a child.
You know not whence you came, nor whither you go.
— CICERO, 64 BC

Every man thinks meanly of himself for not having been a soldier.
— DR SAMUEL JOHNSON

The boundaries of a nation's greatness are marked by the graves
of her soldiers.
— NAPOLEON I

Let us be clear about three facts. First, all battles and all wars are won
in the end by the infantryman. Secondly, the infantryman always bears
the brunt. His casualties are heavier, he suffers greater extremes of
discomfort and fatigue than the other arms. Thirdly, the art of the
infantryman is less stereotyped and far harder to acquire in modern war
than that of any other arm … The infantryman has to use initiative
and intelligence in almost every step he moves, every action he takes on the
battle-field. We ought therefore to put our men of best intelligence
and endurance into the Infantry.
— FIELD-MARSHAL EARL WAVELL

ASSEGAIS, DRUMS AND DRAGOONS

A Military and Social History of the Cape
1510–1806

Willem Steenkamp

JONATHAN BALL PUBLISHERS
JOHANNESBURG & CAPE TOWN

Originally published in South Africa in trade paperback in 2012 by
JONATHAN BALL PUBLISHERS (PTY) LTD
PO Box 33977
Jeppestown
2043

ISBN 978 1-86842-479-5

Also available as an ebook

Twitter: www.twitter.com/JonathanBallPub
Facebook: www.facebook.com/pages/Jonathan-Ball-Publishers/298034457992
Blog: http://jonathanball.bookslive.co.za/

Cover design by Michiel Botha, Cape Town
Text design by Triple M Design, Johannesburg
Maps by William Smuts Maps & Illustrations, Wales
Illustrations by James Berrange, Cape Town
Printed and bound by CTP Printers, Cape Town
Set in 10.75/15 pt Plantin Std Light

CONTENTS

FOREWORD

This book stemmed from a request to the author by the South African Infantry Association that he write an informal history of the South African infantryman of all races through all the eras of this country. The association's requirements were not onerous, but they were very much to the point.

Firstly, the book must be neither a learned treatise on warfare nor a military history textbook. Instead, it must be as readable as possible for both the dedicated military specialist and anybody else, whether of military background or not, who has an interest in the subject – particularly South Africa's soldiers and ex-soldiers themselves.

Secondly, it must not be a hagiography but an attempt to tell the South African infantry story through the ages, without fear or favour. Thirdly, it must tell the story of events, not the exploits of individual regiments, except where this is necessary.

The end result, so it was hoped, would be a narrative, told in an entertaining but instructive way, of South African infantrymen of all races and nations throughout the recorded social history of our country, and in the context of that history.

That was the original intention. Not long after undertaking this task, however, it was apparent that the story of how the South African infantry soldier came to be was more complicated than it appeared, and that to compress the entire story into one volume would be a fruitless exercise.

If it was to serve any real purpose it must start by illuminating a largely lightless corner in South African military historical writing – the period between the 16th century, when parts of what is now South Africa first connected with the outside world, and the beginning of the 19th century, the opening years of what might be called the pre-modern era.

During that period a basic footprint was trodden into the sub-continent's soil as a symbiosis began to take place between indigenous warriors and soldiers trained in European doctrine which was to reach full flower in the 19th century.

What this book is about, therefore, is the genesis of the South African foot soldier of today – that small, usually dirty, frequently over-tired and often hungry figure – without whom an army cannot ring the gong of victory and in warfare there is no second prize. He did not spring up full-grown out of the ground at the wave of some magician's wand. He grew to what he is today through an evolutionary process, both social and military, that took several centuries.

The book has another aim, which is to foster the respect that real fighting soldiers often conceive for one another after they have laid down their arms, a respect that transcends differences of race, religion and belief that politicians, propagandists and others seek to keep alive to serve their own base purposes. They have yet to learn that if you unfairly denigrate your former enemy, you denigrate yourself in the process as well.

It is definitely not the final word on the subject, because there is a great deal that South African military historians have yet to unearth, about both the distant and the recent past. So this book must be seen for what it is, the starting point of a process, and it is hoped that it will serve as a reference work for future military authors delving into the many aspects of our military heritage which remain largely or totally untouched.

Major-General Jack Turner
HONORARY PRESIDENT, SA INFANTRY ASSOCIATION

Brigadier-General John Lizamore
NATIONAL CHAIRMAN, SA INFANTRY ASSOCIATION

INTRODUCTION

When the South African Infantry Association asked me in 2006 whether I would be interested in writing a book about the South African infantryman, it set in motion a sequence of events for which I had been preparing myself in any case.

In January that year I had directed a bicentenary re-enactment of the Battle of Blaauwberg, and it had raised a question for which I had no clear answer. The fiercest resistance to the overwhelmingly larger invading British force in 1806 had come not from Lieutenant-General Jan Willem Janssens' foreign regiments but from a strangely assorted mixture of French sailors, Batavian light horse gunners – and a multiracial army of Cape soldiers: white citizen-warriors from Swellendam, a regiment of coloured infantrymen and a contingent of Malay artillerymen.

Soldiers, particularly volunteers, only fight hard when they are motivated. What motivated the Cape men? I realised I was about to set out on a little reverse engineering when I was approached by the Infantry Association. That provided the spark, and what I discovered resulted in a picture which was considerably different from that painted by various historians of the past.

The result is this book. It is a mixture of social and military history because the men who stood fast on that day of terrifying conflict were shaped by a bewildering variety of influences and events that went back to the beginning of the 16th century. No doubt some readers will take exception to certain statements. All I can say in my defence is that I have gone where the facts have led me.

I have taken the infantry concept to its full extent, to include both foot and mounted soldiers. There is also a good deal about the artillery in it because the infantry and artillery of those days served in close co-ordination – just as the armour and infantry work intimately together in modern times.

Some readers will be disappointed that there is little mention of the great tribal armies of yore in the book. The reason is that the period of the great tribal wars falls outside the time frame within which I worked. All going well, I shall address that matter in another volume; it is a fascinating and vitally important subject about which comparatively little has been written.

Finally, many hands helped to build this book. They include Colonel Lionel Crook, South Africa's foremost artillery historian; Commander Gerry de Vries, founder of the Cannon Association of South Africa; Captain Peter Digby, curator of the Transvaal Scottish Regimental Museum, and a fine historian in his own right; Lieutenant-Colonel Paul Grobbelaar, our greatest expert on the early Cape military forces; Dr Dan Sleigh, the most knowledgeable historian on the early Cape (and the man who first got me interested in Blaauwberg as far back as 1977); and veteran historian Commander MacIan Bissett, a constant source of information.

Then there was Mr Natie Greeff, the ever-helpful curator of the Castle Military Museum; Dr Geoffrey Tribe, who is a scientist by profession but has a passionate interest in the old days; Brent Best, a fine photographer and computer expert, who provided invaluable help with the illustrations; Bill Smuts, an old Blaauwberg enthusiast and cartographer; artist James Berrangé; and Mogamat Hartley and Kammie Kamedien, whom I frequently consulted about the Malay artillerymen of Blaauwberg. I would also be remiss if I failed to mention the indefatigable Ms Louise Jooste of the SANDF Documentation Centre, who supported me from the start; and the committee of the Infantry Association, among them Major-General Deon Mortimer, who made sure I kept going, and Brigadier-General John Lizamore, who gave me a great deal of encouragement.

Last but not least, I would like to give honourable mentions to my wife Andrea, who provided truly vital help with my research and somehow did not get sick and tired of the seemingly endless saga; my publisher, Jonathan Ball and his staff; my editor, Jonathan Downs, a historical writer himself who did a wonderful job of editing the manuscript; and many others, too numerous to name.

Willem Steenkamp

CHAPTER 1

A GOLDEN THREAD IS WOVEN

Many historians date the founding expedition of South Africa to 1652, the year when Jan van Riebeeck arrived at the Cape of Good Hope to establish a ship-repair facility and replenishment station for the Dutch East India Company – better known as the VOC.[1] Here the trading ships could call in on their arduous voyages between the Netherlands and the Company's main trading outpost at Batavia, on the island of Java in today's Indonesia.

However the first strand of that golden thread which winds its way through the chronicles of South Africa's past was woven long before Van Riebeeck set foot on the shores of Table Bay. Historical beginnings can be obscure because they are so often a confluence of different events, large or small; but here we can find four such events which bind the era of the assegai to that of today.

The first was a small but bloody action fought in 1510, almost a century and a half before Van Riebeeck's arrival. At that time Portugal was a major maritime trading nation, its intrepid sailors, fishermen and merchants ranging far and wide in their tiny ships, braving a seemingly endless stream of hair-raising perils, some foreseeable and others not, to establish outposts in the distant corners of the Far East – even as far as the inscrutable and strongly isolationist land of Japan. There they traded in a wide variety of goods, including the pepper, nutmeg and other exotic spices for which Europe had such an apparently inexhaustible appetite.

By the beginning of the 16th century the Portuguese were well established in the Far East, and so it was that on 28 February 1510, a small return-fleet of three caravels heading for home arrived in the bay to take on fresh water and provisions, after the long haul across the Indian Ocean, as passing Portuguese ships had been doing for a number of years.

The commander of the fleet was the nobleman Dom Francisco d'Almeida, who had just spent five years as the viceroy of all Portuguese-controlled areas on the Indian continent and in Ceylon (today's Sri Lanka). His fleet of three merchantmen, the *Garcia, Belem* and *Santa Cruz*, anchored in the bay, probably in the vicinity of today's Salt River, and D'Almeida sent ashore a landing party which duly made contact with an impromptu reception committee consisting of members of a local Khoina clan. It seems to have been an extremely cordial meeting; so cordial in fact that, after successfully trading pieces of iron and cotton cloth for a few head of livestock, a group of 12 or 13 sailors received permission to visit the clan's kraal, which was probably located near the present-day suburb of Mowbray. This second visit started in an atmosphere as cordial as the first, the clan chief reportedly showing great friendliness, but the amicable spirit did not last.

The cause of the sudden breakdown in goodwill has long been lost in the mists of time, and modern theories vary: historian Dr Dan Sleigh[2] quotes Portuguese records, which claimed that the Khoina had pilfered some goods – in response to which the sailors abducted several children to persuade the locals to return the stolen items. Conversely, Lieutenant-Colonel Dr Paul Grobbelaar,[3] says that the sailors did not obtain the quantity of fresh provisions they sought, and abducted a member of the clan to use as a bargaining-chip to get more. Historian PW Laidler[4] claims an entirely different version, that the sailors negotiated with an individual for sheep, then conceived the idea of taking him back to the flagship, dressing him in Portuguese clothes and showing him to D'Almeida before returning him to shore. The Khoina concerned misunderstood their intention and called for help from his clansmen. It has also been claimed that the intention was to take a local to Portugal by whatever means, teach him Portuguese and then return him to the Cape to become a sort of agent-in-place.

Whatever the case, the Khoina did not take this lying down. A hand-to-hand running fight ensued which did not end until the sailors boarded their boats, considerably the worse for wear. On their return to the ships there was some debate among the officers as to the correct reaction. Some took the view that the sailors were to blame and had got what they deserved. Others insisted that the 'insolent barbarians' needed to be punished. At length D'Almeida agreed to take a punitive force ashore the next morning, although not with any enthusiasm; he was 60 years old, a considerable age at that time, and no longer really fit for action. It was a fateful – and, in his case, fatal – decision.

D'Almeida landed with about 150 men who were well-armed with swords, lances and crossbows. It was a formidable force in the circumstances, since the Khoina had no real distance weapons and at most probably numbered no more than a few hundred, women and children included; but their headman (his name, like the exact circumstances that sparked the incident, is now lost beyond recall) had worked out an effective response. He did not attack the Portuguese on the beach, where their crossbows could have been used to the best effect, but let them advance into the heavily bushed coastal area. Eventually the Portuguese reached his kraal, which they found deserted but for some children and a number of calves. Probably feeling considerably uneasy by now, they rounded up the calves and set off back to the beach. Then the Khoina headman made his move. About 150 of his men burst out of the bush and flung themselves on the Portuguese. At first glance it might seem that the Khoina were unduly disadvantaged, but they were armed with fire-hardened spears and poisoned arrows, and they made use of a veritable 'secret weapon' that surprised and disconcerted D'Almeida's men: trained fighting-oxen that could be controlled by whistles or shouts. Above all, they were fighting in familiar terrain and were experts at 'veldcraft'.

The Portuguese were hit by a phalanx of oxen, the Khoina spearmen running behind and between them, effectively protected by the animals from any crossbow bolts that might be fired before they could close in to stabbing range. The Portuguese, their lethal but slow-loading cross-bows almost useless against this sudden and controlled close-quarters onslaught, set off in pell-mell retreat back to the beach. The Khoina kept up the pressure, harassing them with further coordinated attacks. The Portuguese arrived at the beach, having left a number of their shipmates lying dead, and were confronted by yet another disaster: in their absence a stiff breeze had sprung up and the boats had returned to the ships. Backs to the sea, they made a stand while the boats came back for them. But by then between a third and nearly half had died (figures range from 50 to 65), among them D'Almeida himself, as well as several other Portuguese of high birth.

As battles go it was a minor affair, but a noteworthy one. In the short term it was, needless to say, a great embarrassment to the Portuguese, but its long-term consequences affected the history of all of southern Africa and, in fact, territories much further afield. It conferred on the Cape Khoina an undeserved but long-lasting reputation for ferocity, and led to strict enforcement of an earlier directive that banned all Portuguese ships from landings on the lower part of the east and west coasts; this meant that when the Dutch, English and French displaced Portuguese pre-eminence in the Far Eastern trade in the early and mid-17th century, they had free use of the Cape for a replenishment-point, and got to know it well.

Five centuries later, the short, sharp clash between the Khoina and the Portuguese still provides the military historian with some interesting food for thought. The battle plan evolved by that almost forgotten headman, untutored though he was in European military standards of the time, exhibited a sound grasp of what we would now call the principles of war. He fought at a time and place of his own choosing (avoiding the beach, where the Portuguese crossbows would have had the advantage), achieved complete surprise, made good use of the terrain, attacked with maximum violence and speed, did not disengage at any stage but maintained the momentum of the attack and skilfully deployed and coordinated his combat assets, namely his infantry (the spearmen) and 'armour' (the oxen).

The plain fact was that the Portuguese, although doughty fighters themselves, were out-generalled. As a result, a weak local force was able to vanquish a stronger foreign enemy in spite of the theoretical advantages of the relative disparity in numbers (classically, attackers should always significantly outnumber defenders) and the relative qualities of the weapons involved. It was a scenario that in later centuries was to be repeated again and again in southern Africa.

❦

The second strand in this golden thread was drawn a few decades later, when the Dutch nation rose in rebellion against its Spanish overlords. From the early Middle Ages onwards the 17 provinces of the Low Countries (today the Netherlands and Belgium) had once been a fairly independent outpost of the Empire of the Franks. In the 15th century the Low Countries became part of the Habsburg Holy Roman Empire through the marriage of Mary of Burgundy and Maximilian of Austria, who was later crowned Holy Roman Emperor in 1486. In 1555, Maximilian's grandson, Emperor Charles V, made the Low Countries over to his own son, who later became Felipe (Philip) II of Spain.

Philip, ruler of the mighty Spanish Empire, had no great empathy with his subjects in the Low Countries, and in due course his rule over them suffered. The Dutch were a generally peaceful but obdurate people with a history of resistance to foreign domination that went back to the long campaigns of a tribe called the Batavi, waged against the Romans in ancient times; over the years the various indigenous principalities, duchies and bishoprics had developed a vigorous sense of national identity. In the process the area became a hotbed of religious dissent during the Reformation, with Protestantism spreading fast among them. Philip tried to stem the tide by massacring Protestants and unleashing the dreaded Inquisition on the Low Countries – an ancillary aim being to curb the power of the native Dutch nobility. This, however, only made a bad situation worse.

The Spaniards were already as unwelcome as foreign rulers could be. They levied heavy taxes and the Dutch loathed the king's efforts to centralise the ancient and highly devolved regional structures of government, which dated back to medieval times and suited their free-spirited inhabitants. Moreover, the Netherlands were occupied by thousands of arrogant and not particularly well-disciplined Spanish troops who were in the habit of compensating for their low and frequently overdue pay by making free with the lives and possessions of the local inhabitants.

In 1568 a prominent member of the native nobility – William I Prince of Orange, popularly known as Willem de Zwijger (William the Silent)[5] – assumed the leadership of what was to become a general revolt against Spain. The Spaniards soon reconquered the southern provinces of the Low Countries (today's Belgium) but the seven northern provinces, led by Holland, proved a tougher nut to crack. In 1569 they banded together under the terms of the Union of Utrecht; two years later the States-General, which represented the provinces, abrogated its oath of allegiance to Philip II and declared the independence of the Dutch Republic. Then followed eight decades of intermittent warfare that eventually turned the Low Countries into a battleground for virtually all the nations of Europe.

At first sight it must have seemed a laughably uneven struggle: the vast Spanish Empire pitted against a hastily formed federation of seven small provinces with hardly any natural resources or defences between them. However, beneath the surface the picture was considerably less clear-cut. The sprawling Spanish Empire was not as formidable as it appeared, and the rest of Europe was badly disorganised, so that concerted action against the upstart state was not easy. The Dutch, on the other hand, had a strong common purpose. In addition, their extensive world-wide trading activities and a remarkably democratic system of governance for those days had allowed them to accumulate vast wealth with which to finance a long war.

Just as important, they had the good fortune to produce a series of administrative, financial and military leaders of high quality. One of these was Prince Mauritz of Nassau, who had become *stadhouder* or titular head of the United Provinces in succession to his father, William the Silent, assassinated in 1584. Mauritz was a child of the Renaissance, and his particular interest was the reformation of his armed forces. His approach was to review the entire body of military knowledge, starting with the military lessons learnt by the ancient Greeks and particularly by the Romans – the first nation fully to grasp a key fact, over a thousand years before Mauritz's birth, that warfare was primarily a science, and should be prepared for scientifically.

He relied very heavily on the *Taktike Theoria* by the second-century Greek author Aelianus;[6] these writings set out an effective way of controlling infantrymen by a combination of drill movements and commands which made it possible for a body of soldiers to be brought to bear on a target with extreme precision. The decisive 'teeth arm' in Greek and Roman times was the infantry and, very broadly speaking, wars were won mainly by steady, well-disciplined, well-trained, well-handled foot-soldiers.[7]

Mauritz and his think-tank distilled the essence from the accumulated Greek and Roman wisdom, adapted it to the era of firearms and worked out new battle drills, formations and tactics (one of his lesser-known innovations was to standardise small-arms calibres, a great tactical and logistical boon, a given in today's armies). The result was the Staatse Leger, or 'State Army', undoubtedly the best military force in the world at the time.

The efficiency of the Staatse Leger was soon proven. The Dutch began to win victories, culminating in the Battle of Nieuwpoort in 1600. Within a very short time there was not one Spanish soldier left anywhere in the United Provinces. There were still evil times ahead, but in 1648 the Spaniards finally signed the Treaty of Westphalia, which recognised the *de jure* independence of the Dutch Republic.

By that time, the third strand of the golden thread had long since made its appearance on the loom. In 1594 nine Amsterdam merchants had established a joint trading company and sent out a fleet to the Far East the following year, the aim being to break the century-old Portuguese stranglehold on the pepper and spice trade with Asia. The fleet was dogged by misfortune and the pepper it returned with barely covered expenses. But it had proven that the Dutch could use the sea-route around the Cape of Good Hope as well as the Portuguese – and the race was on.

Between 1595 and 1601 at least 15 different companies despatched a total of 65 ships to the East. The money started flowing in, and soon the companies were in fierce competition for the treasures of the spice trade. However, their very success threatened to become a self-inflicted wound: in due course there was an over-supply of pepper and spices, which forced the companies to slash prices to dangerously low levels.

This cut-throat competition posed an obvious danger both to themselves and the Dutch war economy, but they could not bring themselves to do the obvious thing and amalgamate. The situation was saved by the Dutch Government, which was acutely aware not only of the economic danger but also of the fact that the companies were in no condition to assist in the on-going war against the King of Spain (who also ruled Portugal at that time).

The result was that the companies came under irresistible official pressure to amalgamate. On 20 March 1602, the States-General granted a charter to the Generale Vereenigde Geoctroyeerde Oost-Indische Compagnie,[8] or 'General United East India Chartered Company' – today commonly, but not quite correctly, called the Dutch East India Company, and generally abbreviated to 'VOC'.

The VOC consisted of six chambers, each representing a former company, and a board whose directors grandly styled themselves the 'Lords Seventeen'. Its renewable charter was valid for 21 years and stipulated that only the VOC would be able to despatch Dutch ships to transact business anywhere east of the Cape of Good Hope and west of the Strait of Molucca,[9] an immense territory called the *octrooy gebied*, or chartered area.

There were various other provisions which do not concern this discussion, except for one: the stipulation that the VOC would be allowed to maintain a military system modelled on the Staatse Leger, build fortresses where necessary and conclude treaties with local potentates – on the understanding that in time of war all its military assets would be at the disposal of the Dutch Government. For the government, it was a sweetheart deal: in addition to stabilising a vital contributor to the economy, the charter provided a second line of defence at no cost to the nation's coffers. This provision of the VOC charter was to have a decisive impact on the development of the Cape and, eventually, South Africa.

In these days of vast corporations it is difficult to grasp the magnitude of the company that grew from the granting of the charter. Today the Dutch claim that the VOC was the first multi-national company in history, and they are correct. It toppled the Portuguese from their position of commercial supremacy in the Orient, took over their monopoly of contact with Japan and overshadowed its French and English equivalents. Its scale of operations was large even by today's standards: in the 17th century alone it fitted out nearly 1 700 ships, and by the mid-18th century employed 25 000 men at home and abroad, operating a network of trading, ship-repair and replenishment outposts that extended from the Persian Gulf to the China Sea. Even at its demise in 1800, it was still by far the largest trading company in the world. The importance of the huge amount of money it brought into the Dutch economy, particularly during the perilous first half of the 17th century, can hardly be exaggerated.

However, that enormous inflow of wealth did not come easily; to ply between the Netherlands and the outposts at Batavia and elsewhere, the VOC fleets had to undertake long, circuitous and extremely hazardous voyages. In peace-time a VOC fleet, typically consisting of anything from two to five ships, would depart from a port such as Texel and head south, down the English Channel, past Portugal and the Cape Verde Islands. In times of emergency, such as the Anglo-Dutch wars, the fleet would have to battle its way through the inhospitable North Sea and proceed down the stormy west coasts of Scotland and Ireland before taking on the Atlantic. To avoid the contrary winds and currents south of the equator the ships would not hug the coast of Africa but follow a laid-down 'wagon track' across the Atlantic which took them almost to the east coast of Brazil; when they reached the latitude of 30 degrees south, they would swing eastwards towards the Cape of Good Hope.

Voyages were not only arduous but slow, since a typical VOC ship – even the *fluyts*,[10] designed especially for the East India trade – were built for carrying capacity rather than speed, and it could take anything up to four months to make landfall at the Cape. The next leg eastwards and then north-eastwards over the Indian Ocean could take another three months and required precise navigation, no easy task with the

primitive instruments then available[11] or the ships would find themselves heading irresistibly for parts they did not wish to visit, such as
the pirate-infested Straits of Molucca, for example, or the desolate west
coast of the as-yet uncolonised Australia.

It is little wonder that one result of all this was the emergence of a
protean breed of seaman who took in their stride a range of dangers
and difficulties that the modern mariner would blench at. And they
needed that strength and endurance, because the wear and tear on both
ships and men was tremendous. By the time the VOC fleets reached
the Cape on the outward journey the ships were leaking and usually
in dire need of work on hull, masts and rigging, water and provisions
would be scarce, or foul, or both, and each ship's company would have
been decimated by any one of a number of ailments, particularly that
deadly enemy of the blue-water sailor of yore: scurvy, caused by a lack
of fresh food.

It is hardly surprising that the ill-health and loss of life on these
journeys was frequently horrifying. It was not unusual for a ship to
have lost 15% or more of its crew by the time it reached the Cape, with
many of the remainder suffering a range of illnesses. This was not only
tragic but dangerous, as a sail-driven ship relied extensively on skilled
manpower, and a seriously debilitated crew could not operate a vessel
properly. What the VOC needed was a half-way house, an outpost, but
no such place existed. Although VOC ships, like those of other nations,
called in regularly at the Cape on their way to and from Batavia, to collect fuel, replenish their water-casks, cut timber to repair their vessels,
nurse the sick and barter for fresh provender with the Khoina (who
developed into famously sharp bargainers), all of this was done on a
strictly *ad hoc* basis. There was no organised replenishment station.

Then in 1647 the fourth strand was woven into that golden thread
when a VOC merchantman, laden with pepper, the *Nieuw Haerlem*,
was wrecked in Table Bay, near today's Rietvlei.[12] A total of 42 of the
Nieuw Haerlem's occupants made it to shore and set up camp under
two junior merchants (an all-embracing term denoting anything from
administrative officials to actual traders); these two merchants were
Nicolaas Proot and Leendert Jansz or Janzsen.

Most of the *Nieuw Haerlem*'s cargo was salvaged, and the survivors settled down to guard it until they and the pepper could be picked up. They erected tents of timber and canvas for both themselves and the pepper, and constructed a protective all-round earth berm with an impenetrable fence of dried thorn-bushes; they then mounted small cannon on bastions built at strategic places along the earth-shelf of the berm. The survivors spent the next 11 months in their fortified camp, which they named 'Fort Sandenburgh'.

They sustained themselves by hunting, fishing and bartering with the local Khoina, who included the Goringhaicona or 'Strandlopers' (beach-walkers) – led by one Autshomao, also known as 'Harry'. They were a small, feeble pauper-clan whose members owned no cattle or sheep and scratched a living gathering sea-animals from rock pools. Jansz and Proot maintained very cordial relations with the Goringhaicona, and the warmth of these relations is interesting but somewhat puzzling. It is currently the fashion to portray the Khoina of the time as pristine Arcadian folk, uncontaminated by contact with Westerners, but this is not correct.

By 1647 a great number of ships from countries like Portugal, Denmark, France, the Netherlands and England had made landfall at the Cape on their way to or from the Far East. Sporadic incidents of hostility towards visitors had been reported over the years – one point of dispute being an urgent need by visitors for fresh meat, in the face of the Khoina inhabitants' reluctance to part with significant numbers of cattle – but these were not of such a magnitude to justify as drastic an action as the post-1510 Portuguese withdrawal.

It is possible that the Goringhaicona refrained from attacking the shipwrecked crew because they feared their weapons. The Cape's inhabitants were certainly familiar with firearms; as far back as 1595, for example, during the first Dutch expedition to the Far East, cattle that had been acquired by barter at Mossel Bay had been killed by musket-fire, to the astonishment and consternation of the locals. But there were three other clans in the vicinity, two of them so large that they could surely have overwhelmed Jansz and his men in spite of their superior firepower.

Although the Dutchmen's firearms and cannon guarding Fort Sandenburgh provided a strong incentive for peaceful relations, the most likely explanation is that a good trading relationship was more satisfactory to all concerned, given the obviously transient nature of Jansz's and Proot's party and the status it gave to Autshomao and his raggle-taggle band. The fundamentally important fact was that Jansz's party apparently co-existed very comfortably with the Khoina they encountered.

The *Nieuw Haerlem*'s survivors were finally picked up by a return-fleet from Batavia commanded by Wollebrant Geleynsen de Jonge[13] – one of whose passengers was none other than a junior merchant named Jan van Riebeeck, returning home in mild disgrace.

Johan Antoniszoon van Riebeeck,[14] to give him his full name, was a man of considerable experience, although he was only in his early thirties. Born in the Dutch town of Culemborg in 1619, he had followed in his father's footsteps and become an apprentice ship's surgeon at the age of just ten. Later he accompanied his father on at least two voyages for the Dutch West India Company.[15]

In 1638 he accepted a post with the VOC as an assistant surgeon and set off to the Dutch East Indies on 19 April 1639, in the merchant-man *Hof van Holland*, which was bound for Batavia (the VOC's main eastern outpost in Indonesia) with a large sum of money and about 250 soldiers, sailors, labourers, passengers and others. The outward journey was made even longer and more unpleasant by the fact that after three months at sea the *Hof van Holland* ran into a storm and was wrecked on the coast of Sierra Leone. There its crew and passengers spent six miserable months before being picked up by a passing outward-bound fleet.

In September 1640, 15 months after leaving home, Van Riebeeck finally arrived at Batavia, where he laid aside his scalpel and became a 'penner', or clerk. He learnt fast and before long had been promoted to the rank of junior merchant. Then his career was blighted when he followed the example of many of his colleagues and did some private trading to augment his tiny salary. The 'Honourable Company', as it liked to call itself, frowned intermittently on such freelance ventures, although they were quite common. Van Riebeeck was caught in one such crackdown and dismissed from his post, although he stayed in the Company's service and was allowed to retain his rank and salary

– surely an indication that his transgressions had not been taken all that seriously. He was told to return to Amsterdam to await further instructions, and in January 1648 sailed for home in the Indiaman *De Coningh van Polen*. It was on this return journey that they encountered Jansz and his stranded crewmen at the Cape.

For 18 days the fleet lay at anchor in Table Bay while the *Nieuw Haerlem*'s cargo was taken aboard De Jonge's ships. As a supernumerary, Van Riebeeck had no part in this, so he spent his time observing, making detailed notes and holding long discussions with Jansz and Proot. The fleet then sailed away, its departure marred only by an unfortunate last-minute altercation when, having been refused enough livestock for the journey home, some of the VOC men killed seven or eight head of cattle without payment.

This did not prevent Jansz and Proot from describing the Khoina at the Cape as peace-loving, rather than hostile or warlike, when they drew up a *remonstrantie* (memorandum) urging the Lords Seventeen to set up a half-way house at the Cape. Asked for his comments, Van Riebeeck generally endorsed what Jansz and Proot had said, although he was more cautious about the true depth of the locals' love for peace. His observations had convinced him, too, that an outpost at the Cape should include a rather more ambitious fort than Sandenburgh, not just to fend off the Khoina, but also to prevent any attempt from outside to seize the outpost – the specific threat being the English East India Company,[16] the VOC's main rival (and, from 1664 onwards, the French East India Company[17] as well). Perhaps the Lords Seventeen were already thinking about making better use of the Cape, and the memorandum finally swayed them into taking action. The only other operative station known to the VOC at the time lay on the opposite coast.

Outward-bound Portuguese ships customarily sailed around the tip of Africa to the west of Madagascar, to call in at their very effective outpost in Moçambique, (today's Mozambique), but both Dutch and English ships were forced to proceed southeast of the great island and cut directly across the Indian Ocean. As early as 1607 the VOC had tried to capture the Mozambique station, but had been beaten off; had they succeeded, as the historian CR Boxer points out, 'they might never have decided to found a refreshment station at the Cape of Good Hope, and the whole course of South African history would have been profoundly different.'[18]

The VOC's first preference was for St Helena, but acquiring enough fresh meat there was a problem, and its ships had taken to stopping off in Table Bay, where everything they needed was available. Fresh water and naturally occurring fruits and greens, such as the anti-scorbutic wild sorrel, to ward off scurvy were freely obtainable; fish and game were plentiful, and beef and mutton could be had by trading with the indigenous clans. No doubt Van Riebeeck's analysis of the benefits of a Cape outpost struck some sympathetic chords at the notoriously frugal VOC's head office in Amsterdam:

> If, as Leendert [Jansz] proposes, you order your ships to touch at the Cape, I believe that a great deal of preserved provisions would be economised on the outward voyage and likewise wine; for if they pass without touching … the consequence is that the crews are put on short water allowance and the meat and pork are boiled in salt water.
>
> Very little fresh water is given to the crew to drink, but one or two glasses of wine are distributed to make up for it, and though the wine is cordial and strengthening, the sailors remain none the less subject to scurvy and similar diseases in consequence of the staleness of the food.
>
> But refreshed at the Cape, the voyage can, with God's blessing, be safely made to Batavia with the ordinary provisions and wine allowance and fresh water, by which the Company would be greatly benefitted, securing the health of the men and saving a great deal of preserved provisions which are everywhere required in India, while now they are consumed by the crews with the least benefit to themselves.

Whatever the case, on 25 March 1651, the establishment of a Cape outpost was approved, thereby setting in motion a train of events that would drastically alter the history of southern Africa. Van Riebeeck was offered the appointment of commander, and accepted.

It was hardly a plum posting, but the favour of the mighty Lords

Seventeen was not to be spurned, and it is likely that as an intelligent and thoughtful man with experience of the Batavian end of the VOC operation he saw how important the Cape would become in the greater scheme of things. Dr Michael Gelfand suggests one explanation for Van Riebeeck's appointment as commander of the Cape outpost, in spite of his late problem in the Far East:

> While the motivating force behind the settlement of the Cape was economic, it was also intertwined with [the] medical factor, for extension of trade depended on the health of the men who sailed the ships and, to a great extent, the maintenance of their health depended upon winning the battle against scurvy – the sailors' disease.
>
> That the Council of Seventeen were thinking along these lines is underscored by the fact that they put the pioneer settlement under the command of a medical man.[19]

So on the morning of 6 April 1652 Van Riebeeck stepped ashore for the first time after his arrival in Table Bay, accompanied by a small party which included several musketeers carrying the cumbersome matchlock muskets called arquebuses. Their arrival was witnessed by some of the local Khoina, armed with their spears and bows and arrows. The nation of South Africa was about to be born.

CHAPTER 2

THE COMPANY MOVES INLAND: BIRTH OF THE COMMANDO

In popular mythology the arrival of Jan van Riebeeck represents the start of colonialism in South Africa. In fact this is not so. Southward-moving migratory tribal groups and nations, some from beyond the borders of present-day South Africa and others not, had been colonising their neighbours and near-neighbours long before the first Europeans set foot on Africa's southern shores. In fact, the latest of these colonising tribal groups, the Xhosa, was engaged in displacing the indigenous inhabitants south of the Fish River at just about the same time as the VOC's Cape outpost was being established.

This certainly happened at the Cape of Good Hope, which had been invaded and colonised many centuries before the VOC's birth by the people formerly called 'Hottentots' and now known variously as 'Khoi', 'Khoikhoi', 'Khoina', 'Khoisan', 'Khoekhoen', 'Kwekwena', 'Kwena' and 'Quena' – of which 'Kwena' or 'Quena' seem to be the closest phonetic equivalent to what they called themselves, regardless of the currently accepted spelling 'Khoina' (see appendices).

The true origin of the Cape Khoina is a matter of heated controversy, because they have long since vanished as a cohesive population and cultural group. A plausible mainstream theory about how they ended up at the Cape, however, is propagated in the authoritative book

Khoikhoi and the Founding of White South Africa, by the American academic, Prof Richard Elphick of the Wesleyan University, who made an intensive study of the early history of the Cape in the 1970s and 1980s. Elphick holds that they stemmed from certain nomadic hunter-gatherer family groups, roaming in the area of present-day Botswana, who turned themselves into sheep and cattle graziers at some stage in the distant past.

It was a seminal moment in their history. They became skilled at manufacturing spearheads, arrowheads and other implements, and grew taller and stronger than the hunter-gatherers who had remained undifferentiated – possibly because they had more access to milk, a proven growth food (although this is not universally accepted). Elphick speculates that these proto-Khoina did not totally abandon their traditional folk-way. Unlike most other such groups, they did not settle down and become cultivators. They remained nomads who relied on gathering berries and other veld food, but wandered much further afield than their hunter-gatherer forebears because of the perpetual need for water and grazing for their flocks and herds. Separate streams of Khoina started moving south and west at least a thousand years before Jan van Riebeeck's arrival. The westward-bound groups ended up in what is now Namaqualand, while the others meandered southwards and then westwards, which finally brought them to what is now the Cape of Good Hope.

Here they encountered undifferentiated hunter-gatherers and, inevitably, came into conflict with them because of the vastly different paths their cultures and lifestyles had taken.

These hunter-gatherers – whom the Khoina came to label with a variety of insulting names such as 'Sanqua' (which has been variously translated as 'robbers' and 'naked men': see appendices) – probably called themselves by the click-name '!Kung'. A later term for them, 'Bushman', is now considered insulting in some academic circles and is spurned in favour of what Elphick describes as a 'quasi-ethnic' term, 'San'.

The social structure of the San was of the most rudimentary, consisting of family groups of about 25 to 50 people. There was no social hierarchy because all were equal inside that group; they owned nothing and everything, because the riches of the open veld were there for all to harvest according to their needs. However, their Johnny-come-lately opponents, the Khoina, were a different matter altogether. There was no Khoina nation as such; they clustered in large and small clans which could consist of anything from a few score to several thousand members, and which might or might not be connected to others by blood, marriage or common interest – or be bitter enemies. Each clan was strictly hierarchical in structure, with a hereditary chief or headman.

The clans owned no land in the modern sense, but they were no longer pure nomads either, because although they roamed like all livestock-herders, the roaming took place within particular territories to which they claimed customary rights. These rights of occupation were so substantially accepted that it was the practice for strangers to seek permission to use such areas, and hand over some form of gift for the privilege of doing so. This applied particularly to water sources, and simply using a clan's water without going through the traditional formalities was usually regarded as an act of aggression.

The major point of conflict between the Khoina and the original inhabitants was the concept of privately owned domestic livestock. The San hunter-gatherers saw no essential difference between an ox or sheep and a free-roaming antelope. This was intolerable to the Khoina, in whose society a family's wealth and status was measured not by land holdings but by the numbers of livestock it possessed. They clashed repeatedly, and in time the Khoina overwhelmed the hunter-gatherers by a combination of warfare and absorption. Some of the hunter-gatherers became virtual serfs of the Khoina, and every man's hand was turned against those who had not allowed themselves to be absorbed into the conquerors' orbit of influence.

The pre-1652 Cape of Good Hope was not a paradise of peace and plenty. The clans were peculiarly vulnerable to famine and poverty resulting from droughts or livestock diseases, and the constant competition for water and grazing resulted in sporadic cattle-raiding, protracted vendettas and even small wars. Looking back now, there is a curious similarity between the constantly shifting alliances at the Cape and (albeit on a larger scale) those in Europe.

By the time Van Riebeeck arrived, pejorative names were also being applied by more prosperous Khoina to their fellows who had lost their livestock, through war or natural disaster, and had been forced to re-vert to a hunter-gatherer way of life; knowing no better and baffled by the Khoina click-language, the VOC men adopted the names as well, or simply called the hunter-gatherers (or the pauper-Khoina, or both) '*bosjesmannen*', meaning 'Bushmen': people who lived in the bush.

Van Riebeeck and his small contingent of men, women and children knew very little about the Cape, its inhabitants or even its seasons, and part of the steep and often arduous learning curve that awaited them was to make sense of the local military situation with its unsta-ble alliances and deeply rooted custom of preying on others when the circumstances required it. Their ignorance of the traditional protocols concerning land and water use was an added complication.

❦

Neither they nor the Khoina realised just how fragile the long-estab-lished indigenous societal structure was. Up to this time it had not really been affected by the fleeting contacts some of its clans had had with passing ships, but a permanent European presence at the Cape was to cause it to crumble, as a page of an ancient book disintegrates when touched by a human hand.

Richard Elphick identifies two main areas of vulnerability in the Cape's pre-1652 Khoina society. The first was a degree of sophistica-tion after more than a century of trading with passing ships, and the second an extreme individuality resulting from their nomadic cattle-herding way of life, the result being that 'they enjoyed neither the isola-tion of a small-scale society nor the strong traditions and institutions of a large-scale society – both of which can be sources of conservatism':

> The pastoral Khoikhoi were in no way parochial, being well informed of tribes hundreds of miles away to which they were bound by trade, and in many cases common culture. Their perspective was much broader than the local hunting bands which later put up fierce and protracted resistance to European penetration.
>
> Khoikhoi had come to appreciate goods and services which econo-mies other than their own could provide, and consequently they later

showed little hesitation in trading with Europeans. They were familiar with a 'labour' system whereby clients from one tribe worked for employers in another, and they were to have no objections on principle to taking employment in the European colony.

... Confronted by the [European encroachment] on their ancestral pastures, Khoikhoi were to prove comparatively passive; against the threat of rapid social and cultural innovation, they were to offer remarkably little resistance.[1]

However, the 'Honourable Company' of the VOC had a very clear conception of what it wanted at the Cape: a way-station whose primary purpose was not to make a profit but to service the ships proceeding to and from the jewel in the Dutch trading crown, the settlement at Batavia (at today's Indonesian capital of Jakarta). In theory Van Riebeeck's tasks were simple enough, although they were to prove rather more complicated in practice. He was to raise or trade for meat, fruit, grain and vegetables with which to supply passing VOC ships (and other vessels, at a price); establish a repair facility where any damage suffered on passage could be made good; provide for the recuperation of ailing sailors; and generally ensure the safety of the outpost against all internal and external dangers.

He was strictly enjoined against ventures such as establishing a colony, trying to convert the locals to Christianity or making war on them if this could be avoided, since all such pursuits would cost money and be a distraction from his primary task. The VOC was interested in building wealth rather than empires, and what it wanted was a 17th-century version of today's roadside truck-stop, a branch office of Batavia that would be governed according to the Batavian regulations.

The Cape outpost was eventually to grow far beyond what had been planned, and its history was to take several turns not envisaged in the wildest dreams of the Lords Seventeen. This was mainly due to two socio-cultural factors which nobody took into account when the decision to establish the Cape outpost was made.

Firstly, the Khoina were not cultivators, which meant that Van Riebeeck was not able to trade for the large quantities of wheat needed to bake ship's biscuit or bread for the long haul to Batavia; he would have to grow it himself. Secondly, because the Khoina did not regard livestock merely as items of specific value but as status symbols, they were reluctant to barter them away in the numbers Van Riebeeck required.

The fates of nations and peoples often depend on such extraneous considerations: it is conceivable that if Van Riebeeck had been able to obtain enough livestock and grain by barter, the Cape settlement would never have expanded much beyond what the Lords Seventeen had originally envisaged, and the Khoina would have waxed fat during their transition to modern times. As it was, however, the local circumstances gave rise to a number of unforeseen developments that, among other things, soon had military repercussions.

Van Riebeeck came ashore on 6 April 1652 with about 120 men, women and children (including between 70 and 80 soldiers who were also to be used as labourers), a very small number of livestock for breeding purposes, some stores and tools and a set of detailed instructions from the Lords Seventeen in which his priorities were set out.

The origins of his handful of soldiers – the first professional fighting men in southern Africa's history – have always been more or less ignored by most commentators, who have generally assumed that they were Europeans. But it is a fact that at least some of them were '*Mardijkers*',[2] soldiers recruited in Amboina in the southern Molucca Islands archipelago, from which the VOC had earlier expelled the Portuguese. It was not, therefore, an entirely white European force which first landed with Van Riebeeck on the Cape.

Van Ribeeck's first order of business was to bring certain raw materials ashore and construct a 'serviceable wooden building in which to lodge the people and likewise all the tools' as a 'temporary defence against the natives, who are a very rough lot'.[3] One wonders how seriously the Lords Seventeen really were when they wrote this, given the fact that they were virtually marooning him at the edge of the known world with only a handful of soldiers who were also expected to double as labourers.

Once the wooden building had been completed and 'placed in a proper state of defence', he was to construct the 'Fort de Goede Hoop' near the Varsche Riviere, or Fresh River, the stream of sweet mountain water from which generations of passing mariners had refilled their casks. This was to be done in such a way that 'the said river shall be led through or around the fort ... Accommodation shall be provided for 70 or 80 men within the fort in order that the whole garrison may be lodged within it.'

Only then was he to reconnoitre the surrounding countryside for grazing for his livestock and decide on a suitable site where his horticulturalist, the aptly named Hendrik Boom ('Tree' in Dutch), could establish the fruit and vegetable plantation that was such an important part of the outpost's reason for existence.

No doubt he knew from the start just how precarious his situation was. His total military force was laughably small and his resources were even scantier than intended, because a return-fleet that had been scheduled to provide extra provisions and labour had reached the Cape before him, and had not been able to wait for his arrival before departing once again. Van Riebeeck wasted no time. On 10 April 1652, only three days after first going ashore, he had selected the best site for the Fort De Goede Hoop, approximately where part of Cape Town's central post office building stands today, and set his men to work on building the square clay-walled stronghold.

His problems began immediately. The fort's design was not complicated, but late autumn was a bad time of year to start building, and the builders were soon treated to a miserably wet and windy Cape winter, which turned the excavations into morasses of mud, while the newcomers huddled in their leaky tents.

His tiny labour pool soon became depleted by constant illness; in addition, he was short of the high-calorie food required for hard physical labour, and the timber he had brought with him cracked badly in the unfamiliar climate. But the dark, stocky Van Riebeeck was possessed of youthful energy and an unquenchable optimism; by August, the fort had been completed and he and his followers were able to occupy it.

Further improvements and additions were made in the ensuing months. By April 1653 Van Riebeeck was able to report to the Lords

Seventeen that the curtain walls between the bastions had proved adequately weatherproof, although one of the wooden storage and accommodation buildings inside the fort had been unable to stand up to the south-easterly gales; another building he mentions in this despatch is thought to have been the first with a thatched roof at the Cape.

A year later Van Riebeeck managed to fire 60 000 'fine red bricks, like Leyden bricks', and set to work on his first masonry building, a store. Soon afterwards he reported to the Lords Seventeen that it was 'nearly completed … All the houses inside [the fort] we intend to build in the same way, that they may be fireproof.' He added: 'We also, in course of time, intend to cover the outside of the fort with brick, where the sods are now well-fixed with palisades taken from the Cape forest: so that henceforth we require no material from Batavia'.[4]

Brick-making continued on a large scale, and one by one the original timber storerooms, barracks, guardroom and main gateway were replaced by more durable structures. In the end the fort itself was never bricked over, no doubt because the tiny outpost simply did not have the resources to do so, and on several occasions repairs had to be made to portions of the walls which had begun to crumble.

But crumbling walls were only part of Van Riebeeck's concerns: his main problem was finding enough food to feed his people. The provisions he had brought with him ran out in September 1652, and his first attempt at growing wheat yielded disappointing results; it had been planted at the wrong time of year, the soil of the Table Valley was poor and the variable weather conditions did not make for good harvests.

Consequently this first period at the Cape was marked by a constant struggle to obtain enough to eat – and this lasted some five or six years. Van Riebeeck's foraging parties ranged far and wide to catch fish, gather seabirds' eggs and hunt for penguins, seals and other edible local fauna. He even sent an expedition on the perilous voyage to distant Madagascar to obtain rice.

In spite of all his efforts, however, he found himself in the embarrassing situation of having to cadge food from the very ships he was supposed to supply. On one occasion some of his soldiers were actually reduced to devouring a dead and no doubt distinctly aromatic baboon they had found on the slopes of Table Mountain.

The food problem eventually threatened the very existence of the Cape outpost. By 1654, according to Dr Dan Sleigh, 'it was … time to take stock of the situation and to recommend … the shutting down of the station if there were no reasonable hope of success.'[5]

Van Riebeeck's most intractable food problem involved the acquisition of additional livestock, particularly the cattle he needed both as draught animals and as food for both the outpost and passing ships. By 1654 he had managed to accumulate 230 cattle and 583 sheep, but this was still far from adequate for his needs, and protecting the livestock from both human and animal predators was a constant concern. The early records tell of lions and leopards scaling the wall of the fort's southern hornwork (outer enclosure) to make free with the precious cattle and sheep. On Christmas Day of 1652 Van Riebeeck recorded in his journal that 'last night a sheep in the kraal was almost half-devoured by a wild beast, in spite of the fact that one man went about the kraal all through the night with musket and burning slow-match.' On another occasion several marauding lions were chased out of the kraal by gunfire and noise kicked up by the sentries. Another peril was the intermittent theft by local Khoina, who resented the incursion of the Company's cattle on their customary grazing land. Although not habitual rustlers, they had a long tradition of snatching other people's livestock as an act of protest or war.

A solution to the problem of cultivating appropriate quantities of wheat was easier to find, although it was to bring problems of its own. Having learnt from painful experience that the Table Valley would not yield good grain, Van Riebeeck turned to the adjacent valley, through which ran a river he had named the Liesbeeck.

The valley was not only fertile and well-watered but also heavily forested with the sort of tall, straight timber he needed for building and ship repairs. He decided to fence in and fortify the Liesbeeck Valley, then establish two kinds of farms – '*buitenposten*' or out-stations directly managed by VOC officials, and others run by a new class of man, the so-called '*vrijburghers*' or free citizens, (lit. 'free burghers') consisting of Company servants who volunteered to be released from their contracts to work on their own account.

In February of 1657 Van Riebeeck created these first free burghers.

They would be released from their contracts with the VOC and allocated land, livestock and materials. What they harvested and bred would then be sold to the Company. They would also have to contribute to the defence of their holdings if the need arose; if they did not perform as required they could be recalled to Company service.[6]

In the event not all free burghers were farmers. Others became wood-cutters, and yet others were licensed to catch fish, collect seabirds' eggs, kill and salt down penguins or hunt seals for their meat and oil. One group, which came to be known as the 'Saldanhavaarders', or 'Saldanha voyagers', soon established itself at the very safe anchorage of Saldanha Bay, and specialised in transporting such commodities, and any livestock which could be bartered from the sparse population of Khoina in the area. For this purpose they used a variety of small shallow-draught vessels, some privately owned and others the property of the VOC.

The system did not always work as intended – various free burghers abandoned their stated purpose and drifted back to the outpost to set up drinking-shops, while one group absconded on board a homeward-bound ship. But overall it served well enough, and the free burgher class was to have a lasting impact on developments in southern Africa.

Van Riebeeck's plan for the Liesbeeck Valley called for setting up several out-stations, the names of some of which survive to this day. They include Rustenburg, now a famous girls' school in the suburb of Rondebosch, Groote Schuur ('Great Barn'), which much later became the site of one of South Africa's iconic buildings; and 't Nieuwe Land, the current suburb of Newlands or Nuweland, the scene of many famous rugby and cricket matches in the modern era.

In the next three years Van Riebeeck built several small redoubts between the out-stations that were manned around the clock by soldiers of the garrison: Duijnhoop, west of the Salt River estuary, already existed, but nearby two redoubts were added, Kijckuijt and Keert-De-Koe on the opposite bank of the Salt River at the wagon-drift; the Coornhoop guard-house on the lower slopes of Devil's Peak near the Liesbeeck; and the Houdt-den-Bul guard-house.

He also constructed a shoulder-high fence, partly of poles and partly of stacked reeds and shrubs, and along one section of the 13km-long boundary planted wild almonds and thorn-bushes which, he hoped, would grow within three or four years to a strong and well-nigh impenetrable hedge.

There is still some debate about the purpose of the almond hedge, the remnants of which are to be seen to this day. It has been described in some circles as an early apartheid measure the main aim of which was to keep the Khoina out of the Liesbeeck Valley, but there is a certain lack of logic in such an assertion. Since the rest of the boundary fencing was clearly to prevent livestock from straying or being easily driven away, there would have been no sense in making only one section of it people-proof, a manifestly futile task in any case, since no hedge would have stopped a determined intruder. Elphick's opinion is that the hedge was 'aimed not so much at keeping Khoikhoi out of the colony as stopping them from driving out colonial cattle.'[7]

Van Riebeeck's aim was quite clearly to use the various redoubts and guard-houses not just as strongholds but also as bases for mobile patrolling and 'fire brigade' tasks, much like the mile-castles along Hadrian's Wall in Britain. It must be remembered that the outpost had introduced a new species of animal that was to be the boon companion of the South African soldier and civilian alike for centuries to come, the horse.

The expansion along the Liesbeeck, while beneficial to the outpost's ability to perform its primary task, also brought the first serious clash between the Company and the Khoina. The so-called 'Peninsular' Khoina clan had long used the lush Liesbeeck Valley for summer grazing, as had the Cochoqua clan from the Saldanha Bay area. In spite of some reconciliatory efforts by Van Riebeeck friction began almost immediately after the first free burghers established themselves there in 1657.

Sporadically cattle would be stolen, standing wheat damaged and buildings fired when the opportunity presented itself, and the free burghers became increasingly aggressive-minded as they saw the fruits of their labours being destroyed. Van Riebeeck held them in check and persevered with his orders to maintain peaceful relationships with the Khoina, but with ever-diminishing success. In May 1659 a Peninsular alliance, forged by a Khoina leader named Doman, went on the warpath during the typically wet autumn weather, striking at the free burghers' crops, homes, livestock and other property. This is known as the 'First Khoina War'.

The outpost itself was in no danger, since Doman's warriors did not have the ability or presumably even the desire to overwhelm the fort, but by the time the so-called war ended with a negotiated peace treaty the following year, the Company's men had learnt a few salutary lessons.

One was that the main infantry personal weapon in Van Riebeeck's armoury, the cumbersome matchlock musket or arquebus, was totally unsuited to the hit-and-run type of warfare which was clearly the sort of thing to be expected at the Cape. The arquebus was inaccurate, slow to load and so long and heavy that it had to be used in conjunction with a forked rest. Discharging it required a complicated firing sequence: pressing the trigger activated a hammer in whose jaws was gripped a section of burning slow-match cord; the hammer then introduced the burning end of the cord to the priming powder in the pan next to the touch-hole, which led to the main charge of powder in the chamber of the barrel. If all went well, the main charge then went off. Frequently it did not – either because the touch-hole had been blocked by debris from a previous shot or because wet weather had extinguished the slow-match or dampened the powder. The matchlock was, to put it mildly, a distinctly unreliable form of ignition, especially in wet Cape weather. The matchlocks did not even provide a psychological advantage, since long experience with passing ships had made the Khoina thoroughly familiar with both the concept of firearms and their capabilities.

Another lesson was that conventional European-style infantry and tactics served little purpose at the Cape. The typical VOC soldier was heavily laden and trained to fight in ranks and files against similarly organised opponents, his principal methods consisting of tightly controlled volley-firing, followed by hand-to-hand combat with the bayonet or sword.

This meant that he had very little chance of achieving anything when faced with an elusive, fleet-footed Khoina warrior who travelled very light and made use of his local knowledge to mount unexpected attacks, followed by swift withdrawals.

The bottom line was that the regular VOC infantry soldier could provide a static or semi-static guard presence and mount an effective defence against outside attack, but in the bush he was completely out-classed. What was needed was a fast-moving mounted musketeer who could react immediately and take the fighting to the enemy, rather than wage a defensive war. Volley-firing was a waste of time: what counted was hits per shot.

Van Riebeeck set immediately about rectifying his weaknesses. He obtained more horses from Batavia, established a breeding herd, and improved his firepower, urgently requesting more 'snaphaan'[8] muskets, of which he already had a few, to replace the obsolescent arquebus.

The snaphaan, or 'snaphaunce', was an early type of flintlock, then coming into general service in all European armies. It was much lighter and handier than an arquebus, so that the cumbersome forked rest was not required, and had a far superior means of ignition: When the trigger was pulled, the 'cock' with its flint clamped in its jaws, snapped forward against a hinged steel frizzen-plate, causing a shower of sparks and white-hot metal shards. The sparks and fragments then ignited gunpowder in the small flapped pan below the frizzen, and the result-ing flash travelled through the adjacent touch-hole to ignite the main charge.

Although by no means foolproof (misfires could result from several causes, ranging from worn flints to blocked touch-holes) the snaphaan was not only lighter but far less sensitive to weather conditions, and with alterations the flintlock system would remain the principal method of firearm ignition world-wide until well into the 19th century.

Van Riebeeck's innovations, elementary as they might seem to mod-ern eyes, represented a quantum leap in the context of that particular time and place. The snaphaans would provide soldiers and free burgh-ers with a more reliable 'reach' than the Khoina's distance weapons, the spear and arrow, and the horses would counteract their mobility.

The South African mounted infantryman had been born, and he had come to stay. As Lt RJ Haines succinctly put it:

The early history of white South Africa was dominated by the figure of the armed horseman. Not a cavalryman in the accepted sense
of the word, the South African horse-soldier was usually a mounted
infantryman, for he fought on foot but used horses to secure that
mobility which became essential in operations in South African conditions.[9]

More than four decades later, Haines's remarks remain valid except in
one respect: It was not just the early history of *white* South Africa that
was dominated by the mounted soldier. South African wars, regardless
of their causes, have never been uni-racial affairs. In the 18th and 19th
centuries the concept of the mounted infantryman was to spread far
and wide as it was embraced by a variety of tribes, peoples and nations
in what later became South Africa. In the process it changed the course
of common southern African history.

The first part-time 'Burgher Militia' units were established in 1658
or 1659 in direct response to the war with the Khoina. Residents of
Cape Town were enrolled in a more or less orthodox infantry contingent, while the free burghers were organised into mounted groups.
The stage was now set for the evolution of two distinct types of tactics
and organisations. The regular uniformed soldiers and infantry militiamen would retain basic European-style doctrines and procedures,
as their main role was to ward off attack, but the free burghers would
begin to develop a new style of warfare that in essence consisted of
Khoina-style mobility and shock tactics, executed with firearms and
horses. Van Riebeeck did not realise it, but his decision to expand into
the Liesbeeck Valley and establish the free burgher class would lay the
foundation for the blending of Khoina and European military tactics
that was to affect all of southern Africa for the next three centuries.

The development of the new mounted system took place over many
years, and did not always co-exist comfortably with the European or-
thodoxy of the garrison's regulars. During the first decades an expeditionary force would always be led by an officer of the garrison, but the
general lack of manpower of all kinds meant that he would command
a distinctly mixed bag.

Typically his followers would be a combination of regulars from the garrison, free burghers and sometimes Khoina, since various clans had no scruples about allying themselves with or enlisting the help of the VOC against their fellows for the purpose of settling old scores or differences of opinion. Early expeditions achieved only limited success 'because the commanders were not versed in the habits of the Khoi,'[10] and, no doubt, were not very receptive to advice from a bunch of farmers and clansmen who made up most of their troops.

In 1671 there was another series of clashes with elements of the Khoina. By now the new system had undergone further development, and a mixed force of soldiers and free burghers could undertake a follow-up operation that led them a significant distance inland. A similar operation was mounted in 1674, involving 50 soldiers and 50 free burghers, and in 1676 there was an even larger one, consisting of soldiers, free burghers and allied Khoina.

In 1676 these burgher units received a name that still endures with honour everywhere except in the country of its birth: 'commando'. Originally 'commando' meant an order, mission or task, but in time it also came to be used as a designation for a specific type of irregular fighting unit that operated under official authority, as opposed to an *ad hoc* band of vigilantes.[11]

It is not often noted as significant, but this new system involved a quantum leap for the Khoina as well. The allied Khoina who went on such expeditions had now started moving away from the pre-1652 manner of clan warfare with its concentration on spears, bows and fighting-oxen. They had begun to evolve into mounted infantrymen, a role in which they and their descendants were to become expert during the centuries ahead. It is possible that Khoina clansmen played a much more prominent role in the early cattle-retrieving and exploring expeditions than is now recognised, and that each foray included a substantial but unrecorded element of indigenous allies. Lt-Col. Paul Grobbelaar, who has made an intensive study of the early Cape military, has no doubt about the fact that this was so. In correspondence with the author he says emphatically: 'My research indicates that there were no completely "white" commandos. It was the presence of the Khoi that led to the development of commando tactics and provided the great stimulus for the development of the system …'[12]

The commando system continued to expand and evolve as the 17th century moved to a close. The VOC military commander retained overall control over the commandos' activities, but as early as 1688 the free burghers were given the right to respond to a local emergency without having first to run it by the Castle if a rapid reaction were required. This did not give the free burghers *carte blanche*, since they remained subject to military control, but it allowed them to react immediately, eg, to cases of livestock theft, when a swift follow-up could spell the difference between success and failure.

It is generally accepted that the true commando system, as it was later seen in various parts of South Africa, reached its final basic form during the period 1700 to 1715. The Netherlands – and therefore the VOC's army and navy – was becoming involved in hostilities with France, and few regular troops could be spared for anything but essential garrison duties in the Cape defences. This meant that the proportion of regulars in commando expeditions began to dwindle. There was a case in 1701 when a commando sent out against some Bushmen in the Land van Waveren (today's Tulbagh district) consisted of 10 garrison soldiers and 30 irregulars, but control remained firmly in official hands.

However, November 1715 brought about a landmark in the development of the commando, when an officer of the Burgher Militia, Ensign Schalk Willemsz van der Merwe, was nominated to lead a 30-man commando, consisting entirely of irregulars, for operations against Bushman raiders in the Piketberg area. Van der Merwe's expedition did not achieve any great success, but historically it was a watershed event: 60 years after its very small beginnings, the commando system with its mounted citizen-soldiers had finally emerged as a separate concept, and one which later proved that it was not to be trifled with.

CHAPTER 3

A NEW SOCIETY AND
THE PASSING OF THE KHOINA

There is a common belief that, generally speaking, the Cape's early population consisted of a substantial number of increasingly marginalised Khoina and Bushmen, expatriate or locally born whites, people of mixed white and Khoina blood and slaves of mainly Indonesian extraction. This belief might serve the various purposes of certain observers, but it is totally erroneous.

By the beginning of the 18th century a complex demographic mix was emerging at the Cape that exerted a significant influence on society as a whole. This can be seen in the works of researchers such as Dr HF Heese.[1] Heese dug deep into many decades of carefully kept VOC records to sketch the emergence between 1652 and 1795 of a distinct mini-society at the Cape which was based on group or social status rather than race, and allowed for a surprising amount of upward social mobility.

In the early years, broadly speaking, the Cape outpost's population consisted of a very small upper crust in the form of the higher VOC officials, and below them, in descending order of status, the free burghers, lower-ranking Company servants and the like. Off to one side were the Khoina, who remained a free people because it was not Company policy to enslave or oppress local inhabitants, or even quarrel with them except in the line of business – and at the Cape, the main business of the Company was not to found a colony, or fight wars, but to conduct a vigorous barter trade for cattle and sheep. To do that naturally required a substantial free indigenous population with livestock for sale.

Some Khoina maintained their old nomadic lifestyle, while others placed themselves voluntarily under the jurisdiction of the VOC, by taking paid employment with the free burghers or the Company itself, or even invoking its protection against their fellows.

This state of affairs did not, however, solve a major problem: the Cape outpost's need for labour, both skilled and semi-skilled. The Khoina who took service with the VOC, especially in the early days, were skilled herdsmen and shepherds, but the Company needed workers for a variety of other tasks. The only way to address the perennial shortage of labour was to import slaves. Two groups of slaves, totalling 303 souls, were brought in from the Portuguese-ruled colonies of Angola and Guinea in the ship *Amersfoort* in 1658.

These were not the first slaves to set foot at the Cape, which by then had already acquired a grand total of eight women and four men. The very first of them appears to have been one Abraham van Batavia, who arrived as a stowaway in 1653 and claimed to have run away from his owner in Batavia, one Cornelis Lichthart. He was allowed to stay on and was put to work – a reflection, no doubt, of the general scarcity of labour at the Cape.

The other slaves had been brought to the Cape by their owners, and it has been claimed that some Asian convicts were brought to the Cape as early as 1654, as well as others from Madagascar and Java in 1657. But the 1658 contingent seems to have been the first group of significant size, although about 80 were then sent on to Batavia. After objections from the Dutch West India Company, which had the monopoly on trade west of the Cape, later batches of slaves were imported from Mozambique as well as Madagascar. These were followed by Asian contingents of slaves, political exiles and some freemen who came of their own volition.

Contrary to popular belief, the largest single ethnic group, over 50% of the total, according to the respected Cape Malay historian Achmat

Davids, came from Bengal, Coromandel, the Malabar Coast and elsewhere in India, and, he says, formed the embryo of the Cape Muslim
community – often thought to have been founded by the substantial
number of later arrivals from Indonesia (especially the Celebes, Java
and later Macassar) and Ceylon.[2]

In time the Guineans and Asians in particular provided many craftsmen and craftswomen, their skills either learned after their arrival or,
as was often the case with the Asians in particular, brought with them.
The slaves (and, of course, the Mardijkers and others) introduced yet
another element into the Cape's increasingly tangled demographic and
economic mix.

Their arrival unintentionally helped to ease yet another pressing
problem at the Cape outpost, a great shortage of unattached women.
Only a handful of the people in the outpost, mainly members of the
VOC's upper-crust, had been able to bring their families with them,
while the traditionalist Khoina clans frowned on marriage and casual
sexual liaisons between whites and their women.

This is not to say that such liaisons did not happen, but the first
official marriage between a white and a Khoina did not take place until 1660, when Van Riebeeck's Danish assistant surgeon, Pieter van
Meerhoff, married Krotoa/Eva van de Caab. Inevitably, therefore, the
arrival of female slaves soon resulted in interracial sexual relations.

This does not seem to have been as widespread as some earlier accounts indicate. Elphick and Shell[3] note that these early reports are
inaccurate because they concentrated on tales of the admittedly licen-
tious goings-on at the Company's slave lodge, rather than at the outpost as a whole.

The ultra-respectable VOC frowned on such leisure-time activity,
although apparently without great effect. Given human nature, this
is hardly surprising, and most of these fleeting pleasures were probably indulged in not by people in the Company's area of influence but
by voyagers travelling to and from the Far East. As Elphick and Shell
point out, 'thousands of single Company soldiers and sailors disem-
barked each year at Cape Town for 10 days or three weeks of recrea-
tion. For example, from 1701 to 1710 an average of 68 ships visited
per year, and in the 1780s this rose to 133. On each of these ships were

70 to 300 or more sailors, most of them with money in their pockets and only a brief time to spend it.' The result was inevitable.

Resident Company employees certainly indulged in similar casual pleasures of the flesh but over the years many formal marriages also took place, between the free burghers and Company servants on the one hand, and enfranchised slave-women on the other. It is not difficult to see why. To many of these men from war-torn Europe the Cape represented a fresh start, and they were interested in acquiring helpmeets rather than mere concubines. Provided that the women in question had first been freed and baptised, the VOC did not discourage such marriages, no doubt because it would result in a more stable labour force, which was a problem in most of its other outposts, and according to Elphick and Shell they took place steadily throughout the period.

According to Heese the first such marriage at the Cape took place in 1656, *before* slaves started arriving in significant numbers. One Jan Woutersz, late of Middelburg in the Netherlands, married an Indian woman called Catharina Anthonis van Bengale when the return-fleet on which they were travelling to Europe called in at the Cape. Woutersz and his new bride contrived to stay behind when the fleet sailed – among the first, but certainly not the last, birds of passage who arrived at the Cape on the way to somewhere else but chose to go no further. Since freemen could not marry those in bondage, this means Catharina van Bengale was probably also the first slave to be freed at the Cape.

Other interracial marriages soon followed, with 'Bengalis [continuing] to be the favourite pure-blood marriage partners in the 17th century, but Cape-born women, many of whom were likely of mixed ancestry, rapidly overtook their Asian counterparts,' according to Elphick and Shell.

JH Hoge[4] found that between 1660 and 1705 a total of 191 German VOC servants 'married or lived with women who were not pure-blood Europeans; of the 191 women, 114 were Cape-born, 29 were Bengali, 43 were from other Asian regions and only five were Madagascans or Africans.' Heese notes that 'the children and descendants of these marriages between whites and imported slaves were *all* absorbed into the

35

white society, and numbers of present-day Afrikaners are descended through the male and female lines from these Oriental founding mothers.'[5]

In 1685 Commissioner Hendrik van Reede van Oudtshoorn gave the Cape melting-pot yet another stir when he laid down the procedure by which slaves owned by the VOC could be manumitted, or freed. These regulations stayed more or less unchanged right to the end of the Company's sway in 1795. Foreign-born slaves with 30 years' diligent service who could speak Dutch, had been confirmed in the Dutch Reformed Church and could prove that they were able to support themselves financially, could buy their freedom for 100 guilders (roughly the equivalent of eight months of a soldier's pay). Since new arrivals averaged 16 years of age, such slaves could qualify for freedom in their mid-40s. Cape-born slaves qualified slightly earlier, at the age of 40.

Slaves of mixed descent, on the other hand, could buy themselves out for 100 guilders at the age of 25 for men or 150 guilders at 22 for women, providing that they had been confirmed in the Dutch Reformed Church and could speak Dutch. From 1713, too, any slave taken to the Netherlands was automatically manumitted on arrival (the British East India Company instituted a similar policy, but not until nearly 60 years later).[6]

According to Cape Town's Iziko Slave Museum researchers, the VOC preferred that a female's manumission fee be paid by a free citizen whose aim was marriage – the thought being, no doubt, that this would promote good morals. The Iziko researchers also make note of another little-known fact, namely that yet another accepted alternative was to offer a substitute slave, who 'could be bought either from the slave's own income or by free family or friends.' What this meant was that slavery did not necessarily equate to life-long servitude, and before long two other significant socio-cultural groups began to emerge from the melting-pot.

One was made up of the so-called 'free blacks', former slaves who had bought themselves out or been manumitted by other means, and were now free to indulge in their own pursuits. Various researchers have differed about whether 'free blacks' meant ex-slaves of African

origin, ex-slaves of Asian origin or ex-slaves generally. Since no specific terms for the various ethnic categories existed, it seems likely to
have been a generic name. The other group consisted of people of any
of a variety of backgrounds and ethnic mixes who had been born free,
whether in or out of wedlock.

The second factor in the shaping of this new and strange population
mix came early in the 18th century by way of what is undoubtedly the
greatest human tragedy in the history of the Cape of Good Hope. By
the time it was over, everything had changed, not least the composition
of the Dutch East India Company's future military forces at the Cape.

❦

Less than 15 years into the 18th century, a cataclysmic event resulted
in the virtual disappearance of the Khoina as a coherent ethno-cultural
group in the southern and south-western Cape – and, eventually, the
impoverishment of many of those Khoina living further afield. In
recent years there has been talk of an alleged 'Khoi genocide' at the
hands of the VOC, but no such event ever took place. The Khoina demise actually resulted from a fell combination of happenstance, disease
and societal structural failure.

One day in 1713 a small return-fleet arrived in Table Bay from the
Far East, after suffering an outbreak of smallpox on board. This was
bad news but not necessarily a real problem, except for those in the affected ships, since the VOC had an early-warning system in place that
was designed to cope with just such an emergency.

The system varied slightly in different eras, but the essentials remained the same. During the daylight hours a *vlaggeman*, or look-out,
was posted permanently on top of Lion's Head, armed with a bronze
signal-gun, a powerful telescope, an enormous Dutch flag and an as-
sortment of other national banners. When the *vlaggeman* spotted ships
in the distance he sounded the alert by firing as many shots as there
were vessels in sight. This was then repeated by a second gun-posi-
tion located on the 'Leeuwen Bil', or 'Lion's Haunch' (Cape Town's
present-day Signal Hill), since experience had showed that if a south-
easter was blowing, the Lion's Head gun might be inaudible at the

Castle. Then, when the ships were close enough for their origin to be identified, he hoisted the appropriate national flag. At one stage the system also allowed for the hoisting of a coded sequence of flags on the Leeuwen Bil to advise approaching VOC ships that it was safe to enter Table Bay, because the outpost was still in Dutch hands.

At the right moment a boat was then sent out with a surgeon on board who would either give the ships a clean bill of health or quarantine them in the bay, the most infectious cases being isolated just offshore on Robben Island. The system seems to have worked well enough, except for that ghastly day in 1713.

The *vlaggeman*, it has been said, was either drunk or seriously hung over. No warning shots were fired. Whatever the case, the ships eventually arrived unannounced in Table Bay, anchored and apparently sent some infected linen ashore to be washed. The smallpox went ashore with it and before long an epidemic was raging on shore.

It is surprising that nothing like this had already happened at the Cape, given the fact that ships had been calling there for more than two centuries. But now the time had come for the catastrophe to take place, and catastrophe it was.

The devastation of a full-scale smallpox epidemic is almost inconceivable to a person of the 21st century, but at that time it was one of the greatest killer diseases known to mankind. It is believed to have originated in ancient Egypt, and in succeeding centuries spread to Europe, China, India, Africa and the Americas, wreaking havoc wherever it went. Highly infectious and almost always fatal, it was capable of destroying virtually entire populations.

Being an organised mini-society, the Cape outpost managed to survive in spite of grievous losses, but enormous devastation was visited on the indigenous population. Completely non-resistant to the disease, the Khoina in the Western Cape succumbed *en masse*. Uncounted numbers of corpses lay rotting by the roadsides, while desperate refugees fled inland to their home-kraals, only to be turned away or even killed by their own people. The VOC operation at the Cape came near to collapsing. Herds, flocks and fields were left untended, and starving refugees banded together to steal livestock in order to survive.

Meanwhile the pox marched remorselessly northwards, to the

borders of what is now Botswana. There it attacked the BaThlaping, a Tswana tribe, then moved southwards again to sweep through the north-western Cape and devastate the Namaqua and Grigriqua as well. 'Smallpox viruses continued to circulate among southern African peoples for a century,' Elphick comments, 'causing disruption whose scale and historical significance may never be fully known. However, for the Western Cape Khoikhoi it was the plague of 1713 that did the decisive damage. Not only did it kill the majority of the population but it also eliminated [the] vestiges of traditional Khoikhoi social structure.'[7]

The epidemic was thus both a physical and cultural death-blow for traditional Khoina society at the Cape, which had been coming slowly apart ever since the arrival of the VOC. Given its crucially important location on the sea route between West and East, the Cape was fated sooner or later to become an outpost of one of the great trading companies, and the local indigenous society simply could not handle the consequences of the new era rung in by Jan van Riebeeck and the VOC.

The Khoina could not or would not adapt, possibly because the crumbling of their society was gradual, taking place over six decades. Ironically, the process was unknowingly helped along by the losers themselves, who did not realise that they were actually sowing the seeds of their own traditional society's destruction; Elphick avers that the Khoina social structure was not crushed by the Dutch but collapsed because of a number of factors.

More and more Khoina had started taking employment with the Company at the turn of the 18th century, at first mainly as superlative herdsmen; this was either through sheer necessity or because they perceived it as offering them greater benefits and economic stability than their intermittently precarious traditional lifestyle.

The result, Elphick says, was that 'within 60 years of 1652 the traditional Khoikhoi economy, social structure and political order had almost entirely collapsed,' adding that this collapse

> ... cannot be explained purely in military terms, for the whites in this period were few in number and yet had to resort to arms against Khoikhoi only infrequently and briefly. Neither can it be seen merely

as a result of the smallpox epidemic of 1713, though this swept away the bulk of the Western Cape Khoikhoi population. Khoikhoi decline was far advanced and probably irreversible well before this final catastrophe.[8]

One of the contributing factors, Elphick says, was the continual bartering of cattle or labour for European goods: 'When a Khoikhoi sold his heifer to a Dutch bartering expedition, or his labour to a colonist, he was exploiting the colonial situation for his own ends; but, though he did not know it, his immediate interests were incompatible with the continuing autonomy of his traditional society.' Though our records show episodes of conquest, Elphick continues, they fail to give witness to these minor actions which, in the end, brought about the decline of the Khoina:

> It is a fact worth pondering that the European subjugation of southern Africa began not because statesmen or merchants willed it, nor because abstract forces of history made it necessary, but because thousands of ordinary men, white and brown, quietly pursued their goals, unaware of their fateful consequences.[9]

There was yet another factor which helped to doom traditional Khoina society for all time. The first wave of smallpox had barely subsided in 1714 when the Cape was struck first by two years of severe drought and then seven years of rampant livestock diseases in both the VOC area of influence and beyond.

Both the Company and the surviving Khoina lost most of their cattle, but the passing ships' requirements did not diminish. The Khoina came under great pressure to sell more of their animals than could be replaced by their herds and flocks, already depleted by Bushman raids and sickness. The smallpox had struck the Khoina at their moment of greatest weakness. Exactly how many died will never be known, but in another of his writings Elphick tentatively accepts the contemporary calculation of a staggering 90% fatality rate in at least some areas. 'Khoikhoi [in the south-western Cape] virtually disappeared from the records of subsequent years ... A society which had been in a protracted phase of social and economic decline was now almost annihilated.'[10]

The Khoina in this area came so close to total extinction that, according to the Canadian historian John Laband the Company's population in its area of influence actually outnumbered the remaining clanspeople by the end of the century. He adds that many remnants of the broken clans took employment as herdsmen or labourers, although along the VOC's frontier 'others continued to resist the intruders by plundering their cattle and burning their farmsteads.'[11]

Whether 'resist' is the most appropriate word in this context is, perhaps, a moot point. The rapidity with which the free burghers spread outwards during the 18th century has always been something of a conundrum in military terms, since the presence of a substantial indigenous population (and the fact that the Khoina lacked neither fighting spirit nor expertise at bush warfare) should surely have resulted in the extinction of just about all of the tiny early trek parties. The only logical conclusion is that the free burghers encountered little or no resistance to their outward movement – because in many areas there were very few people to resist them, Khoina or not.

In his analysis of Khoina society immediately before Jan van Riebeeck's arrival Elphick hints that the most intransigent resisters were actually Bushmen, not Khoina. The 1970 edition of the *Archives Yearbook of South African History* notes that the 1713 smallpox epidemic 'resulted in a drastic numerical reduction and detribalisation of the Hottentot population. The remaining Hottentots posed little threat to the burghers. In many cases they became the burghers' allies against the predacious Bushmen in the interior.'[12]

The 'trekboers', as the outlying free burghers were now called, were another factor in the general Khoina decline. They were the result of a distinct social evolutionary process that had started after Van Riebeeck first released Company servants from their contracts to farm for themselves. As Stephen Taylor puts it, in his account of the wreck of the *Grosvenor* East Indiaman: 'As well as cultivators and officials … the little colony bred a tough brand of frontiersmen who ventured eastwards beyond the Langeberg and Zwartberg mountains, as hunters and – like the tribal people they came increasingly to resemble – nomadic pastoralists.'[13]

A second smallpox epidemic in 1755 repeated the pattern of 1715, with many deaths in and around Cape Town and among the remnants of the Khoina population. Naturally this does not mean that there were no Khoina left, as Laband has pointed out, but they were few and hard-pressed to survive. The overall result of all these catastrophes and changes was disaster for the Khoina. Elphick and VC Malherbe write: 'All 18th-century descriptions show these people in a lamentable condition: poor, disunited and in fear of "Bushman" robbers. Many poor Khoikhoi were forced to become hunters and robbers themselves.'[14]

In essence the two wandering cattle-owning groups, the trekboers and the remaining Khoina, were competing for the same resources, just as the Khoina clans had competed with one another before Van Riebeeck arrived, and faced a common enemy, the 'free' Bushmen, who had certainly not been converted to the culture of private livestock or land ownership. To make matters even worse, the outlying eastern Khoina also started to feel pressure from the Xhosa national group in its advance southwards and westwards as the century wore on.

The emergence of the trekboers changed the demographic landscape even more: as the years went by, the VOC administration in Cape Town had less and less real control over them. This, in turn, affected the military geography of the country as well, because it meant that the commando concept started to ripple outwards to tribes and nations far beyond the VOC's sphere.

In the meantime Cape society had begun evolving into its final form, one that was not based on race *per se*. The system of slavery was relatively flexible in the context of the times, not so much because some slaves could and did attain their freedom (this was not unknown in slave-owning societies) but because, at the Cape, a slave background did not necessarily constitute a serious stigma, as far as either freed slaves or their descendants were concerned. 'Free blacks' and free-borns of colour, descended from free blacks, appear to have had no qualms about owning slaves themselves in spite of their own experience – even if quite recent. A contributing factor to this phenomenon, a strange one to more sophisticated 21st-century eyes, is, of course, that slavery was not unique to the Cape but was common in most parts of the world.

The VOC's main concern seems not to have been racial, or whether one was of slave origins, but religious persuasion and legitimacy of birth. The only real official obstacle, at least for the purposes of this discussion, apparently was the stipulation that freed slaves could not serve in the Burgher Militia, although their children had a full obligation as long as they had been born in wedlock after their parents' release, and had been baptised. Otherwise, free blacks were more or less at liberty to move up or down the social scale. Thus by the early 18th century Cape society had long since become the melting-pot of races and cultures that it is today – it even included some Chinese 'free convicts' who had ended up on Robben Island, stayed on after expiry of their sentences and generally prospered.

Usually, a slave was given a suffix to his or her name, such as 'Van de Caab', for a person born at the Cape, or 'Van Bengale', indicating Bengali origin. But many persons of colour adopted the typically European names of the families into which they had married or been born; one 17th-century bridegroom was called Christoffel Snyman, but in spite of his name was of full-blooded Indian descent, being the son of the free blacks Anthony van Bengale and Catharina van Palicatte.

With one exception these groups were totally Westernised in their customs and practices. The lone exception was the group generally known today as the Cape Malays, who were mainly of Indian and Malay/Indonesian origin. This group was able to maintain its separate culture and ties with its religious roots, because not all of its members had arrived at the Cape as slaves. Some had come out as craftsmen and servants, while others like the famed Sheik Yusuf of Macassar,[15] (who is still revered because of his work in strengthening and fostering the local Islamic culture) were political exiles who lived in a reasonable state at the Company's expense.

In later British times, of course, the Cape also gave refuge to numbers of what became known as 'remittance men' – mostly well-born scapegraces whose families paid them to stay as far away from England as possible, sometimes under assumed names. A rather different type of remittance man was George Rex, the fruit of a morganatic marriage between the Prince Regent, later George IV, and a woman named Hannah Lightfoot. Some remittance men were downright scoundrels and drunkards, but many others suffered from no more than an excess of wild spirits, and fitted well into the free and easy colonial lifestyle.

VOC policy was to allow Muslims to practise their observance in private, although they could not build any mosques, a situation that would not change until the Batavian Republic took control of the Cape in 1803 and instituted total religious equality before the law. They could not belong to the Burgher Militia because of their religion, but were obligated to man the fire brigade, a vital task in a town where most houses possessed thatched roofs; one might regard this as South Africa's first example of 'alternative service'.

The effect of this heterogeneous demographic make-up on the military system is something to which very few historians, military or otherwise, have paid much attention. What is quite clear is that, in the 18th century, many formal ethnic lines of descent had become hopelessly blurred, and that for most people social mobility both inside the military and out of it was dictated by religion and birth-status rather than racial concerns. Consequently there was a nearly universal obligation to render compulsory military service in time of emergency. Freeborns of whatever ethnic background were liable for service in the Burgher Militia, provided only that they were Protestant Christians and of legitimate birth. Starting in 1722, free blacks were also liable for part-time military service in a separate company of their own, the Compagnie der Vrijswartzen, or 'Company of Free Blacks', commanded by its own officers. So were the Chinese free convicts, following Governor Maurice Pasques de Chavonnes' reorganisation of the Cape's defences.

The tasks of the Company of Free Blacks are nowhere clearly defined, although it is known that it took its turn with the other Burgher Militia companies in night patrols of the various wards. Its primary duty was to put out fires and prevent the looting of shipwrecks.[16] Logic dictates, however, that this 'support to the civil power', as it would be termed today, was the unit's *peace-time* emergency role, and that in war-time its members would be mobilised for auxiliary support of combat forces.[17]

44

As the century progressed, the administration also addressed the problem of the growing number of free people who had been born out of wedlock. Since it was not considered appropriate to have them render service in the Compagnie der Vrijswartzen, a unit called the Corps der Vrijen, or Free Corps, was established. It was commanded by officers of the Burgher Militia; it had its own regimental colours, and by regulation paraded immediately to the left of the Burgher Militia on formal occasions. This indicates that it was a properly organised and structured unit.

It appears that in the outlying districts of Stellenbosch and Drakenstein the free blacks' former slave status was not taken all that seriously when it came to service in the Burgher Militia (possibly because manpower was too scarce for niceties about birth-status), but in the Cape Town district more attention was paid to origin. Heese quotes the case of a free burgher named Jan Gerrits of Hamburg, whose wife applied in 1724 for her stepson to be registered for militia service. Her request was turned down because the boy had been born into slavery, and he was placed in the Compagnie der Vrijswartzen instead. However, that same year the Political Council conferred free-burgher status on a blacksmith named Christiaan Victor, who had also been born into slavery. This might have had something to do with the fact that he was the illegitimate son of a prominent burgher named Jacob Victor, who had submitted an impressive 'request' or petition to support Christiaan's case and, no doubt, pulled some strings.

Naturally the integration process had its hitches, although not always for what might seem the most obvious reasons. For example, in 1736 one Evert Colyn was charged with refusal to render military service. Colyn's defence was that he was not unwilling to do his duty, but he refused to serve under one Philip Constant because the latter was a former slave. Heese comments on the Colyn–Constant case:

It is ironical, however, that it should have been Colyn of all people who complained – a case of the pot calling the kettle black. Evert Colyn's father was Johannes Colyn, who was married to the daughter of Margaretha van de Caab – a freeborn or free black woman. In addition, Johannes Colyn's mother was Maria Everts, the daughter of Evert and Anna of Guinea, who presumably had been among the first group of negro slaves brought to the Cape in 1658.[18]

The Colyn case provides an interesting illustration of the attitudes of the time. Colyn's objection was based not on race but on social status. No doubt he was a man of swarthy complexion himself, given his immediate ancestry, but what was important, at least in his own estimation, was that he was a second-generation freeborn. Heese adds:

> What is under discussion here is therefore not physical appearance or colour but whether a person was born free or in slavery. In spite of his negro origins Colyn was accepted as a burgher and was not considered a free black … In addition, cultural differences or places of origin were not … a disqualifying factor as regards rendering burgher service with the white or European inhabitants. If a person had been born free he enjoyed the same status as a white free burgher or former official.[19]

A surprising example of societal integration, if Heese is to be believed, is to be found in the case of Sheikh Yusuf. Heese says that although Sheikh Yusuf gained enduring renown for his efforts to strengthen and root the Islamic culture at the Cape, all of his children eventually converted to Christianity. In 1721, long after his father's death, Ibrahim Adahaan was baptised as Abraham de Haan, followed by his sister Sitina Asia in 1726 as Maria Dorothea Sultania, and his brothers Mochamat Dayan (David Sultania) and Mochamat Aserk (Isaac Sultania) in 1739 and 1746 respectively.

The brothers identified fully with the VOC culture, language and religion, Heese says. Both Abraham de Haan and David Sultania served in the mounted section of the Burgher Militia, and it appears Isaac also rendered service. Heese says that 'an investigation of the Burgher Military Council's minutes for the period in question shows no evidence of discrimination against these brothers – including Isaac Sultania, who was probably born in Batavia.'[20]

Heese's overall conclusion is that as far as the military was concerned, as with the civilian population, status was defined not by physical descent but by birth, in or out of wedlock:

> But generally speaking, the status-groups nevertheless did have a connection to physical descent, appearance and cultural grouping, especially of the mother. Thus by 1795 most members of the citizen force would have been white *by appearance* [author's italics], born in wedlock and members of the [Dutch] Reformed Church or Lutheran Church …
>
> Finally – until 1795 [ie, the end of the period covered by Heese's treatise] the colour of a person born free, or the racial type he represented, was not a legal obstacle to material and social progress in Cape Town and its immediate environs.[21]

There were two other groups, however, which were outside the official parameters during most of the Company's rule at the Cape. One was the so-called 'Bastaard-Hottentotten' (Bastard Hottentots), the illegitimate offspring of, for the most part, male slaves and Khoina women on the outlying farms. They were not considered slaves because the Khoina were freeborns, but otherwise fell through the official cracks and, as Heese says, 'occupied the lowest rung in the society of free people.'

Considerably better off were the '*Basters*' (Bastards), the results of liaisons between whites and Khoina women. Most were christened and some were absorbed into the 'white' citizenry, but according to Heese the majority ended up in groupings such as the later Griquas, who were to become daring frontiersmen and bushveld mounted fighters in future years.

By the closing decades of the 18th century the Cape's armed forces had developed in a very different fashion from that which has been portrayed in subsequent times, in so far as it has been portrayed at all. Firstly, lines of descent were now so entangled that, to a greater or lesser extent, all the different groups were related to one another by blood. Secondly, religion and birth-status, not racial origin or appearance, were the main benchmarks for differentiation between various groups in both the civil and military fields. Thirdly, all the groups had a common heritage of language, customary usages and religion which transcended the normal societal ills and inequalities, including the Bastaard-Hottentotten and Basters, even though they were not yet fully on the official radar. The only partial exception was the Muslim group, which had managed to retain a good deal of its cultural and religious heritage while simultaneously slotting itself comfortably into the general societal structure. Fourthly, the top military and civil structures – the free burgher class and its military arm, the Burgher Militia – were open in both theory and practice to people of all races, provided that they were baptised Protestants, of legitimate birth and born of free parents; and fifthly, every free male in the Company's orbit, irrespective of ethnicity or culture, or whether he was a freeborn or a manumitted slave, had an obligation to render part-time military service of some kind (or a form of alternative service in the case of the Muslims). This would eventually include the Bastaard Hottentotten, who were destined to render good service against the British invader in 1795 and 1806.

This last highlights a question which non-military historians have hitherto ignored or overlooked. No administration in history has ever deliberately absorbed into its military forces any sector of the population that was likely to turn against the established order. The fact that the VOC did not hesitate to incorporate almost every group in its control, even freed slaves, indicates its confidence in the existence of a common identity. This could not have been anything but deliberate. The VOC's administrators were not naïve do-gooders but hard-headed officials of great experience who would not have embarked on a policy of this kind without careful consideration – and they were later proved right during two British invasions in just over a decade.

What had happened, of course, was that in its ancient way Africa had swallowed the motley array of people cast upon its southern shores, stirred in some of the local genes and given birth to what amounted to a new tribe or nation; it would not happen again on such a scale until Moshoeshoe I forged the remnants of half a dozen tribes into a new nation called the BaSotho in the early 19th century.

They had even coined a name for themselves: Africaander, or 'African'. Originally this was a term that specifically denoted the offspring of liaisons between whites and slaves, but it also carried a note of pride, as witnessed by the case of Hendrik Biebouw.

In 1707, the 16-year-old Biebouw (also spelt Bibault) and three of his friends went on a drunken rampage in Stellenbosch that soon got out of hand. Like most other local inhabitants they were celebrating the downfall of the corrupt and tyrannical Willem Adriaan van der Stel, possibly the worst governor ever to be inflicted on the Cape, who had been recalled to answer to the Lords Seventeen for his sins. Biebouw and his friends celebrated so thoroughly that they were arrested for public drunkenness, foul language and presumably destruction of property. The local landdrost, or magistrate, an expatriate German named Johannes Starrenberg, rebuked Biebouw and his three followers and told them to go home. When they refused he struck Biebouw with his cane, at which Biebouw cried: 'I will not go. *Ik ben een Africaander* (I am an Afrikaner)! Even if the landdrost beats me to death, even if he puts me in jail, I will not be silent!'[22]

Noting the specific meaning of the term up to this time, the historian Hermann Giliomee comments that this was the first recorded occasion on which a white had used it to describe himself, rather than more generally used terms like 'Christian' or 'boer'. The poet-writer Breyten Breytenbach speculates about whether it mirrored Biebouw's estrangement from a purely European identity like that of Starrenberg's, and whether the fact that his father had earlier sired a daughter by a slave named Diana had anything to do with it. Giliomee concludes:

> All that we can say at this stage is that in his indignation it was not about the fact that his honour as a free burgher, a white or European or Christian had been injured. He was rebelling against an official who was a German and not a son of Africa, who was affecting his entitlement to a specific place, position and status, for which he used the term '*Afrikaner*' … The fact that there were people calling themselves Afrikaners who were partly of European and partly of slave descent, did not hold Biebouw back from taking the name for himself as well.[23]

All these factors were to have a significant effect in the turbulent years that were to come at the end of the 18th century.

CHAPTER 4

GUARDING THE CAPE

The '*Caabse Vlek*' (the Cape Hamlet) was founded during a perilous time in Europe. Soon after Van Riebeeck stepped ashore at Table Bay in April 1652 the English and Dutch engaged in a short but fiercely fought naval struggle, now known as the First Anglo-Dutch War.[1] The war stemmed from commercial and political pressures arising in the English Civil War, which saw the execution of Charles I, the rise of the self-styled 'Lord Protector', Oliver Cromwell, and conflict with British commercial concerns in North America.

The nascent outpost at the Cape of Good Hope was not directly affected by the war, but the conflict loomed in the background until hostilities ended in August 1653 after an English victory at the Battle of Scheveningen. After another eight months a formal peace treaty was signed in May 1654, but it must have been obvious that another round of fighting lay ahead.

This was part of the reason why Van Riebeeck began building up a part-time burgher militia as early as 1658, but the onus of defending the Cape outpost from external aggressors – the likeliest candidate being the English East India Company – rested squarely on the shoulders of the regulars, most of them infantry and artillerymen.

This strategic preoccupation can be clearly deduced from the design of the Fort of Good Hope, which was far more elaborate than what was needed for a fortification aimed at dealing with local violence. It was what would today be called a conventional-warfare installation: modest in size, it is true, but intelligently located and laid out for defence against an amphibious landing in Table Bay.

Static warfare in those days called for successive lines of defence, the aim being to fend off an attacker or, at the very least, bloody his nose and dampen his fighting spirit before the decisive assault; this allowed the defenders to retain the option of launching a limited counter-attack (this is why old fortifications have 'sallyports', and the expression 'to sally forth' remains in current usage). If the attackers overcame the external lines of defence and broke into the fortress itself, the defenders could withdraw to a 'keep' or internal fortification and fight on, possibly launching further counter-attacks aimed at clearing the attackers out of the fortress again. Once one grasps these principles the final form of the fort's layout makes perfect sense.

The fort's outer line of defence was a moat, fed by the Varsche Riviere, or Fresh River, whose only crossing-point was a drawbridge on the seaward side that led to a sturdy arched stone gateway with heavy timber doors. The drawbridge connected the fort with an outlying hornwork, or enclosure, that lay between it and the sea.

This hornwork consisted of a large square, bounded to left and right by long thatched buildings, one containing the hospital and the other various stores and kitchens. On the seaward side it was bounded by a wall, a stone's-throw from the beach, with another entrance which was guarded by two flanking gun positions. The only landward approach to the hornwork's entrance was by way of a standing bridge that crossed the Varsche Riviere as it emptied from the moat into the sea.

Inside the moat lay the fort itself, a square construction around an internal courtyard, or bailey, about 24m across, with tapering walls nearly 6m thick at ground level and four metres high, all constructed of the earth dug out of the moat and covered with sods. There were four corner-bastions, connected by a walkway, which Van Riebeeck named 'Dromedaris', 'Walvis', 'Oliphant' and 'Reijger' after the ships in which he and his followers had travelled to the Cape. Each mounted several naval guns, and most probably had switch positions so that the guns could fire outwards and also provide supporting fire for the adjacent bastions if necessary.

Built into the fort's southern wall was a small square tower, or 'Kat',[2] whose primary purpose was to serve as a keep into which the garrison could retire if attackers were to capture the rest of the fort. This 'principal stronghold' had stone or clay walls 1.2m thick, a flat fireproof roof of heavy timber on which guns were mounted, and a stone parapet nearly two metres higher than the curtain walls. On the roof was also a small hut to accommodate a look-out post. The kat was flanked by thatched buildings housing Van Riebeeck's quarters and assorted storerooms, while other lean-to buildings against the eastern and northern walls contained kitchens, a mess hall, guardrooms and similar facilities.

On the landward or southern side of the moat was another large hornwork, basically the livestock kraal and stables. This southern hornwork had a separate entrance, but was commanded by the guns on the Dromedaris bastion, and there was no access over the moat.

What all this meant was that any aggressor force landing from the sea would be subjected to withering long-range fire from the northern hornwork and the Walvis and Reijger bastions. Any landing parties would meet close-range bombardment with grape-shot and musket fire, while at their most vulnerable, disembarking from their boats. If they succeeded in penetrating the northern hornwork, they would be channelled into its large open space, which would become an ideal 'killing ground' for the fort's musketeers and gunners. Crossing the moat to get at the stone archway would further delay them and present the defenders with yet another densely concentrated target. Assuming they finally got across, they would have the moat at their backs while at the same time being subjected to direct and supporting fire from the bastions. Any flanking attacks from the east and west would have to run the same sort of gauntlet, and any encircling attack by way of the southern hornwork would have to cross the moat in the face of fire from the roof of the Kat, the Dromedaris and Oliphant bastions and the top of the curtain wall between the bastions. In short, the fort was a more than adequate deathtrap for any aggressor.

Generations of commentators have been led astray by the undeniable fact that for all its virtues the small, clay-walled fort was a feeble thing by the standards of the sturdy stone fortifications of Europe and elsewhere, and would not have lasted long in the event of a serious bombardment from the sea; but the issue is not necessarily as simple as that.

Firstly, the Cape started as a comparatively low-budget operation which was designed to yield rapid results, and which could be abandoned without too much damage to the Company's fiscus if it did not prove worthwhile. This meant that there would have been no sense in building a more durable fortification in 1652, even if Van Riebeeck had had the time, resources and manpower to do so. So the fort could be seen as a compromise solution that was right for its particular circumstances.

Secondly, the most likely external aggressors were the English and French East India Companies, or perhaps the odd pirate flotilla. While the fort would not have been able to withstand a determined assault by a substantial national naval force, it would certainly have deterred aggressors like its commercial rivals, which would be as reluctant to cut into their profits by mounting large military expeditions as were the Lords Seventeen. The same principle would apply to pirates, who preferred soft targets and did not operate in significant numbers in the southern oceans in any case.

The fort was, in truth, not very sturdy. The walls might be neatly washed inside in the VOC's standard light ochre shade, but the homemade bricks soon became brittle from being hollowed out by rain, and structural collapses were not uncommon. In the early hours of one August day, for example, the inhabitants were roused by a 'dreadful crashing noise' and found that a gable on one building had given way after suffering slow but fatal damage at the hands of the heavy rains and north-west gales.

The fort was not the outpost's only defensive position against external aggression. Van Riebeeck started fortifying the coastline from the earliest days, a process that continued after his departure a decade later. He founded the Cape's first-ever gun battery soon after his arrival in 1652, in the shape of two small field-guns, probably 4-pounders,[3] which he placed on the beach to protect the wooden jetty which had been one of his first projects. This was followed in the same year by the Tranenborg Redoubt with two small guns at the mouth of the Salt River, replaced two years later by the Duijnhoop Redoubt a little to the west when it became clear that Tranenborg was too isolated and windswept.

In 1654 Van Riebeeck placed two 6-pounders on Robben Island and two 3-pounders on Dassen Island; these weapons would not have been able to contribute to the physical defence of the outpost, but would nevertheless have played a valuable role as signal guns to warn of approaching ships.

❦

The soldiers who formed the Cape garrison during the VOC's sway were, to put it mildly, a mixed bag, with only one thing in common: all were mercenaries who had been trained in one or other army and then recruited by the Company. The proportion of native Dutchmen and Flemings was quite low at all times, but there seems always to have been a very substantial percentage of Germans from several points of origin (particularly areas speaking the Low German dialect, which was similar to Dutch), as well as Frenchmen, Scandinavians, Irishmen, Scots and others from a variety of military backgrounds. As shown earlier, given the VOC's indifference to racial origins, at least some of them were men of colour. Dr Dan Sleigh points out that many such – either full-bloods or people of mixed descent – served in the VOC's eastern forces, and it is likely that some were enlisted in their homelands or drifted to Europe and were welcomed by the Company's recruiters. The mulatto Mardijkers who accompanied Van Riebeeck to the Cape in 1652 provide a case in point.

The Company clearly did not completely trust its mercenaries, except the Germans, to stand firm in the event of a foreign attack. As early as 1657 Commissioner Rijckloff van Goens directed that only Dutchmen and Germans be admitted to the garrison – at the time neither the cultural nor political differences between 'Dutch' and 'German' were as distinct as they are today, and this may have played a significant part in such a proclamation. How thoroughly this edict was obeyed is another question, given the outpost's chronic lack of trained manpower, but sources suggest there certainly came to be a very strong German representation in the Cape outpost's military and civil population in later years.[4]

Trustworthy or not, this motley crew was what the Company had, so it made sure that they were stringently disciplined and kept busy with a continual round of training, ceremonial duties, military construction work and the manning of its out-stations. Not surprisingly, there were occasional desertions, but these were few; absconding was a capital offence and there was nowhere to go.

Garrison life for the VOC regular soldiers at the Cape was most likely not unpleasant, with fine temperate weather during most of the year, game and imports aplenty, a reduced likelihood of incurring wounds, or worse, and the opportunities for earning extra money were more plentiful at the skills-starved Cape.

It is certainly a fact that the first six decades or so after 1652 were uneventful from a military point of view, with only three minor local wars and a number of armed cattle-retrieving expeditions, all on a small scale and resulting in very few casualties on either side. This is a remarkable record, considering the inevitable strain resulting from the interaction of vastly different cultures, and certainly a distinct departure from the sanguinary clashes which were later to take place elsewhere in Africa.

Several reasons can be found for this. One was undoubtedly the fact that the Khoina, generally a peaceful people unless provoked, had been trading with passing ships for a century and a half. Thus they had long had a window to the outside world and were thoroughly acquainted with the material benefits of peaceful co-existence. Another was the Company's lack of enthusiasm for such money-wasting distractions from their primary mission as making war, colonising for the sake of colonising, or trying to convert the locals to Christianity. Yet another important ingredient, according to Elphick, was the legacy of Jan van Riebeeck himself.

Van Riebeeck was not antipathetic towards the Khoina as a whole, as has often been claimed, although he certainly disliked one group, the so-called Peninsulars, because they had tried to secure a monopoly to prevent other clans from trading directly with him. But he admired and was on good terms with the leaders of various other clans, and 'through his friendliness, patience and insight, he gained the confidence of Khoikhoi in a way no other Dutch official was able to do in the 17th century.'[5]

Barring the occasional clashes with the Khoina and Bushmen, therefore, the garrison soldiers' time was taken up mainly with labouring on defensive works, training, providing guards and sentries, lookout duty, patrols, drilling and routine parades. The last included the daily opening of the fort's main gate by a small party of soldiers and a drummer, followed by a less noisy closure in the evening.

The garrison's off-duty soldiers were known to indulge in moonlighting tasks, while others were loaned out to free burghers who needed help on their farms, and becoming a free burgher's '*knecht*', or worker, was sometimes a passport to greater prosperity than the average soldier could normally expect. A *knecht* was not well-paid at all, but the Cape chronicler OF Mentzel, himself a former soldier who had gone this route, writes that in the early 18th century 'this form of employment was a stepping stone to wealth for competent men ... such men frequently married their master's daughter or widow. In fact, I have known cases where widows engaged *knechts* with a view to matrimony.'[6] The result was that a number of them became free burghers themselves in a very short time.

Bandsmen were also an integral part of the Cape's regular garrison from the start, the earliest being trumpeters, drummers and possibly 'pypers' (fifers), although as time went by new instruments such as flutes, hautboys (the forerunners of the modern oboe, although much higher in pitch), clarinets, hunting horns and kettledrums also made their appearance. Military musicians of those days acted in many roles, and were essential to the smooth functioning of the armed forces. As a result, bandsmen were classed as fighting soldiers, because instruments like the trumpet and drum were used for signalling as well as keeping soldiers in step. They often marched with the regimental colours into battle as visible rallying points amid the smoke, noise and general confusion. In and around the fort they acted also as the equivalent of public-address systems by sounding calls which ranged from summoning soldiers to action stations, warning them of imminent parades or recalling them to barracks at sunset, giving notice that a ship was about to set sail.

They also provided appropriate music for a number of private or official occasions, ie dance music for social functions, or outside the commander's or governor's residence during dinner parties or even to play at funerals. In April 1658, for example, a Company official was accorded a semi-military interment at which two drummers and three trumpeters played. At such times they might be augmented by musicians from within the ranks of the Company servants, slaves or freedmen. In later years they even 'supplied small "chamber groups" to perform classical music for those of more refined taste.'[7]

Collapsing walls or no, the fort remained the centre of all activities as the *Caabse Vlek* expanded in response to its circumstances. The Council of Policy sat within it to govern the settlement, as did the Council of Justice, which meted out punishments which were often very harsh by modern standards but no different from those of Europe, and when Van Riebeeck established the Burgher Militia in the late 1650s its members drilled in the fort's square on Sunday afternoons, no doubt under the expert tutelage of the garrison's non-commissioned officers.

The children who played within its walls would one day become figures in South Africa's history books. One was Bernert Willemsz Wijlant, the son of the sick-comforter Willem Wijlant, who was the first white child to be born at the Cape; another was Abraham van Riebeeck, the commander's younger son, who was destined one day to become Governor-General of the Dutch East Indies. Yet another was Eva, otherwise known as Krotoa, the young Khoina girl whom Van Riebeeck brought up in his own home and who, at the age of 21 in 1664, became the first indigenous woman to marry a VOC man, the garrison's Danish assistant surgeon, Pieter van Meerhoff. Their daughter, Pieternella, married another Company servant and thus became the ancestral founding mother of the large Saayman family in modern-day South Africa.

Here, too, Van Riebeeck received emissaries and notables from the surrounding clans, fingered specimens of rich copper ore they brought him and gave the orders that launched several expeditions into present-day Namaqualand to look for the outer reaches of the legendary golden empire of King Monomotapa.

Monomotapa's kingdom, with its great cities of Davagul and Vigiti Magna, was a subject of much interest to early geographers. They believed it to be in the fabled biblical Land of Ophir, where King Solomon was said to have mined gold for his marvellous temple, and – like many other educated men of his time – Van Riebeeck was convinced of its existence. On the basis of the existing 'evidence' he concluded that it was to be found in the vicinity of present-day Pretoria, a startlingly accurate prediction when one considers the location of the Witwatersrand gold mines developed two centuries later.[8]

According to Dr Geoff Tribe of Stellenbosch, a long-time researcher into Cape history, Van Riebeeck's imagination was fired by his foster-child Eva, who soon learnt to speak fluent Dutch and proved helpful in fostering trading relations with the substantial Cochoqua clan. Eva told him stories about a wealthy civilisation to the north, and from 1660 onwards he sent a number of expeditions into the interior to find the outposts of the non-existent empire. Although these attempts would not bring home the gleaming wealth of El Dorado, they served an important historical function: they drove the men of the Cape outpost into the interior.

Most of these expeditions were led by seasoned non-commissioned officers of the garrison, and they needed every ounce of their endurance and experience. The daring and determination of these men can scarcely be comprehended by modern South Africans. Hair-raisingly ill-equipped, almost totally ignorant of vast tracts of country which even now can daunt a nervous traveller's heart, they marched on foot with their baggage carried on pack-oxen, navigating with compass, cross-staff and astrolabe as if they were sailing to India. Because they travelled in summer to avoid being thwarted by rain-swollen rivers, they were usually tortured by heat and thirst; every aboriginal inhabitant they encountered was a potential and sometimes very real enemy; their guides and interpreters frequently swindled them; predatory carnivores posed a constant danger and at times they came close to starving.

The first expedition was led by Jan Danckaert, who set off in November 1660 with 13 men, one of them the surgeon Van Meerhoff, and eventually made it all the way to the Olifants River (Oliphants Reviere – so named because Danckaert saw a large herd of elephant on its western bank). Weakened by illness but still resolute, Danckaert pressed on until he reached the vicinity of present-day Clanwilliam, but was then forced to turn back.

Danckaert had failed in his primary mission, but he had brought back much invaluable information, and just ten days after his return another expedition set out, consisting of Corporal Pieter Cruijthoff, 12 soldiers and Van Meerhoff. Cruijthoff trekked west of the Olifants River and reached the vicinity of present-day Graafwater before turning back. A third expedition, led by Van Meerhoff this time, returned to the area in April 1661 and established warm relations with the local clan potentate, a chief called Akembie. In November 1661 yet another expedition was sent out to invite Akembie to Cape Town, this one led by Pieter Everaert, the garrison's sergeant of militia, but could not make contact with him and returned after suffering great privation. But a fourth sortie, led once more by Cruijthoff, set off in October 1662 at the behest of the new commander, Zacharias Wagenaer, who was as enthused about Monomotapa as his predecessor had been.

Cruijthoff penetrated deep into the unknown marches of lower Namaqualand before turning back empty-handed and in some disgrace because he had come close to destroying a Bushman kraal after a nocturnal attack on his party. But he brought back with him a gem of information: the existence, so the locals had told him, of a 'great river' only a few days' trek further to the north. This later became the Orange.

The last of the early expeditions, 14 men under Sergeant Jonas de la Guerre, set out in October 1663. He went even further than Cruijthoff, but also failed to reach the great river, and returned with nothing to show for his efforts except some scraggy cattle he had bought from the locals on the way back. Neither De la Guerre nor anyone else realised that he had come within striking distance of Namaqualand's immensely rich copper deposits, and for the next two decades no expedition ventured northwards again.

But their efforts had not been totally in vain. True, they had not found even the outskirts of Monomotapa's kingdom, but, as Elphick points out, 'the main effect of the exploration was the opening up of relations with new Khoikhoi groups, chiefly Guriqua and Namaqua. The Dutch were becoming increasingly less dependent on the Peninsular Khoikhoi for their meat supplies.'[9]

❦

The fort outlasted Jan van Riebeeck, but not by much. On 2 April 1662, just four days short of ten years since first setting foot on Cape soil, his successor, Zacharias Wagenaer,[10] arrived from Batavia with a return-fleet. He was formally read into office, and the following day Van Riebeeck and his family set sail for the Far East.[11]

The elderly, grave and phlegmatic Wagenaer was a total contrast to the young, energetic and positive-minded Van Riebeeck. Fresh from the luxuries of Batavia, where the VOC's high officials lived in great style, he was also extremely dissatisfied not only with his fairly rough-and-ready living quarters but with the fort in general.

His jaundiced view of the fort was justified; the little stronghold was obviously on its last legs, finally done in by the ravages of time and weather, not to mention the inferior building materials that had had to be used in its construction, and in any case the Lords Seventeen were justifiably worried about the looming threat of another war with England.

The outpost had now shown itself to be indispensable to the profitable conduct of the Company's eastern business, and it was decided that the time had come to build a proper Castle or stone-walled fortress which could defend Table Bay and the *Caabse Vlek* against all comers.

This decision marked an almost unnoticed but significant milestone in the military history not just of the Cape but of the southern oceans. Up to this time the importance of the sea route around the Cape had been mainly commercial, but things were changing in Europe as the 17th century began to move into its final decades. During the coming 18th century the Cape sea route, the key to control of the Indian Ocean and thus the Far East, would start to assume a strategic politico-military importance to the great European powers which would remain a major factor until the Cold War ended in the last few years of the 20th century.

In June 1665 plans for the new Casteel de Goede Hoop (Castle of Good Hope), a large, five-sided building, designed according to the latest fashions in siege warfare, were sent out by the Lords Seventeen with Isbrand Goske, commander-designate of the Eastern VOC outpost of Cochin, who broke his journey to launch the project.

By this time the Second Anglo-Dutch War had broken out, following the restoration of the English monarchy under Charles II. Much as the first war, it stemmed from political disputes and commercial rivalry with the mighty Dutch trading empire. The English, prominent among them James, Duke of York, brother of the newly restored Charles II and head of the Royal African Company, wanted to take over the Dutchmen's trade routes and outposts, then exclude them from the English foreign possessions. A slightly less piratical aim was to cut down on the clandestine (and thus untaxed) shipping from colonies in North America and Suriname, an enclave on the South American continent which had hundreds of rich sugar plantations. The Dutch, on the other hand, considered it their right to trade with anyone anywhere, although this did not deter them from enforcing their monopoly in the Dutch Indies and threatening to expand it to India after they had expelled the Portuguese from that area.

Backed by Lord Arlington, a favourite of Charles II, the Duke of York first tackled the Dutch West India Company (GWC), whose trading area covered everything to the west of the Cape of Good Hope. The result was a carefully orchestrated series of provocations, coupled with a campaign to gain the English population's support for a war with the Dutch.

Privateers captured about 200 Dutch merchantmen, English ships refused to salute the Dutch flag, and in mid-1664 the Duke of York sent a Royal African Company expedition to seize all the Dutch trading posts along the west coast of Africa. In August 1664 a surprise attack ended in the capture of all the Dutch outposts in New Netherlands, the West India Company's North American territory, among them the outpost of New Amsterdam, which was renamed 'New York' in the duke's honour.

The Dutch responded by despatching a fleet under the renowned Admiral Michiel de Ruyter, which promptly recaptured the West African colonies. This was followed by an English attack on a Dutch merchant fleet. The attack was beaten off, but the following month Dutch ships were authorised to open fire on British warships at the outposts when threatened, and Charles II used this order as a pretext to declare war on the Netherlands. Two years of fierce sea warfare followed, which, no doubt, lent a certain urgency to the construction of the Castle of Good Hope.

Goske disregarded a survey which had been carried out as early as 1661 and in August 1665 identified a slight rise, about 230m south-east of the fort as the most suitable location (one story has it that Wagenaer selected the site by using a convenient freshwater spring as the centre-point; whether or not this is true, it is a fact that the Castle's well lies exactly at the centre of the fortress).

Tactically its location was not ideal, since it would be overlooked by high ground on which a determined enemy could mount artillery, and since the water table was high in the vicinity, it would also suffer from dampness in its cellars (something which occurs to this day). But there was nothing for it, since the Castle had to be virtually at the water's edge so that its guns could command the anchorage.

Like the fort, the Castle was clearly designed for conventional warfare. Many modern-day tourists are disappointed by its lack of features like turrets and a towering keep which are so common in Europe and elsewhere, but the fact was that by the 1660s the medieval European castles had been overtaken by progress, specifically the developments in heavy ordnance. By contrast to the intricate wonders of Europe, the Castle was a state-of-the-art fortress, all sharp angles to ward off round shot and a minimum of upward-projecting features which would be vulnerable to gunfire.

The first step was to set 200 soldiers (the garrison had been temporarily increased to provide labour) to clearing and levelling the area and digging the massive foundations, 5m wide and 3.5m deep. At this stage Goske set off on the rest of his interrupted journey to the east, leaving the actual construction to his assistant, the master builder Peter Dombaer, and Dombaer kept up the pace set by Goske. It was a tremendous task for so small an outpost. Every available able-bodied man was put to work on it – soldiers, sailors, volunteers, slaves, paid indigenous labourers, recaptured deserters and convicts chained to their wheelbarrows, among them a few Khoina who had been jailed for offences committed inside the outpost's jurisdiction.

Some quarried granite from the Leeuwen Bil and dressed it for construction, while others cut timber from the forests. Yet others ferried blue slate and seashells from Robben Island, the former for the Castle's flagstone floors and the latter to be rendered into lime for the mortar.

The work was so hard that the Council of Policy rather grudgingly decided to give the soldiers a higher rate of pay to keep them more or less content with their arduous lot. But it all paid off, so that by 2 January 1666, preparations had progressed to the point where Wagenaer was able to lay the foundation stone.

This was done with much pomp and ceremony; there was even an amateur poet on hand to recite a dreadful ode he had composed for the occasion. The administration temporarily relaxed its grip on its pursestrings to throw a party for all those involved, who took advantage of this rare concession to consume two head of cattle, six sheep, a hundred loaves of bread and eight barrels of beer.

Slowly the Castle began to take shape, in spite of considerable negativity from the Lords Seventeen. The gentlemen in distant Amsterdam were not convinced that their new fortress was in the best location, complained about spiralling costs (which now included hiring free burghers to haul stone from the Company's quarry) and fretted about soldiers being kept at the Cape when they were urgently needed in the Far East.

The wisdom of fortifying the Cape outpost against the VOC's commercial rivals was brought home in December 1666, however, when a French East India Company squadron arrived at Saldanha Bay to look at the possibility of laying claim to the excellent natural harbour there. A detachment of soldiers was hastily sent out from the Castle to avert any such attempt, and they stayed there until the French ships sailed eastwards a month later.

The Second Anglo-Dutch War ended in July 1667 after a number of extensive sea battles and the capture of Suriname. What brought it to a finish was a daring raid in which De Ruyter captured the fort at Sheerness at the mouth of the Thames, then sailed up the estuary and attacked the British fleet where it lay at anchor on the River Medway. By the time he was done 15 English warships had been burnt, sunk or scuttled, while the largest, the flagship *Royal Charles*, had been captured without a shot being fired and towed away by the triumphant Dutchmen – the ultimate embarrassment. All that prevented the raid from being a complete catastrophe for the English was that De Ruyter's marines did not manage to destroy the Medway's Chatham Dockyard, the country's largest military-industrial complex. But it was the greatest naval disaster the English had ever suffered, and it had a far-reaching ripple effect.[12]

England was almost bankrupt, and still unsettled after the Great Fire of London in 1666, which had destroyed most of the capital. In London itself there was also such a strong mood of popular rebellion, owing to the extravagance of Charles's court, that he feared it might break out into open insurrection. The result was the hastily signed Treaty of Breda of 1667, a stop-gap measure which would not be ratified until 1674, one war later. The treaty confirmed English rule over the Dutch outposts in North America, in return for which the Dutch received possession of Run, a small and remote but rich spice island in the Far East as well as the formerly English Suriname, with its valuable sugar plantations.

At the Cape, work on the Castle slowed after the Treaty of Breda was signed, but not for long. Anglo-Dutch rivalry had clearly not reached its conclusion, even though England joined the Netherlands and Sweden in a 'Triple Alliance' against France in 1688. England still had its sights on the Dutch trading outposts and routes, while Charles II felt personally humiliated by the results of the second war, and specifically De Ruyter's raid on the River Medway. Just two years later, in 1670, he formed a secret anti-Dutch alliance with France that was designed to induce Louis XIV to invade the Netherlands. Now a third war was on the cards – one that, like its forerunners, might have grave consequences for the VOC and therefore the Cape outpost.

That same year the French gave the *Caabse Vlek* a bad scare. In 1669 a detachment of VOC troops had been sent to Saldanha Bay to occupy its two best water sources after intelligence had been received that the French were taking a renewed interest in formally annexing it. Nothing had actually happened, but now a squadron of six ships put in there and landed troops who attacked and overwhelmed the small VOC outpost. Inexplicably, however, the French did no more than erect a marker proclaiming the bay as French territory before sailing on to Madagascar.

All this contributed to a frenetic increase in the rate of construction, and in January 1671 the hard-driving Commissioner Isbrand Goske, who was now returning from the Far East en route to the Netherlands, dropped off some 300 more soldiers and sailors to work on the Castle. In October 1672 he was back again, this time to take command of the Cape with the title of Governor, an indication of how important the outpost had become to the VOC.

By this time, the Third Anglo-Dutch War was in progress. The French had invaded the Netherlands, Charles having promised them the cities of Amsterdam (then the richest in Europe) and Rotterdam, and he immediately joined them, together with the German princely states of Münster and Cologne.

Initially the French made large gains, but eventually the Dutch stopped them by taking the drastic step of breaching the sea dykes and flooding large parts of the countryside. Admiral De Ruyter was turned loose on the Anglo-French naval forces and won a series of spectacular victories in four battles.[13] This foiled an English plan to blockade the Dutch coast, and they found themselves barred from the vital wood and tar trade with the Baltic states. The Dutch then allied themselves with their recent enemies the Spaniards, and in 1673 the French withdrew.

In the meantime Goske's exertions at the Cape were yielding results. By early 1674 the Leerdam, Buuren and Catzenellenbogen bastions were complete and the Nassau bastion was at its full height. In November that year the war came to an end after the British Parliament flatly refused to vote any more money for further fighting. An exasperated Charles II was obliged to agree to the Treaty of Westminster, which did little but ratify the stop-gap Treaty of Breda.

It had been a largely fruitless exercise which had achieved little of immediate benefit for the English. The Dutch had repeatedly humiliated them at sea, disrupted their Baltic trade and seized more than 550 of their ships. When the spoils were shared out the only English gain was the New Netherlands outpost, while the Dutch walked away with two lucrative overseas territories and retained not only their West African outposts but also the vital half-way house at the Cape of Good Hope.[14]

Despite the end of the war, work continued on the Castle. The Oranje Bastion was within three months of completion when Goske handed over to Governor Johan Bax van Herenthals[15] in March 1676, and by 1678 the Castle could be occupied, although it was still in the final phase of construction. This spelt the end for the old fort, which was now more ruinous than ever, and it was demolished without further ado. The following year, in April 1679, the Council of Policy officially declared the Castle to be complete.

The appearance of one of Cape Town's most enduring features, the Wapenpleyn (Parade Square) or military exercise ground, which is known today as the Grand Parade, is closely linked with the construction of the Castle. The Wapenpleyn had been identified as a potential training area for the VOC garrison even before the Castle's completion, and eventually the rough, hillocky tract was levelled into a grassy meadow, intersected by a number of meandering streams, that probably looked something like today's Rondebosch Common. For nearly 150 years it was to be Cape Town's largest open space – extending from the Castle all the way to the Heerengracht ('Gentlemen's Canal', the upper part of which is now Cape Town's Adderley Street), and bounded on either side by the Keisersgracht or 'Emperor's Canal' (now Darling Street) and the shores of Table Bay. The historical evidence indicates that from the earliest days Capetonians took a proprietorial interest in the Wapenpleyn, so that it ended up being used for many purposes other than military exercises.[16]

The Castle did not acquire its final form for a long time to come. Before the turn of the century it had undergone two major alterations and additions at the hands of Governor Simon van der Stel,[17] who took over from Goske during the year of its completion. Van der Stel was a very considerable person. A man of mixed race, born in the East Indies, he had been a soldier, merchant, farmer and wine-grower in his time, had read widely and was interested in scientific matters; and some aspects of the Castle over which he cast his trained eye did not please him.

One was the main entrance, which faced directly onto the beach and was difficult to defend, hard to reach when the sea was up, and liable to result in the flooding of the Castle during spring tides and stormy weather. Van der Stel closed it and replaced it with another on the western side, today's imposing Van der Stel Gate. He was also the man who built another iconic feature of the Castle, the immensely thick 'Kat', or cross-wall.

The Kat was not Van der Stel's brainchild alone. The vulnerability of the Castle's open bailey to plunging cannon-fire from the mountain's slopes was clear to all trained soldiers, and during his visit in 1685, Commissioner Hendrik Baron van Reede tot Drakenstein[18] authorised Van der Stel to construct the 12m-high Kat between the Catzenellenbogen Bastion and a point mid-way on the curtain wall between the Leerdam and Oranje Bastions. The baron's reasoning was that the Kat would strengthen the Castle's ability to defend itself and also allow the creation of more accommodation by the addition of buildings on either side.

The Kat was not finished until 1695. When it was, it radically changed not only the defensibility of the Castle but also its interior appearance and functionality. There were now two baileys: the main yard inside the new Van der Stel Gate, known today as the Voorplein, or front square, and a rearward yard still called the Wapenplaats, or 'Arms or Weapon Square'. In the event of cannon-fire from higher up the mountain, at least one of the baileys would be sheltered, allowing the Castle to continue functioning, and in case of attack the garrison would still be able to offer resistance, even if the Castle's defences were breached. In time, too, buildings would be erected against either side of the wall to provide a new council chamber, storerooms, offices and residences for the governor and his senior staff.

A prominent feature was 'de Nieuwe Kat' (the new Kat), a graceful pillared stoep or veranda, that was officially taken into use on 1 May 1695, when it was used for divine service. The balcony soon became an indispensable feature of the Castle, being variously used for posting official notices, making announcements and holding auctions.

Van der Stel's next major contribution to the Cape defences was, of course, the founding of Simon's Town. While touring his new domain he laid eyes on what was known as Van Ijsselstein's Bay and immediately saw its potential as a fishing outpost and possibly a secondary harbour for the VOC's fleets. He was right on both counts, and 300-odd years later Simon's Town remains the foremost naval base of the southern oceans.

The other equally famous locale which bears his name is Stellenbosch, lying to the east of the city, in the interior. The founding of Stellenbosch in 1679 was a significant moment in both the social and military history of the Cape. The ships' insatiable demand for meat and the reluctance of the Khoina clans to part with too much of their livestock forced the outpost to cast its net further and further afield. This meant that an outermost staging and collection point was needed, along with an armed presence, both for theft prevention and retrieval of stolen animals. As a result Stellenbosch became a buffer zone between the *Caabse Vlek* and the interior, and therefore bore an extraordinary military burden.

The founding of Stellenbosch was also a milestone in the social development of the Cape. Van Riebeeck's original outpost had rooted itself by building the Castle, a far more permanent thing than the clay-walled Fort de Goede Hoop. Now its reach extended some 70km beyond the *Caabse Vlek*, and here, too, deep roots were being sunk. The VOC could not do without the Cape anymore, and the outpost had turned into a long-term settlement.

The Burgher War Council seems to have wasted remarkably little time in organising the local militia.[19] On 30 July of that year Van der Stel appointed the officers, a sergeant and an ensign, and by the time he returned on 12 October the Stellenboschers were able to parade 88 infantrymen and dragoons, who greeted him with three musket-volleys, after which he inspected them. By the following year the number had grown to 27 dragoons and 74 infantrymen, and a little later they received further reinforcements when the Huguenots arrived and were settled in the Drakenstein area. It would appear that this was the first appearance of the dragoon proper on the Cape scene.[20]

Military activities were the backbone of the annual Stellenbosch festival, with its famed 'parrot shoot' competition. This was an all-comers event, in which marksmen fired at a target depicting a parrot and won prizes according to their accuracy. The entire Burgher Militia contingent would turn out to drill and would mount a final muster parade and inspection.[21] The parrot shoot had a broader purpose, namely to encourage Stelleboschers in general to hone their musketry skills. The importance Van der Stel attached to musketry practice at the competition can be seen from the fact that in 1686 the ever-frugal Council of Policy authorised a considerable amount of 'in kind' assistance, namely 75kg of gunpowder, 50kg of lead bullets and 300 flints for the event.

The emphasis on marksmanship can be taken as an indication of the influence of local conditions on conventional doctrine. In those days the line infantry soldier was usually not a good shot; the smoothbore muskets then in use were not accurate beyond almost point-blank range because the need to reload rapidly in spite of heavy fouling dictated that the ball must fit loosely in the barrel. This meant that much of the gas resulting from the exploding charge leaked around the ball instead of pushing it down the barrel.

As a result not much attention was given to individual marksmanship development. The preferred modus operandi centred on concerted volleys into the mass of the enemy force at close range, followed by hand-to-hand combat with the bayonet. Thus great attention was given to the infantryman's ability to load and fire rapidly under all conditions, but not much to his personal shooting skills.

At the Cape, however, it had become clear that volley-firing and fighting with bayonets served no purpose in irregular campaigning, one of the militia's two roles. What counted in a commando was not shots per minute but hits per shot. It is likely, therefore, that by this time the Burgher Militia's soldiers were using the hunter's stratagem of wrapping their bullets in thin cloth or leather patches to reduce the gas leakage. Such patched balls made for slower loading, but this was irrelevant because bush fighting did not require rapid concerted volleys.

As to training, Grobbelaar makes the interesting comment that 'at this stage [the 1680s] training was arranged in such a way that it would be seen as a pleasure rather than a burden.'[22] The compulsory annual eight-day refresher training in skill at arms 'was an important military and social occasion':

> All burghers between 16 and 60 who were liable for service had to report. The youngest among them had first to take their burgher or musketeer's oath. Then they were allocated to companies and the military exercises began. On the last day the muster or *'wapenskou'* was held [and] two members of the Council of Policy were in attendance to see that all went properly and in an orderly fashion.[23]

The winners of the various competitions for muskets and pistols were rewarded with prizes and public acclaim. After the best pistol-shot among the dragoons had received his prize he was escorted to his house by the entire mounted force, while the winner of the musketry competition was acclaimed 'king of the marksmen and given the prize, [and also] ceremonially escorted to his home.'

To maintain and promote popular enthusiasm for shooting, the senior officers of the Cape Town and Stellenbosch militia were also allowed to go hunting twice a week, and Van der Stel even established a type of compulsory cadet system for children. As a result, by 1687 the Cape could boast 50 well-mounted horsemen trained in conventional battlefield cooperation with foot infantry, and Van der Stel believed that if a thousand such dragoons[24] were available the Cape would not have to fear being overrun. Needless to say, this was hardly feasible, since there was not even that number of Company servants at the *Caabse Vlek*.

A mounted militiaman's official military 'home' was the dragoon company in which he was enrolled. This meant that members of dragoon companies could be mobilised to form fairly informal and independent commando-style expeditionary units, but they were also trained in Staatse Leger[25] doctrine so that they could be slotted into the regular forces in time of war. It was only much later, after the burgher dragoons had been abolished following the second British invasion, that commandos became specific bodies bearing the names of their towns, wards or districts. The militia's duties extended to civil policing as well from 1686, when it took over the nightly street patrols in Cape Town.

The Burgher Guard was organised into six 30-man companies which were each required to provide street patrols for two months a year.[26]

❦

Like Jan van Riebeeck and Zacharias Wagenaer, Van der Stel was a firm believer in the existence of Monomotapa, and his scientific interest was excited by specimens of copper ore given him by a visiting party of Namaqua. He sent the specimens to the Netherlands for analysis, and they were so rich that he had no trouble obtaining the sanction of the Lords Seventeen to carry out further explorations.

The first expedition he sent out consisted of 30 soldiers under a 39-year-old Swedish officer, Ensign Olof Bergh. The party suffered from thirst and found itself entangled in warfare between the Nama clans, but travelled all the way to the location of the present-day town of Garies before Bergh was forced to turn back. In August 1683 Bergh tried again, with the largest expedition so far, 42 whites and 10 Khoina. Once again he penetrated deep into Namaqualand's unknown vitals before being forced to turn around because of drought.

Four months later, Van der Stel, told by another party of visiting Namaqua about a mountain of copper just 15 days' travel from Cape Town, sent off a third expedition under another of his soldiers, the veteran Sergeant Izaak Schrijver. In spite of suffering great hardship Schrijver and his men reached their destination and returned with samples of what was undoubtedly rich ore.

Fired by these discoveries, Van der Stel talked the Lords Seventeen into letting him take a look for himself and set off in August 1685 with more than 100 men and a number of slaves and interpreters. In just under two months Van der Stel got all the way to what is now the town of Springbok and dug prospecting shafts that are visible to this day. But he concluded, correctly, that the physical obstacles to transporting the ore were insurmountable, and mining did not start at Springbok for nearly two centuries more. However, a huge amount of knowledge had been gained, mainly as a result of the sturdy infantrymen of the Castle garrison who had risked life and limb to push as far into the unknown as they could.

The quest for Monomotapa's kingdom seems to have ended at this point. The fact was that the Golden Kingdom did not exist, or at least not in the form the chroniclers claimed. But the Company would soon have dealings with another nation that was definitely not the figment of a distant cartographer's creative talents.

Called the amaXhosa, it had crossed the Limpopo River some centuries earlier and had been drifting inexorably south-westwards ever since in its never-ending search for more water and grazing. Around 1660 or 1670 it had reached the region now called the Eastern Cape Province, brushing aside the scattered groups of indigenous Khoina and Bushmen in its path in order to colonise the lush, well-watered land along the eastern Cape coast.

It was inevitable that at some stage the intrepid forward elements of the Xhosas would make contact with the small groups of equally intrepid free burghers who were going out eastwards on hunting and cattle-bartering expeditions, far beyond the outermost reaches of the Company. In 1702 these two groups came head to head for the first time at the edge of the Tsitsikamma forest, near the later town of Knysna, and indulged in a brisk little bout of hostilities. It was the opening chapter of a long interaction, sometimes cordial and at other times not, which was to last throughout the rest of the Company's rule and far beyond.

CHAPTER 5

MILITARY LIFE AT THE CAPE
IN THE EARLY YEARS

Other major alterations and additions were still to be made to the Castle, but by the early years of the 18th century it was a formidable fortification. The moat had been deepened, and ravelins (outer defensive works) had been constructed to defend the Van der Stel Gate as well as the Buuren and Catzenellenbogen bastions; in the years to come the Castle would be the central node of a network of coast artillery batteries and redoubts.

With the main work on the Castle completed, the garrison resumed its daily round of routine which included ceremonial duties, particularly when important dignitaries came visiting. Paul Grobbelaar notes that from the very beginning, a dignitary such as a visiting VOC commissioner en route to or from Batavia, who automatically outranked the local hierarchy, would be met on board his ship by the commander (or later the governor) at the Cape. He would then be escorted ashore, from where he and his host would proceed to the fort, accompanied by a guard of honour and the firing of salutes. The following day before a full ceremonial parade, the newcomer's 'commission' or instructions to the governor would be read aloud to the assembly.

Then and later, the Company set great store by ceremonial obligations, both its own and those of arriving or departing visitors. When a ship entered the bay it was expected to fire a salute, the number of shots depending on its degree of importance. The Catzenellenbogen bastion would then reply with a smaller salvo. The number of shots fired varied according to the rank of the honoured visitor; a report of 1685 stipulated that a member of the Council of India was entitled to nine guns, admirals of return-fleets to seven and other important personages to five.[1] By the beginning of the 18th century an admiral's flagship was entitled to 21 guns, with correspondingly lesser salutes for commanders of lower rank.

The firing of salutes was a matter that the VOC took very seriously, as the captain of an English ship discovered on one occasion early in the century, when he entered the bay without honouring the ceremonial requirements. When he came ashore, an emissary from Governor Louis van Assenburgh icily informed him that if he did not observe the usual courtesies he would be blown out of the water. The captain hastened back and did the necessary, after which Van Assenburgh received him with the greatest courtesy.

Another English captain named Edward Reddix, who committed a similar *faux pas* a few years later, was made of sterner stuff. He not only refused to observe the customary courtesies but when rebuked demanded that the Castle fire first because the flag of the King of England surely enjoyed higher status than that of a mere chartered company. The matter, Grobbelaar says, was 'eventually settled to the satisfaction of both parties.'[2]

The salute *faux pas* was not limited to the English. Early in the century the French ship *Hirondelle*, 'firing to celebrate the arrival of the new year, just missed the Castle with a live round. The governor had the cannon-ball ceremoniously returned to the captain of the ship.'[3] Then again, 'Governor of the Cape, Maurice Pasques de Chavonnes … was a great proponent of the gun-salute and took exception to any irregularities in the appropriate protocol. When the English ship *Marlborough* anchored in the roadstead without offering the customary 11-gun salute, De Chavonnes threatened to drive her from the anchorage by gunfire. Only the captain's plea for an exception to the rule, as they had a live elephant on board and did not want to enrage it, placated the governor.'[4]

In the early days the Cape's ceremonial assets were scanty, but in later years the self-conscious magnificence of such occasions assumed considerable proportions. Consequently, parade-ground work played an important part in the Cape regular soldier's working day. Although in modern armies parade drill is now mostly ceremonial in nature because of sweeping changes in weaponry and tactics, in the 17th, 18th and most of the 19th centuries parade-ground evolutions were also battle drills. In an era of linear battle formations and complicated loading sequences it was necessary to pay great attention to proper dressing of the ranks and concerted, orderly movement. These were hammered into the infantry soldier's mind by constant repetition so that he could be trusted to carry them out even when starved, exhausted or terrified. A well-drilled soldier, therefore, was a well-trained one.

Discipline at the Cape was modelled, like the training, on the Staatse Leger's example, and was harsh. Mutiny and other offences against good order were punishable by death, as were transgressions such as sleeping on duty or threatening an officer with a weapon, although some offences and their punishments ring strangely in modern ears: a second conviction for blasphemy, for example, could lead to the offender's tongue being pierced with a red-hot iron. There was a death sentence for entering a military installation by any other than the authorised entrances, and is, perhaps, more understandable. Grobbelaar speculates that it 'might have had to do with the vulnerability to infiltration of the fort or camp. Any person entering or leaving the place by a route other than the authorised one could be an enemy.'[5]

The Cape garrison began falling into its final shape around 1700, when it was re-formed as 'De Caabse Regiment' (The Cape Regiment); at this stage it numbered about 200 rank and file which included 14 corporals, about 160 musketeers, four drummers and six hautboyists.

The Cape Regiment was to display plenty of stamina and would serve for nearly a century until just after 1795, but in the early years of the 18th century it still had a long way to go.

The Cape defences improved significantly and rapidly after the arrival in March 1714 of a new governor, Maurice Pasque, the Marquis de Chavonnes, whose staff included his brother, Captain Dominique Marius Pasque de Chavonnes.

The new governor was a man to be reckoned with. Born in The

Hague in 1654, when the *Caabse Vlek* was only two years old, he was the grandson of a Protestant French nobleman who had settled in the Netherlands after the infamous St Bartholomew's Day Massacre in 1572.[6] He served from an early age in the renowned Staatse Leger, among other things commanding an infantry battalion during the 1701–1713 War of the Spanish Succession and rising to staff rank. When the war ended with the Treaty of Utrecht and the Staatse Leger began to return to peace-time strength, the 60-year-old De Chavonnes retired and took service with the VOC. Given his record as a soldier and administrator, it was hardly surprising that he was soon named to replace Governor Van Assenburgh, who had died at the end of December 1712.

De Chavonnes was not satisfied with the state of the Cape garrison and immediately set about tightening it up. He appointed his brother Dominique captain of the garrison, and on 1 May 1714 he sought and gained the approval of the Political Council for new regulations for both the garrison and the Burgher Militia.

Among other things garrison activities and daily routine were formalised, while individual drill, mass evolutions and weapons training were revised to conform more closely to the new Staatse Leger pattern of the day. Although the Cape garrison had always based its practices on those of the Staatse Leger, it is reasonable to assume that the local regular soldiery had become somewhat slack and ignorant of doctrinal changes, owing to 60-odd years of isolation from the military mainstream, their variety of non-military tasks, and a measure of complacency bred by the lack of immediately visible threats.

De Chavonnes set about sweeping all these cobwebs away, although, it appears, not without some difficulty in getting his message across. Grobbelaar quotes a case where the garrison adjutant neglected to enforce certain new regulations while the governor was absent from the Castle, for which he duly received a thorough tongue-lashing.

He also made an early start on the question of distinctive military uniforms, a matter which had been raised earlier by the then Governor-General of the Indies, Jan van Riebeeck's son, Abraham. In a letter to De Chavonnes' predecessor, acting Governor Willem Helot, Van Riebeeck had said that soldiers serving in VOC ships should have proper uniforms, his concern being that otherwise it would be difficult to distinguish friend from foe in any close-quarter encounters with enemy boarding parties.

Van Riebeeck died shortly thereafter, however, and nothing had come of his advice. Now De Chavonnes addressed the matter in typically decisive fashion. Apart from deficiencies in training and the like, the Cape Regiment presented a rather untidy appearance as they wore a variety of clothing and equipment imported from Europe, with no laid-down dress code or uniform. In a letter to the Lords Seventeen dated 30 May 1714 he pointed out that the rag-tag appearance of the Cape's soldiers militated against a sense of pride and prestige. He would be obliged, therefore, if the Lords Seventeen could provide proper uniforms like those worn in Europe. Officers' and sergeants' uniforms would be made of fine linen, he proposed, and those of other ranks of good-quality English serge or Dutch-made 'carsay' or kersey, a coarse woollen cloth. The cost would be negligible, he added, thanks to the standard practice of docking the cost of uniforms from the soldiers' pay, at cost price, and whatever was spent would be amply repaid by improved morale and the consequent advantage to the VOC.

Appealing to the directors' well-developed corporate ego was obviously just the right approach, and on 19 March 1716, he received a letter from the Lords Seventeen that approved all of his proposals, on the grounds they would help to increase the prestige of the VOC.

When the cloth arrived De Chavonnes set immediately to work on getting his soldiers suitably clothed. The garrison's tailors started making the uniforms, and a '*placaat*' or proclamation, was posted to inform all concerned that the Company's soldiers would in future be clothed in a uniform of blue serge. The soldiers would not be allowed to sell items of uniform to civilians, and civilians in turn would not be permitted to buy such items from the soldiers. The uniforms were issued to the garrison on 2 September 1716.

Exactly what they looked like is a matter of speculation, since no original examples seem to have survived, but it is accepted that they were probably very similar to those worn by European infantry regiments of the time, and thanks to De Chavonnes' regulations it is possible to create an accurate picture of how his soldiers looked: a braided black tricorne hat with a cockade on the left front brim; a thigh-length flared blue collarless coat without contrasting piping or facings; white shirt; blue knee-breeches, blue hose and buckled shoes – all in all, a sightly enough uniform, and economical to make.

That indefatigable observer, OF Mentzel, provides valuable additional details. For ceremonial occasions officers wore a coat of 'rich scarlet cloth braided with silver … the hat is ornamented with a broad band of Spanish silver lace.'[7] Each officer also wore a solid silver gorget – the last remnant of traditional body armour[8] – around his neck, and on parade subalterns (junior officers) carried a spontoon, an elaborately bladed short pike, in addition to their swords. Sergeants wore the blue uniform, the coat boasting a 'red silky lining … faced with a double row of gold braid about half an inch wide. The hat is rimmed with a single row of similar braid.'[9] Corporals, bandsmen and private soldiers wore a blue uniform consisting of 'a coat, a sleeved doublet and breeches of blue kerseymore lined with blue East Indian linen – called Salemporis. The hat has an inch-wide rim of gold braid.'[10]

All non-commissioned ranks wore short swords, including each company's drummer, while the sergeants of each company also carried halberds, the ferocious axe-headed pike then in use both as a weapon and as a badge of office. The rank and file were each armed with a flintlock musket,[11] together with a satchel containing three spare flints, 12 paper cartridges and 12 musket balls/bullets.

De Chavonnes embroidered on this basic pattern, when he turned one of the garrison's four companies (each nominally 55 men of all ranks) into grenadiers. In those days grenadiers were an elite group, formed from the tallest and boldest men in a unit, and wore distinctive uniform accoutrements to mark their special status.

In this case De Chavonnes used locally available materials to add some swagger to his grenadiers. The grenade-satchels on their right hips were made of sealskin, and their tall European-style grenadier caps were fronted with leopardskin. With further differentiation afforded by hose colour, thus was born the first distinctively South African military uniform.[12] How long this lasted is a moot point, though one tantalisingly vague glimpse is afforded by a famous painting depicting the wreck of the VOC ship *De Visch* on the shores of Table Bay. One of the onlookers is a soldier, perhaps stationed there to discourage looters, who is wearing hose of a pumpkin colour.

❦

De Chavonnes' uniforms and regulations might have become fragile, yellowed relics of past events, but his greatest legacy endures still: the Chavonnes Battery in the heart of Cape Town's Waterfront, the first major defensive work at the Cape after the Castle.

The Castle of Good Hope was a formidable state-of-the-art fortress, quite capable of giving a bloody nose to any likely attacker rash enough to attack the *Caabse Vlek*'s anchorage, but it had an Achilles heel: there was little to prevent an assault force landing at any of several places on its western flank, beyond the range of its guns, and then marching on it through the dunes where the suburb of Green Point now stands.

This weakness had long been known, but during the outpost's first six decades no serious attempt had been made at developing a western defensive shield. To an experienced soldier like De Chavonnes the situation was unacceptable, and once again he applied himself to sweet-talking the Lords Seventeen into spending money, even though he had been instructed to be frugal because the Cape was absorbing far too much funding.

To deter any aggressor from attacking the ultra-valuable outpost from the west, he said, it was necessary to build a strong elevated battery on a rocky promontory at the water's edge where the lower slopes of the Leeuwen Bil ran down into the sea. Once again the Lords Seventeen fell in with his proposal, and De Chavonnes personally laid the battery's foundation stone on 20 February 1715.

It was a major project for the small outpost and took 11 years to complete, partly because of a perpetual shortage of stonemasons and partly because of the large quantities of lime needed for making enough special lime mortar. But De Chavonnes and his builders persevered, and it was by a sad twist of fate that he died suddenly in September 1724, 17 months before the battery was completed.

De Chavonnes – kindly, far-sighted and incorruptible – is recognised today as one of the best of all the Cape's governors. In addition to strengthening the defences, he had built schools and churches, improved the wine industry developed by the Huguenots four decades earlier, enlarged Simon van der Stel's vineyards at Groot Constantia and placed the economy on a sound footing by various fair and even-handed financial measures.

So it was that people came from near and far to attend when he was buried with much ceremony in the vaults under the Groote Kerk (Great Church) six days after his death. It was a genuine outpouring of feeling for a man who had won the regard not only of the people he had ruled so well, but also of those distant eminences, the Lords Seventeen, who in 1721 had paid him the rare accolade of appointing him a Councillor Extraordinary of Netherlands East India.

The funeral procession included military and civilian mourners. His spurs, sword, gloves, helmet and cuirass were carried on cushions and his horse, draped in black, preceded the coffin. Two companies of the Burgher Militia – one infantry, the other mounted – were in attendance, as was the Cape Regiment, which provided the guard of honour and fired a salute. Minute guns boomed from the Castle's ramparts from the moment the coffin left the Van der Stel Gate until the military escort returned after the funeral, while for the next six weeks the bells of the Castle and the Groote Kerk were tolled for an hour every morning, midday and evening. No doubt the mourners at his funeral sang the traditional hymn 'Thank God That He Is Dead', a song of thanksgiving for the fact that a good man would now receive his just reward in Heaven. It was, as Agnes van Loon writes, 'an impressive and honourable farewell to a Governor who was loved and respected by all'.[13]

Work on De Chavonnes' brainchild continued after the funeral, and it was inaugurated in April 1726 – an immensely strong construction of granite quarried from Table Mountain, blue slate from Robben Island for the flagstone floors and small bricks fired at the Cape or brought in as ballast by passing ships. Holding it all together was lime mortar created from Robben Island's seashells.

The 'Water Casteel' (Water Castle), 'Groote Batterij' (Great Battery) or 'Mauritius Batterij' – it was not officially named 'Batterij Chavonnes' (Chavonnes Battery) until 1744 – consisted of a massive stone-faced rampart in the form of a splay-legged 'U', facing the sea and built directly on the rocks at the water's edge. On the front wall were mounted a number of heavy guns (typically eight), with several more guns on each slanting side-wall. Behind and below this armament was the necessary infrastructure the battery needed in both peace and war – casemates for storing ammunition and equipment, powder magazines, various workshops. At the top of a long flight of steps was a small barracks block that included a lock-up for convicts sentenced to hard labour. At the rear it was open and defenceless, since its main purpose was to prevent a seaward landing.

By today's sophisticated standards the battery seems almost laughably simple. But when it was built it posed a deadly danger to any force with ambitions of undertaking a landing or even entering the bay. In the early 18th century ships were the equivalents of today's airborne forces, as they could land troops at any spot along a hostile coast where boats could go ashore, and a well-placed battery like this was the best possible counter to such an event.

Its rampart, about 5m high, could ward off any projectiles, and it was capable of much more accurate fire than any ship as its guns were mounted on a stable firing platform, rather than a rolling deck. It had more ammunition available than any attackers (it should be remembered that the most likely hostiles were armed merchantmen, whose first priority was their cargo) and it out-gunned them by a large margin.

The average armed merchantmen of those days would most likely have mounted nothing heavier than 9-pounder guns, while the battery deployed great 18-pounders, 24-pounders and 36-pounders, which could fire a variety of ammunition: solid iron round-shot to smash holes in ships' hulls or batter in their gun ports, bar and chain-shot to destroy their sails and rigging, and man-killing grape or canister-shot for close range, whose loads of small musket balls sprayed out like those of a giant blunderbuss or shotgun. Later, the Chavonnes Battery, like the others which followed it, was also equipped with shot-ovens which allowed its gunners to heat cannonballs to make red-hot 'hot shot', a terrible threat to the ships of the day with their highly flammable tarred wooden hulls and huge spreads of canvas sail. It is also likely that at various times the battery was equipped with mortars, high-angle weapons which fired large explosive shells.

OF Mentzel, a soldier in the Castle garrison from 1733 to 1741, later wrote that the battery

> ... [was] best situated for a bombardment of enemy ships. It is built upon rocks and surrounded by them, while its guns are placed low down over the water. If the gunners did but train them in a directly horizontal position on their carriages ... it would scarcely be possible for them to miss an enemy ship, while the holes that the balls would make would be close to the waterline, and therefore very dangerous.[14]

The Chavonnes Battery was the first of a chain of strong coastal fortifications to be built over the next 70 years and which would turn the Cape into one of the most heavily defended ports in Africa. Yet with one or two minor exceptions neither the Chavonnes Battery nor those built later were destined ever to fire a shot in anger, and were probably never fully manned except on rare occasions. However, the first duty of any armed force is not to fight wars, but to deter aggressors, and the big guns grinning from the Cape batteries' ramparts certainly fulfilled that requirement. During the Company's 143-year rule at the Cape no hostile naval force ever ventured anywhere near the anchorage.[15]

Mentzel is less complimentary about the crews who manned the Chavonnes Battery. According to him there were few trained artillerymen in the garrison, and in time of war about 100 'totally unskilled' local sailors would be conscripted as gunners.[16] The battery's peace-time complement amounted to no more than a handful of men: a sergeant, who was the full-time post-holder, a corporal, and nine gunners who came out daily from the Castle, spending much of their time on maintenance and repairs to keep the battery ready for immediate operation – although this work was not too onerous, given that resident convicts were available for the more arduous tasks.

In the early 1700s the Cape's total military presence was a small one: roughly some 200 full-time members of the active garrison and about another 400 in various civilian occupations who were available for call-up in time of dire need – presumably members of the Burgher Militia, since Mentzel notes that they had not had 'regular military training'. It seems that the VOC's strategy was to maintain a prepared defensive system which could be manned by reinforcements from the Far East or Europe, or simply commandeered from passing fleets.

❧

The Cape's regular garrison might not have smelt much powder during the first half of the 18th century, but its members were not idle. The Castle was the epicentre of all military and civilian activity, since it housed not only the garrison but also the Governor and his staff. As a result it was very firmly secured and the scene of constant routine and special ceremonial drills.

Thanks to Mentzel we have a rare and finely observed picture of a Cape infantryman's daily routine. Mentzel makes many cogent comments about weaknesses in the Cape defences (of which a number had been attended to by the time his book was published in 1784), but adds that 'for a man who loves method it is a veritable joy to observe the excellent order maintained in the Castle. The whole work of the day is mapped out by the clock and is performed with the utmost punctuality.'[17]

According to Grobbelaar, the garrison consisted of the captain, two lieutenants, two ensigns, one adjutant, eight sergeants and 14 corporals, plus the rank and file. These were divided into three infantry companies, each with two sergeants; one artillery battery, commanded by another sergeant; and the Governor's Guard, which, with the remaining sergeant, was the responsibility of the senior lieutenant, who was also the garrison second-in-command.

The Governor's Guard consisted of two corporals, all six hautboyists, 12 grenadiers, six musketeers, and drummers and trumpeters. Among other things it provided the sentries who paced solemnly back and forth with fixed bayonets in front of the governor's quarters and escorted him when he sallied forth on his official rounds.

In Mentzel's time the Castle began to stir before dawn, at 4am. Those responsible for dragging the garrison into the new day were the corporal of the night-guard and the duty '*rondegangers*', or watchkeep-ers. Watchkeeping appears to have been a specific appointment for eight of the garrison's *rondegangers*, two of whom were always on duty in the guardroom at night. Being a night watchkeeper was no sinecure; the duty shifts were regulated by an hourglass that had been set during the day from the sundial in the Voorplein, and every hour on the hour one of them would climb into the tower above the Van der Stel Gate and strike the bell by hand. The fortress was locked up for the night at 9.30pm, though the Castle never really slept.

In 1743, during the governorship of Hendrik Swellengrebel,[18] the first 'African' (ie, locally born man) to assume the outpost's highest office, the Castle acquired another outer defensive work, the formi-dable Imhoff Battery. When the new Governor-General of the VOC's Eastern outposts, Gustaf Baron van Imhoff, passed through on his way to take up his new position he expressed his dissatisfaction with the fact that enemy ships could easily land troops and artillery to the east, out of range of the Castle's guns. Van Imhoff knew only too well that this would leave the Castle, and Cape Town itself, in a very precarious situation. Not only would they be sitting targets for plunging artillery fire, but it would also be possible to sabotage the pipes carrying fresh water from Table Mountain to the town.

This had been a concern for decades, but Van Imhoff had the power to do something about it, and in the next few years the Castle's inner and outer defences were substantially extended and strengthened. He authorised the construction of a modest square-shaped fort, consist-ing of earth ramparts on stone foundations and named Fort Knokke, near the site of Cape Town's present-day Woodstock railway station. Fort Knokke was linked to the Castle by a series of smaller batteries, called Elizabeth, Helena, Charlotte and Tulbagh, which were collec-tively known as the 'Sea Line'.

The Sea Line gave the Castle's eastern flank some protection against amphibious landings and also against a landward advance along the coast from False Bay, or from the other side of Table Bay, although the problem of the heights of the mountain-slopes would only be ad-dressed four decades later. A small battery was also erected at Rogge Bay, Cape Town's fishing harbour, located slightly to the west of where

Jan van Riebeeck's statue on the Foreshore stands today, and is now buried under Thibault Square.

Van Imhoff's major contribution, however, was the construction of a defensive work immediately in front of the Castle's seaward aspect that was even more formidable than the Chavonnes Battery. The Imhoff Battery, as it came to be called, linked up with the ravelin which protected the Van der Stel Gate and mounted eleven 24-pounder guns and six 18-pounders – heavy ordnance for those days. At its southern end was a well-guarded '*barrière*' or gate, similar to the one at the Castle's front entrance, the Lion Gate, through which all wheeled traffic to and from Simon's Town had to pass.

Thanks to Van Imhoff the approaches to the Castle were now defended in front and on both flanks. Much remained to be done, both in the environs of Cape Town and further down the coast at False Bay, but the Cape's defences had come a long way in the 90-odd years since Van Riebeeck's men had constructed the little sod-walled Fort De Goede Hoop.

At this stage of the Cape's military development the regular garrison had come to depend on the part-time soldiers of the Burgher Militia to provide a substantial depth element, and the militia had made significant progress since its tiny beginnings. By the mid-18th century its men were properly organised and trained to fight in two different roles, depending on the requirement.

The beginning of the 18th century had seen a certain change of direction for the Burgher Militia, with more emphasis being placed on formal drill movements and battle formations. By 1740 the militia had grown to such an extent that when the Cape went on the alert during the War of the Austrian Succession (1740–48), 50 part-timers could be mobilised every month to support the regular garrison in manning the outpost's defences. Five years later, when the district of Swellendam was created, part of the establishment was a company of militia dragoons, which was to grow into three companies with 315 rank and file within the next 50 years.

The Company's reliance on its citizen-soldiers in the 1700s was underlined even further by the creation of a long chain of signal guns by which members of the Burgher Militia in the outlying areas could be called to arms in the event of an emergency. By the 1730s about 20 such guns were emplaced on various prominent terrain features, linking the Castle to Citrusdal in the north, the sub-drostdy[19] of Tulbagh (today's town of Worcester) in the north-east and Swellendam in the east.

The system was designed to be simple and cost-effective. Each signal gun was located within hearing distance of an occupied farmhouse, settlement or outpost. When the occupants heard the nearest gun in the chain, they collected their equipment, went to their gun and fired it. Theoretically this process would then be repeated by the next gun in the line although there were some differences at different stations: in the event of a general mobilisation the 'Prinsevlag', the orange, white and blue battle flag under which the men of the Princes of Orange had fought during the war of liberation from Spain, would be hoisted over the Plattekloof position near Cape Town, after which the Plattekloof gun would be fired, setting off the chain of signals. At first the system did not work as planned, but it was gradually improved and more guns were added. Within a short time the summons would have been heard wherever there was a VOC presence. What it signified was that the Burgher Militia had finally developed from a more or less scratch-depth element into a first-line defence force that could be thrown into battle at minimum notice.

CHAPTER 6

THE FINAL FLOWERING

The second half of the 18th century saw the final flowering of the VOC military establishment at the Cape – ironically, just at the moment that the Company itself began its final decline. The heyday of the great East Indian trading companies was almost over, and the name of the new game was international politics, military strategy and maritime power.

The French East India Company was long gone by the latter decades of the century, dissolved in 1769 when it was no longer able to pay its way. The Swedish East India Company, once such a lucrative enterprise, was fading out. The Danish East India Company had lost its monopoly charter in 1772, and by 1779 its Indian possessions had become a British crown colony; the destruction of the Danish fleet at Copenhagen in 1807 would ring the first peal of its eventual death-knell. Britain's 'John Company' was destined to hold out the longest, thanks mainly to British domination of the oceans, but it, too, was fading. In 1813 it would lose its trade monopoly, and although it would still rule a vast stretch of India for decades to come, the writing was on the wall.

The new scheme of things resulted in a strange contradiction at the Cape of Good Hope. After almost one and a half centuries of doing pretty much what it pleased, the once-indomitable VOC was nearing the end not only of its prosperity but of its very existence. Yet its military establishment at the Cape of Good Hope continued to grow as the Company became more and more enmeshed in international power politics.

The Netherlands was no longer the dominant maritime and economic power, and the seeds of yet another downward lurch were sown in the 1770s when the Dutch expressed their resentment at the increase in British power by supporting the American rebels. The direct result of this was that in December 1780 the Dutch 'blundered into a war[1] with England for which they were totally unprepared, militarily and economically ... The ensuing war was wholly disastrous for the Dutch and led indirectly to the ruin of the VOC.'[2]

In the years to follow, the Dutch built scores of new warships for their neglected fleet (although the English built even more), but the end of the old alliance with Britain left them vulnerable to attack from their large neighbour, France. The most serious future effect on the Netherlands, and therefore on both the VOC and the Cape of Good Hope, was that the war provided more fuel to inflame the passions of the republican revolutionary 'Patriotten', or Patriots, made up of both middle-class supporters of the French revolutionaries and members of the proletariat, who were opposed to the aristocrats and plutocrats of the existing regime.

The VOC, as FS Gaastra of the TANAP research project graphically puts it, now entered 'a long drawn-out death agony ... the Company was engulfed by such colossal financial problems that the chambers in Holland had to request suspension of payment. The Company could no longer go ahead under its own steam. It was only thanks to the government, who guaranteed repayments and the payment of interest on any financial obligations that the VOC would undertake, that the directors were able to keep the Company afloat.'[3]

The government now had its hand firmly on the wheel, and its grip on the VOC would keep tightening as the Company became more and more dependent on it. But the VOC, though growing increasingly feeble with each passing year, continued to lay down an ever-expanding military footprint which was so deep that it would continue to influence developments in southern Africa for centuries to come.

At the same time it had to keep track of the free burghers' outward movement along the distant eastern frontier, on the outermost rim of the Company's sphere of influence – if 'influence' is the right word to apply to its weakened presence there – where considerable friction was building up between the trekboers and various clans of the Xhosa nation.

The Xhosas of that time could probably best be described as a tribal confederation rather than a cohesive nation, a fact that was to have a definite influence on what was to come. They had a typical structure, with a paramount chief who ruled over a number of tribes or clans of various size, but unlike the Zulus under Shaka three decades later, their society was not highly centralised, and as a result each of its components enjoyed a greater or lesser degree of autonomy.

Military historian Ian Knight notes a Xhosa custom which was to have a discernible effect on the future eastern frontier situation: 'The Xhosa state had a tendency to expansion through fragmentation, each son of a chief being encouraged to set up a chieftainship of his own. This process in itself sent Xhosa bands across the frontier.'[4]

This innate flexibility was echoed in Xhosa fighting tactics. The typical Xhosa warrior of the time did not go to war decked out in gaudy martial raiment. Typically he would be wearing little more than a small loincloth, a supple leather cloak and beads around his neck and arms. Generally speaking heads were bare, though men of a more flashy temperament often wore upright wing feathers tucked into either side of a headband. Chiefs were distinguished only by leopard-skin cloaks and a brass armband on the right arm.

Xhosa tactics and battle drills were much more flexible and individualistic than the monolithic phalanx favoured by Shaka and the Zulus in later times. The Xhosa warrior would be armed with a number of light throwing spears – '*assegai*', in the universal South African usage, although he would have used the term '*umkhonto*' – a smallish oval shield of oxhide and a *knobkierie*[5] or club which was both a short-range throwing weapon and a ferociously effective fighting tool in close combat.

When fighting in the open the Xhosas used a winged battle formation that resembled the famous 'horns of the bull' which was later used with such merciless efficiency by Shaka, but with some important differences. A Xhosa warrior bent on hand-to-hand fighting would launch all but one of his assegais when within effective range, 30m or so, and then charge in with the last, part of whose shaft he might break off for greater handiness in close combat.

But the Xhosas were not wedded to the concept of mass close-quarter action, because in an important aspect their military mindset was inherently different from that of the Zulus. The Xhosa warrior's preference was to skirmish as the circumstances demanded. This philosophy of flexibility and willingness to adapt to changing circumstances was to make the Xhosas tenacious opponents in their two fairly minor clashes with the VOC and seven more serious ones with the British in the next century or so.

Looking back on past southern African wars, it would not be wrong to say that the three groups which offered the most sustained resistance to British imperialist expansion before their inevitable subjugation were the Xhosas, the Boers and the BaSothos – citizen-soldiers almost to a man, all tactically flexible and ready to adapt to changing circumstances.

By 1730 the nomadic trekboers had reached the Great Brak River, and by 1743 they had established themselves along the Gamtoos. Cordial contacts or no, events were now moving towards a classic African *casus belli*, involving two separate pastoralist groups competing for the same watering and grazing resources, and it was clear that at some stage friction would result.

The Cape Government, mindful of the VOC's aversion for profitless conflict, went to considerable lengths to rein in its independent-minded frontiersmen, and in 1743 declared the Great Brak River the outpost's official eastern boundary. But the eastern free burghers, who were virtually a law unto themselves by this time, paid little heed and kept moving ever further.

In the meantime the Cape garrison continued to grow as the situation in Europe began to deteriorate once more, although some of the steps taken clearly illustrate the Company's increasingly desperate financial situation. In 1743, for example, it was decided to form a 'Corps des Invalides', consisting of soldiers who had been discharged due to age or infirmity but could still be utilised in time of war; in this case to act as a sort of gendarmerie while the active soldiers were otherwise occupied.

The Cape military took yet another innovative step. Khoina had been involved in the commandos from the earliest days of the Cape outpost, albeit on a more or less *ad hoc* basis, but this state of affairs had begun to change when Governor Swellengrebel had directed that in the event of attack from outside, the free burghers were to attach both themselves and their workers to the garrison forces. This was followed in 1759 by an order that in time of military emergency the free burghers of the Swellendam and Stellenbosch districts were to report for duty along with any of their slaves and labourers who were trained in the use of firearms.

This directive had deeper implications than might be visible at first glance: once again it proved that the VOC administration at the Cape had no qualms about the military reliability of people of colour – not even slaves. The shadows of the Spanish Inquisition still hung heavily over the Low Countries, and what clearly still concerned the Lords Seventeen far more than race was whether a person was a baptised Protestant. And people of colour were not just involved in what might be called the statutory military.

By mid-century, the Cape's ever more racially blurred population had given rise to two distinct groupings of people of clearly mixed race, outside the official military parameters – the 'Bastaard Hottentotten' of the official documents – which were both destined to make a name as mounted infantrymen.

One group was made up of the people who would later become known as the Griquas. The founder of the later Griquas was an exceptional man of mixed ancestry named Adam Kok (1710–1800). Born a slave, Kok was a man of such personality and industry that he was manumitted and allowed to settle on a farm near St Helena Bay. Kok had greater ambitions, however, and around 1750 he led a group of like-minded people into the sparsely populated interior of

Namaqualand, which at that stage was still largely untouched by out-siders except for hunters, cattle traders and a few vagabonds who had fled from the settled Cape districts.

Kok settled in the lower part of the Kamiesberg, the long mountain range which runs parallel with the sea and divides Namaqualand into two regions, the Sandveld to the west and the Bushmanland to the east. There Kok blended a many-hued group of Bastaard-Hottentotten with ethnic Grigriqua and Namaqua clanspeople into what amounted to a new tribe.

Eventually renamed the 'Griqua' (after a missionary pointed out with some truth that 'Bastaard' had rather a negative connotation), it was recognised by the VOC government, and Kok was presented with the brass-headed staff of office given to every clan chief as a token of that recognition.

Kok's people were independent in every sense of the word, living a semi-nomadic life and existing mainly by raising livestock and hunting, as well as plundering the locals from time to time. However reprehensi-ble some of their activities might have been, they are of specific interest because essentially their social organisation and military activities were not much different from those of the free burghers.

The historian JS Marais provides us with a graphic verbal snapshot of the Griquas: 'They were, in fact, typical frontiersmen, more so than many of the Boers themselves, whom they nevertheless resembled in a number of ways. They fought in the Boer manner … and their leaders were often at loggerheads with one another.'[6]

By 'fought in the Boer manner' Marais means the classic commando system with its characteristic hard-riding, sharpshooter horsemen, and many decades later, after the Griquas had moved eastwards from Namaqualand, an action involving one of their commandos was to have an important effect on southern Africa's military development.

The other group was composed of people who tended to have a higher proportion of white ancestry than the Kok clan. Led by one Barend Barendse and his brother Nicolaas, they too moved towards the north-western frontier but struck slightly further eastwards, to-wards today's Prieska Drift.

Like Kok's people they were products of the new population evolved at the Cape, with separate cultural structure, language and military organisation; and decades later, when the majority moved into what is now Namibia and founded the town of Rehoboth, they were to have a distinct influence on military structures and tactics north of the Orange River as well.

At Cape Town the Corps des Invalides limped along, in more senses than one, until 1762 – by which time it also included past members of the Burgher Militia – when those still capable of some form of active service were separated and formed into the 'Compagnie des Reserves', their task being to defend the Imhoff Battery. Still later inactive reserve components were formed for the Burgher Militia detachments at Swellendam and elsewhere.

The late 1760s saw a further formalisation of the Burgher Militia. By 1763 it was properly organised with well-planned defences. The signal system now worked well, and Stellenbosch had four companies of dragoons and one company of infantry which could swiftly be called up to assist the Cape garrison in time of war. Five years later, the Burgher War Councils had been granted certain punitive powers and made responsible for the maintenance of public order, the appointment of their commissioned and non-commissioned officers, and the enforcement of ordinances and Burgher Guard regulations – all part of a stricter regulation.

The new governor arrived at the Cape in 1773, but was in no position to enact any further changes. Baron Pieter van Reede van Oudtshoorn tot Nederhorst[7] had set sail for the Cape in the merchantman *Asia*, but was taken fatally ill on board, and well before the *Asia* arrived in April 1773 Van Oudtshoorn had gone to his eternal rest, though not yet to his grave. This last matter was attended to as soon as the *Asia* anchored in Table Bay. The gubernatorial funeral is regarded as the most spectacular interment ever to be staged at the Cape in the earlies.[8]

During this period the commando system underwent yet another overhaul. By 1774 there were 13 field corporals, each representing a different ward, and it was decided that an improved chain of command was needed. This led to a Council of Policy decision to appoint Godlieb Rudolph Opperman as *veldkommandant*, or field commandant, for the Stellenbosch area. This was an appointment title rather than a rank, however, so it was also decided to institute the notch of *kornet* (cornet) to denote the leader of a commando and give Opperman the necessary authority over the various field corporals in his jurisdiction. By 1776, the existing field corporals were elevated to the new rank of *veldwacht-meester* (field watch-master, the equivalent of a sergeant) and made commando leaders themselves, their replacements becoming what would now be called sub-unit commanders.

It is not difficult to see why this happened. The Cape outpost had now expanded, more or less of its own volition, to an extent far beyond the wildest imaginings of the Lords Seventeen. It had taken on a life of its own, with the more enterprising spirits putting as much distance as possible between themselves and the dread hand of the VOC's bureaucracy; the ability of the Company to control and secure its outlying areas was weakening rapidly. Yet the extent of the VOC's area of influence, real or imagined, by that stage can be judged by the fact that in 1774 a large commando was formed to undertake an expedition to the Hantam area and parts of the Karoo and Sneeuwberge, hundreds of kilometres from Cape Town.

There are graphic depictions of the lawless conditions in the Koue Bokkeveld, the Roggeveld and the surrounding regions in the 1770s to be found in Lt Donald Moodie's monumental *Record*, first published in 1838; this contains verbatim reports from the *veldwachtmeesters* and *veldcorporaals* (or 'sergeants' and 'corporals', as he calls them) which were lodged at the drostdy of Stellenbosch, under which the region fell at that time. It is clear that there was a fierce four-sided struggle in progress in which little quarter was given, involving the farmers, Khoina and organised bands of Bushman livestock rustlers (although the latter might well have included or consisted mainly of Khoina).

The relevant reports date from October 1775 to April 1777, and speak of sheep and cattle being carried off in their hundreds, Bushman attacks on farmers, commando members unable to attend owing to the defence of their homes, and a harsh, hot guerrilla war. 'On 1 October 1775 veldcorporaal Willem Steinkamp[9] from the Onder-Roggeveld reported that "I have to inform you that here in my district, since the commando of last year, all is still in peace and quiet with the Bushmen."'[10] But on 9 February 1776, Gerrit Putter reported:

This is to inform you that the Bushmen have again stolen at Jacob Naude's; they have stabbed sheep dead, and also taken away, how many is not known, and on the 13th March we attacked the kraal, shot 17 and took 10 ...[11]

But on 29 April 1776 the same Corporal Steinkamp who 'had earlier reported that his district of the Onder-Roggeveld was quiet', now informed the landdrost:

The undersigned makes known that the following: mischief has been done by the Bushmen :- lst. At J Louw's, murdered a slave, killed 3 horses, stole 82 oxen and 200 sheep. 2d. At C Mouton's, when sitting at supper with the door open, they shot arrows into the house, and wounded a slave girl and a Hottentot. Mouton then closed the door, but they did not cease to shoot at the house all night, until at length they drove the cattle off the homestead, to induce the men to come out of the house, but stole nothing. 3d. They broke open the house of J. Mouton in the night and destroyed every thing. The said Corporal further states, that 4 persons have already left their farms, that, if no support be given, the others and he himself must fly also; and requests a commando ...[12]

One of the men in a retaliating commando 'was wounded with a poisoned arrow, but recovered.' The final report details that Pieter van Wyk was

... robbed of 200 sheep, and the shepherd murdered; Stevanus Naude robbed of 15 oxen, and the herdsman murdered [sic]; the same night a Hottentot of Naude's ran off, hid himself about the farm for some days, and coming to the farm by night, killed Naude's principal Hottentot with a poisoned arrow; this thief was caught, but W Pretorius, gave him over to Joubert, who then sent him to the Sergeant D S van der Merwe, but he got loose on the way, and ran off, when the person in charge of him was obliged to shoot him; from W. Engelbrecht 700 sheep carried off ... [A commando] fortunately found the kraal, in which there were 300 Hottentots, but having too few men they only shot 20 ...[13]

In the meantime the eastern free burghers were still moving out-wards. By 1770 they had settled throughout the Great Karoo, the Roggeveld and Nieuweveld Mountains, the plateaux behind them and the Camdeboo area (today's Aberdeen district) to the east. In the next 10 years they went even further, to the areas of Bruintjieshoogte and Tarka, which were to become springboards for the Great Trek two generations later.

At the same time events in Europe were claiming much of the VOC's remaining attention and financial energy. The Cape's total military manpower now consisted of about 1100 trained regular and militia soldiers in Cape Town, several thousand militiamen who were scattered far and wide in the outlying districts, and several hundred civilian VOC employees who could be pressed into service in an emergency, although obviously not to great effect. With these scanty assets it was expected to present some sort of credible deterrent. This meant, in turn, that there was little to spare for the outlying areas.

When Governor Joachim Ammema, Baron van Plettenberg,[14] paid a personal visit to the eastern frontier area in 1778 he found both trek-boers and Xhosas living in the fertile Zuurveld (Sour Veld) on either side of the official border, in such close proximity that some of the tribesmen were actually in the employ of the farmers.

Van Plettenberg did what he could to stabilise what was quite clearly a very volatile situation. Among other things he directed that without his express permission no commando expedition should be undertaken against the Xhosas, and he negotiated, or so he thought, an agreement with local Xhosa chiefs that designated the Fish River as the boundary between the two groups.

The governor set great store by this agreement, but the Xhosas did not, and later repeatedly crossed the Fish River to raid either the farm-ers (in retaliation for violations by the latter, they claimed, accurately or otherwise) or settlements of the original Khoina inhabitants, of whom they had a low opinion and regarded as their natural prey. Eventually they went further and actually occupied territory on the western side.

The reason for this apparent exhibition of bad faith is not necessarily as obvious as it might appear. It is certainly likely that the Xhosas, who tended to move in whole communities, did not take serious account of the farmers, who were very few in number – but it also seems clear that Van Plettenberg made the mistake of speaking to the wrong people – or to not enough of the right people. Given the decentralised nature of the Xhosa groups, an agreement reached with certain chiefs would certainly not be regarded as binding by other chiefs who had not been involved. Another invisible but potent factor propelling the Xhosas westwards was the pressure being exerted on their rear by other south-ward-migrating tribes, not to mention internal strains resulting from intermittent outbreaks of civil war between various clans.

The first sizable armed clash between the trekboers and Xhosas was not long in coming. By December 1779 Xhosa cattle raiding had reached such a pitch that some of the trekboers along the Bushmans River were retreating while they still had something to lose. The exact cause of the clash is obscure, but is thought to have resulted from the actions of certain trekboers, conceivably in reaction to a Xhosa cattle raid.

Early the following year two commandos under Josua Joubert and Pieter Hendrik Ferreira were mobilised and seized a large number of Xhosa cattle, but could not overcome the tribesmen. By October the chorus of complaints from the frontier – where the farmers were being raided also by Bushmen – reached such a pitch that Van Plettenberg felt compelled to take action.

He appointed the experienced Adriaan van Jaarsveldt[15] as field commandant and directed him to expel the Xhosas who had settled on the western side of the Fish River. He soon amended this directive and ordered Van Jaarsveldt to negotiate the Xhosa settlers' departure but, as before, this course of action did not work well because each chief was more or less a law unto himself, and only one actually withdrew. Van Jaarsveldt then stripped off the velvet glove and went on the war-path with a commando of about 90 burghers and 40 allied Khoina. The combination of horses, guns and veldcraft proved irresistible, and by mid-1781 he reported that he had captured a great number of cattle and claimed that no Xhosas remained in the Zuurveld.

Thus ended the so-called First Frontier War, which was not a war so much as a series of skirmishes and cattle raids. But the respite was to prove strictly a temporary one, since neither the trekboers nor the

Xhosas were willing to let go of the Zuurveld or desist from the cattle bartering of which the VOC continued to take a dim view. And the Xhosas, as they had proved already, were not people to be trifled with.

The fighting had exposed some weaknesses in the commando system. Developed to address a specific set of operational requirements, it naturally did not work as well against the Xhosas as it had against the Khoina clans and Bushman groups. The Fish River area was difficult fighting territory for the commandos: easily fordable in most places, its heavily wooded banks provided much natural cover for cattle raiders and ambushes. Tactically this suited the Xhosas very well, since the commandos' horses and guns were less of an advantage than they had been further south. The result was that just after the end of the 'war' the system underwent extensive restructuring.

There would now be two field commandants, ranked as lieutenants, one for the eastern and one for the northern district, each with a second-in-command. Van Jaarsveldt was field commandant for the eastern districts, now raised to the rank of lieutenant in the militia, with Cornet Dawid Schalk van der Merwe as his second-in-command. Below him were five *veldwachtmeesters* and five field corporals. The northern and north-western field commandant, Lieutenant Charl Marais,[16] would have a cornet as his second-in-command, two *veldwachtmeesters* and two field corporals, and in times of emergency the *veldwachtmeesters* of the Roggeveld, Bokkeveld and Hantam districts would be under his control as well.

To add to Governor van Plettenberg's troubles the military situation in Europe was deteriorating even further, and before long the Dutch were firmly allied to France and thereby to the new revolutionary American nation. But since their days of maritime might were long past, the Cape was vulnerable to an attack by the British, to whom it had now assumed considerable strategic importance.

One result of this was that in March 1781 the expanded involvement of people of colour in the military went an important step further when the Council of Policy proclaimed that all free burghers must compile a yearly statement of the number of Khoina and persons of mixed blood in their service. The following month Van Plettenberg – surely the instigator of the Council of Policy's proclamation – declared that as far as he was concerned such persons would be excellent defenders of the Cape.

The very next day the Council of Policy directed that all Khoina and persons of mixed blood were to be sent to Cape Town for military service. Barely a week later the Corps Bastaard Hottentotten was established, and within a month had 400 serving members. The Corps did not last long, however, because the Lords Seventeen had already concluded that the only way the Cape could be defended against England would be to call in the help of the French.

Learning of a British plan to seize the Cape, the French undertook to loan them the Régiment Pondichéry – a battalion of infantry with its own artillery company – and on 22 March, the same month as the creation of the Corps Bastaard Hottentotten, the regiment sailed from Brest in the care of one of France's best young fighting sailors, Commodore Pierre de Suffren.[17]

It was not a moment too soon, because British preparations were well in hand. A certain Commodore George Johnstone,[18] who was due to leave Spithead for South America in mid-March on a punitive expedition against enemy privateers,[19] was ordered instead to invade the Cape. With 46 large and small warships, transport vessels and troopships carrying about 3 000 regular soldiers, Johnstone had more than enough muscle to overwhelm the VOC's defences, but fortunately for Van Plettenberg his plans came rather unstuck.

Resting at anchor in Porto Praya in the Cape Verde Islands, his fleet was surprised by De Suffren's squadron of five heavy ships of the line on 16 April 1781. Caught badly arrayed at anchor, Johnstone's fleet suffered severe damage from De Suffren's attack, and there followed a brief but inconclusive battle, resulting in De Suffren's *Artésien* being boarded, her captain killed and 25 crew captured, and another French man-o'-war, the *Annibal*, being completely dismasted. With the loss of some 200 men, De Suffren broke off contact, yet captured several of the British ships including two East Indamen; owing to his poorly arranged fleet lines Johnstone could not give effective pursuit and called off the only attempt to do so in order to effect repairs, believing the French would head for the West Indies instead of the Cape – Johnstone's second greatest mistake. *Annibal* managed to rig a jury mast, De Suffren abandoned the captured British ships and beat Johnstone to the Cape despite his handicap.

On 29 May the French frigate *Serapis* dropped anchor in Table Bay, and a few days later the remainder of De Suffren's ships arrived and made for False Bay, disembarking the Régiment Pondichéry's infantrymen and gunners at Simon's Town, from where they marched to their quarters in Cape Town. In the blink of an eye the tactical situation had swung in the VOC's favour.

De Suffren's lurking fleet and the newly reinforced garrison behind the heavy coastal batteries made an attack on the Cape Town–Simon's Town area a poor proposition, and an overland advance from Saldanha Bay was an even worse prospect, given the distance involved and the terrain which would have to be covered – about which little was known except that it was distinctly unfavourable. The bottom line was that the odds were now stacked against Johnstone, so he contented himself with attacking Saldanha Bay, where he captured five valuable Dutch merchantmen – a sixth was set alight by its crew and blew up – while some of his troops carried out a small unopposed landing operation.

Having inflicted a painful but not crippling blow on the VOC, Johnstone sent his troops and five of his warships on to India, and returned to England with the rest of his fleet and his prizes.[20] Even this last enterprise went wrong when an on-passage hurricane sank three of the Dutch merchantmen, thereby substantially reducing the amount of prize money Johnstone and his men were due from the disposal of the captured ships.

Thus failed the first British attempt to capture the Cape. The incident is almost forgotten now and usually earns no more than a passing reference,[21] but it might have changed the course of southern African history if De Suffren had not won the race to the Cape and landed his infantrymen and artillerymen in the nick of time. They had not fired a shot in anger, but they had demonstrated once again how effective a credible deterrent could be in averting war.

An interesting, albeit unverified, footnote to this crisis is a story told by travel writer José Burman in which, as he says, 'the Chavonnes Battery was able to prove its worth'. Apparently a Danish ship, anchored in Table Bay, came under suspicion of gathering information for the British. The Port Captain, a Dane named Staaring, decided to make some personal enquiries, so he had himself rowed out to the suspect ship after first arranging a clandestine signal with the Chavonnes Battery in case of any dastardly stratagems on the part of his fellow countrymen. When Captain Staaring hauled himself on board, the Danes decided that discretion would be the better part of valour and hastily made sail with their visitor still in place. Staaring's reaction to this cavalier treatment was to give the pre-arranged emergency signal, at which the great guns of the Chavonnes Battery opened fire and the Danes wisely struck their colours rather than run the risk of being sunk.

The arrival of the Régiment Pondichéry eased the immediate military manpower crisis, and the situation improved even further in May 1782 with the arrival of another French unit, the Régiment Luxembourg. The Corps Bastaard Hottentotten was now disbanded, but an important milestone had been reached and passed: a group which up to this point had been largely ignored had now become part of the military establishment.

In just over a decade this was to lead to the creation of an infantry regiment whose soldiers – almost all recruited from the formerly marginalised Bastaard Hottentotten – would prove their mettle before the most unforgiving taskmasters of all, the red gods of battle. The Régiment Pondichéry and the Régiment Luxembourg were the first of a number of foreign regiments to serve at the Cape; the American Revolution and Johnstone's attempt at invasion had persuaded the Lords Seventeen that the outpost needed a garrison of at least 2 000 officers and men.

Several other French regiments were to be stationed at the Cape during the next three years. The Régiment Luxembourg was posted to the Far East in 1783, but by then another French unit called the Régiment De Waldner, or Waldener, had arrived and gone into camp at Diep River, outside Cape Town. The Régiment De Waldner was soon posted to Batavia, but the Régiment Pondichéry stayed in situ until 1784 before it too was posted, to Île de France (which was later to be captured by the British and renamed Mauritius).

Though brief, the French presence was to have an immense

influence not only on the Cape's defences but also on its civil society. 'For three years,' Grobbelaar says, 'the French virtually occupied the Cape [and] a period of false economic progress resulted. During this time the Cape gained a thorough acquaintance with French military tradition ... Cape Town blossomed and was known as 'Little Paris'.[22]

In his book 'Masters of the Castle', Hymen WJ Picard writes:

> Cape Town became a different place altogether ... Apart from protection, the French brought ... a prosperity in which every Capetonian could participate. Everybody made money – from the black shoe-shine boy on the Parade and the 'free black' wigmaker in Dorpstraat to the wagon-maker in Rondebosch and the wine merchant in Wynberg.
>
> Dressmakers and milliners had to work overtime; tailors [had] to hire larger premises ... one ball after another was offered in honour of the French protectors, and romance blossomed as it had never done before.[23]

By this time the VOC's military commander at the Cape was Robert Jacob Gordon,[24] an unusual combination of thoroughly professional soldier and dedicated natural scientist and geographer – and ultimately a tragic figure who was driven to an early death by his unwavering loyalty to the House of Orange.

Described by contemporaries as 'a very fine jovial fellow' and 'a tall, stout, soldier-like man', Gordon's grandfather was a Scotsman who had joined the Dutch navy – not an unusual act in those days, given the close ties which existed between the Netherlands and Scotland at the time – and never returned to his homeland. Gordon's father joined the Scots Brigade, a most unusual unit of ethnic Highlanders that served as the Prince of Orange's personal bodyguard (see Appendix 3), and eventually rose to the rank of major-general.

Gordon, described as being possessed of 'indefatigable spirit and an eager thirst for knowledge', went to university at the age of 16, excelled at nature studies and actually published some articles in the renowned Buffon's *Histoire Naturelle*. In 1765 he was commissioned into the Scots Brigade as a lieutenant, but transferred into the VOC's army in 1780. He was appointed captain of the Castle garrison, thereby automatically becoming president of the Burgher War Council. By 1782 he had leapfrogged to full colonel's rank and was a member of both the Council of Justice and the Council of Policy.

Gordon laboured mightily at building up the Cape's defences. He improved the standard drill manual and then applied the improvements, persuaded Van Plettenberg's successor to lay hands on a shipment of muskets destined for Batavia, designed a new type of tent which was better suited to local conditions (although as far as is known it was never manufactured) and replaced the cumbersome standard drill for firing red-hot shot with a better one, which resulted in a dramatic increase in the coastal batteries' rapidity and effectiveness of fire. His talents were clearly recognised: within two years of Van Plettenberg's replacement taking office, Gordon rose to become commander of all Cape military forces, the governor's chief of staff, and the designated coordinator of military forces in time of war.

In between all this Gordon found time to mount two extensive expeditions into the interior, one to the east and the other northwards into Namaqualand, gathering great amounts of knowledge about the topography, flora and fauna. During the Namaqualand trip he reached the great river known as the Gariep that had so tantalised Jan van Riebeeck, and re-named it the Orange River.[25]

In 1784 Van Plettenberg's term was up, and the Lords Seventeen concluded that his successor should be a specialist who would be able to administer and deploy the swollen armed presence to the best military – and financial – advantage. Their choice fell on Lieutenant-Colonel Cornelis Jacob van de Graaff.[26]

Van de Graaff was a complete contrast to his well-meaning and courteous but occasionally somewhat indecisive predecessor. Reputedly descended (via the wrong side of the blanket) from a Dutch nobleman of the 15th century, he was a soldier's son who became a cavalryman but then transferred to the engineers and rose to the senior post of Controller-General of Fortifications, marrying a countess's daughter along the way.

By various accounts – admittedly written mostly by his enemies, of whom there were many – Van de Graaff was not a very likeable character. Among other things his contemporaries describe him as arbitrary, headstrong, unpredictable, and violent of temper (on one famous occasion he reportedly drew his sword on an obdurate member of the Council of Policy, although he refrained from actually running him through). He was careless in financial matters, extravagant both in official spending and in his personal lifestyle, tactless and lacking in administrative skill – though this latter charge is unlikely, given his rank in the Dutch army engineers.

He was also a lifelong snob, which derived, perhaps, from his reputed descent and a close personal relationship with the Prince of Orange, and in general got along badly with the ever more independent-minded free burghers. One of his tasks was supposed to consist of calming them down and restoring some sort of unanimity of opinion, but this enterprise did not work well because he regarded his new subjects, so Picard says, as 'soldiers who had to obey their commanding officer, and for the rest keep their mouths shut.'[27] Not surprisingly this did not go down well with the free burghers.

The great improvements in the Cape defences during his tenure speak for themselves, though it is true he enjoyed the help of expert French engineers like Lieutenant-Colonel PH Gilquin and a lieutenant named Louis-Michel Thibault[28] – whose name was to be writ large in later Cape history – but Van de Graaff's was the directing hand, and his zeal and energy were boundless. He demanded numerous improvements to the existing batteries and was involved in the design of new ones, intensified training of both infantry and artillery, and made sure that his coastal gunners were expert at firing red-hot shot.

Although Van de Graaff was under orders from the cash-strapped VOC to be as frugal as possible, the first six years of the 1780s saw immense amounts of work being carried out on strengthening the Cape defences, a leading role being taken by Gilquin and Thibault. The overall aim of the work was to provide Cape Town with a credible defensive system against two threats. One was a landing in Table Bay, the other an overland attack by one of two routes. An enemy could seize Hout Bay or Simon's Bay, or both, then advance by way of the existing road, or he could land at Camps Bay on the other side of the peninsula and make use of the only other route to Cape Town at that time, through the cleft between Table Mountain and Lion's Head which was known then as Vlaggemanskloof and is today's Kloof Nek.[29]

Van de Graaff's response to these threats was to fortify Cape Town and its approaches as heavily as possible and equip Camps Bay and the Hout Bay–Simon's Town front with enough weaponry to delay any attack so that the main garrison in Cape Town would have time to prepare for defence or a counter-attack.

To this end two batteries called Boetzelaar (mounting four 24-pounder and four 8-pounder guns) and Zoutman[30] (with four 24-pounders) were erected at Simon's Town; Hout Bay was fortified by means of the West Battery on the western shore, mounting eight 24-pounder guns, and the East Battery on the mountain slopes opposite with eight 18-pounders.

Another small battery, known as the Conway Redoubt, or the Constantia Nek Redoubt, was erected on the southern slopes of Constantia Nek, along the only route from Hout Bay to Cape Town, while two small earth-walled batteries were built at Camps Bay and armed with 18-pounders to prevent an enemy force from landing there and then marching up to Vlaggemanskloof. Vlaggemanskloof itself was protected by two more seaward-facing batteries which enfiladed the road.

The outer seaward approaches to Cape Town were given some teeth. The French upgraded (or 'up-gunned') the modest Kleine Battery, constructed by the VOC at Three Anchor Bay in 1779 (the bay's name derives from three large ship's anchors which were embedded at various places in the little inlet to hinder boats from landing), and renamed it the Heine Battery. They also erected a heavily armed sod-and-earth battery at Mouille Point which mounted four 36-pounder and five 24-pounder guns. It was supposed to be a temporary defensive work, but the guns were still there in 1809, according to cannon expert Commander Gerry de Vries.

The Castle's eastern outer defences were strengthened by up-gunning Fort Knokke with three new 36-pounders and giving it flank protection in the form of two batteries, located between it and the mouth of the Salt River, the Nieuwe and Intermediaire Batteries. From the little fort, too, three new strongpoints – the Holland, Centre and Burgher

Redoubts, collectively known as the Fransche Linie or French Line – were constructed up the lower slopes of Devil's Peak and connected by zigzag trenches, thus providing the Castle, for the first time, with a measure of real protection from enemy activities on the heights at its back.

As an added precaution, a line of earthworks connecting two re-doubts named Gordon and Coehoorn were raised behind the French Line as fall-back positions. Two substantial stone batteries were also built along the coast west of the Castle at Rogge Bay, and armed with 18-pounder, 12-pounder and 8-pounder guns.

The most lethal of all the new fortifications, however, was the mas-sive Amsterdam Battery, designed and built by Gilquin and Thibault, which arose from 1784 onward, between the Rogge Bay batteries and the Chavonnes Battery on the bones of a smaller gun position with the peculiar name of 'Heer Hendriks Kinderen' (Master Hendrik's Children).

When it was eventually completed in 1787 the new battery towered over the beachfront, its fourteen 24-pounder guns and five 18-pound-ers commanding a wide arc of fire which not only plugged the exist-ing gaps between the Chavonnes and Rogge Bay Batteries but posed a threat to any enemy force which might land at today's Green Point and then approach across what was then open ground to attack Cape Town.

The Amsterdam Battery got off to a disastrous start at its first test-firing – a ceremonious affair at which the VIP guests included Governor Van de Graaff. One of its smaller weapons, a 12-pounder, exploded and killed two gunners, wounding not only another five but Van de Graaff himself, although not seriously. Neither he nor the others in at-tendance appear to have been unduly perturbed, however, presumably because the artillery pieces of those days tended to explode from time to time.[31]

The heavy emphasis on coastal artillery made absolute sense ac-cording to the nature of war at the time. For a distant outpost like Cape Town, not very heavily manned by infantry and far from any reinforce-ments, a successful seaborne landing was particularly dangerous. Ships could drop off troops and even light artillery wherever a landing was possible; each reasonably sized British warship also carried a contingent of marines who specialised in landing operations, and the sailors of those days were accustomed to fighting on land as light infantry if the need arose.[32]

❦

When the French regiments departed, the VOC began to hire mercenary regiments. The first to arrive in 1784 had been the Régiment De Meuron, recruited from the French-speaking cantons of Switzerland. The Cape was destined also to be the regiment's training base, and a depot was set up where recruits could be brought up to full standard before being shipped off to the Far East.

It would appear that the Swiss soldiers had some difficulty adapting themselves to the VOC's army. Grobbelaar quotes a German officer who was struck by the newcomers' language difficulties – commands were given in Dutch, which was incomprehensible to most of the rank and file, so that it was necessary for every order to be given first in French, then repeated in Dutch.

Although the fight between England and France was over for the time being, a second mercenary unit was called in, Colonel Theodor von Hugel's German-speaking Regiment Württemberg, and this arrived at the Cape in 1786. In those days mercenaries did not have the stigma under which they suffer today, and soldiers for hire prided themselves on their professionalism.

Grobbelaar quotes a chronicler of the regiment as saying that when it was being raised

> ... it was regarded as a particular honour to obtain an appointment in this new regiment ... applications were also received from the Wurttemberg Military Academy, and various officers and officials were recruited. The regiment was regarded as a show regiment by the Dutch [which] would serve as an example for the sharpening-up of the whole military system in East India. They were thus to ensure that only experienced soldiers were recruited ... [and] the regiment was to be manned only by good officers and non-commissioned officers.[33]

Just as with the Swiss regiment, all commands were given in Dutch, a dispensation to which the Württembergers easily adapted, the language having common roots with German. The regiment's smartness, general efficiency and tight discipline rapidly gained the respect of the general population, the Council of Policy, and even the perfectionist governor. Van de Graaff became very friendly with Colonel von Hugel, although he did not always approve of the Germans' methods – while a strict disciplinarian himself, he was horrified on one occasion when two soldiers who had been convicted of mutiny were sentenced to a mock execution which involved being marched out to face a firing squad, only to be officially 'reprieved' at the last moment.

Meanwhile, the situation on the eastern frontier did not improve. In 1786 the Governor established a new town in the eastern area, named Graaff-Reinet for himself and his wife, Cornelia Reynet, and consulted with the sagacious Adriaan van Jaarsveldt about the next step.

Van Jaarsveldt decided to concentrate on curbing Bushman raids to the north while adopting a conciliatory policy towards the Xhosas in the east. This carefully considered decision resulted, however, in considerable disgruntlement among the free burghers in the area, who felt that his priorities should have been the other way around. Farming folk were beginning to rebel against the heavy burden of continual call-outs to curb Bushmen raids, which seriously disrupted their economic activities.

The inhabitants of Swellendam had already made their feelings abundantly clear, and when the new district of Graaff-Reinet was proclaimed along the eastern frontier in 1785, the town's free burghers came into conflict with the landdrost; he believed that the military effort should be focused on the Bushmen, whereas they felt that there should be more aggressive action against the Xhosas.

Experience had shown that the carrot worked better than the stick, and the authorities instituted a new system: this allowed for burghers who went on commando against the remaining Khoina to be rewarded with captured livestock and the right to indenture captives. But there was no slackening of the burden of obligation.

In 1786 the field commandants were ordered to ensure that no eligible burgher was absent from the annual training exercises without express permission. It was not a particularly onerous obligation, though, since it was deemed adequate for a burgher to attend only one such exercise every four years. But this easy-going attitude did not apply to call-outs for active service.

During these years an unofficial but condoned paramilitary grouping arose among people of colour, this time under the leadership of one Jager Afrikaner, who was born near Tulbagh in the Roodezand Valley and was based in the Witzenberg area. Historians differ as to whether Jager and his followers were of pure Khoina or mixed descent, but it is common cause that he possessed some cattle of his own.

In addition to running cattle, Jager and his followers were paid and supplied with arms and ammunition by the VOC government for many years, rendering valuable service in fighting the Bushmen, the traditional enemies of the Khoina as well as the free burghers; as the historian GPJ Trumpelmann says, he 'virtually became a member of the Dutch East India Company's police force.'[34] Jager Afrikaner was later destined to turn himself into a ferocious robber baron, but that still lay years into the future. His immediate significance for the purpose of this book lay in the fact that he too used the commando system he had come to know so well, on his punitive expeditions.

In 1789, with Europe in turmoil and evil times approaching, the VOC sent a military commission to the Cape to investigate the condition of the defences, the costs of which by now far outstripped the revenue that was being generated. It was also specifically tasked to evaluate the Regiment Württemberg, since the Prince of Orange, the States-General and the Lords Seventeen all wanted to know if the Germans were providing a good return on the money spent on them.

Germans aside, by now one of the earliest enterprises Van de Graaff had launched, the 'Militaire Kweekschool' (Military Seminary), the first dedicated officers' training establishment in South African history, was up and running. There had been a serious shortage of well-trained artillery and engineer officers at the Cape, and he had been directed to set up a suitable establishment as soon as possible after his arrival; in fact, when the Regiment Württemberg was raised provision was made for its organic artillery company to establish the school.

Characteristically, Van de Graaff had wasted little time in doing just that. He appointed Lieutenant-Colonel Gilquin as commandant, and by April 1786 selection criteria for officer-cadets had been formulated; cadets were to include people of colour, and the selection of suitable slaves was also to be considered.

By 1788 the Militaire Kweekschool had been in full operation. Officer-cadets selected from the serving rank and file were exempted from other duties to ensure regular attendance at classes every weekday from 9am to noon, where they were instructed in such subjects as algebra, trigonometry and topographical surveying. When it landed, the commission saw a very professional army indeed.

Similarly, the commission arrived at an interesting stage of the Burgher Militia's evolution as well. In the urban centres the classical foot infantryman still predominated, but outside Cape Town the mounted dragoon was clearly becoming the fighter of choice. The Cape Town area's militia comprised seven infantry companies and 250 dragoons, but Stellenbosch had one infantry and four dragoon companies, Swellendam had two companies of dragoons and no infantry at all, and Graaff-Reinet three companies of dragoons. Altogether there were now 2 893 militiamen available for service, many of them mounted infantry; it had taken all of a century, but Simon van der Stel's vision of 1687 had finally come to pass.

The team made a thorough evaluation of the Cape's defences and departed after being treated to a grand review of all the Cape units on 31 July, having expressed their particular satisfaction with the Württembergers' state of preparedness. As it turned out, the Württembergers never fired a shot in anger while at the Cape as they were eventually transferred to the East Indies well before 1795, when they were most needed. Picard quotes an exasperated Van de Graaff, angered by cuts in his budget and the departure of the Württembergers, warning prophetically: 'This will cost you the Cape!'[35]

One of the recommendations subsequently made by the commission broke new ground in the evolution of the South African military. In addition to the existing full-time garrison and Burgher Militia, the commission said, a regular full-time force of 200 dragoons should be established.

The commission's reasoning was firstly that the dragoons would be more effective in counteracting an enemy landing because invaders would not be likely to have any heavy cavalry available; secondly that they could be sent out on particular tasks at short notice, and thirdly, being mounted infantry they could fight on foot if circumstances required.

It was an eminently sensible and long overdue suggestion. As Grobbelaar notes, 'it is interesting that the utility of a regular dragoon force [operating] over the lengthy distances of the Cape was not comprehended at an earlier date'. Evidently the Lords Seventeen agreed, and the dragoon force was established the following year.

The commission's recommendation must surely have been influenced by the trend towards mounted infantrymen in the part-time forces outside Cape Town. It would appear that the regular military establishment, by the very nature of its main task, guarding the Cape's facilities against attack from outside, had not taken full cognisance of the fact that military operations in African conditions were dictated by time, distance and lack of infrastructure to an extent unknown in Europe.

During this time the eastern frontier continued to simmer, with new tensions arising as the latest round of the intermittent outbreaks of civil war among the Xhosa tribes and clans resulted in increased settlement in the Zuurveld. But the eastern frontier situation and the growing discontent among the Graaff-Reinetters, those long-standing thorns in the Cape government's flesh, would soon cease to be Governor van de Graaff's problem.

During his tenure at the Cape he had managed to offend everyone except, it seems, the Prince of Orange. The long-suffering Lords Seventeen had finally had enough of his profligate spending, his disdain for the Company's meticulous bureaucratic ways and his disastrously bad relations with the general population, both high and low.

Given Van de Graaff's connections with the House of Orange,

however, getting rid of him required rather more than the peremptory summons to Amsterdam that had sufficed up to that time. Months passed before he was recalled in 1791, and as a face-saving measure he was not officially sacked, but recalled to the Netherlands in his gubernatorial capacity for consultations.

Van de Graaff handed over to his *Secunde*, his second in command, Johan Isaac Rhenius, and sailed away, no doubt not displeased with what he had wrought – his legacy, after all, included the vastly improved Cape defensive system and the eastern town of Graaff-Reinet. It is doubtful whether he was perturbed by the well-nigh universal dislike for him and, more importantly, the VOC, which he had managed to generate in the process. But this was also part of his legacy, and one that was to have disastrous ill-effects in the near future.

CHAPTER 7

COUNTDOWN FOR THE VOC

The following year, while the Cape awaited its new governor, the terminally ill VOC sent out yet another commission of enquiry from the Netherlands, this time a two-man team consisting of its senior advocate, Sebastiaan Cornelis Nederburgh,[1] and a naval captain, Simon Hendrik Frijkenius[2] – it was 'one last attempt … to halt the rot,' as FS Gaastra puts it.[3] Their specific mission was to sort through the situation Van de Graaff had left in his wake and see what could be done about reducing costs and increasing revenues. The VOC was now so badly off that the Lords Seventeen had lost the virtual omnipotence they had formerly enjoyed; 1790 saw the establishment of a political supervisory body called the Hollands-Zeeuwse Staatscommissie (Committee of the States of Holland and Zeeland), consisting of four members from Holland and two from Zeeland, each appointed by their provinces. It was the beginning of the end for the Company.[4]

Nederburgh and Frijkenius found the Cape in a poor condition in every way. The free burghers' mood ranged from discontented to downright rebellious about the VOC administration and the burden of the various taxes it levied, while the eastern frontier was on the brink of all-out war. They did not waste any time in addressing the situation, but unfortunately their efforts only made the problems worse.

They alienated their most influential potential allies by refusing to recognise the members of the Burgher Council as representative of the free burgher population. The free burghers responded by holding a series of protest meetings and bombarding the commission with petitions. By the time the commissioners eventually softened their attitude and accorded the council the recognition it felt it deserved, the point at which meaningful dialogue could take place was long past.

They trimmed almost every section of the bureaucracy drastically and introduced two new taxes, one on auctions and the other on stamp duty, which infuriated the free burghers anew. Frijkenius and Nederburgh stood firm, however, and unnecessary expenditure dropped noticeably, although at the cost of burgher discontent – and this would have a bearing on events in the not-too-distant future. The main object of their dislike was neither the Prince of Orange nor the States-General, but the Company. Nederburgh was uncompromising on this subject, however. Although not a Dutch colony, the VOC was the local legal representative of the States-General; therefore, disloyalty to the VOC amounted to disloyalty to the States-General.

The commissioners compounded their errors by making one Honoratus Christiaan David Maynier[5] the new landdrost at Graaff-Reinet. It was an unfortunate choice, since Maynier was a prickly character who had been at odds with the eastern free burghers since his arrival at Graaff-Reinet in 1789, as secretary to his predecessor, MHO Woeke.[6]

Soon after his arrival, he and Woeke had travelled to the Zuurveld to negotiate with the Xhosas, and get them to leave the area. Needless to say, the Xhosas showed no enthusiasm for any such thing, and the two men returned empty-handed, having decided not to pursue the matter. Maynier was one of the people Nederburgh and Frijkenius consulted when they launched their enquiry. He conceded that the free burghers were having some difficulties, but told the commissioners that in his opinion peace with the Xhosas was desirable at any cost, although some action should certainly be taken against the Bushmen.

Whether Maynier truly believed this or was playing to the gallery is a moot point (Giliomee makes the point that Maynier was not pro-Xhosa but a faithful Company servant whose main aim was to prevent money-wasting military action), but his opinion was favourably received by the cost-conscious commissioners, and they duly appointed him as Woeke's replacement at Graaff-Reinet.

To say that the appointment was unpopular would be an understatement; the veteran Adriaan van Jaarsveldt and three others walked out in protest at the next meeting of heemraden[7] and military officers. Maynier was unmoved. He made it clear to the free burghers that he was the undisputed ruler in Graaff-Reinet, and that he regarded their troubles with the Xhosas in the Zuurveld as being largely of their own making.

That same year saw the outbreak of the Second Frontier War.[8] In spite of the tense situation, however, it resulted not from the friction between white and black but from an ongoing succession squabble among the rulers of two Xhosa tribes. The main instigator was one Ndlambe, of the western Rarabe tribe. The tribe's paramount chief, Phalo, had had two sons, his rather lacklustre heir Gcaleka and Rarabe, an outstanding warrior with a large popular following. When Phalo died Rarabe decided to make a bid for the throne. Civil war broke out, during which Rarabe and his followers were defeated and forced to flee to what is now Tembuland, west of the Kei River.

This area was already heavily populated, but Rarabe trounced the smaller local clans, expelled them and started settling in. Rarabe was still consolidating his hijacked territory when both he and his heir, Mlawu, were killed. The chieftainship now devolved to Mlawu's teenage son, Ngqika (or 'Gaika', as the whites called him), The tribe took Ngqika's name, as was the custom, but he was too young to rule, and his uncle Ndlambe was appointed to act as regent until the boy was old enough.

Although Ndlambe had no real statutory authority, as it were, he set about expanding the clan's size and military capability, the reason being that he had ambitions of his own which went well beyond that of playing caretaker while Ngqika grew up: he wanted to usurp Ngqika's chieftainship as a stepping stone to becoming paramount chief of the Xhosa confederation.

To achieve this aim he began systematically whittling down his competitors, and enlisting the support of some of the less scrupulous local whites against three other clans. But this was only the opening gambit of his campaign for the paramount chieftainship. His next target was the Gqunukwebe, a distinct ethnic group which had resulted from wholesale intermarriage between the local Khoina and the Xhosas. The Gqunukwebe had long been established in the Gamtoos River area, but in 1778 had started to drift to the Fish River, settling in the coveted Zuurveld. This turned out to be a serious mistake on their part, as they were soon to discover.

While Ndlambe was preparing to deal with the Gqunukwebe, the VOC administration in Cape Town was gripped with fear for the future. The French Revolution of 1789 had upset the entire political balance in Europe and created a situation that was intolerable to the Continent's crowned heads. The revolutionaries were like the Biblical Ishmael, with every man's hand turned against them, and an armed struggle between the revolutionaries and supporters of the *status quo ante* was clearly on the cards.

It broke out in April 1792, when the new French republic declared war on the mighty Austrian empire after Austria's threats in the Declaration of Pilnitz.[9] Six months later, on 20 September, to the horror of all the surrounding monarchies, they then proceeded to inflict a decisive defeat on the Prussian Army and their Austrian allies at the Battle of Valmy.[10] The shots fired at Valmy heralded the start of more than two decades of almost constant conflict in Western Europe.[11]

Although the Netherlands was not yet involved, there was no doubt that sooner or later hostilities would break out between France and England, to which the Dutch were currently allied. Given the Company's close association with the House of Orange, which went back nearly two centuries, the likelihood of an eventual French assault on the Cape was therefore anything but remote.

The new threat came at a moment of grave military weakness. The departure of the mercenary regiments had stripped the Cape of most

of its full-time military manpower, and the chances of obtaining reinforcements were small. Long-term mobilisation of the Burgher Militia
was not a viable alternative, since the removal of a substantial part of
the civilian labour force for an extended period would have serious effects on the economy and the outpost's ability to service passing ships.

Nederburgh and Frijkenius concluded that the only way to expand
the Cape's military manpower was to establish a full-time locally recruited light infantry unit as well as a part-time infantry company,
manned by VOC administrative employees; this would not only be
economical but would also allow the VOC to deploy most of its forces
elsewhere – particularly in the Far East, which was so crucial to the
Netherlands economy.

The Pennisten Corps (Clerical Corps) was duly founded, officered
by members of the Council of Policy and manned by clerks from the
VOC administration, who were likely none too pleased at their sudden
conscription. In its final form the corps was to be about 150-strong
and was commanded by Baron Willem Ferdinand van Reede van
Oudtshoorn,[12] son of Baron Pieter van Reede van Oudtshoorn who
had been buried with such pomp and ceremony in 1773.

Much more significant, as it turned out, was the establishment of
the Corps Pandoeren, to a certain extent a resurrection of Governor
van Plettenberg's Corps Bastaard-Hottentotten of 1781. Like its predecessor it was largely manned by men from the Baviaanskloof (later
Genadendal) mission, but it was not an emergency levy by any means.
The aim was to create a well-trained, adequately equipped unit of light
infantry, and that is what the administration set about doing.

The VOC administration's concern about events at home and abroad
turned out to be fully justified. Louis XVI of France was condemned
to death by the revolutionary assembly on 16 January 1793, and five
days later he was guillotined with Queen Marie Antoinette. Now there
was no doubt about it: a fight to the death between the intransigent
revolutionaries and their equally intransigent opponents was inevitable
and, within weeks, Britain declared war on France.

As if this were not enough, the eastern frontier boiled over once again. Ndlambe recruited some very dubious allies in the shape of a party of outright rogues under Barend Lindeque, one of whose followers was the notorious Coenraad Buys,[13] then attacked the Gqunukwebe. The result was almost instant chaos in the Zuurveld, with free burghers fleeing their farms and cattle being carried off in large numbers.

Two government commandos were mobilised, one led by Maynier and the other by his colleague from Swellendam. They penetrated a considerable distance into Xhosa territory, drove out several smaller Xhosa clans eastwards over the Fish River (where the refugees were promptly pounced on by Ndlambe) and recaptured a large number of stolen cattle. Apart from that they accomplished little else, possibly because of a lack of military expertise, since neither Van Jaarsveldt nor any of his associates would have anything to do with an enterprise in which Maynier was involved.

The result was a stalemate peace of sorts that settled nothing. The western Zuurveld remained in Xhosa hands and cattle raids continued. When the farmers complained to Cape Town, Maynier responded by contending that their claims were exaggerated, and that in any case they had only themselves to blame for the unsettled conditions. Naturally this did little to lessen the tension.

And in fact this did not end the Second Frontier War, except in the minds of the Political Council members in Cape Town, because Ndlambe was still engaged in fostering his greater plan to seize the paramount chieftainship. Young Ngqika had now turned 18 and was ready to assume the chieftainship, but Ndlambe was not prepared to relinquish his grip. He tried to persuade the Ngqika clan to support his case, failed and turned to the Gcalekas west of the Kei River, whose chief was Phalo's rightful heir. Gcaleka, fearing that Ngqika would resurrect the old succession quarrel if he won, threw in his lot with Ndlambe and provided him with modest support in his latest attempt at usurpation.

Unfortunately for the Gcalekas, he backed the wrong horse. Ngqika showed that he was his father's son by not only defeating the usurpers in a famous battle which is now part of the Xhosa folk legend but also taking Ndlambe prisoner. Ndlambe was nothing if not a survivor, however, and as it turned out the eastern frontier had not heard the last of him yet.

☙

In Europe the crucial early struggle with Revolutionary France was for control of the major French naval base and arsenal at Toulon, on the Mediterranean coast. Heavily fortified, it was garrisoned by French royalist troops, reinforced by British, Spanish and Italian contingents, while a combined Anglo-Spanish fleet lay at anchor in its harbour – it was a vitally important objective for the revolutionary forces, and a formidable one.

There followed an intermittent battle that lasted from 18 September to 18 December 1793, with neither side willing to concede defeat. The stalemate was finally broken through the efforts of a young Corsican captain of artillery, named Napoléon Bonaparte.[14] Bonaparte conceived a plan to take the gun emplacements on the heights overlooking Toulon, overran them and turned Toulon's guns on the Anglo-Spanish fleet, driving it out of the harbour and the enemy troops from the town. Now Toulon and all its great resources, including more than 100 guns, were in the revolutionaries' hands – and the young Corsican's reputation was made.

Just prior to the battle for Toulon, Nederburgh and Frijkenius departed the Cape, having appointed a temporary governor, Abraham Josias Sluysken.[15] It was an unfortunate appointment, driven by the press of circumstances, and it fell on a very reluctant and totally unsuitable nominee.

Sluysken was a veteran East India hand who had finished his term as director of the outpost of Surat and was on his way home to retirement when the return-fleet with which he was travelling stopped off at Cape Town for the customary replenishment. Nederburgh and Frijkenius had no great confidence in the existing *Secunde*, Johan Rhenius, and recommended Sluysken take over the administration of the Cape, at the rank of commissioner-general, until a new governor could be found.

It was a classic example of the wrong man being in the wrong place at the wrong time. What the Cape needed at this trying time was a De

Chavonnes, a Simon van der Stel or even a Jacob van de Graaff. What it got was a worn-out administrator on the verge of retirement who, no matter what other good qualities he possessed, lacked the decisiveness and capacity for command that the Cape's dire situation demanded. But, like any good company man, Sluysken acceded to the request and took his place in the chair of Van Riebeeck, but with no great enthusiasm. He would have had even less if he (or Nederburgh and Frijkenius) had known that his stay at the Cape would be far longer and entirely more harrowing than any of them anticipated.

Nederburgh and Frijkenius sailed away on 2 September 1793, no doubt with relief at being rid of the troublesome outpost with its cantankerous inhabitants, and Sluysken got down to wrestling with his problems. His only consolation, one presumes, was that the momentum generated by Van de Graaff (and latterly Gordon) continued in spite of the tightening official purse strings, so that within the next year, the Cape's sea defences became stronger than they had ever been before.

The Castle was no longer the almost invulnerable fortress it had once been because firepower had improved considerably since its erection nearly 150 years earlier, but it remained an installation to be reckoned with, and the Cape Peninsula now boasted at least 400 artillery pieces.[16] Shot-ovens had been installed in 19 batteries between Camps Bay and Fort Knokke, so that between them the batteries could fire 450 red-hot round-shot in just 14 minutes, and Potgieter says that Gordon's gunners 'were apparently quite crack, and since they exercised often, they were apparently proficient in the use of red-hot shot.'[17] He quotes the captain of the Dutch frigate *Scipio* saying that the fortifications were 'formidable', so that even if there were no more than 2 500 soldiers to defend the Cape it would be very difficult to capture it from the sea.

It was a brave show, but it had a weakness. False Bay, on the shore of which lay Simon's Town and the starting point of the two overland routes to Cape Town, was virtually undefended except for the Zoutman and Boetzelaar Batteries, which overlooked the anchorage but were not well-sited, providing poor fields of fire. The back door to Cape Town could easily be kicked in.

Potgieter rightly describes this situation as 'inconceivable'. Given the undoubted expertise of Cape military commander Robert Gordon, the charitable assumption is that he had planned to strengthen the False Bay defences but had been overtaken by events and a lack of resources. Gordon's main problem, however, was manpower.

To man the Cape defences he had what can only be described as a motley crew, and a scanty one at that. The only full-time infantry element, apart from the Régiment De Meuron and Regiment Württemberg training depots (which could muster just 57 men between them), consisted of the 210-strong Corps Pandoeren and the inappropriately named Nationale Battaillon,[18] which was manned almost exclusively by foreign mercenaries, mainly Germans. Led by Lt-Col CMW de Lille, Gordon's second in command, it was also sadly understrength, with only 25 officers and 546 other ranks. For the rest he had between 400 and 600 infantrymen of the local Burgher Militia, well over 1 000 burgher light dragoons (who turned out to be among the most spirited of his troops) all from the outlying districts, 90 members of the Corps des Invalides, the Pennisten Corps, and a half-company of 43 or 44 *sepayers*,[19] soldiers recruited by the VOC in Indonesia or more likely Ceylon.

Gordon also had at his disposal a full-time artillery component of 27 officers and 403 other ranks under one Major Kuchler, and 20 Burgher Militia part-timers. It appears that he was also entitled to call up another 340 'discharged or otherwise employed servants of the Company serving with the artillery' and 200-odd men whose civilian occupations ranged from wharf employees and tradesmen to construction men working on the fortifications. In all, a total of roughly 3 500 men.

As the last months of the VOC's 150-year sway at the Cape of Good Hope ticked away, a serious divide yawned between the evermore rebellious free burgher population and the solidly Orangist leadership of the Company – and the burgher light dragoons were a problematic component in this mix, as neither Gordon nor Sluysken could be sure of where they stood. By this stage the Cape was riven by political dissension which extended into the core of both the full-time and part-time military. All this was to have a discernible effect in the saga of double-dealing, heroism and personal tragedy which engulfed the southernmost tip of Africa before 1795 reached its end.

Previously there had been no doubt about the free burghers' ultimate loyalty; their support for the States-General and the Prince of Orange had never been questioned. Now, however, many of them turned their backs on the House of Orange and openly inclined towards the French-inspired spirit of republican revolution that had taken hold among a large section of the Dutch population, whose members called themselves 'Patriotten'

The frontiersmen in particular had taken to mouthing revolution-ary slogans and wearing tricolour cockades in their hats. Other free burghers, according to Potgieter, wanted the Cape to be ruled directly by the States-General, while yet others wanted nothing less than com-plete independence. It is tempting simply to blame all this disaffec-tion on the frontier problems and the incorrigible intransigence of the free burghers, but in fact it was mainly the explosion of generations of pent-up grudges against the VOC administration which had finally been brought to boiling point by the new concepts of egalitarianism flowing first from the American and then the French Revolutions.

At bottom of it all was the fact that the Cape outpost was a consti-tutional anomaly. Although it had expanded much further afield than had been intended in Jan van Riebeeck's day, it was still run very largely as it had been since 1652, as a subordinate branch office of the VOC's Far Eastern headquarters at Batavia. No systematic attempt had been made to turn it into a colony, or to conquer or make allies of the local inhabitants outside the outpost's orbit; it would be fair to say that as a result the Cape was not governed so much as managed.

The VOC controlled every commercial aspect of the settled com-munity's lives, although in the more remote areas, of course, its writ did not run strongly, if at all. The Swellendammers in particular had an extensive list of genuine grievances, chief among them being the latest round of taxes instituted by the Nederburgh-Frijkenius commission and their long-standing resentment at the ban on doing business direct-ly with passing ships – everything still had to be sold to the Company at the less-than-generous prices it determined. An aggravating factor was that times were leaner than normal because the war had greatly reduced the number of passing merchant ships from which much of the free burghers' income was ultimately derived.

In point of fact the VOC was already in its death throes, teetering on the edge of bankruptcy as a result of the European wars, so that the *rijksdaalders*[20] or rix-dollars in circulation at the Cape were hardly worth the paper they were printed on, because they were no longer backed by adequate reserves of gold and silver. The final blow came when the Company was deprived of its main patron, the Prince of Orange.

The architect of the Prince's – and with him, the VOC's – final undoing was a French general named Jean-Charles Pichegru,[21] The son of a peasant, the friars of his birthplace, Arbois, sent him to a military school, after which he joined the artillery in 1783 and was soon commissioned – a considerable feat in the class-obsessed royalist French Army. Pichegru's meteoric rise and election to lieutenant-colonel and then brigadier-general is similar to many who, freed by the revolution from the social handicap of low birth, rose by sheer merit to become outstanding combat leaders.[22]

Pichegru got his opportunity to shine when he was made commander-in-chief of the French Army of the North in February 1794. He fought successfully against allied Coalition forces on several occasions in a series of coups that secured his military reputation: the general pattern at that time was to go into winter quarters until fighting conditions improved, but Pichegru decided to make the weather work for him. To this end he avoided what would inevitably have been a bloody amphibious operation by waiting for the Meuse River to freeze. When this had happened, he dashed across with horse and foot to chase the Austrians to the other side of the Rhine. Then he did the same at the Waal River and expelled the British from the area as well. But this was only the precursor to his most famous exploit, which is still unique in the annals of warfare.

He marched on the major naval base at Den Helder, where the

Dutch warships lay trapped in the ice, sent his hussars clattering out over the frozen surface of the harbour and captured the entire fleet, almost without a shot being fired. That sealed the fate of Orangist Netherlands. On 19 January 1795 he entered Utrecht and next day Amsterdam fell, followed by the rest of the Netherlands in the next few months.

The Dutch Government sued for peace, the Prince of Orange fled to England and the Netherlands became the Batavian Republic, ruled by the revolutionary Patriotten. The Netherlands was now bound firmly to France, not just by national self-interest, but by a common political ideology which automatically pitted both countries against virtually every crowned head in Europe. Overnight the main enemy of the Netherlands became not France, but England.

The installation of the new Batavian regime was also the beginning of the end for the Lords Seventeen, who had ruled the VOC with such authority for almost 200 years, and set in motion the decay and ultimate death of the Company itself. This did not happen immediately, however, and at the Cape the increasingly harried Sluysken had his hands full with a much more pressing crisis involving the disgruntled free burghers of Graaff-Reinet.

Beset by debt, their salvoes of complaints directed at the administration consistently ignored, the Graaff-Reinetters finally went into open rebellion. On 6 February 1795 Adriaan van Jaarsveldt and 40 others confronted Landdrost Maynier and gave him three days to quit his post in the drostdy (the administrative centre). Maynier realised that his customary obduracy would not suffice this time, and retreated to his nearby farm.

At Swellendam a similar spirit of insurrection was brewing, and strong divisions existed within the Cape garrison as well, since the officers of all units were strongly pro-Orange, while the artillerymen and most of the free burghers favoured the Patriotten. It is hardly surprising, therefore, that Sluysken did not take decisive action about the Graaff-Reinet rising. He appointed a commission of enquiry under

one OG de Wet, the aim of which was to record the farmers' grievances, but this did not resolve the situation.

When it became clear that De Wet would not countenance the expulsion of the Xhosas from the Zuurveld, a commando of 200 men
ordered him to go back to Cape Town forthwith, which he did. The
burghers also resolved not to pay any taxes to the VOC because they
regarded themselves as being under the direct authority of the States-
General.

In August 1795 Sluysken appointed Friedrich Carl David Gerotz[23]
as provisional landdrost at Graaff-Reinet. Gerotz was a German from
Stuttgart, but he had been at the Cape since arriving as soldier in the
VOC's army in 1767. In time he had gravitated to Graaff-Reinet, where
he had been appointed a lieutenant in the Burgher Militia and became
a farmer. Described as a 'worthy person, full of good faith', he was to
prove a valuable moderating influence.

Sluysken had other urgent fish to fry, however. His greatest preoccupation at this time was the state of affairs in Europe, but he had almost
no information on which to base any conclusions because all his news
was several months old by the time it reached Cape Town. In February
1795 he had received an alarming four-month-old letter from the
VOC's senior legal adviser, warning that the Netherlands might suddenly change sides. Then in mid-April the Dutch frigate *Medenblik*
arrived with the equally alarming news that Pichegru was making serious advances. But Sluysken was still ignorant of the most devastating
tidings of all, because the *Medenblik* had sailed before the capitulation
of the Netherlands Government and the flight of the Prince of Orange.

The result was a state of confusion in the ranks of Sluysken's administration. Where did the VOC, with its traditional links to the States-
General and the Prince of Orange, stand amid all this chaos? Was the
Netherlands still allied to England, or had Europe's notoriously unstable alliances shifted once again? This uncertainty was to play a major
role in the events of the next few months.

The truth of the matter was that the British Government was already laying plans for seizing the Cape. Horse Guards HQ[24] and the
Admiralty had been concerned about its future for several years, and
between 1785 and 1787 an officer named Colonel William Dalrymple

had twice visited the outpost to glean information about its military weaknesses and assess the chances of a successful invasion, after Commodore Johnstone's failure in 1781.

Free access to the Cape's facilities was an absolute requirement for the British Honourable East India Company, (HEIC), whose trade with the Orient remained a pillar of the national economy. Moreover, control of the Cape would safeguard India from French attack and neutralise the French-held Indian Ocean islands of Île de France and Réunion, their nearest source of supply.

The directors of the HEIC had laid a proposal for an invasion before the Secretary of State for War, Henry Dundas,[25] as early as 1793. They had clearly found a receptive audience, because the government instituted negotiations with the Dutch that same year. The negotiations did not result in anything concrete, because the Dutch were willing to consider a British naval squadron at the Cape but prudently would not countenance any troop presence.

By the end of 1794, with an Orangist defeat becoming an increasing likelihood, the matter of the Cape was uppermost in Dundas's mind, and he is on record as stating his belief that if France ended up in control of the Netherlands 'their first act will be to send a French force to the Cape ... we must be beforehand with them.'[26] Consequently, Dundas was ready to listen in mid-January 1795 when Sir Francis Baring, chairman of the HEIC's board of directors, wrote to him to point out that the Cape 'commands the passage to and from India as effectively as Gibraltar does the Mediterranean,'[27] and implored him to consider taking it. As Dundas's under-secretary trenchantly noted on 25 January, if the French took control of the VOC outpost 'a feather in the hands of Holland [would become] a sword in the hands of France.'[28]

Thereafter events moved swiftly. Within a few days the Prince of Orange signed a letter authorising loyal Dutch naval commanders to permit the Royal Navy's warships to defend the Cape against the French,[29] and instructed Sluysken to let British troops land and enter the Castle. Two days later the British Government tied up another loose end by directing the Royal Navy to seize any Dutch ships it encountered, with the understanding they might now be allied to France.

So important was the capture of the Cape that the Admiralty

appointed one of its finest sailors, Admiral Sir John Jervis,[30] as commander of the South Atlantic expedition and commander-in-chief of the entire Indian Ocean. However, Jervis was seriously indisposed, and delegated the task to one of his associates, Admiral George Elphinstone.[31]

Then 50 years old, Elphinstone was well thought of by his colleagues and had considerable operational experience which included commanding a ship in the American War of Independence and taking part in the siege of Toulon under the legendary Admiral Hood.

He did not allow the kelp to grow under his feet, as it were. On 16 February he ordered Captain John Blankett to the naval base at Plymouth with his four-ship squadron – the *America*, *Ruby* and *Stately*, all 64-gun ships of the line, and the 16-gun sloop HMS *Echo* – to embark Major-General JH Craig[32] and 515 soldiers of the 78th Highlanders,[33] then set sail for the Cape.

Elphinstone himself set off on 3 April with three 74-gun battleships, the *Monarch*, *Arrogant* and *Victorious*, a fast frigate called the *Sphynx* (24 guns) and the *Rattlesnake*, another swift 16-gun sloop. On 15 May a squadron of troopships followed with the third component of the task force, Major-General Alured Clarke,[34] with the main body of combat troops.

On 10 June Elphinstone met Blankett off the Cape. Next day, without identifying themselves, his ships sailed into False Bay, where the *Medenblik* was still riding at anchor along with the merchantmen *Willemstad en Boetselaar*, *De Jonge Bonafacius* and *Geertruyda*. Elphinstone's fleet was an intimidating sight, no doubt, to the modest Simon's Town garrison of 110 infantrymen and 50 gunners.

The *Medenblik*'s commander, a Captain Dekker, sent his first lieutenant over to the English ships, armed with a flag that he was to wave if they were friendly. The lieutenant did not return. The VOC official in charge at Simon's Town immediately despatched an urgent message to Sluysken. That evening Sluysken called a meeting of the Council of Policy, and at midnight Lt-Col De Lille was sent off to Simon's Town with 200 men of the Nationale Battaillon and 100 artillerymen to strengthen the garrison there. Sluysken also ordered that the signal-guns be fired to summon the outlying Burgher Militia companies, for whatever that was worth.

The response was poor at first, because the free burghers, particularly the more distantly located ones, saw no reason why they should assist in keeping the Cape in the hands of the VOC. 'Many of the discontented burghers on the frontier,' as Potgieter says, 'felt that the evils of a foreign yoke might not exceed those existing. Furthermore, many thought that if the current government could be overthrown, a new and independent one could be established.'[35]

On the afternoon of 12 June Sluysken convened another special meeting of the Council of Policy to discuss a letter from Elphinstone, inviting Gordon and himself to a meeting on board the flagship, HMS *Monarch*. He had important information to pass on to them, Elphinstone wrote, as well as a letter from the Prince of Orange. He added that he particularly desired a private conversation with Gordon, if that were possible.

There can be little doubt as to what course that private conversation was intended to take. Gordon's sympathies were so clearly evident that Colonel Dalrymple had reported in 1787 that 'the colonel has an English heart tho' born in Holland and is strong in the Prince of Orange's interest', and that if the British attacked, Gordon might well go over to them.

In addition, Potgieter points out, that same year the HEIC's agent at the Cape, John Pringle, had reported that Gordon would be replaced if the French overran the Netherlands, and that if suitable help were given to him (Gordon) it was possible that the Cape garrison could be persuaded to join hands with the British.

It is likely that this latter conclusion is wrong, at least to some extent. Even a superficial reading of Gordon's character leads one to believe that if given a straight choice his allegiance to the House of Orange would not have wavered, and that he would not have changed sides simply to retain his appointment – and because the prince was the ally of King George, the British could not be considered enemies.

But of course Gordon's options were hopelessly muddied because the Prince of Orange was now being supported by Britain, his independence quite possibly compromised to suit British aims. Some commentators hold that the prince was little more than a hostage of the British, though he had turned to them for aid against the revolutionaries. Thus, for Elphinstone, there was a rare opportunity of suborning or at least fatally weakening the resolve of a man who was by far the best soldier at the Cape, an opportunity of which Elphinstone was naturally to take as much advantage as possible in the days ahead.

Sluysken declined Elphinstone's invitation, suggesting instead that the letter and information be sent to him by a trusted officer. In the meantime he gave permission for the British ships to take on badly needed provisions and water, and land a large number of sailors who were suffering from scurvy, on condition that no armed troops came ashore.

On 14 June, Captain Temple Hardy of HMS *Echo* and Lieutenant-Colonel Mackenzie of the 78th Regiment arrived at the Castle with the Prince of Orange's letter and a report from Elphinstone and Craig on events in the Netherlands. The report confirmed Sluysken's worst fears by sketching the Dutch surrender and the subsequent flight to safety of the Prince of Orange, but otherwise, according to Potgieter, was somewhat economical with the truth:

> They ... reported that Britain and her allies were amassing large ar-
> mies to drive the French from Holland. This information was deliber-
> ately incomplete ... since they did not want to reveal the enthusiastic
> welcome the French received from the Dutch *Patriotten*, that the
> Dutch government had changed, that the States-General [had con-
> sequently] abolished the stadholdership and that the majority in
> Holland saw the French as friends. The British version concentrated
> on the ruthless French conquest.[36]

Although there was much popular support for the revolution in the Netherlands, and a new Batavian Republic had been declared, the Cape was possibly the only territory which could be retained by the exiled Prince of Orange, using the military might of their British allies. This, of course, suited British aims perfectly. However, Elphinstone had to tread carefully. He would have a full-scale landing on his hands if the Cape officials discovered the truth: that neither the old States-General nor the prince had rights over them any longer.

The Council of Policy wrangled at length about Elphinstone's documents. Gordon accepted the report and proposed that Elphinstone's force be made welcome, provided that the Cape be held in the name of the Prince of Orange, that the VOC Government stay in place and that Elphinstone be under Sluysken's command, so that, as Potgieter says, 'the situation [would] basically be the same as during the early 1780s, when French troops were stationed at the Cape.'[37]

Other members of the council were less amenable. The letter did not draw much water, they pointed out, given the circumstances in which the deposed *stadhouder* had signed it, and they would not countenance the landing of British troops. The best course would be to play for time.

The council finally decided on a guarded reply which expressed gratitude for Britain's willingness to protect the Cape and welcomed Elphinstone's help in repulsing a French assault, but added that they believed the Cape was perfectly capable of defending itself from any foreign attack.

All this took some time, which Lieutenant-Colonel Mackenzie spent profitably in the company of two locally resident British East India Company officials named Owen and Cust, covertly examining defensive works and gathering information about all aspects of the military situation. His conclusion in a report to Craig was that 'we can get safely round behind [the defensive works].'[38]

At the same time, Captain Hardy had a meeting with Gordon at the latter's house. Gordon told him that he would resist a British attack, but would welcome Elphinstone's force if it intended to protect the Cape for the Prince of Orange. Gordon was now venturing into very murky waters indeed. Potgieter quotes from a letter he wrote to Elphinstone in which he welcomed British protection of the Cape, inveighed against French revolutionary principles and blasted the Dutch Patriotten as indoctrinated dupes. He emphasised that he was a loyal Orange supporter who would serve 'the Common cause' to the maximum, but if the Netherlands surrendered 'then I am a Greatbritainer'.[39]

It was a courageous, or perhaps foolhardy, stand. There was no secret about his staunch loyalty to the House of Orange and the fact that he favoured a British protective presence against the French, their mutual enemy, meant that he was regarded with grave suspicion by the ever-bolder local Patriotten. The distrust of the VOC's administration had reached the point where, on 17 June, the Swellendammers followed the Graaff-Reinetters' example and rose in rebellion. Led by the commander of the local Burgher Militia contingent, they occupied the drostdy, ejected Landdrost AA Faure and proclaimed an independent republic – surely the world's smallest ever. Gordon was skating on very thin ice indeed.

Elphinstone was not interested in the Council of Policy's preferences; nothing less than total control over the Cape would suffice. So on 19 June he sent General Craig in person to clarify matters. Craig – a short, muscular soldier of considerable experience, who had a tendency towards pomposity and tended to make enemies because of his quick temper – presented the council with a detailed offer.

The British force had been sent to occupy the Cape to protect it from the French, he said. Laws and customs would not be altered, and officials would stay in place until an eventual decision about their future was made by the British government. The VOC troops would be paid by the British, but they would have to take an oath of loyalty to the British crown.

The Council of Policy flatly rejected this proposal, which probably did not surprise the British too much, since it would have amounted to little short of total surrender. Undismayed, Craig toured Cape Town in the company of Owen and Cust, no doubt taking careful mental notes of both the defences and the terrain.

These visits and information from local sources – 'humint', or human intelligence, in 21st-century military jargon – enabled the British local high command to start building up a detailed intelligence picture about the VOC's defences and the general topography along the route from False Bay, which would obviously be their approach-route of choice if the Cape had to be taken by force.

On 21 June, 10 days after Elphinstone's arrival, Captain Dekker decided to take the *Medenblik* to the Far Eastern headquarters at Batavia. To avoid hostilities that might upset the fluid local situation and eventually benefit the French, Elphinstone let him go after extracting a promise that Dekker would not visit any French ports en route.

The next day Elphinstone tried to circumvent the Council of Policy by issuing a proclamation directly to the Cape population, inviting it to send a delegation to discuss British protection for the Cape. He also sent a copy to Gordon, whom he still regarded as an ally, with the request that he pass it on to the VOC troops.

The proclamation served no purpose other than to ratchet up the tension. Gordon refused to accede to Elphinstone's request, and the Council of Policy ordered him to make sure, in the interests of maintaining morale, that the proclamation did not reach the troops. The council also ignored Gordon's advice and broke off the negotiations. The VOC's resident agent at Simon's Town was told to increase local security measures and desist from supplying the British, who were now to be regarded as enemies; he was also to remove all horses, oxen and other draught animals from the area to deny them to the British.

The VOC's battle plan, Potgieter says, was that if the British landed 'Simon's Town was to be defended, mainly from the Zoutman Battery and, if overpowered by the British, all gunpowder was to be dumped in the sea, guns [were to be] spiked and everybody should withdraw to Muizenberg.'[40] Quite clearly, though, there was very little 'if' about this plan: if the Zoutman Battery resisted a landing attempt it would be pounded into dust by Elphinstone's ships before any British soldier set foot on shore.

On 28 June Elphinstone's deception about the true state of affairs in the Netherlands was revealed when two American ships arrived with mail and official papers. The British promptly confiscated all documents and newspapers and clamped a tight guard on the two ships, but some private mail and a newspaper made it to shore, and now the cat was thoroughly out of the bag.

The newspaper contained an official notice from the States-General which freed Dutch citizens everywhere in the world from their allegiance to the Prince of Orange, and the mail made it clear that the stadholdership was no more, in a Netherlands which was now firmly allied to the French.

Elphinstone cast aside all further pretence of reasonableness. When the Council of Policy told the three Dutch merchantmen in False Bay to leave and ordered the Zoutman gunners to fire on the British if they interfered, he ordered them to remain at anchor, and positioned two of his men-of-war directly opposite the battery. This heavy hint had the desired effect. Nine days later Elphinstone went even further and sent boarding parties to seize all three ships. The *Willemstad en Boetzelaar*, which carried a respectable 26 guns, considering she was primarily a merchant ship, was taken into Royal Navy service as HMS *Princess*, under command of Captain Hardy. This outright act of war signalled the arrival of the *moment critique*.

Sluysken and Gordon now had just two choices: fight or surrender. Potgieter makes the point that 'the correct thing for the Cape authorities to have done would have been to defend the Cape against the British on behalf of the legitimate Dutch Government.'[41] But they were faced with a double dilemma.

On the one hand they were staunch Orangemen who were so repelled by the French revolutionary doctrine now governing the Netherlands that they preferred an outright British occupation of the Cape. On the other hand, most of the free burghers and a significant part of the armed forces held precisely the opposite sentiment. 'Therefore,' as Potgieter says, 'the Cape needed to be handed over to the British in a more subtle way.'[42]

Like various other historians, he has little doubt that this is precisely what happened. If one accepts the general belief that the members of the Council of Policy were all dedicated Orangemen and therefore wanted to facilitate a British takeover, he says, 'was a scheme not devised for the handing over of the Cape after a feigned defence, a scheme in which Gordon was to play the leading part?'[43]

But then he asks a second pertinent question, which he does not attempt to answer: If this were the case, how would one explain the council's forthright declarations on several occasions that they would defend the Cape against a British attack?

One possibility is that such declarations were meant mainly to pacify the local Patriotten. Another is that the council's members were hedging their bets in case the Prince of Orange were to be restored to power; a possibility which could not be ignored, given the fact of revolutionary France's array of powerful enemies. Yet another is that at least some members were full of fighting spirit – Van Reede van

Oudtshoorn, for example, who was to urge resistance to the very end – and the declarations were a compromise to preserve unanimity among the Cape's administrators.

It is also possible that discussions were held at a top-secret level to which only the Council of Policy – in whole or in part – was privy; Potgieter states that 'it is also evident that letters from the British commanders (the contents of which are unknown) were delivered to Sluysken and Gordon by a certain Alexander Farquhar.'[44]

A great weight now bore down on Gordon in particular as he faced a dilemma that penetrated to the very core of his being as a professional soldier, an Orange loyalist and a man of honour. Should he obey his principles and refuse to defend the Cape, or stand to his duty and fight on behalf of a regime he abhorred but who now legitimately claimed his allegiance following the States-General's abolition of the oath of loyalty to the House of Orange?

If Potgieter's theory about a feigned defence is accepted – and the circumstantial evidence is very strong – Gordon would have to play a leading role in what would be not only an act of doubtful military morality, not to say outright treason, but would also mean that he would risk having soldiers die needlessly while acting out what their leaders knew to be a sham.

The last would be anathema to any military commander of Gordon's stamp, and particularly so in his case when one considers that he grew up in the close-knit Scots Brigade. In that era Scottish units of the British Army always tended to feature a strong personal and emotional relationship between officer and man, and by all accounts this bond was equally strong in the Scots Brigade, especially in view of its expatriate status.

Then on 29 June the Council of Policy took the step that finally set the wheels of invasion in motion. Acting on the advice of Gordon and De Lille, it decided to evacuate its forces from Simon's Town. In accordance with their earlier orders the infantrymen and gunners spiked the guns and threw their charges of gunpowder into the sea, then melted away to re-form at Muizenberg. Simon's Town became a ghostly place, inhabited only by the VOC resident and a handful of slaves.

The stage was now about to be set at Muizenberg, the greatest obstacle to a British advance, for what could have been the first classic infantryman's battle in recorded Cape history. But it turned out to be something else altogether, something unthinkable to many honourable soldiers serving the VOC.

CHAPTER 8

INVASION

For just over two weeks the evacuation of Simon's Town elicited no reaction from the British. Then, on 14 June Craig landed with 450 men of the 78th Regiment, with 400 marines following a week later. No doubt some energetic foraging took place after the landings, since food was so short that shipboard rations had had to be cut by a third. There was no question of marching on Cape Town immediately though, and it is not difficult to see why: at this stage the cards were still stacked in the VOC's favour.

For one thing, Craig's force on the ground was adequate for establishing a strong beach-head, but far too small to risk a confrontation against an opposition that might not prove to be as feeble as it was hoped. With only 850 or so soldiers and marines at his disposal, he was badly outnumbered. He could augment his force with drafts of seamen from the ships, but this was hardly an ideal solution. Although sailors of those days were used to hand-to-hand combat and lightning shore raids, they were not accustomed to an orthodox overland advance.

It was one thing for a captain to assemble a contingent from his crew for a quick in-and-out shore expedition, but quite another to endanger his ship by leaving it undermanned for an indefinite time.[1]

To make matters worse, Craig had no field artillery except a few light guns, and no siege artillery of any kind. Neither did he have any horses, barring the officers' chargers, or other draught animals with which to draw even the few guns he did have. Elphinstone's heavily armed ships, so fearsome a threat to the Zoutman Battery, did not make up completely for this lack: their 18-pounder and 24-pounder guns had a maximum range of perhaps 2 000m, but their effective or accurate range was no more than 500 or 600m. This meant that they could only provide supporting fire while the British land force or its opponents were near the shoreline.

There was also no question of their venturing into Table Bay itself. They would have to run the gauntlet of volleys of red-hot shot fired by the Amsterdam and Chavonnes Batteries, as well as the smaller positions at Kijk-in-de-Pot (today's Fort Wynyard)[2] and elsewhere, and then face the guns of the Roggebaai Battery, the Imhoff Battery and the Sea Line.

The only way to make up for the lack of artillery was an overland infantry attack in overwhelming force. And, although he and Elphinstone believed that the Nationale Battaillon would not fight with enthusiasm and might even roll over without firing a shot, this was certainly not enough of a sure bet. There was nothing to be done except wait for the arrival of Major-General Clarke with the main body of their troops, due to collect a further contingent from St Helena.[3] But of the task force there was no sign.

At the same time Craig was becoming ever more conscious that time was running out. The limited food supplies were diminishing by the day and his spies were reporting that parties of militiamen kept arriving from the interior (including members of the Swellendam dragoons) in spite of the internal political divisions. Every day's delay meant more time for the VOC to strengthen its defences.

However, the situation would have been much worse if the VOC leadership had not withdrawn its forces from Simon's Town. Although VOC forces would have found it difficult to repulse a concerted naval and amphibious attack after Clarke's arrival from St Helena, it is conceivable that dragoons supported by the Simon's Town batteries could have prevented Craig's force from landing, or at least inflicted heavy losses, before they in turn were destroyed by Elphinstone's naval guns.

This might well have affected the final political dispensation. Instead, as Potgieter says, 'the evacuation of Simon's Town was a blessing for the British and the lack of proper defences a grave military error by the Dutch.'[4]

The stage was now set for a confrontation at Muizenberg, the greatest obstacle to a British advance, blocking the overland route from Simon's Town to Cape Town. Here, too, the VOC forces started off at an advantage with a relatively favourable situation. Tactically Muizenberg was a good defensive position, since its flanks were protected by the Steenberg mountains on one side and the Sandvlei marshes on the other. This meant that Craig would not be able to come in from the side and roll up the Dutch positions, but would have to send his men in to attack on a narrow front. With a strong defensive line and stubborn resistance on the seaward side, as Potgieter points out, the British force with its lack of transport or heavy land weapons 'would have [found] it very difficult to force the Dutch from the Muizenberg position.'[5]

But the VOC's preparations to hold it were anything but impressive, in spite of the resources at its disposal. There was a suspicious lack of enthusiasm about setting up a credible defensive line, in spite of the ample preparation time resulting from the British force's inability to move. A 50m-long trench was dug across the road from Simon's Town, and two 4-pounders on field carriages from the Castle's artillery park were deployed at the landward end. But in spite of ample warning time no earthworks were erected at the seaward end to protect the Dutch infantry from the naval bombardment which would obviously cover any British land advance, and initially no guns were deployed there either.

As the days passed a trickle of extra artillery pieces arrived from Cape Town: a 13-inch mortar – presumably laboriously transported from the Amsterdam Battery on Table Bay, which mounted six of these cumbersome weapons – and a howitzer, thought to have been of 4½-inch calibre, which might have come from either the Amsterdam or Chavonnes Battery. Last came two more 4-pounders and finally a brace of the fearsome 24-pounders from one of the coastal batteries. Accompanying the howitzer was a portable powder magazine that was intended to supply all the guns. This consisted of a box-bodied wagon clad in metal plates, with a steeply sloping roof that was intended to ward off explosive shells or other incendiary devices. It was a strange, niggardly mixture of weapons and equipment for such a serious business, one that did not make sense then and does not do so now.

Too heavy for the purpose, the mortar was most definitely out of its element. A field gun needed to be highly mobile and capable of dealing with a variety of changing battlefield situations. Typically it was a light weapon of no more than 9-pounder calibre, mounted on large wheels to cope with uneven terrain and equipped with trails so that it could easily be swung around to meet an unexpected development, or hitched up and galloped away to another position if the occasion demanded. It had a limber carrying its first-line ammunition and was drawn by a team of six or eight horses that could move it to a new location or take it out of danger at short notice.

The mortar, by contrast, was an indirect-fire weapon whose best use was as siege artillery. Its barrel was fixed at a 45-degree angle and instead of a carriage it had an immobile bed that did not allow it to be traversed or even moved with any sort of speed in response to a changing situation. The howitzer – basically a mortar with a slightly lengthened barrel, mounted on a field carriage – was somewhat better, but it, too, was an indirect-fire weapon which had been deployed in a situation where the two sides would be exchanging direct fire at close quarters.

However, an additional complication must surely have been that the portable magazine would have to cope with distributing ammunition of four different types.

Nevertheless, as Gerry de Vries and Jonathan Hall point out, the field guns, howitzer and mortar would likely have been able to blunt any attack Craig might launch, seeing that his approach was limited to the narrow strip of open land between the mountains and the sea. This, in modern infantry parlance, would have provided an ideal 'killing ground' because the British troops would have been bunched up instead of being able to advance in open or extended order. The only great advantage of the mortar and howitzer in this situation would have been that their ammunition consisted of explosive shells – fused, hollow round-shot, filled with a bursting charge of gunpowder.

The 24-pounders were another story altogether. They were correctly placed – at the seaward end of the VOC line – but their potential was reduced almost to nothing by a blunder so egregious that one finds it hard to describe it as anything but deliberate. Namely, they faced the wrong way: *towards Craig's expected line of advance.* In other words, Gordon's plan was to use the 24-pounders as field artillery, a role for which they were unsuited in every way.

24-pounders were naval guns, ship-killers *par excellence*, and their natural environment was a coastal battery. There they had all the odds in their favour. They had no limitations on space for supplies of ammunition and could be loaded with a variety of projectiles with which to wreak havoc on hulls, gun ports, sails, rigging and crew, or to set the ships themselves on fire. In a land battle, however, they were truly fish out of water. They were simply too cumbersome and heavy for field use. A typical 24-pounder's barrel alone was usually about 3m long and weighed up to three tonnes, and the sturdy carriage needed to support this mass of iron contributed substantially to the gun's overall weight.

Their carriages were also wrongly configured. A 24-pounder was normally mounted on a small-wheeled garrison carriage that stood on a long wooden platform of trapezoidal shape, usually about 5m long, which was built on top of a stone foundation. To tame the 24-pounder's violent recoil the platform sloped upward at the rear, and strong breeching ropes lashed the carriage to the battery's ramparts to stop the guns from running back more than about 4m.

Coastal guns of the time were not traversed to any great extent, but fired as they bore on their targets because they had to recoil more or less perpendicularly to the rampart or they would run off the platforms. This meant that their carriages had no need of trails by which they could be swung to left or right to deal with swiftly changing situations, and they could not, of course, simply be hooked up and towed away to another location if this was required.

Preparing a 24-pounder for action in the field was a laborious business because it was necessary to recreate part of its normal environment by constructing a quasi-parapet out of stone to which the breechings could be attached, then installing the wooden platform on which it would be run in and out. The 24-pounders arrived at Muizenberg minus these platforms, without which they would dig themselves into the sand with each shot. This meant that the gunners had to construct makeshift platforms of stones and tree branches that, inevitably, did not work as well as proper ones.

Logically, therefore, the 24-pounders should have faced seawards, behind protective earthworks, at the seaward end of the VOC position in order to protect the Dutch line from a flank bombardment by the British ships. Even worse, they had only been supplied with round-shot – even if there had been a last-minute change of plan and they had somehow been swung round to engage the British fleet, they would still not have had any bar or chain shot to hurl at Elphinstone's ships.[6] And it would surely also have been possible to improvise ovens for heating the round shot, yet nothing was done.

Most of all, more than two guns should have been brought in. Admittedly the new defensive works erected in the recent past had left the VOC with no spare guns in storage, but some could have been withdrawn from the existing batteries around Cape Town – particularly from the well-armed Amsterdam Battery, which mounted a great number of large-calibre cannon. In addition, there was no shortage of gunpowder, since the VOC had literally tens of thousands of pounds of it stored in the various magazines, enough for about 30 000 shots.

As it happened, the only time the British put their noses into Table Bay was two days before Craig landed, when a small squadron entered the roadstead on what was obviously a scouting expedition to assess the batteries' state of readiness. The Kijk-in-de-Pot gunners fired several shots at the British ships and they sheered off, having got their answer.

The Dutch cannon at Muizenberg would certainly have faced a large number of British naval guns – possibly 60 to 80, but De Vries and Hall point out that the 24-pounders would have been 'firing from a steady platform at relatively large ships which were stationary. The British [would have been] firing from a rolling platform at a relatively small-profile target.' That being said, Royal Navy gunners were the most technically proficient in the world – and Muizenberg was a sitting target.

The positioning of the 24-pounders was therefore the complete opposite of what the situation demanded and cannot be put down to ignorance or the press of circumstances, since the VOC had ample time on its side and did not lack for experienced and well-trained artillerymen.

The way the 24-pounders were deployed was so blatantly wrong that a number of Dutch officers, whose spokesman appears to have been one Lieutenant PW Marnitz,[7] approached Gordon and stated their concerns to him. Gordon duly inspected the position and then, to their utter astonishment, declared himself satisfied with the preparations.

They were so astonished, in fact, that they committed the cardinal military sin of openly questioning a superior's judgment and pressed for a second opinion from the French engineer Louis-Michel Thibault, who was now a captain in the VOC garrison. But Potgieter relates that Gordon told Marnitz that no further entrenchments were necessary because 'the English are too much our friends to cause us the least fears.'

So no further work was done on the seaward end of the line, even though Elphinstone had made his intentions quite clear by sending boats to take soundings for his ships directly opposite the VOC positions. They did so with impunity because De Lille, to the rage of his gunners, forbade them to fire. This could be interpreted as the correct response, seeing that the negotiations were still in progress, but De Lille's subsequent actions tend to indicate that this was not quite his motivation for the order.[8]

The size of De Lille's force was also curiously unimpressive. He had started out with just under 1 000 soldiers of various kinds, but as the weeks passed some of his regular infantrymen – idle, bored, distrustful of their leaders and enticed by British promises of higher pay for any deserters from the Dutch side – had trickled away. The desertions eventually stopped after a Burgher Militia patrol captured two runaways, who were promptly executed by firing squad, but the damage had been done.

By the beginning of August De Lille had only 700 troops left: about 200 infantrymen of the Nationale Battalion, 150 artillerymen, 200

Burgher Militia dragoons and 150 Pandoeren. Yet his Muizenberg force could have been double that number. Burgher Militia dragoons were still arriving in Cape Town from the hinterland, so that by the time of the battle there were more than 1 100 of them available. Since one of the dragoons' main virtues was their mobility, it would have been possible to deploy most of them at Muizenberg, from where they could have been rushed back to Cape Town in the unlikely event of the British changing their minds about a landing there. This 'fire-brigade' mode was precisely the role for which the dragoons had been trained since Simon van der Stel's time. But most of them were held back in camp at Cape Town and Wynberg. One could ascribe this to excessive caution, but only by a stretch of the imagination.

By late July General Clarke and the British main body had still not arrived, and Elphinstone and Craig were forced to start preparing to move without him, the former having satisfied himself that if wind and sea conditions were satisfactory his ships would be able to get close enough to shore to bombard the VOC positions accurately.

On 7 August Craig set off for Muizenberg in a reasonably sanguine frame of mind. Side drums beat out the time for his force. Its back-bone was made up of his stolid Highland infantrymen in the short red coatees, loose white pantaloons and black semi-toppers or 'round hats' which in hot weather replaced the colourful but uncomfortable uniforms of Europe. Marching alongside them were several drafts of red-coated Marines and two 500-man battalions of seamen, one under the command of Captains Hardy of the *Echo* and Spranger of the *Rattlesnake,* veterans of boarding parties and the cutting-out raids in which the Royal Navy excelled.

As they advanced, Admiral Elphinstone transferred his flag from the *Monarch* to HMS *America* to lead the bombardment, and with the *Stately, Echo* and *Rattlesnake* (commanded by their first lieutenants), and a small gunboat called the *Squib,* set sail for Muizenberg from Simon's Bay. Craig was still on the march to Muizenberg when the ships reached Kalk Bay and put a VOC piquet there to flight. The ships arrived off Muizenberg at approximately 1pm, anchored themselves fore and aft, and set about the laborious task of winching themselves into position for firing broadsides.

At 2.20pm they were ready. The *Squib* began bombarding De Lille's position, followed by HMS *Echo* and the *Rattlesnake*; 40 minutes later the *America* and *Stately* joined in as well.[9] The Royal Navy was renowned for the speed and accuracy of its gunnery, and in short order the VOC position – bereft as it was of any protection on its seaward flank – was turned into a small hell on earth. It was a brutal and unnerving introduction to full-scale conventional warfare, and the VOC soldiers broke – or were allowed to break.

In fact, according to JJ Oberholster, quoting CJ Barnard in the 1950 *Archives Year Book*, the disintegration started *before* the British opened fire, when De Lille 'set a deplorable example by beating a disorderly retreat at the head of his infantry' towards Sandvlei with the 4-pounders, abandoning the mortar, the howitzer and the 24-pounders without even spiking them. Left completely unsupported, the Burgher Militia, Pandoeren and most of the artillerymen followed in De Lille's wake.

The only ones to stand fast were Lieutenant Marnitz and a colleague named Kemper, along with a few of the artillery rank and file, who heroically manhandled the two 24-pounders around so that they bore on the ships. Thanks to the lack of proper recoiling platforms and the guns' *mis*orientation, serving them was a frustrating business. Because the platforms faced the wrong way the guns ran off them when they were fired, so that soon their barrels pointed drunkenly skyward. Since there was no way of getting them back on to the platforms, Marnitz's party compensated by inserting more quoins (wooden elevating wedges) under the breeches. This worked for a few shots, but the guns dug themselves deeper each time, and Marnitz soon ran out of quoins.

In an action worthy of any nation's highest honour, Marnitz and his men, deserted by their leaders and bereft of all support, managed to score direct hits on HMS *America* and HMS *Stately*. Then, battered by the storm of fire directed at them and defeated by the impossibility of training the hopelessly dug-in guns any further, they spiked the 24-pounders and retreated as well.

Admiral Elphinstone later wrote that two men were killed on board the *America* and four wounded when one of her guns took a direct hit and was disabled; one man was wounded on board the *Stately* and several other shots passed through the ships without inflicting any serious damage. Compared to what might have been – if the VOC had had four or six 24-pounders, properly mounted and dug in, and equipped with shot-ovens, during the hour and 20 minutes it took to bring the ships into position – Marnitz's brave effort was a paltry response indeed.

Craig's men occupied the Muizenberg position without encountering resistance, staggered by the Dutch failure to fight. An eyewitness to the incident, Captain Robert Percival, spoke for all when he later wrote that 'the Dutch on our approach neither behaved with courage or prudence, nor took proper advantage of their strong positions ... and with a degree of folly scarcely to be accounted for ... abandoned the important place which they should have defended to the last extremity.'[10]

The British soldiers and sailors advanced through the VOC position and kept up the chase, but when the Dutch forces had retreated far enough to be out of range of the ships' ordnance a party of Burgher Militia, Pandoeren and artillerymen armed themselves with one of the 4-pounders and counter-attacked. This unexpected sally succeeded in forcing the forward British elements to withdraw to Muizenberg, but that was the sum of resistance. Soon the redcoats were moving inexorably over the abandoned battlefield again, the sullen thudding of their snareless side-drums the passing-bells for the VOC's long sway at the Cape of Good Hope.[11]

De Lille and his men did not stop running until they reached Lochner's Farm, near the present-day suburb of Diep River. There they were visited by Sluysken and Gordon, who pacified the near-mutinous burghers by ordering De Lille to go back to Sandvlei and take up a defensive position. He deployed his force in a line with his own infantry in the centre, the burghers and Pandoeren on either flank and several guns out in front, securing the Steenberg flank with two burgher dragoon companies under Captain Myburgh and Captain Cloete, plus a 50-strong infantry company and 36 gunners with two guns. But it was strictly for show.

When Craig launched a two-pronged advance next morning – the sailors crossing Sandvlei and the soldiers edging along the foot of Steenberg – De Lille ordered a general retreat without a single shot being fired. He wasted no time in putting his order into effect, his destination not Diep River this time but the far more distant military camp at Wynberg, an inconsiderable distance from Cape Town itself. Along with him went Gordon, who had not only been present when all this happened, but, Potgieter points out, had 'made no attempt to calm his troops and approved the retreat to Wynberg, although he knew it could not be justified.'[12]

The burgher dragoons and Pandoeren were made of sterner stuff, however. While De Lille disappeared into the distance they carried out a flanking attack on Craig's men which so disconcerted the British that they began to fall back, with the dragoons and Pandoeren in hot pursuit. It had to be called off, however, when the Cape men came under fire from some of the unspiked guns which had been abandoned the previous day and had then been pressed into service by the British. Their daring enterprise foiled, the dragoons and Pandoeren withdrew to Wynberg as well. Gordon did what he could to calm things down and then, according to Thibault, 'returned to Cape Town, laughing like a madman.'[13] Was it the laughter of despair or the sign of an incipient nervous breakdown? Perhaps both, when one considers subsequent events.

Potgieter comments that Gordon's and De Lille's conduct during and after the fiasco at Sandvlei 'make it altogether clear that the defence of the Cape was sabotaged. Not Sluysken, nor Gordon nor De Lille made any significant effort to hold the line or organise an effective resistance before withdrawal to Wynberg.'[14]

On 9 August a British ship finally arrived from St Helena, bringing Elphinstone and Craig almost 400 more soldiers, nine field guns and ammunition and also a substantial sum in silver coin. Now the die was cast in no uncertain terms; the blunder at Muizenberg had doomed the Cape, even if the Council of Policy had been of a mind to do something about offering further resistance.

Next day the Burgher Militia officers, incensed by what they saw as De Lille's cowardice, accused him of treason and he was arrested. The Fiscal cleared him of this charge, but public opinion, Oberholster says, 'was so violently against him that he was detained in the Castle for his own safety.'[15] But De Lille's removal from the scene was merely a cosmetic gesture; it was too late now to make any meaningful stand against the British, and in any case his replacement was Captain BC van Baalen, another Orange supporter.

On 11 August the free burghers, acutely conscious of the fact that the British advance would soon be resumed, disgusted by the conduct of their military leaders and angry because nothing had been done to fortify Wynberg, demanded – and got – a mass council of war at the Burgher Watch-House in Cape Town, the seat of civil government. Attended by a great number of Capetonians, the meeting was an extremely tense occasion. The free burghers resolved that the 'whole task of defence now rests on the shoulders of the citizens'.[16] A tearful Sluysken pleaded for unity and discouraged any thoughts of precipitate action, stating that attacks were expected both in Table Bay (which he must have known was highly unlikely) and overland from Simon's Town. Once again he promised that the Cape would be defended to the last.

The following day Elphinstone and Craig increased the pressure a little more with a letter saying that they were waiting for Clarke to arrive with 3 000 men and repeating their offer to place the Cape under the protection of Britain; if Sluysken did not comply, their troops might get out of control and they could not be held responsible for what might happen to the inhabitants. Once more the Council of Policy's official reply was that any British take-over would be resisted.

It was to be several weeks before the British continued with their advance on Cape Town, but once again no good use was made of the delay to improve Wynberg's defences, although it was obviously Craig's next target. The commanding officer, De Lille's replacement Van Baalen (now promoted to major), rejected pleas from the Burgher Militia officers and Marnitz and his colleagues to strengthen his poorly organised defences, claiming he had no authority to do so. Gordon, meanwhile, was nowhere to be seen: he was spending all his time strengthening Table Bay's defences against an amphibious attack which was obviously destined never to take place. To a disillusioned Marnitz this misdirected energy was a transparent stratagem to keep the military engineers too busy to put them to work at Wynberg.

Craig's men had now dug in at Muizenberg, but they were still vulnerable to attack, and repeated requests were made to fall on them before Clarke and his troops arrived. All were ignored until the agitation reached such a pitch at the end of August that Sluysken reluctantly ordered Gordon to design an assault. Gordon took his time in drawing up the plans, and, Potgieter says, they were 'openly and frequently discussed, to such an extent that the British probably knew what to expect.'[17]

The fighting spirit of the burghers and Pandoeren remained high all the while, and they were involved in a number of small-scale actions, the most telling of which took place on 1 September, when volunteers raided the British positions at Steenberg and seized five prisoners after wounding two officers and 12 other ranks. But Gordon's main attack never took place. On 3 September Clarke and his 14 ships full of troops, weapons and supplies arrived. Gordon's operation was called off and Sluysken immediately ordered the return to Cape Town of some guns that had earlier been deployed at Wynberg.

Some up-country members of the Burgher Militia began to drift away because they feared for their families as a result of rumours that the Bushmen were rising in the interior and that there was a possibility of a slave revolt. Now others gave up hope and left as well. Most stayed in place, however, so that about 900 of the original 1 000-plus dragoons were still available.

On 14 September Clarke marched out of Muizenberg and headed for Cape Town with between 4 000 and 5 000 soldiers, marines and sailors. Volunteers from the newly arrived ships' crews dragged his guns because no solution had yet been found to the extreme lack of transport vehicles and draught livestock. A party of Swellendam dragoons under Lieutenant Daniel du Plessis carried out a daring harassing attack on Clarke's columns. It failed when the dragoons were driven off by heavy fire, although Clarke was so impressed that later he invited Du Plessis to dinner, where he complimented him on his conduct.

It was the only praiseworthy aspect of the VOC resistance to Clarke's advance. At Wynberg Major van Baalen mounted what can only be described as a token defence – 230 Nationale Battaillon infantrymen in the centre of his line, some of the nine dragoon companies on the left flank and the rest, together with the Pandoeren, on the right. What few

The fight on the beach near the Salt River mouth in 1510 which resulted in the Portuguese shunning the Cape for almost a century and a half. In the background can be seen the trained Khoina battle oxen which were used to such devastating effect.

By permission of the Castle Military Museum, Castle of Good Hope

Jan van Riebeeck arrives at the Cape of Good Hope in April 1652 and exchanges gifts with waiting Khoina inhabitants. In the background are some of the characteristic *matjiehuise*, or mat houses, which can still be seen in South Africa.

GS Smithard's illustration in Ian D Colvin's *The Romance of Empire*, 1909

At various times any of three flags could be seen at the Cape. One was the national red-white-blue horizontal tricolour. The second was the VOC house flag, the tricolour with the VOC logo and the letter 'C' to denote the Cape outpost. The third was the revered orange-white-blue 'Prinsevlag' under which the Dutch had fought and won their 80-year war of liberation from Spain. This was the 'blood flag', hoisted only in times of war.

Jan van Riebeeck entertains a party of visiting Khoina in his austere quarters in the little Fort of Good Hope, while at left one of his staff provides background music on a *muselaar*, an early form of harpsichord. Visitors like these showed him lumps of copper ore from Namaqualand and spurred his desire to find the mythical Monomotapa, the kingdom of gold.

JS Skelton's illustration in Ian D Colvin's *The Romance of Empire*, 1909

Sheikh Yusuf of Macassar – Indonesian nobleman, soldier, statesman and holy man – and 49 followers disembark from the VOC ship *Voetboog* at the start of his Cape exile in 1693. Well treated at the VOC's expense, he was settled on the farm Zandvliet (later renamed 'Macassar' in his honour), where he formed the first cohesive Muslim community in South Africa. By the time of his death in 1699 he had become the most revered Muslim holy man in the country's history.

GS Smithard's illustration in Ian D Colvin's *The Romance of Empire*, 1909

The increasingly diverse population of the Cape acquired another ingredient when a party of industrious Huguenots, driven from their French homeland because of their Protestant beliefs, arrived to make a new life for themselves in 1687. In the process they not only turned the small local wine-making industry around so that it eventually became one of the world's best, but also left a legacy of French first and surnames which are borne by millions of modern South Africans.

GS Smithard's illustration in Ian D Colvin's *The Romance of Empire*, 1909

The small exploring parties Jan van Riebeeck and some of his successors sent out northwards in search of the outskirts of Monomotapa faced an array of dangers and hardships – thirst, hunger, attacks by predatory wild animals and, on occasion, by some of the local inhabitants they encountered. However each expedition brought back more knowledge of the unmapped hinterland.

JS Skelton's illustration in Ian D Colvin's *The Romance of Empire*, 1909

An enraged rhinoceros attacks Governor Simon van der Stel's coach during his trek into Namaqualand in 1685 to make a personal inspection of the copper fields. After an investigation, which included tunnelling into the hills of today's Springbok, he reported that getting the copper ore over the mountains to the sea would be too difficult. He was right – mining did not start there till the 1850s.

JS Skelton's illustration in Ian D Colvin's *The Romance of Empire*, 1909

Governor Maurice Pasque, the Marquis de Chavonnes, who not only radically upgraded the VOC's administration but also whipped its military garrison into shape, outfitted it with a uniform he designed himself and built a formidable battery west of Cape Town, which is now a museum in the V&A Waterfront, – the first of a series of fortifications which made the Cape Peninsula among the most strongly defended localities in sub-Saharan Africa.
By permission of the William Fehr Collection, the Castle of Good Hope

The retreat to Sandvlei
The map depicts the position after the Batavian collapse at Muizenberg. General Craig had advanced from Simon's Town and broken through the perfunctory Dutch defensive works at Kalk Bay, when Lieutenant-Colonel CMW de Lille fled precipitately with most of his forces. Swellendam burgher dragoons and the Corps Pandoeren mounted an *ad hoc* counter-attack but were forced back; so was the valiant artilleryman Lieutenant PW Marnitz, who collected some volunteers and fired De Lille's two stranded 24-pounder guns at the British ships lying off-shore. Now the ships have moved up the coast to cover Craig as his soldiers, sailors and marines head for Sandvlei – and another feeble defensive line. De Lille will soon abandon Sandvlei and head northwards, essentially leaving Craig's path to Wynberg wide open. ©William Smuts

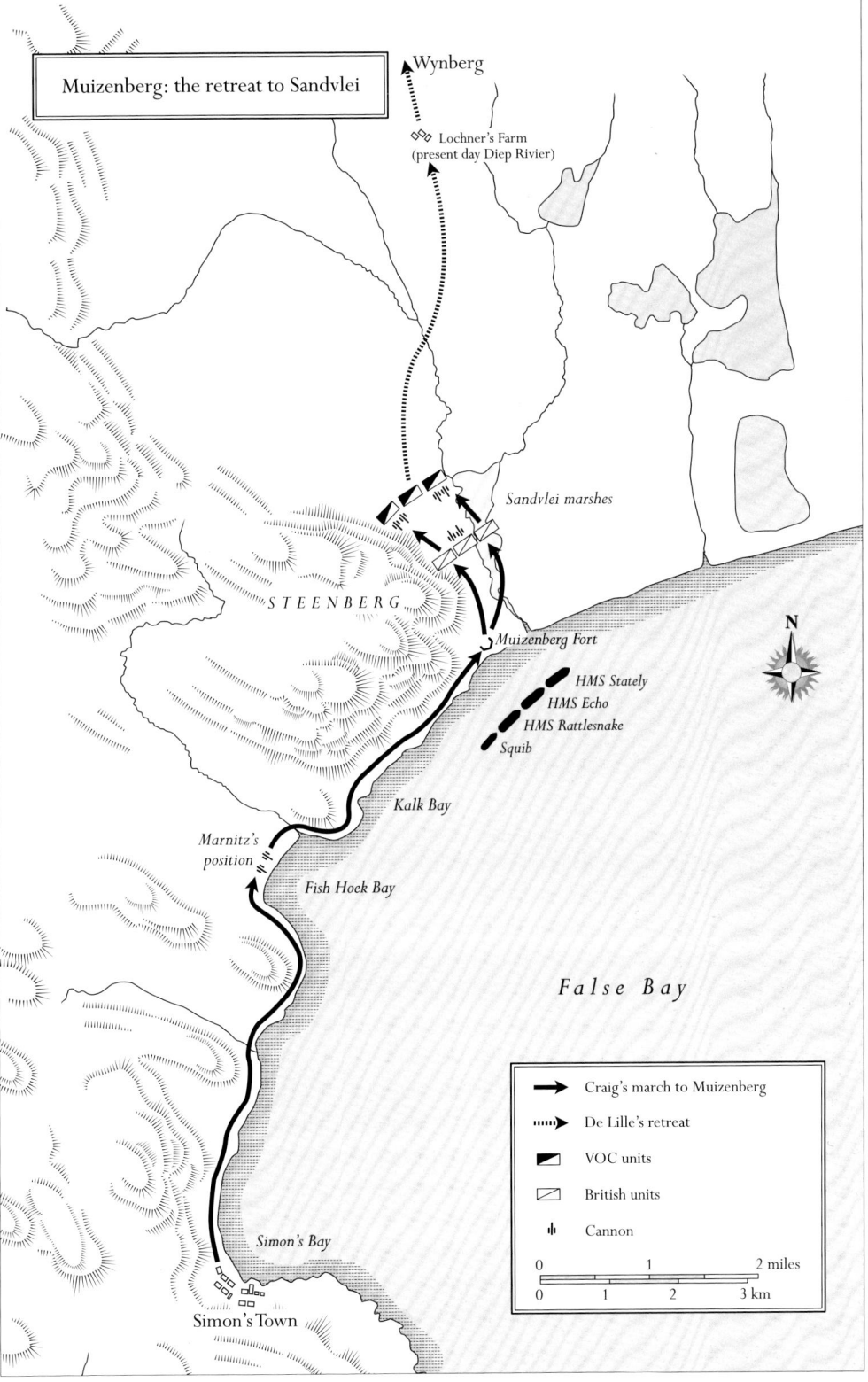

Muizenberg: the retreat to Sandvlei

Wynberg

◊◊◊ Lochner's Farm
(present day Diep Rivier)

Sandvlei marshes

S T E E N B E R G

Muizenberg Fort

HMS Stately
HMS Echo
HMS Rattlesnake
Squib

Kalk Bay

Marnitz's
position

Fish Hoek Bay

False Bay

N

Simon's Bay

Simon's Town

→ Craig's march to Muizenberg

⇢ De Lille's retreat

◣ VOC units

▱ British units

⫟ Cannon

0		1		2 miles
0	1	2		3 km

The Rev John Barrow, clergyman, traveller and confidant of Governor Lord Macartney, whose unashamedly partisan reports exacerbated rather than improved conditions on the unstable eastern frontier. Barrow loathed the frontier free burghers, his information-gathering ability was poor because he could not speak Dutch, the *lingua franca* at that time, and he knew little about the Cape's history and its peoples. In future years he would also campaign for the British to recapture the Cape, and even wrote a book on how best to do it.

Lieutenant-General Jan Willem Janssens, the Cape's enlightened last Batavian Governor, who strove mightily against his lack of resources to make it defensible against the British, but when the invasion came was defeated by a combination of ill fortune and overwhelming odds.

Commissioner-General Abraham de Mist, respected Batavian humanist, political scientist and administrator, who brought sweeping changes to the administration at the Cape, set the abolition of slavery in motion and introduced a brief period of liberal democracy at the Cape – the first in Africa – whose influence lasted for generations after his departure.

In June 1803 General Janssens travelled up to the Eastern Cape, where he met with the young Xhosa chief Ngqika, who was engaged in fighting his usurper, Ndlambe. The meeting was most amiable, but the volatile situation on the eastern frontier was not defused, and partway through Janssens had to return to Cape Town with all possible speed – war had broken out between Britain and France once more. In the background are Batavian soldiers, probably a contingent of the 5th Waldeck Regiment, and on the left members of the regular Batavian dragoons wearing the distinctive Tarleton helmets.

By permission of the William Fehr Collection, the Castle of Good Hope

Heinrich Lichtenstein – a traveller, writer and natural scientist – and a confidant of General Janssens.

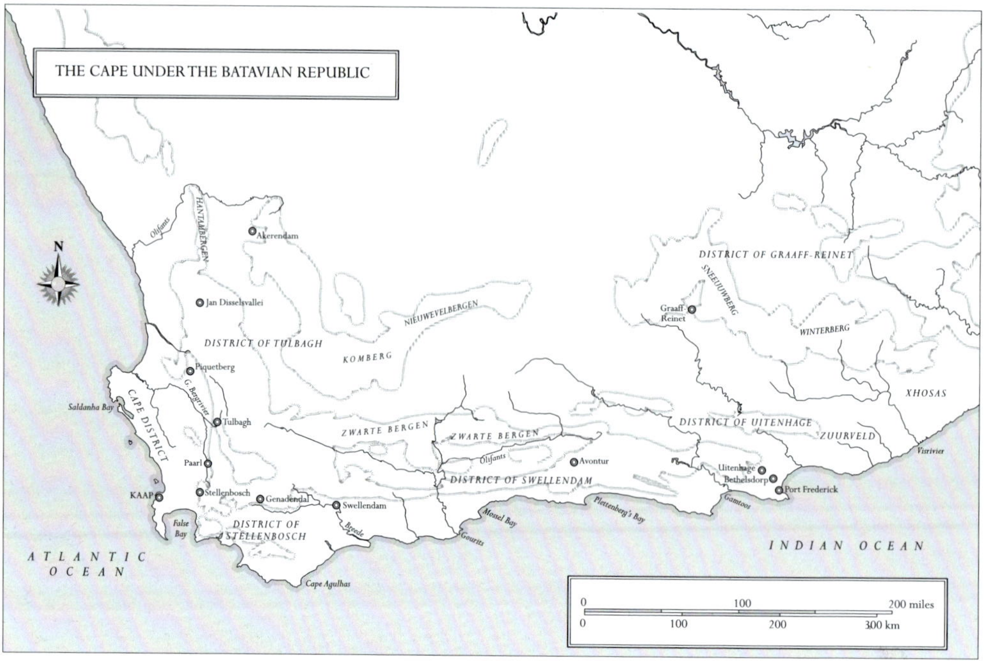

The Cape under the Batavian Republic (1806)
At the end of Batavian rule the Cape Colony's writ extended in the north to the Olifants River, although numbers of Cape people, including both whites and Griquas, had been living beyond it since the 1760s; in the east, the border was supposed to be the Fish River, but the Xhosa nation had been pressing westwards over it for decades. ©William Smuts

The Hottentot Light Infantry, consisting mainly of coloured men from the Genadendal mission, conducted themselves so well at the Battle of Blaauwberg that Janssens commended them to Baird, who incorporated most of them into a new regiment.

Popham's thrust southwards
Commodore Sir Home Popham set a dogleg course to the Cape, not only to preserve secrecy but also to take advantage of favourable winds and spare his troops the worst effects of tropical heat. Meanwhile Admiral Pierre-Charles de Villeneuve, frustrated in his effort to facilitate a French invasion of Britain by luring Royal Navy ships away from the British blockading fleet, was returning from Martinique, on his way to his date with destiny off Cape Trafalgar. ©William Smuts

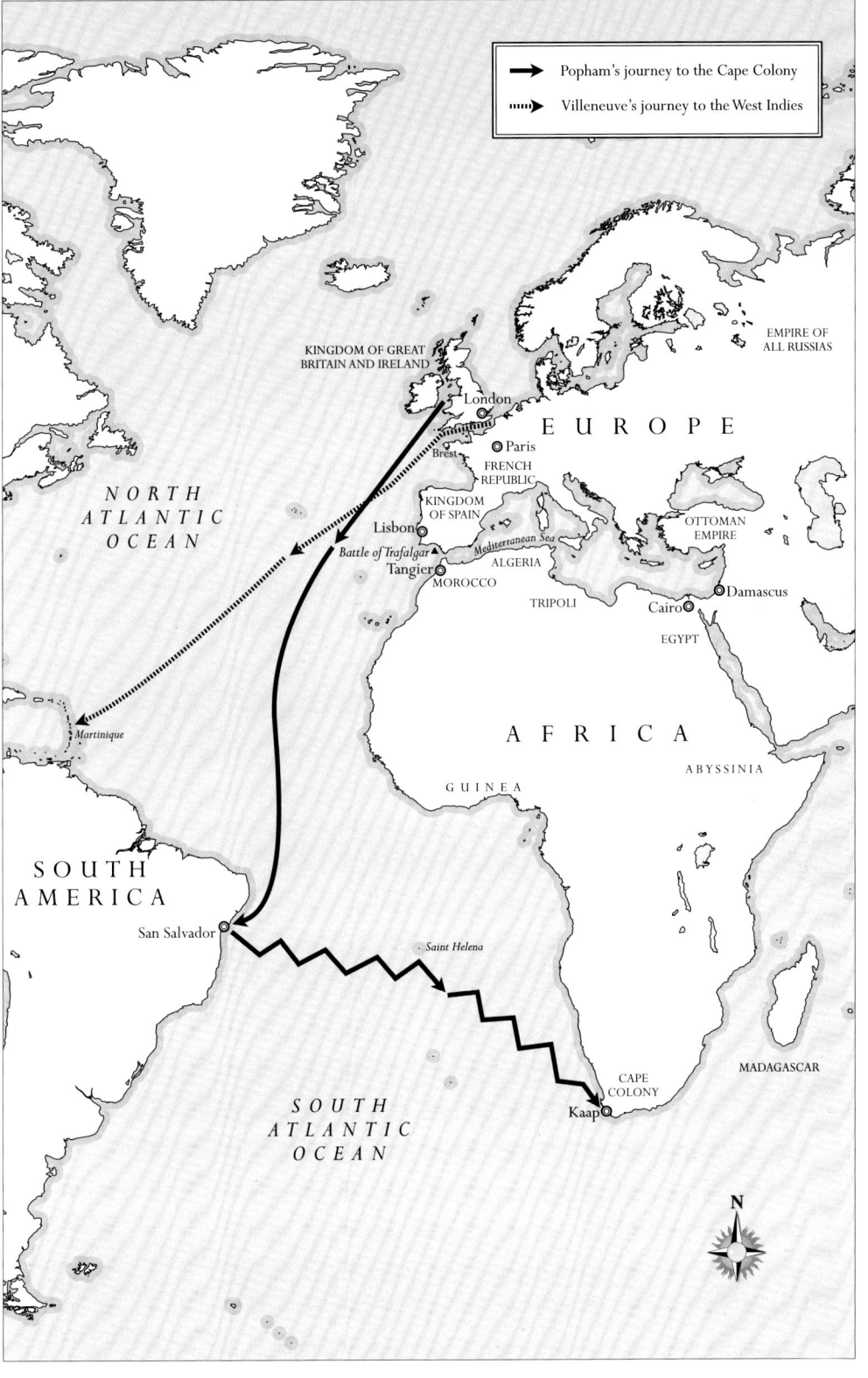

Major-General Sir David Baird, a veteran soldier of the Indian wars, who led the second British invasion of the Cape in 1806, and became a wise post-1806 governor … and then almost destroyed his career by an ill-informed decision to carry out an unauthorised expedition to South America.

Lieutenant-Colonel Robert Wilson of the 20th Light Dragoons, a famous soldier and military writer who accompanied Beresford to Saldanha Bay and, to his frustration, arrived too late for the battle.

Commodore (later Admiral) Sir Home Popham, who brought Baird's force to the Cape in a fleet of warhips, troopers and transports, worked with him on executing an efficient landing … and after the invasion persuaded him to give orders for the ill-fated expedition to South America, but survived the ensuing scandal because of his political connections.

The Rev Henry Martyn, a young preacher on one of the troopships, for whom Blaauwberg was to be a ghastly introduction to the gruesome reality of the battlefield.

Popham's fleet arrives in Table Bay. Now the invasion is only days away. This depiction was published in June 1806 by a London print-seller, Edward Orme, and it is clear that by this time some of the facts about the Cape's geography had filtered back.

Brigadier-General WC Beresford (seen here in later life after being ennobled), one of Baird's capable subordinates, who was sent off to land at Saldanha Bay when it appeared that the sea was too high in Table Bay – and thus missed the Battle of Blaauwberg.

An accurate reconstruction of the shako and jacket worn by the 22nd Batavia at Blaauwberg. These would have been worn with a white waistcoat and loose white trousers over short black spats or gaiters.

The fruitless dash from Saldanha Bay
Beresford successfully lands his force at Saldanha Bay, then sets off on the arduous but fruitless dash to Cape Town, led by Lieutenant-Colonel Wilson and his light dragoons. In the meantime, Janssens and his field army march to the Rietvallei camp and then head for the Blaauwberg.

© William Smuts

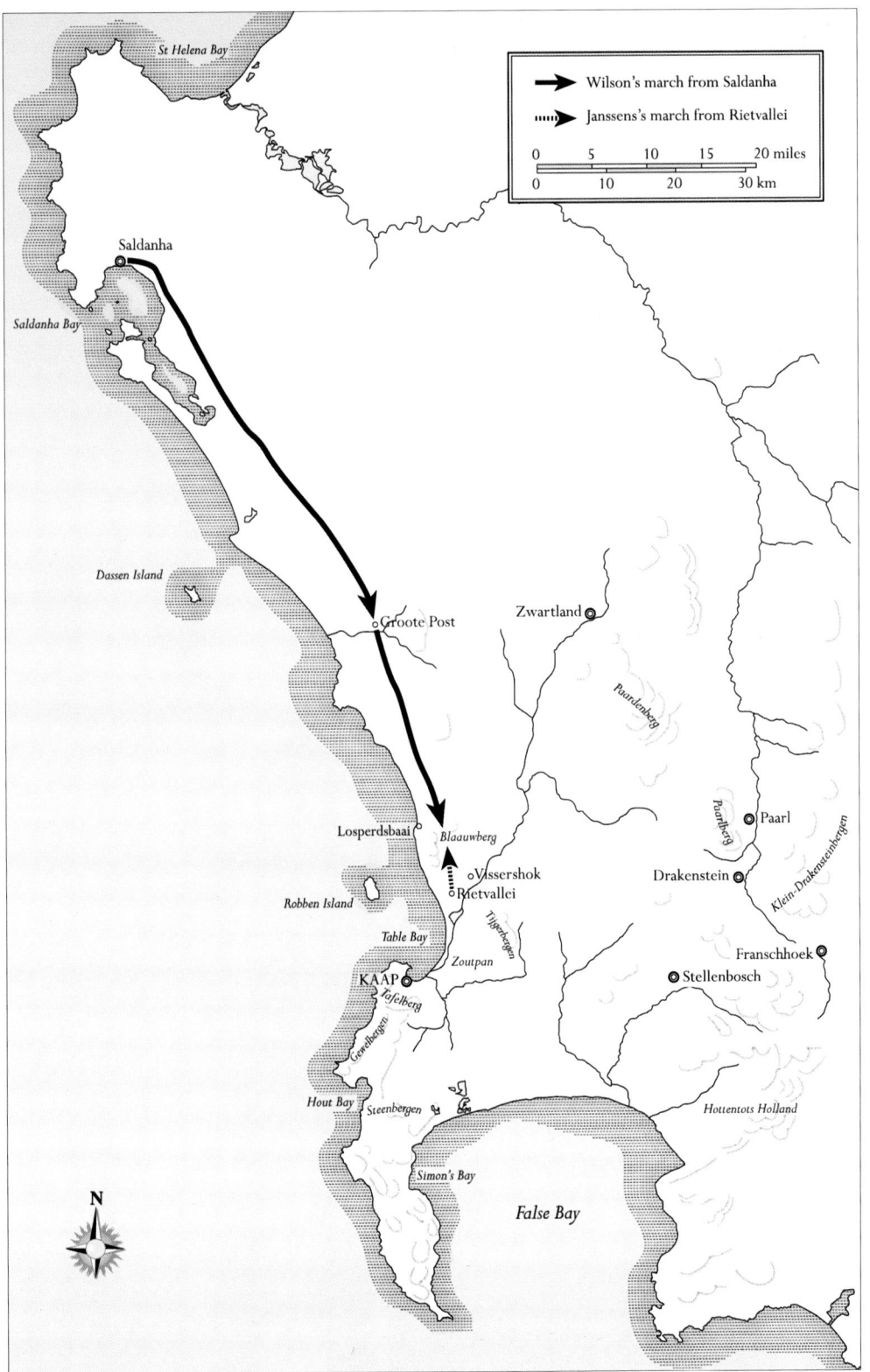

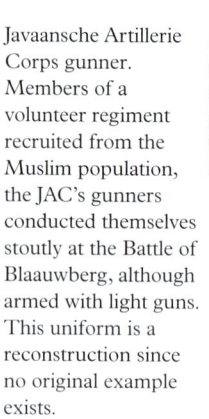

Javaansche Artillerie Corps gunner. Members of a volunteer regiment recruited from the Muslim population, the JAC's gunners conducted themselves stoutly at the Battle of Blaauwberg, although armed with light guns. This uniform is a reconstruction since no original example exists.

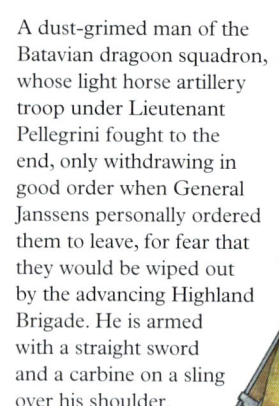

A dust-grimed man of the Batavian dragoon squadron, whose light horse artillery troop under Lieutenant Pellegrini fought to the end, only withdrawing in good order when General Janssens personally ordered them to leave, for fear that they would be wiped out by the advancing Highland Brigade. He is armed with a straight sword and a carbine on a sling over his shoulder.

Swellendam burgher light dragoon. The Swellendammers had a reputation for intransigence, but at Blaauwberg – as at the Muizenberg during the first British invasion – they showed themselves to be daring and efficient warriors who fulfilled Janssens's faith in them. This is a reconstruction of their probable field uniform since no original is known to exist.

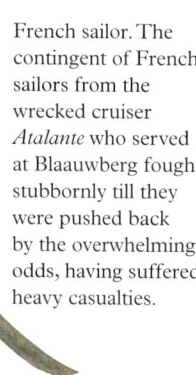

French sailor. The contingent of French sailors from the wrecked cruiser *Atalante* who served at Blaauwberg fought stubbornly till they were pushed back by the overwhelming odds, having suffered heavy casualties.

A wildly inaccurate depiction of the landing at Losperd's Bay, prior to the Battle of Blaauwberg, which is inaccurate in almost every respect.

An even more fanciful depiction of the landing, published in the British *Martial Register* in 1806, presumably without the benefit of any eyewitness descriptions.

A more accurate sketch by Royal Marines officer Robert Fernyhough, drawn on board Popham's flagship, HMS *Diadem*, of what the landing at Losperd's Bay probably really looked like. Contained in a letter to his family, it was first published in 1829, by which time the myths and legends around Blaauwberg had been firmly established.

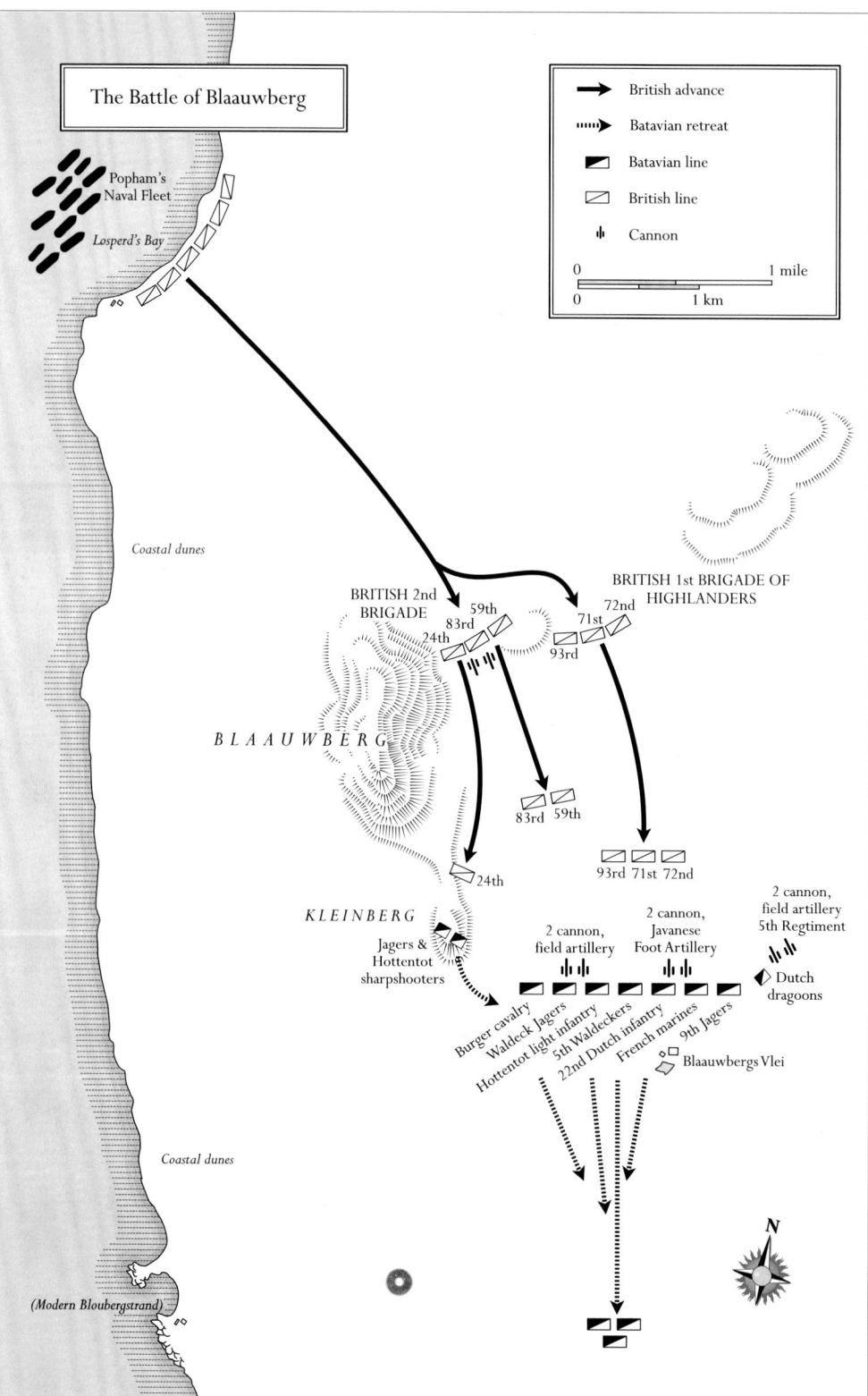

The Battle of Blaauwberg

British advance
Batavian retreat
Batavian line
British line
Cannon

0   1 mile
0   1 km

Popham's
Naval Fleet

Losperd's Bay

Coastal dunes

BRITISH 2nd
BRIGADE

BRITISH 1st BRIGADE OF
HIGHLANDERS

59th
83rd
24th

72nd
71st
93rd

B L A A U W B E R G

83rd   59th

93rd 71st 72nd

24th

KLEINBERG

Jagers &
Hottentot
sharpshooters

2 cannon,
field artillery
5th Regtiment

2 cannon,
field artillery

2 cannon,
Javanese
Foot Artillery

Dutch
dragoons

Burger cavalry
Waldeck Jagers
Hottentot light infantry
5th Waldeckers
22nd Dutch infantry
French marines
9th Jagers

Blaauwbergs Vlei

Coastal dunes

(Modern Bloubergstrand)

N

The Battle of Blaauwberg

The Battle of Blaauwberg begins. On Baird's right, the 24th Regiment attacks the handful of Swellendam Dragoons holding Kleinberg and forces them to retreat and join the Batavian line. On Baird's left the Highland Brigade advances straight towarrds the Batavian with bayonets fixed. Now the stage is set for the 5th Waldeckers to turn and run, destroying the integrity of General Jan Willem Janssens's line and setting an inevitable withdrawal to Rietvallei in motion because the flanks of the units on either side are now threatened. The left of the line – the burgher dragoons, the Hottentot Light Infantry and the Javaanse Artillerie Corps – will still hold out, as will Lieutenant Pellegrini's horse gunners on the right flank, but the end is inevitable.
©William Smuts

Brigadier-General RC Ferguson, whose Highland Brigade flung itself at the centre of the Batavian line at the Battle of Blaauwberg in the face of a storm of fire and sent the mercenaries of the 5th Waldeck Regiment running for their lives.

The only depiction of the Battle of Blaauwberg known to exist, this panoramic anonymous painting graphically (and fairly accurately) depicts the early stages of the fighting. The Waldeckers are still standing fast in the centre of the Batavian line, but in the distance burgher dragoon reinforcements are galloping towards Kleinberg as the 24th Regiment advances on it. The mounted officer in front of the Batavian line, sword drawn, is presumably Janssens himself, whose reckless courage in the face of British fire gave his staff great concern.

Ritmeester Jan
Zacharias Moolman,
one of the valiant
Swellendam burgher
dragoons who held
the Batavian left
on Kleinberg, and
reportedly left the
battlefield with an extra
horse after shooting
its owner, Captain
Andrew Foster, out of
his saddle.

By permission of the owner,
Mrs Marina van Dyk

An enlargement of Orme's print shows
General Baird (on the white horse) sending
off a hastily saluting galloper with orders
for one of his regiments, while Baird's
brother, Lieutenant-Colonel John Baird –
temporarily commanding the 2nd Brigade in
Beresford's absence at Saldanha – mounts.
Virtually at Baird's feet lies the corpse
of Captain Andrew Foster of the 24th
Regiment, earlier shot dead by Ritmeester
Moolman at Kleinberg.

A raging General Janssens tries vainly to halt the fleeing mercenaries of the 5th Waldeck Regiment as they desert the vitally important centre of his line, thereby dooming his plan to give the British a bloody nose with a massed volley from all his troops. The uniform details in this painting are thought to be wrong, as the Waldeckers have been described as wearing typical Batavian uniforms of blue coats with yellow facings and white breeches or pantaloons.

From JS Skelton's illustration in Ian D Colvin's *The Romance of Empire*, 1909

Robert Fernyhough's sketch of the Royal Marines landing at the Rietvallei camp (at left) in an attempt to cut off the retreating Batavians after the Battle of Blaauwberg. But they were too late – Janssens was already moving to his fall-back position in the interior.

The long-vanished 'Treaty House' in Cape Town's Woodstock suburb (then known as Papendorp), where the capitulation of Cape Town was decided. This picture was taken many years later, before it succumbed to urban sprawl. But the tree next to it still survives.

Landdrost WR van der Riet of Stellenbosch, who received one of Janssens's last directives as the final days of Batavian rule at the Cape slipped past – that to prevent futile suffering and damage to property, the people there must not offer any resistance to General Beresford's troops.

Landdrost WS van Ryneveld, who was adept at trimming his sails to the prevailing political winds (he had served the British faithfully during the first occupation) was made chief magistrate by General Baird, but it was not a token appointment – he had a reputation as a capable and hard-working administrator.

guns he had were so deployed that according to the historian George McCall Theal 'they were practically useless'. Marnitz went even further in his condemnation, later accusing Van Baalen of exposing the infantry and dragoons unnecessarily to British cannon fire.

When Clarke attacked in the early afternoon there was a reprise of the disaster at Sandvlei. As soon as the British got within range Van Baalen took to his heels with most of his infantry. The remaining infantrymen and gunners stood fast and tried to fight back, but the British advance was unstoppable and they had to withdraw, getting clean away only because Clarke's men were too exhausted to pursue them past what is now the suburb of Newlands.

Convinced now that they had been betrayed by their superiors and the Council of Policy, the burgher dragoons finally gave up hope. They ignored orders to man the French Line on the slopes of Devil's Peak and went home rather than take the chance of being made prisoner in what was obviously a totally lost cause. The battle for the Cape, to all intents and purposes, was over.

The Council of Policy met after the retreat from Wynberg, and 'the general atmosphere at this meeting was one of desperation and defeat', according to Potgieter.[18] Van Reede van Oudtshoorn still wanted to fight, but he stood alone. The Cape could not be defended, the council was told by Sluysken and Gordon, the latter adding that the French Line could not be held and that further resistance was pointless.

The council resolved (with Van Reede van Oudtshoorn dissenting) to ask for a 48-hour truce in order to negotiate the best possible terms of capitulation, and sent off Sluysken's aide-de-camp with the request. Around midnight on 14 September Clarke announced that he would grant a truce, but only for 24 hours. If ever there was a clear sign of the contempt in which he held the VOC forces' ability to resist, this was it.

The Council of Policy spent most of 15 September working out terms of capitulation, while the demoralised remnants of the VOC army manned the French Line and coastal batteries; there was a brief exchange of gunfire at Hout Bay when Captain John Blankett carried out a previously arranged mock attack in apparent ignorance of the truce, but that was all.

In the evening the completed surrender document was sent to Elphinstone to sign, which he and Craig did next morning at their camp. Ironically they were encamped at Rustenberg, one of Van Riebeeck's original outposts. And a surrender it was, not any sort of protective occupation – it must be remembered that, to the British and the Orange loyalists, defending the Cape was the act of revolutionary Dutch Patriotten, with whom Britain and the prince were wholeheartedly at war.

All VOC property was to be confiscated and the Company's troops would become prisoners of war. Their officers – no doubt as a reward for services rendered – would be given the choice of remaining at the Cape or being repatriated, on condition that they did not serve against the British for the remainder of the war. Attempts to keep the terms from the VOC troops inevitably failed, and many of them were enraged by what they saw as treason on the part of Sluysken and particularly the once deeply respected Gordon.

Concerned for public order, and doubtless the safety of his office, Sluysken[19] asked Clarke to occupy Cape Town as soon as possible, and later that day he took over the French Line, then marched into Cape Town with 1 400 men. As a sop to their feelings the VOC garrison's soldiers were allowed to march out of the Castle with their drums beating and colours uncased. Then the British Union flag[20] was hoisted over the fortress that Isbrand Goske and his successors had built so long ago; 143 years of VOC rule had ended, once and for all time.

For Gordon it was an especially bitter moment. The courtesies extended to the garrison did not pacify his troops, and when they marched out of the Castle his appearance was greeted by a storm of jeers and curses. Gordon stayed in position, however, and marched them on to the Wapenpleyn. There he halted them, though not without some difficulty, drew his sword and ordered them to present arms and then lay down their muskets.

This was too much. The troops flung down their muskets, cursing their officers for traitors and criminals; one broke ranks and tried to assault Gordon himself. Worse was to come a few days later, when, according to Thibault,[21] Gordon was actually beaten up by another group of soldiers. It was the bitter nadir of a lifelong and hitherto shining military career.

For Admiral Elphinstone the virtually bloodless capture of the Cape would bring fulsome plaudits from London,[22] but for Gordon it meant a descent into the depths of despair. He was a professional soldier, a 'man under authority' like the Biblical centurion, but he had allowed his personal political convictions to come between him and his loyalty to the legitimate government, to the point of being willing to sacrifice the lives of his men and the defence machine he had built up.

By so doing he had destroyed a lifetime's worth of professional honour, without which a true soldier is less than the dust under his boots. On 25 October, little more than a month later, Robert Jacob Gordon went out into his garden and shot himself.

Let Potgieter have the last unequivocal word about this tortured man:

> The first loyalty of officers and military men should be to their lawful constitution and legitimate government of the day ... It is self-evident that the incapacity of the VOC officers to do their military duty ... should be regarded as treachery. Gordon thought he acted in the best interest of the House of Orange when he offered and organised no effective resistance against the British occupation. This again, according to some recent observers, is not outright treason, since Gordon [was] true to his principles. But in the final analysis, as a soldier and a military man *he did not do his duty!*

This is the orthodox view, not an incorrect one, but in the context of his time and circumstances, worth examining; Gordon was a fervent king's man who abhorred the Patriotten and their action in dethroning the Prince of Orange. Like many other kings' men in Europe he would not have recognised a revolutionary government as the legitimate successor to a monarchy which had been overthrown not by consent but by force of arms – and *foreign* arms, at that. For a soldier pledged by oath to his prince, this last must have seemed an intolerable insult.

Gordon was a career soldier who had always lived by a simple credo of unquestioning loyalty to the established order, which consisted of the

Prince of Orange and the States-General, over which he reigned but did not rule. Then that seemingly immutable order had crumbled. Left rudderless in a sea of contradictions, he adhered to his original loyalty. His reward was to be hated and despised by many of the soldiers who had once revered him, and doomed to be remembered as a leader who had ignominiously abandoned the battlefield to the enemy.[23]

By contrast, Gordon's chief military co-conspirator, Lieutenant-Colonel de Lille, stifled any such qualms he might have had and speedily turned his coat to enter the British service.[24]

It is surprising to note how little has been written about the lessons learnt from the invasion, mainly inglorious and almost devoid of serious combat though it was. However, several noteworthy conclusions and observations can be drawn from it.

Firstly, the locally born dragoons and militia had proved their mettle by attacking Clarke's vastly superior column in one of the few occasions when opportunities had presented themselves, although it was their first taste of battle against arguably one of the best armies in the world.

Secondly, the value of the dragoon or mounted infantryman as a force multiplier had been proven. The same can be said for the Cape-style light infantry concept, as personified by the Corps Pandoeren.

Thirdly, a strong Cape identity which transcended social barriers seems to have grown up during the VOC years, as evidenced by the fighting spirit of the Pandoeren and their close cooperation with the burgher dragoons. Although some observers might say they were merely paid by the VOC to fight, they fought despite their commanders' reluctance.

In regard of Elphinstone's ships and their inability to support Craig's infantry beyond the shoreline, the advantages had been, or should have been, on Gordon's side, even after the arrival of the British reinforcements from St Helena. He had far more artillery, light and heavy, and unlimited supplies of ammunition, his forces not only outnumbered Craig's but were fighting on their home ground, and he had a formidable force of hard-riding mounted troops. Thus a clear lead by Sluysken and Gordon would most likely have submerged all these differences *pro tem.*

❦

The immediate imperative for the British was to establish the supremacy of British naval power in the southern oceans, and secure the route of the all-important East India Company for the first time.

The first step towards this aim was to make sure the French did not take control of the only organised and properly equipped replenishment and repair station between St Helena and the Far East. This, without question, the British had done with some efficiency. Given the wide support for the Patriotten among the locals, Elphinstone and Craig had acted none too soon.

The true intentions of the British become quite clear in the text of a laudatory message to Elphinstone from the First Lord of the Admiralty, Earl Spencer, congratulating him on an acquisition which was 'one of the most advantageous we have ever made'. Potgieter points out there was 'no mention … of the Dutch claim or the protection of the Cape on behalf of the House of Orange. The conquest was for British interest alone; the timely presence of a fugitive Prince of Orange in England was only a stroke of good luck.'[25]

It would be fair to say that the hoisting of the British flag over the Castle's ramparts signalled the beginning of a new career for the Cape of Good Hope. It had long been an important commercial target; now it had become a politico-strategic football for the major powers in the struggle for world domination, a role that was to last right up to the end of the Cold War in 1989 and, for all we know, might yet resume at some time in the future as new power-blocs arise.

CHAPTER 9

OATHS AND INSURRECTIONS

As far as General Craig was concerned the military situation at the Cape was very clear. Within a week of the British take-over he wrote: 'It is certain that the great Body of the People are at this moment infected with the rankest poison of Jacobinism … should a french [*sic*] force appear tomorrow, I have not a doubt that every assistance would be given to it.'[1]

It was an accurate summary of the situation. From Craig's perspective things were very unstable in the immediate post-invasion period. The British controlled Cape Town, Simon's Town and the surrounding areas, but the military assets they had available in the event of a French intervention were scanty.

Many free burghers in the interior did not regard the conquerors as anything but enemies, and still cherished the hope that a Dutch or combined Franco-Dutch force would wrest the Cape back from the British. Swellendam was within reasonable reach and its commercial ties to Cape Town made it easier to keep in line, but the even more quarrelsome Graaff-Reinet free burghers, led by the veteran frontier fighter Adriaan van Jaarsveldt, were far tougher nuts to crack.

By this stage Graaff-Reinet had enjoyed more than a year of virtual independence, the only burgher with any sort of official status being the provisional landdrost, Goretz, whom Sluysken had appointed to replace the expelled Honoratus Maynier. The Patriotten sentiment was still strong, and the farmers continued to consider themselves Dutch citizens bound by an oath of loyalty to the States-General, the legitimate heirs to the VOC's authority.

Their intransigent attitude was not as rash as it might seem. Past experience had shown how difficult it was for the administration in distant Cape Town to enforce any edict on them, and they believed that they were too important a source of slaughter stock to be dismissed lightly. Their position was weaker than it might have seemed, however. A fierce struggle with the Bushmen during most of 1795 had led to the wholesale abandonment of farms and large-scale livestock losses in the Tarka and Renosterberg districts, as well as part of the Sneeuberg district. On top of that the official coffers were empty and the burghers were still chained to Cape Town by their all-important need for gunpowder, without which they would be at the mercy of their competitors and opponents.

It is a classic illustration of the importance of logistics in war. If the Graaff-Reinetters had been able to make their own gunpowder or obtain it from another source they would have been in a vastly stronger position. They had never needed to do so; now it was too late to make other arrangements, and supplies were running low because shipments from Cape Town had been cut off for many months.

Their need emerged very clearly in a letter dated 29 October which Goretz, Van Jaarsveldt and five others sent to Craig. The letter was a mixture of supplication and defiance. They requested the appointment of magistrates, the despatch of a preacher to Graaff-Reinet, instructions on how to proceed in the critical circumstances and a resumption of the supply of ammunition. They also informed him that by popular vote they had decided to choose representatives to watch over the burghers' interests, and that these representatives would be sitting members of the local government.

Craig replied in a characteristically blunt letter dated 23 November. He had appointed a permanent magistrate, one FP Bresler, to take Goretz's place, he said, and while he would overlook everything that had happened at Graaff-Reinet during VOC rule, any further disruption of the public order would be severely dealt with.

The appointment of Bresler was, as Giliomee says, 'a tactical error', because he was related to OG de Wet, who had earlier been expelled from Graaff-Reinet; the Graaff-Reinetters 'apparently were convinced that British rule over the eastern frontier would be a continuation of the Company's policy.'[2]

The Graaff-Reinetters responded in typical fashion. The burgher council instructed Goretz not to allow Bresler to take over as magistrate and sent a round-robin letter to the surrounding areas which called on farmers to refuse to sell any slaughter stock until the supply of ammunition had been resumed.

Just how intransigent they were became clear when Bresler was barred from entering the drostdy when he arrived in late February 1796, accompanied by a former Graaff-Reinet Dutch Reformed preacher called Von Manger. Bresler did not allow himself to be intimidated by this hostile reception, however. He called a public meeting at which he hoisted the British flag and read himself into office.

It was a brave but futile exercise in resistance. Inflamed by republican sentiment and wild rumours about British reverses and Craig's lack of military manpower, the burghers promptly hauled the flag down and made it plain that they did not accept the authority of the King of England, Craig, or Bresler himself.

On 25 March Bresler gave up and headed back to Cape Town with Von Manger. With him he took a letter to Craig. Once again it was a strange mixture of supplication and defiance which displayed a singular lack of understanding about the bigger strategic picture which had led to the British invasion. The Graaff-Reinetters were so wrapped up in their parochial concerns that they did not realise that they, like everyone else in what would later become known as southern Africa, had become hostages to fortune, mere pawns in a much greater struggle. It was a scenario which was to be repeated again and again in the next two centuries.

The burghers said that they had not risen against Britain; it was just that they were still bound by their oath of loyalty to the States-General. They complained about the state of official finances, asked for forgiveness of long-standing arrears, assuring Craig that they were willing to obey all reasonable laws and furnish Cape Town with their products, as long as they were able to obtain clothing, ammunition and other necessities. Finally, they asked Craig for help in regaining the farms from which some of them had been driven by the Xhosas. At the same time, however, they refused point-blank to accept Bresler (instead, they suggested, Craig should send them an Englishman who did not have a foot in any party's camp) or people like Maynier or De Wet, whom they regarded as the enemies of all free burghers.

In the meantime Craig had been hard at work preparing the Cape to face dangers from without as well as within. He had persuaded General Clarke to leave the entire invasion force in garrison and petitioned Secretary of State for War Henry Dundas for more troops, not only to deal with any future Franco-Dutch threat but also, if the worst came to the worst, to deploy against any local insurrection.

Having ensured continuity of efficient administration by retaining most of the local bureaucracy, he began strengthening or expanding some of the Cape Peninsula's existing fortifications. He could do nothing about the Castle's less than ideal location below the high ground, but in due course he repaired some of the surrounding installations and erected three blockhouses – the King's, York and Prince of Wales's Blockhouses – on the slopes of Devil's Peak, each armed with two 24-pounder Dutch guns brought up from the Imhoff Battery. In combination with Fort Knokke and the two VOC-era defensive lines, this would ensure that a more concentrated cross-fire could be brought on hostile ships (the York Blockhouse was later abandoned because it was found to be badly situated and replaced by another nearby, the Queen's Blockhouse).

At the mouth of the Salt River he built another battery with a cannon-proof tower which became known as 'Craig's Tower', and erected an earth-walled temporary battery mounting three heavy mortars between Kijk-In-De-Pot Battery and Mouille point. At Simon's Town he raised a fortification which is unique in South Africa and endures to this day, the Martello Tower.[3]

Based on a fortification on Cape Mortella in Corsica which had defied the Royal Navy's attempts to subdue it, Craig's copy at Simon's Town was built because he had taken note of how easily Elphinstone's ships had managed to force the VOC gunners to abandon their batteries during the invasion.

Later he would also erect and garrison a stronghold at Algoa Bay which he called Fort Frederick, although the internal situation, especially along the restive north-eastern frontier with its competing groups of cattlemen and marauding bands of Bushmen, presented a well-nigh intractable problem which could not be solved or even eased by putting up stone walls.

To deal with the more fiery Batavian sympathisers near at hand he applied both the carrot and the stick. He attempted to foster goodwill by relaxing restrictions on internal trading and facilitating the importation of goods, and at the same time set about building up a reliable locally enlisted military presence to nip any future insurrections in the bud.

To this end he established a light mounted unit which was intended to serve as a sort of gendarmerie or military police force – a British version of the regular dragoons formed by the VOC – and in February 1796 also ordered the formation of a 300-strong infantry unit of coloured men officered by British regulars, raised partly from the now-defunct Corps Pandoeren, commanded by Lieutenant (later Captain) John Campbell.[4]

Designated the 'Cape Corps' – the first but certainly not the last time that this regimental name was to feature in South African military history – the new unit was outfitted in a smart uniform of broad-brimmed black hat with the right side turned up, a hip-length red jacket and dark blue trousers.[5]

The Cape Corps was to be trained as a conventional light infantry unit which could take its place in the defence of the Cape from external aggressors, but there was a less obvious subtext: they were to be used for intimidating the whites and cultivating the Khoina as allies against the free burghers.

Craig was perfectly aware of the permanent tensions along the eastern frontier in particular, thanks to information passed along by spies such as the traveller and writer John Barrow,[6] although Barrow's input was anything but objective. He was violently antipathetic towards the free burghers and in addition was hardly comprehensive when it came to fact-gathering, since he could not speak a word of Dutch and relied for most of his information on Honoratus Maynier, who felt very much the same way as he did himself.

Craig's conclusion was that if the frontier farmers could not be persuaded to be loyal citizens, they must be coerced, and so he fell back on the traditional divide-and-rule approach. 'Nothing I know would intimidate the Boers of the country more,'[7] he is recorded as saying about the establishment of the new regiment, and it was no more than the truth. As Giliomee remarks, this and other steps were aimed at 'trying to gain the Hottentots as allies. Possibly humanitarian considerations also played a role, but the most important motivation for the establishment of [the Cape Corps] was undoubtedly political in nature.'[8]

In hindsight Craig's decision to play off ethno-cultural groups against one another in such a heterogeneous and unstable population mix was extremely unfortunate, and it would have long-term repercussions. Up to 1795 the population inside the VOC's orbit was divided partly by class and social status and partly (particularly along the eastern frontier) by race and culture, but there was a certain degree of commonality as regards language, social usages and (except for the Malays) religion. Certainly, to judge by the conduct of the Pandoeren at Muizenberg and Sandvlei, the issue of overall identity and common loyalty seems not to have been in doubt.

This being the case, It would be fair to say Craig's stratagem did great damage to that incomplete commonality because it used the issue of race to pit members of the community concerned against one another in the crudest and most offensive way (it is to be remembered that many recruits to the Cape Corps were not aboriginal Khoina clanspeople but people of mixed race and acculturated Khoina who had abandoned their traditional lifestyle).

Whether Craig was aware of the longer-term implications of this is a matter for speculation. The chances are that even if he had been, it would have made no difference to his actions, because his first and most urgent priority was the need to secure the routes through the southern oceans against the French at almost any cost.

Craig's fears in this regard were not exaggerated. The Cape was the jewel in the southern oceans' crown, and it was to stay British, at least for the foreseeable future. This could only be guaranteed by a strong defence. Indeed, an attempt at re-conquest was already underway.

At the end of 1795 the Batavian Government had opened negotiations with its French counterpart about a combined expedition to re-conquer the Cape. For obvious reasons the French had been very interested in such an operation, but it had proved difficult to get any commitment from them, no doubt because they were under heavy military pressure themselves.

Be that as it may, in February 1796 – the very month the Cape Corps was founded – the Batavian Navy's Admiral Engelbertus Lucas set out from Texel with a squadron of two ships of the line, three large frigates and four smaller ships, one of them a transport, and just under 2 000 soldiers.

Lucas was under the impression that when he reached the Cape he would rendezvous with a French squadron at Saldanha Bay or either of two other places and then launch an assault on the British. But the Batavian Government had failed to inform him that no French help was in the offing, and that the only allied presence in the southern oceans was a small five-ship squadron which had left European waters after him and was tasked not with attacking the Cape but with freeing slaves at Mauritius and Reunion.

Thanks to this incredible communications failure the hapless Lucas sailed straight into the lion's jaws, because the British had got early wind of the Franco-Dutch intentions and were making hasty work of strengthening the Cape. Between May and the end of July 1796 there arrived seven Royal Navy warships under HMS *Monarch*, flying the flag of Craig's old colleague of the invasion days, Admiral Elphinstone. They brought with them more than 5 000 soldiers, mainly infantrymen; with a rough total of over 8 000 soldiers and a fleet of 13 warships in place, the Cape was now more heavily garrisoned than at any previous time during its existence.[9]

Craig was also heavily engaged at this time in trying to keep the lid from blowing off the internal situation. By April 1796 he had subdued the quarrelsome Swellendammers by stationing a 300-man force in Stellenbosch and threatening to arm the coloured population against them, thereby striking another blow at future race relations.

160

These measures had allowed cooler heads to prevail, though, and British authority was accepted, albeit reluctantly by some. But the Graaff-Reinetters were far from tamed, and had now been reinforced by a party of Swellendammers who had migrated to the interior rather than submit to Craig.

As early as mid-June Craig had also taken the precaution of warning local representatives and officials that Lucas's force was far too small to threaten the Cape, and that it was therefore in the local population's own interests to refrain from any actions which might force him to apply punitive measures against them. According to Giliomee, 'this step did much to apply a *coup de grace* to all the rumours about the arrival of a Franco-Batavian force which had been going the rounds in 1796.'[10]

In addition Craig made certain other internal-security preparations which could be activated at the right time. By now the new Cape Corps was 171-strong, and since many of its men were trained soldiers recruited from the rank and file of the defunct Corps Pandoeren, it was swiftly turning into a first-class unit with a high standard of drill, musketry and general turnout. The frontier free burghers, beset on every side, watched all this with foreboding and continued to hope that a Dutch or joint Franco-Dutch force would appear to rescue the Cape from the British.

The long-awaited Batavian force finally made landfall at Saldanha Bay on 3 August. It was somewhat less than formidable. Lucas was not, it seems, an inspired leader, but that was only one of several serious disadvantages. He was so badly outnumbered in both ships and men that his lack of command qualities hardly mattered, and the morale of his ships' companies was poor, because the leaders were staunch Batavians but most of the ratings were equally staunch supporters of the House of Orange. On top of that he was still under the impression that he was about to join hands with a French force.

Lucas then compounded all this by a fateful decision to anchor in the bay to wait for his non-existent French allies, thus relinquishing his freedom to manoeuvre on the open sea. Meanwhile in Cape Town Craig immediately implemented his internal-security measures. All access routes to Cape Town were blocked off, and burghers living within

10 hours' ride from the town were compelled to despatch all their horses and livestock to the interior.

Craig brooked no opposition to his preparations. An order was published which proclaimed that any contact with the Batavians would be punishable by death. Local representatives whom he regarded as tardy in supplying horses and wagons for a forced march he intended to make to Saldanha Bay were informed that unless they responded in satisfactory fashion each would have 12 British soldiers quartered on him – a very considerable expense and inconvenience in those days.

On 14 February Craig marched on Saldanha Bay at the head of 2 500 men, leaving a garrison of 4 000 to defend Cape Town. The following day, 15 September, Elphinstone set sail with his entire fleet. A day later he was there, and promptly sealed off the bay with his ships and invited Lucas to surrender 'to spare an effusion of blood'.[11]

Lucas tried to stall in spite of the obvious hopelessness of his situation, but the murmurings of his disaffected sailors seem finally to have persuaded him, and on 17 September he surrendered. The last word had finally been spoken about the Cape's future.

Well, not quite. There was to be a brief Batavian resurgence, but that still lay almost eight years away.

August 1796 also marked the end of the Graaff-Reinetters' resistance to British rule. Internal dissension played a role, but as Giliomee says, 'most important of all, there was no more ammunition at the drostdy to fend off the Bushman threat along the northern frontier.'[12]

This meant that farmers had to rely on their own sparse stocks, and their situation soon became untenable. The writing was on the wall as early as 20 May, when a call-out for a commando against the Bushmen, with burghers expected to supply their own gunpowder, received such a poor response that it had to be cancelled.

In mid-July the burgher representatives met and decided, albeit only after acrimonious debate, to send a deputation to Cape Town to negotiate the healing of the breach. At a subsequent meeting, called by Van Jaarsveldt's colleague Marthinus Prinsloo, leader of the Zuurveld and Bruintjieshoogte wards, the best way of doing so was discussed.

According to Giliomee 'it appears as if the plan was to despatch 500 Graaff-Reinetters to place demands before Craig in co-operation with the Swellendammers', after having deposed the landdrost and other officials there.[13] No decision seems to have been taken, however, and at another meeting on 22 August representatives of all wards, except the Zuurveld and Bruintjieshoogte where resistance to British rule remained strong, unanimously decided to inform Craig that they wished to submit themselves to British authority.

Early in September Craig belatedly received tidings of the Prinsloo meeting and despatched 800 troops to Swellendam under Major Fielder King, 150 of them men of the Cape Corps. This last was obviously a deliberate propaganda ploy, because Craig explained to King that the aim of the expedition was 'more to impress the people with terror and to convince them of the practicability of our reaching them, than in any hope that it will be in your power to chastise the Inhabitants of Graaffe Reynette, [*sic*] who will probably keep at such a distance from you as to preclude the possibility of your affecting it.'[14]

But the precaution was unnecessary. Before King had even reached Swellendam Craig received a letter of capitulation from Graaff-Reinet, and was so impressed by the fact that the signatories included Adriaan van Jaarsveldt, one of the most obdurate resisters, that he recalled King's force and responded in a generally conciliatory way to the Graaff-Reinetters. It was agreed that Goretz would stay on as landdrost until a replacement was sent, and that the heemraden and members of the burgher war council who had been serving when the revolt broke out would resume their seats. All would be forgiven, except in the case of one of the greatest agitators of anti-British feeling, JP van Woyer, on whose head a reward of 100 *rijksdaalders* was placed.[15]

Craig also allowed the Graaff-Reinetters a supply of desperately needed ammunition, 300lb of lead for casting bullets and 300lb of gunpowder, although he made no bones about the fact that he did not believe armed action against the Bushmen was really worthwhile; considerate treatment was the way in which they could gradually be weaned from their tendency to rob and plunder. The Graaff-Reinetters were frankly sceptical of Craig's approach, although future events were to bring an interesting development in this regard.

The bitter-enders in the Bruintjieshoogte and Zuurveld wards now found themselves isolated. In a last flicker of defiance they sent Craig a letter on 12 November in which they declared themselves willing to submit to British authority provided he met certain demands. The live-stock stolen by the Xhosas must be returned, permission must be given to occupy a tract of land east of the Fish River, Craig must not appoint a former VOC official or Bresler as landdrost, and the burghers must elect the heemraden.

Craig's reply was short and sharp. He rejected the proposed conditions, warned the two wards not to act aggressively towards the Xhosas and told them in so many words that they would receive no government ammunition until they had placed themselves unconditionally under British authority. To this there could be only one response, and on 12 January Prinsloo and his followers sent Craig a letter pledging their obedience.

Just afterwards, Giliomee recalls, one last hope of fanning the embers of Batavian resistance into flame guttered out. Van Woyer had persuaded the Governor-General of the East Indies to send a ship to Algoa Bay, laden with 36 000lb of gunpowder, eight artillery pieces and various supplies for the Graaff-Reinetters.

There can be no doubt that if this shipment had arrived the frontier free burghers would have gone into rebellion again and presented Craig with an almost insuperable problem because they would have unlimited supplies of ammunition and would be fighting on their home ground. But the ship was delayed by storms and eventually had to put in at Delagoa Bay, further up the coast, where a British warship seized her.

With the submission of the Prinsloo party the stage appeared set for orderly government of the former VOC settlement, and the British were careful, at least in the first phase, not to rock the boat too much. They made certain administrative and other changes, and people of colour were given greater protection by the local courts (in theory, anyway – like the VOC, which had had the same approach to non-whites, the British did not possess adequate means to enforce the measure), but they did not depart from the VOC style of government. In the end, the take-over did not, in fact, alter the local social or military situation in any real sense.

They did not, for example, take any steps to abolish slavery or even forbid the importation of slaves; as Giliomee says: 'There is no evidence that the British ... concerned themselves about the plight of the slaves in any particular way.'[16] For example, Lord Macartney,[17] who became Governor of the Cape in May 1797, made his priorities quite plain in a letter to the Secretary for War, Henry Dundas:

> It appeared to me an indispensable obligation rather to provide for the subsistence of the People committed to my care, and of His Majesty's fleet and army ... than to argue with myself what might be the possible felicity of freedom to unknown Blackamoors.

Although, in all fairness, Macartney had just as little sympathy for the frontier farmers and made no effort to disguise his feelings towards them. However, Giliomee points out,

> ... the impression must not be created that the government actually took the side of the Hottentots against the colonists. [It] was not interested in overthrowing the existing colonial co-existence. Apart from the government's desire, for the sake of security, to keep the dominant population group in the interior satisfied, the regular supply of meat to Cape Town was always one of its most important priorities.
>
> The government thus approved the colonists' actions against stock theft and was prepared to supply ammunition for this purpose. For the same reason the government did not contemplate making large tracts of land available to the Hottentots at the cost of the colonists.[18]

Giliomee's remarks are particularly interesting because they show the synergy which was forced on both the British and the farmers by the prevailing circumstances. At the end of the day the British could not do without the farmers because of the overriding priorities of the war against France; conversely, the farmers were firmly chained to the logistical line to Cape Town because they could not manufacture gunpowder or obtain it from any other source.

The appointment of Macartney, an experienced and able colonial administrator, clearly signalled Britain's intentions. The Cape was not merely a temporarily occupied territory but would be turned into a fully fledged crown colony. The British had come to stay, and any action by the local population which smacked of a lack of enthusiasm for the Crown would be harshly and immediately dealt with.

Combined with Craig's intimidatory tactics, the result certainly was a distinct lack of enthusiasm. Even Barrow admitted that 'few of the male inhabitants associate with the English, except such as hold employments under the government.'[19] Some inroads were made as time went on, particularly by the lovely and charming Lady Anne Barnard,[20] wife of the Colonial Secretary, and through efforts by the British which included cash rewards and appointments, but the divisions were never fully overcome.

By late 1797 the local forces which Craig had established had become substantial entities. The mounted corps had grown to 150 men, while the Cape Corps numbered seven officers, 12 corporals, 13 buglers and 265 rank and file, all enlisted for a year at a time, and was generally regarded as having exceeded expectations. As yet neither unit had been put to the ultimate test of combat, but both the north-eastern and north-western frontiers remained volcanoes, constantly rumbling and occasionally erupting.

In the north-west a number of white farmers had moved into Namaqualand from 1761 onwards, in the wake of Adam Kok's arrival. Some members of the local Khoina clans accepted their presence as an accomplished fact and traded or took service with them, but others resisted the new arrivals; according to Giliomee 'it appears as if they regarded the Olifants River as the border between themselves and the whites and wanted to drive the whites back over it.'[21]

Soon after the British invasion, one such group, led by a certain Piet Baster – a man of mixed blood, to judge by his name – had taken advantage of the temporary vacuum of power to launch a campaign of arson and cattle theft. Craig authorised the formation and despatch of a commando to deal with Piet Baster, preferably without bloodshed. Nothing is now known of what transpired, but no more was heard from Baster's group.

While all this was happening the situation on the north-eastern frontier was in a process of gradual deterioration. The question of Bushman raids had received new attention after the arrival in 1797 of Lord Macartney. Macartney had been advised by a senior Dutch official who was now in British service, WS van Ryneveld, that the Bushman territory lay beyond the Zeekoe River and that they should be encouraged to return there, peacefully if possible, forcibly if that was the only way.

FP Bresler, who was on the point of leaving, belatedly to take up his appointment as landdrost of Graaff-Reinet – he had originally been appointed in 1796 and then promptly expelled by rebellious free burghers opposed to taking the British oath of allegiance – expressed doubt that anything except punitive action would succeed. But Macartney persevered. He ordered Bresler to follow Van Ryneveld's approach, and as a sweetener to burghers who had been driven off their farms he offered six years' exemption from farm tax to any who returned to their abandoned homesteads in the Tarka, Swagershoek, Sneeuberg and Nuweveld areas.

After Bresler arrived at Graaff-Reinet, therefore, he and Barrow undertook an extensive journey on the frontier to make contact with the Bushmen, the aim being, according to Barrow, 'to bring about a conversation with some of the chiefs of this people; to try if, by presents and persuasion, they could be prevailed upon to quit their present wild and marauding way of life.'[22]

It was a quixotic quest, since the Bushman social structure was extremely simple, being based on the extended family group. Not surprisingly the expedition was anything but a roaring success. They encountered very few Bushmen, and those they did manage to engage in discussion said truthfully that they had no chiefs.

This sparse information did not prevent Barrow – whose dislike for the trekboers was so deep that he did not shrink from telling deliberate falsehoods about them – from informing Macartney (with whom he had great influence) that the nomads were 'mild and manageable in the highest degree', and that they were merely taking revenge from having their land invaded and their children abducted. No more commando expeditions should be sent out, he advised, because this would only cause further bitterness and confirm the farmers in the righteousness of their trespasses.

It was such a total misreading of the situation that one can only assume it sprang from a combination of Barrow's loathing for the free burghers and a generous dose of sheer ignorance. In addition, Barrow either did not know or ignored the fact that the antagonism was a replay of the situation that had existed between the Bushmen and the Khoina long before the Company's arrival at the Cape. The Bushmen had been at odds with the Khoina because they did not recognise or accept the principle of private livestock ownership. All that had changed was that the cattle herders were now mainly the trekboers.

Just after Barrow's return Macartney proclaimed a northern and eastern frontier. Like earlier proclaimed borders, it failed to achieve anything. Thousands of sheep, cattle and horses were stolen in raids, and attempts to stop the haemorrhage proved unsuccessful. On one occasion in February 1798, for example, so Giliomee records, a commando chased after an unusually large band of about 300 Bushmen who had just plundered a farm in the Sneeuberg district, but were forced to retreat when their quarry turned on them. Another commando expedition was sent out the following month and proved equally unsuccessful; an even larger one in August of 1798 returned after two weeks with almost nothing to show for its efforts.

Macartney now came up with a radical new approach for dealing with the Bushmen. Craig's long-held belief – probably fostered by Barrow – was that armed action against the Bushmen was not really worthwhile, and that considerate treatment was the way in which they could gradually be weaned from their tendency to rob and plunder. The Graaff-Reinetters in particular had grave doubts about this belief, but they were only partly right.

The farmers contributed generously to the scheme, so that by the end of 1798 Louw was able to hand 460 sheep and goats over to the Bushmen. Many frontier farmers considered the scheme hopelessly naïve, but it had been conceived by two experienced frontiersmen, and in several places actually worked (although not in the Roggeveld district and elsewhere, where several punitive expeditions later took place). Giliomee comments that Macartney's proclamation was 'the start of a conciliation policy regarding the Bushmen which was to have more success during the next century than the commando system had had during the 18th century.'[23]

In 1798 there was another upheaval, when some of the Namaqua clans threatened to rise because of a new government directive that the '*opgaaf*' or census should be applied to them as well. They believed that this was the first step towards enslaving them, and in December that year several hundred banded together, plundered five farms, killed one man and seized livestock, 21 firearms and a quantity of ammunition.

Efforts to make peace were rejected; urgent appeals for reinforcements went out and after a long delay a small number of reinforcements arrived from Piketberg in February 1799, comprising 18 whites, two coloured men and one Khoina. A commando now numbering 37 whites, 20 coloureds and seven Khoina set out and cornered the insurgents in a *kloof*, or ravine.

Although the Namaqua clansmen speared one member of the commando to death when he approached them to open peace talks, a settlement was finally reached. The rebellious clansmen gave back part of their plunder and returned whence they had come, except for a number of their leaders, who moved to the northern side of the Orange River because apparently they did not think the peace would hold.

And indeed it did not, so that 1799 marked the start of renewed eruptions on both frontiers that were to last in places until 1802. One particular trouble-spot was the north-western frontier, thanks to Jager Afrikaner, the erstwhile VOC mercenary and Bushman raider of the 1780s. Three years earlier, in March 1796, Jager and his brother Titus murdered the Tulbagh *wachtmeester*, their employer Pieter Pienaar, for whom they used to ride out against the Bushmen. Killing several members of his family as well, they hurried northwards with Pienaar's livestock, firearms and whatever else their gang could cart away.

When he reached the Orange River Jager set up a stronghold on a large island, from which he and his men – trained and experienced mounted infantrymen from their former service with the VOC and later with Pienaar – launched a long reign of terror over whites, coloureds,

Griquas, Khoina and Bushmen alike within a radius of several hundred miles. The plundering surpassed anything the region had seen before, and was one of the reasons why Adam Kok's Griquas eventually trekked eastwards to what later became Griqualand. In May 1799, Jager set off on his most ambitious venture to date: nothing less than a raid deep into the Hantam district.

Given Jager's well-deserved reputation for ferocity, there was surprisingly little loss of life – one white man and four Khoina ended up dead – but his men seized 3 700 sheep and goats, 446 head of cattle, eight horses and three guns. A commando was immediately raised and sent after him, but could not catch up with him.

Major-General Francis Dundas, the acting governor since Macartney's premature departure due to ill-health in November 1798, heeded the anguished calls for help and sent out a 200-man commando drawn from far and wide – a large force by frontier-warfare standards. This formidable group could not lay Jager by the heels either, and he was free to pursue his untrammelled life of crime for almost two decades more.

Jager's 1799 raid is something of a milestone in South Africa's military annals, because it was the first time that both sides consisted of *veld*-wise, highly mobile irregular commando soldiers, the quintessential southern African mounted infantrymen of the late 18th century, fighting in a way unknown in Europe. It is interesting to note that in this case, as in many others, no attempt was made to use regular British cavalry. One assumes that at least one reason was that the authorities realised the futility of sending conventional European-style soldiers out against wily local bush fighters.

Things were no more tranquil along the eastern frontier. By 1798 the farmers had re-occupied the northern part of the coveted Zuurveld, but, partly as a result of the on-going struggle between Ngqika and his would-be usurper Ndlambe, the southern portion remained in the hands of a number of Xhosa groups, some of whose members probed as far down as the Swellendam district. Inevitably tensions began to arise, not only between the frontiersmen of various racial persuasions but also between the farmers and the British.

In January 1799 the Graaff-Reinetters' grievances had boiled over once more when Bresler had Van Jaarsveldt arrested on a charge of falsifying a receipt. Van Jaarsveldt's followers broke him out of custody and went into rebellion. Craig responded by sending an expeditionary force under Major-General TP Vandeleur to the eastern frontier. Vandeleur landed at Algoa Bay and made quick work of quelling the rising.

By April 1799 it was all over. Van Jaarsveldt, his son Zacharias and 14 others, including Marthinus Prinsloo, one of the leaders in the first rebellion, were arrested and carried off to Cape Town. At their subsequent trial Van Jaarsveldt and Prinsloo were sentenced to death (which was later commuted) and the others given long jail terms.

Then fighting broke out on the eastern frontier once again. The history books call it the Third Frontier War, but it was essentially a continuation of the second one, because the stalemated 'peace' of 1793 had solved nothing and thus condemned the eastern frontier to continued turmoil which involved so many conflicting interests that new conflagrations kept breaking out in the next few years.

Among other things a number of discontented Khoina joined forces with the Xhosas in the Zuurveld and began attacking white-owned farms. Raiding parties penetrated as far to the south-west as the town of Oudtshoorn, and while Vandeleur was marching back to Algoa Bay he was attacked by one Gqunukwebe clan, whose main motivation was fear that Nldambe would now take care of some unfinished business and expel them from the Zuurveld.

Commandos were mustered at Graaff-Reinet and Swellendam, and after a series of running fights the 'war' came to an end with a peace which allowed the Xhosa clans to remain in the Zuurveld, thus diminishing the chances of a general Khoina rising. As in 1793, however, the alleged peace merely sowed the seeds for the next frontier war, and the first of its malign fruits was born in 1801.

It started when the Khoina rose under three leaders, Klaas Stuurman, Hans Trompetter and one Boesak. Widespread raids resulted in many farms being hastily abandoned. Several commandos from Graaff-Reinet, Swellendam and Stellenbosch were mobilised and saw action, Commandant Tjaart van der Walt of Swellendam being killed in June 1802. Then the rising fizzled out without any clear-cut results – although the prospect of further fighting remained abundantly clear.

But the eastern frontier with its troublesome denizens of all colours was now within months of becoming someone else's problem.

'DE KAAP IS WEER HOLLANDS!'

The first major effect of the British seizure of the Cape was that it forced France to seek an alternative route to the East Indies. The French did not have sufficient naval power to invade England directly, but they could conceivably attack England's source of wealth: India. In July 1798, Bonaparte's forces landed in Alexandria and within thirty days had conquered Cairo. The plan was to cut out the ancient Suez Canal and move a battle fleet through the Red Sea and into the Indian Ocean. However, Nelson's victory at the Battle of the Nile[1] had marooned the French in their new colony; the French Directory Government abandoned the politically dangerous Bonaparte and his devoted men, forcing his return to Paris in 1799. He took power in a coup in October, and instituted a new government, the Consulate, becoming First Consul himself. That same year, Bonaparte made overtures of peace to the British but, considering the weakness of the French position in Egypt, these were summarily rejected.

After Bonaparte rectified the reverses suffered by France in his absence, most dramatically through the victories at Marengo and Hohenlinden in November and December 1800, Britain's allies – Austria, Russia and Naples – asked for peace in 1801. Now, so he believed, Bonaparte could prepare for his long-planned invasion of Britain.

Certain events conspired against him, however – specifically the counter-invasion of Egypt by British and Turkish forces in March that year, and the assassination on the 23rd of Tsar Paul of Russia, whom he had hoped to rope in as an ally. Five days later, Nelson attacked the Danish fleet at Copenhagen and effectively destroyed it. After decisive defeats in Egypt, which led to the surrender of Cairo and the siege of Alexandria, Britain was set to capture Bonaparte's entire 'Army of the East', the Armée de l'Orient. The invasion of Britain was postponed *pro tem* and in July 1801 Bonaparte initiated formal peace negotiations with the British Government. By the end of that summer, the remaining French forces in Egypt besieged in Alexandria capitulated, and signed the formal surrender in September.[2]

After an initial ceasefire agreement in London the negotiations were continued at Amiens, and on 25 March 1802 a 'Definitive Treaty of Peace' between France and the United Kingdom was signed, confirming 'peace, friendship, and good understanding' between the signatories. It provided for the return of prisoners and hostages and stipulated the complete withdrawal of French forces from the Papal States, and British forces from Ottoman Egypt, (most of which had already departed in November 1801 after defeating the French) and the restoration and protection of the Knights Hospitallers to Malta, which was to remain neutral, though effectively wound up under the aegis of the British. Most important, it called for the return of the Cape of Good Hope and parts of the West Indies to the Batavian Republic.[3] In return, Britain was granted Trinidad, Tobago and Ceylon, and the republic would recompense the House of Orange-Nassau for its losses during the revolution – but above all, the Cape was to be 'free to all', French and British alike.

The treaty – the only period of peace between the start of the 'Great French War' and its end in 1815 – was actually anything but definitive, however, and was clearly doomed to failure, since it left a number of important commercial and military issues unresolved, and certainly did not change the strategic situation in the southern oceans.

In Britain a powerful school of thought, whose members included Henry Dundas' successor as Minister of War, Lord Hobart, and the country's greatest naval hero, Lord Nelson, felt that the Cape was now of little strategic value because Britain controlled the seas. But another influential group – which included Dundas and the former Prime Minister, William Pitt the Younger,[4] who had resigned in 1801 – believed that the British had conceded too much, because the struggle with France was far from over.

Their opponents carried the day, however, and preparations for the British withdrawal were put in hand. But Pitt, Dundas *et al* were right. The Peace of Amiens solved nothing; a disdainful Napoleon Bonaparte regarded it as a mere mechanism for furthering his aims, including his postponed invasion of Britain, and did not even try to make it work.

In his incisive 1970 Master's dissertation for the University of Potchefstroom, Lourens Johannes Erasmus points out that

> If ... Napoleon had ceased alarming the British and opened French harbours for British trade the peace might have been more permanent in nature and the enlarged French empire might have continued to exist ... Britain was concerned not only about Malta and Trinidad, or control over the mouths of the Schelde and Rhine Rivers, but also about the stability of the European state system which had been overpowered by the French. Britain desired free trade with Europe to obtain a sales outlet for her industrial products. Until these problems could be resolved the war must be prosecuted, in the absence of other ways to solve [them].[5]

In the end the treaty was to last for only 14 months. But it would have enormous consequences for the Cape of Good Hope and later southern, Central and East Africa (not to mention other outlying places like Haiti after it was reoccupied by the French). Thus, as was to happen so often in later centuries, the destiny of the southern tip of Africa was once more determined by events taking place thousands of kilometres away.

In the meantime, however, the process of handing the Cape over to the Batavian Republic was set in motion. On 24 December 1802 a

Dutch naval squadron consisting of the *Bato* (a 74-gun battleship), the *Pluto*, the *Kortenaar* and the *Maria Reifersbergen*, as well as six troop and transport ships, arrived at the Cape; two other ships, the *Vreede* and the *Zeenimf*, had been lost at sea on the way to the Cape, together with a substantial number of soldiers and a large amount of equipment and supplies.

On board the *Bato* were Commissioner-General JA de Mist (1749–1823), a leading politician and specialist in civil governance on temporary assignment to the Cape, and Lieutenant-General Jan Willem Janssens (1762–1838) of the Batavian Army, who had been appointed governor and military commander-in-chief but would not assume full civil control until De Mist returned to the Netherlands.

By all accounts the arrival of the squadron gave rise to considerable rejoicing among the populace, among many of whom the British had not been popular (particularly the free burghers, who had regarded them with the same ill-will as they had felt for the VOC). A popular cry was *'de Kaap is weer Hollands!'* (the Cape is Dutch once again), an expression to indicate general satisfaction that endures in South Africa to this day.

The unusual tandem arrangement resulted from the States-General's realisation that there were two important tasks which had to be tackled simultaneously. De Mist's role would be to bring some unanimity and patriotic feeling back to a population riven by the political strains and isolation of the past decade, and at the same time introduce it to the rules and usages deriving from the radically new principles espoused by the Batavian Republic.

Janssens' first task, on the other hand, was to upgrade and strengthen the Cape's defences as best he could – an unenviable task indeed, since although the Cape was, militarily speaking, in a bad way, it could expect little material aid from the impoverished Dutch revolutionary government. Then he must govern the Cape according to the new scheme of things after De Mist had completed his task and departed.

History provides numerous examples of how easily such a divided command can lead to self-defeating discord, but these two intelligent men – very different in personality and approach but 'spiritually akin', and, says the historian WJ de Kock, 'both inspired by the political ideals introduced into their country from revolutionary France'[6] – were able to work together in a spirit of cooperation that overcame most of their various private differences, sometimes quite serious ones, on the formulation and implementation of policy.

At 40 Janssens had been a soldier since becoming an army cadet at the age of 12. As a captain he had fought against the French in 1793–94, sustaining such a serious wound that he was later given a pension and transferred to administrative duties. His talents – later amply demonstrated at the Cape – were recognised when he was made commissioner-general of French troops stationed in the Netherlands, and in 1800 became secretary to the Ministry of War as well, holding down both tasks until his appointment as governor and military commander of the Cape.

De Mist, then aged 54, was a graduate of Leyden's famed university, and had carved out a name for himself as a political activist and thinker, a long-time fighter against corruption and an Aristotelian rationalist who rejected the nihilism of radical French revolutionary thinking. Essentially his political philosophy was based, as the historian AH Murray says, 'on the three principles of the sovereignty of law, the continuity of historical institutions and a plurality of autonomous local bodies.'[7]

De Mist's tenure at the Cape gave him the opportunity to implement the principles he had consistently argued for in the Batavian parliament, and he intended to waste no time after the formal handover. This was due to take place on 1 January 1803, but there was an unscheduled delay when a message arrived from London at the last minute, temporarily halting the process (this, Erasmus says, was due to William Pitt, who was laying plans to resume the premiership in the immediate future, and had persuaded his successor to postpone the hand-over in case the war resumed). Pitt's plans did not succeed, however, and the result was another message in February, giving the green light to General Francis Dundas, nephew of the Secretary of War Henry Dundas, and acting Governor of the Cape since 20 April 1801 (he was also acting Governor between 21 November 1798 and 9 December 1799).

On 21 February the Batavian flag was duly hoisted on the Castle's

Leerdam Bastion to a triumphal thunder of guns, and four days later the Batavian and British representatives attended a sumptuous dinner at which King George III and the Batavian Republic were saluted with 21 guns each. Then on 4 March Dundas and his followers finally departed to the accompaniment of full military honours.

After thanksgiving services in the Dutch Reformed and Lutheran churches Janssens was immediately sworn in at the Castle to music and cannon fire, and held a dinner and ball for the Cape's notables. According to DW Krynauw, there was 'a spirit of satisfaction and joy everywhere.'[8]

One can imagine that Janssens and De Mist were not as full of satisfaction and joy as the general public, however, since they knew very well that the Batavian Republic was in very enfeebled shape and could not be relied on to contribute anywhere near as much help as would be needed at the Cape.

Since the overthrow of the Prince of Orange in 1795 the Netherlands had had to pick sides in the ongoing struggle between France and Britain. Owing to the politics of the revolution, the choice fell on the French, and it cost the Dutch dearly. They had to pay substantial war reparations, cede certain territories to France and take responsibility for the cost of maintaining a 25 000-strong resident French army.

This relationship brought even more catastrophic financial consequences, because it eventually dragged the Batavian Republic into a new war with the British which led to the loss of merchantmen worth 120 million guilders – a savage blow for such a dedicated trading nation – and most of the Dutch battle fleet, destroyed by the British in the Battle of Camperdown in 1797, while by 1801 the British had taken over all of its outposts and colonies with the exception of Java.

Worse was to come. When First Consul Napoleon Bonaparte crowned himself Emperor in May 1804, he created Marshals of the Empire to secure the allegiance of the vast revolutionary army. The way was now clear at last for launching his grand plan to dominate Europe, which required that first he defeat Britain. Essentially he had three options – to attack Austria, Britain's ally, to seize British posses-sions in India (a long-held dream) or to invade England itself (his other long-held dream).

He opted for an assault on Britain, and had been plotting such as early as 1802. From May 1803 onwards he set about concentrating a large invasion force at Boulogne, the only barrier to his invasion fleet (which eventually numbered some 2 200 small vessels) being the Royal Navy ships blockading the French coast. In the meantime he made sure of the Batavian Republic's unwavering support by presenting it with an ultimatum: change the constitution to concentrate all executive power in the hands of one individual, or be incorporated into France.

The Batavians chose the lesser of these two evils, nauseating as it was to their freedom-loving souls, and Napoleon appointed an able advocate from Amsterdam named Rutger Jan Schimmelpenninck[9] as the chief executive officer of the country with the strange title of 'Raadspensionaris' or Council Pensioner. It was a sad day for the Netherlands. A proud, fiercely independent nation had become, as Lourens Erasmus notes, 'a satellite state of France, [which] had to dance to Napoleon's tune.'[10]

In spite of all this, Janssens' and De Mist's arrival at the Cape was a significant moment in South African history. For 143 years it had been no more than a commercial outpost of the VOC – the 'Honourable Company', as it liked to call itself, like its British equivalent – sur-rounded by a scattering of surviving Khoina clans and, along the east-ern frontier, the Xhosas; a mere appendage of the VOC's Far Eastern headquarters. Then for eight years after 1795 it had been in limbo as a defeated territory occupied by the British army.

Now, all of a sudden, it had a national identity for the first time, with all that that implied. The former VOC outpost and its area of influence had become part of the Batavian Republic – not a fully-fledged prov-ince as yet, but, as De Mist saw it, a territory linked to the Netherlands in what AH Murray describes as 'a contractual relationship with mu-tual privileges and obligations.'[11] In other words, the Cape was now to be governed for (and to some extent by) its new citizens rather than simply managed as a virtual branch office of the Dutch East India Company's headquarters in Indonesia.

Lesser men than Janssens and De Mist might have made merely a nominal effort at transforming Cape society, given the circumstances and lack of support from *Patria,* the motherland, but they were not lesser men, and laboured mightily to carry out their mandate. Due to a lack of resources De Mist was destined to achieve very much less than he had intended, but he and Janssens nevertheless effected an amazing transformation in the three brief years of Batavian rule.

The Batavian Republic was governed by an ethos that was totally different from the VOC's. The most important component of that ethos was a written constitution, a great rarity in those days, and an almost unprecedentedly liberal one at that, certainly ranking with that of the new United States of America. It enshrined such liberties as freedom of speech and lawful assembly, a non-racial qualified franchise and protection for the ordinary citizen against being arrested or having his home searched without a court-issued warrant. What it amounted to was that in the next three years the Cape became the only country in Africa (and, one of the few anywhere in the world) to be governed according to what would now be described as liberal-democratic principles. It was not that the concept of the 'Rights of Man' was unknown in other countries – it was just rare for it to be so unambiguously enshrined in the statute books.

De Mist was an active and energetic administrative reformer who immediately began to implement a sweeping range of changes to the existing shape of things. His measures were not always agreeable to the inhabitants; he did not like to change his mind once it was made up and at times he tended to make bad appointments because the candidates had political influence in the Netherlands (an unfortunate necessity from his point of view but a frequent source of dismay for Janssens, the quintessential professional soldier).

But their efforts resulted in an indelible democratic footprint being left on South African soil. As the historian HJ van Aswegen puts it, 'the Batavian era was a period of change and rejuvenation at the Cape. Enlightened European ideas of the time took root here.'[12] AH Murray points out that many of these principles were later exported to the hinterland by the Voortrekkers. The almost anarchically decentralised constitutional structures adopted by the two Boer republics half a century later can be traced back directly to the Batavian ethos De Mist and Janssens introduced at the Cape.

Having released the imprisoned Graaff-Reinetters (except for Adriaan van Jaarsveldt, who had died in the interim), De Mist got down to applying the provisions of the Batavian constitution. Firstly, the constitution forbade slavery – 'the greatest affront to our nature', as it had been described in 1793 by the National Convention of post-revolutionary France, decades before the rest of the world came to the same conclusion.[13] Secondly, it institutionalised religious tolerance, an almost unheard-of phenomenon in those generally bigoted days, by guaranteeing equal recognition and protection before the law for all religions. It also introduced another startling innovation, that civil marriages could be performed by a landdrost and two heemraden, or local councillors, without benefit of clergy.

It was an enormously significant moment for the Malay community in particular, whose Islamic faith had been tolerated but not officially recognised by either the Company or the British. Religious tolerance was not unknown in the world, but it depended everywhere on the whim of rulers or governments (which was why, for example, the Huguenots had had to flee France in the 1680s when the king's protection was summarily revoked). Now it was entrenched by statute.

The true significance of this is sometimes misunderstood because the provisions of the Batavian constitution are not as well-known as they should be. For example, Ebrahim Mahomed Mahida, in his *History of Muslims in South Africa*, states that 'by 1804, the number of the Vryezwarten or Free Blacks, [the] majority of whom were Muslims', had reached such significant proportions that 'the Dutch rulers changed their policies in order to enlist their support, pending the British invasion of the Cape. They granted religious freedom to the Vryezwarten ... on July 25, 1804.'[14]

But in fact this is incorrect, since religious freedom was not a privilege or concession granted by the government to buy Muslim support, but the exercise of an inalienable right guaranteed by the Batavian constitution. There is also evidence that Janssens and De Mist were genuine liberal humanitarians who were strongly influenced by the theories of the French philosopher, Jean-Jacques Rousseau,[15] one of which was that all men were born free and equal but were everywhere in chains. Subsequent gifts to the Muslim community which were *not* required by the constitution provide some proof of this.

De Mist's approach to tackling the difficult task of abolishing slavery was a strictly practical one, because he was aware of the fact that it was such an integral part of the local economy that the process of abolition would have to be achieved without causing a financial upheaval. His method was a phased approach – an immediate ban on the importation of more slaves, together with a decree that henceforth slaves' children would automatically be born free. Essentially this meant that, given the existing avenues for manumission and the shorter life expectancy of the time, slavery would die out quite rapidly by what might be described as assisted attrition.

De Mist promoted free trade, so that the Cape's inhabitants could do business directly with any passing ship or even with Europe, thereby encouraging individual enterprise and eliminating a grievance which dated back to the earliest days of the free burghers. He brought in an expert from the Rhineland to advise local farmers on improving their viticulture, while an official was appointed to encourage the production of merino wool. Unsuccessful attempts were also made to grow rice and olives.

He reorganised government and created a centralised structure with built-in checks and balances, while at the same time granting a great measure of autonomy to religious corporations, magisterial districts and local authorities, and set up a free judiciary and other bodies, including a loan bank.

He placed education under local control and instituted partial temporary government support for the educational system. Schools were placed under a government-appointed council, whose avowed aim was to establish a system driven by Rousseau's humanist philosophy, rather than undiluted Calvinism. Teachers were brought in from the Netherlands; De Mist established a grammar school for boys and an intermediate school for girls, and started planning to found a teachers' training college.

To assist and advise Janssens he created a four-man Political Council, two of whose members were local inhabitants. He appointed a watchdog body to prevent official misappropriation of funds, and reformed the justice system. The VOC-era Council of Justice, or high court, returned, but this time as a politically independent body consisting of a president and six members, all legally trained; the traditional legal office of Fiscal was replaced by that of the Attorney-General, who was the public prosecutor, and appeals could be made directly to the Supreme Court in the Netherlands.

The sprawling districts of Stellenbosch, Swellendam, and Graaff-Reinet were reduced in size and thus made more manageable, by the creation of two new ones, Tulbagh and Uitenhage. Each district was governed by a full-time landdrost and six heemraden, chosen from the local burghers, who also dealt with minor civil and criminal proceedings. The guardians of law and order were field cornets selected from the local inhabitants, who were not paid but were exempted from taxes and quitrent.[16]

It was altogether a period of extraordinary change. But one important thing De Mist could not achieve was improving the Cape's financial situation. In spite of all his efforts the Dutch *rijksdaalder* continued to lose value, and this was to play a crucial role in weakening the Cape's ability to defend itself.

The new dispensation came at a time of sweeping changes in the broader scheme of things. In the preceding century and a half the Cape's main value had been economic in nature. Now the great trading companies were dead or dying, and while the East India trade still had tremendous importance, the Cape had become a vital part of a greater area that was of strategic concern to two great powers, the British and the French.

South African history books have long used the word 'occupation' to describe the two British invasions of the Cape. This might be technically correct as regards the 1795 invasion, the first priority of which was to keep the French out of the Cape (although the British had had no intention of relinquishing their grasp any time soon) but in the first half-decade of the 19th century the stakes were changing.

There was a realisation now that it was not enough simply to prevent the French from controlling the Cape; the British needed to lay hands on it permanently to protect their growing empire in India.[17] With the

Cape as a secure base and Mauritius – which was dependent on the Cape for food supplies – also in British hands, the Royal Navy would be able to dominate the Indian Ocean and its trading routes. Given the situation in Europe, a Cape controlled by the French, therefore, constituted a clear danger.

The French were just as aware of this paradigm as the British; Napoleon's ill-fated invasion of Egypt in 1798 had been meant to be the first stage of a phased onslaught on British holdings in India. With this door closed, the only other approach was by dominating the eastern sea route. In addition, the Cape was the only real gateway to the vast, unexplored southern African interior, and all the riches it might contain.

While De Mist concentrated his attention on civil governance, Janssens took advantage of the precarious peace resulting from the Treaty of Amiens to acquaint himself with the state of affairs along the eastern frontier, which was still suffering from the aftermath of the Third Frontier War, and the northern border area with its problems involving the trekboers and the Bushmen.

On 3 April 1803, less than a month after Dundas' formal departure, Janssens set off eastwards with a sizeable party which included his aide-de-camp, the able artilleryman Captain WBE Paravicini di Capelli,[18] and the wealthy explorer Dirk Gijsbert van Reenen,[19] plus an escort of regular dragoons and infantrymen. They trekked past Algoa Bay to the Kat River, where he met Ngqika on 24 June for what appears, from Van Reenen's journal, to have been generally cordial negotiations and discussions.

Understandably, Ngqika adamantly refused to make peace overtures to his would-be usurper, Ndlambe, with whom he was still in a state of war. Ndlambe had twice wounded him because he had refused to kill Christians (meaning freebooters like Ndlambe's erstwhile ally, Coenraad Buys), he said, and had also tried to bribe him to do so, but he had refused because he had always lived at peace with them, as his father had. Ngqika stressed that he wanted to live in peace with the Batavians as well.

The upshot of this and a follow-up meeting was a formal agreement of friendship, with the Fish River being declared as the formal boundary between the Xhosas and the Batavians. Ngqika promised that only his official messengers would be allowed to cross it, and also gave an undertaking that he would not harm Xhosas currently living in the Zuurveld if they returned, even though they had been fighting against him.

It was also agreed that those freebooters living among the Xhosas would be sent back to Batavian jurisdiction, with the exception of Coenraad Buys, who had undertaken to return to the Batavian area of his own volition, which he did a few months later (some of these rogue adventurers were duly handed over to the Batavians, but a few others took up residence with more distant tribes).

The two leaders parted on cordial terms after an exchange of gifts, and on 25 June Janssens set off for the northern frontier. But he got no further than the beacon which Governor van Plettenberg had erected along the Zeekoe River in 1778, when a messenger from Cape Town caught up with him on 23 July, bearing urgent tidings: on 12 May the Treaty of Amiens had become a dead letter, so that Britain and France were once again at war.

It was ominous news, given the Batavian Republic's close relationship with the French, and Janssens cut short his trip to return to Cape Town at all possible speed by way of Graaff-Reinet. He told Van Reenen and Paravicini di Capelli to carry on and 'make a note of all events, and particularly of the petitions of the inhabitants and to report them to him on our arrival at the Cape,'[20] as Van Reenen noted in his diary. Then, accompanied only by his physician and his manservant, Janssens set off for the Cape on horseback.

Back in Cape Town, the troubled frontier went on to the back burner as Janssens tackled the vexed matter of how best to use the meagre resources at his disposal to strengthen the Cape's defences in view of the very real possibility of another British invasion. De Kock relates that from time to time Janssens suffered from bouts of despondency, so that 'De Mist often had to encourage and console Janssens and remind him of his proven ability'[21] – and indeed Janssens had every reason to be despondent.

In the first place, after De Mist's departure he would be expected to govern a large, unruly territory with an intermittently unstable eastern frontier whose inhabitants were still unsettled. There was widespread suspicion, particularly among the outermost farmers, that the new regime would simply be a continuation of the old VOC. Others, particularly the soldiers of the disbanded Cape Regiment or Cape Corps, in the absence of Craig's protection, were uncertain about their future in the new Batavian-ruled Cape, *inter alia* because of several wildly inaccurate rumours about retribution connected with Craig's use of them as an intimidation measure. In fact, as it transpired, there was no official retribution, and Janssens was not at all averse to absorbing some of them into a new locally recruited full-time coloured regiment.

Secondly, he would have to make plans to defend the Cape against an attack by a major military power although sadly lacking in the 'sinews of war' – men, money and matériel. Both he and De Mist also knew very well that they could expect little help from the Batavian Government, because the formerly prosperous Netherlands was now an economic ruin. The ongoing war had disrupted the trade that was its very life-blood, and Napoleon had long been looting its military and financial resources to sustain his endless campaigns.

De Mist had arrived with some cash funds and bills of exchange, but these were fast running out and no more could be expected, while the Cape itself yielded up an annual revenue of only about 370 000 *rijksdaalders*, then the equivalent of about £61 000 sterling. This was a paltry sum, even when it is adjusted to present-day values, if one considers the magnitude of Janssens' task. The only bright spot in this depressing financial picture was the confiscation on 29 September 1803 of a large amount of property in Cape Town, a very large consignment of salted provisions, and about £11 000 in cash belonging to the British East India Company, all of which was now enemy property.

De Mist and Janssens also knew that the Batavian Republic was acutely aware of the need to hold on to the former VOC holdings in the Far East, the nation's most important financial asset. ('Java is everything,' as J Spoorz summed up when he was acting president of the Batavian Republic. 'Without Java even the Motherland has nothing but a precarious existence.') This meant, in turn, that Java's military needs would always enjoy a higher priority than the Cape's.

Janssens' primary concern was not the existing fortifications, although many of them were in poor condition because they had not been maintained by the British, who had preferred to build a number of their own, and which he would be hard put to repair because of his limited resources. The fact was that the Cape was a difficult place to defend because of its plethora of potential landing sites, far too many for all to be fortified. In the preceding few years a number of possible invasion scenarios had been developed by both British and Dutch commentators, and the potential landing sites stretched all along the coast, from Simon's Town to the other side of Table Bay.

He concluded quite rightly that the only way to conduct any sort of meaningful defence was to create a mobile field force of infantry and mounted troops which could be marched to areas of threat at short notice. According to his calculations he would need at least 6 000 regular troops to mount any sort of credible defence – even this was actually a low-end calculation: estimates by the British ran as high as 10 000.

But in this respect too, he was handicapped by a lack of resources. What he actually had – thanks partly to the Batavian Republic's ruinous finances and partly to the loss of the *Vreede* and the *Zeenimf* on the journey to the Cape – was the 3 000 or so regulars he had brought with him, and it had been made clear to him that he could expect little or no reinforcement from the home country. For the rest he would have to rely on whatever forces he could raise locally. In the latter connection it is to be remembered that the old Burgher Militia system – which had been carefully designed to provide both organised line troops and light irregulars – had been totally dismantled by the British, except for some aspects of the lightly armed commando organisation.

The backbone of his puny regular force consisted of three 'heavy' infantry regiments: the 22nd and 23rd Battaillons van Lignie, the 5th Battalion of the Regiment Waldeck, and a light infantry unit, the 9th Battalion Bataafsche Jagers (Batavian Jagers/Rifles). In addition he had the 5th Artillery Battalion, consisting of four companies, and a squadron of regular Batavian Kaapse Dragonders, or Cape Dragoons (apparently also known as the 5th Regiment of Dragoons), which had its own horse-artillery troop with four light guns and provided an official bodyguard to the Cape commander.

The quality of his regular infantry units was uneven. The 22nd and 23rd Battalions, for example, had been formed in the Netherlands in early February 1802 by re-mustering surplus *scheepsoldaten* ('ship soldiers': marines). All seem to have been trained men, and the two battalions were quite well armed, since it is recorded that they carried the late-model 1799 infantry musket in addition to the standard side arms of bayonet and short sword.

But each was grossly under-manned. Originally the two battalions had had one grenadier company and seven fusilier companies apiece, but by the time they were posted to the Cape later in the year each had had its grenadier company and three of its fusilier companies bled off to strengthen the Dutch home army. They had then been thinned out even more when some of their men went down with the *Zeenimf* and *Vreede* on the way to the Cape.

The most fully manned of the two was the 23rd, with almost 800 rank and file – although this was still several hundred short of full strength. And the 22nd had barely half that number. The Bataafsche Jagers was in similar straits. Formed in 1802 from four former marine light companies, it was the youngest of the Dutch army's justly respected rifle battalions. Its soldiers carried the rifled *jagerbuks*,[22] which far surpassed the common smoothbore musket in both range and accuracy. But it, too, was far below its authorised strength.

The joker in the pack was the 5th Waldeck, comprising one light and six fusilier companies. The last mercenary troops ever to serve at the Cape, the Waldeckers were the best trained of Janssens' infantry; Janssens thought so highly of their efficiency that he took some of them along on his later trips into the interior and at times used them to train his other troops. But, perhaps because of their mercenary roots, they lacked that most essential ingredient: the will to fight. The Waldeckers were to become a byword for cowardice during the forthcoming Battle of Blaauwberg, but the matter is not as simple as that. Even the best troops will not fight well unless they are motivated, whether by regimental spirit, patriotism, vengeance or survival, or anything else; and the Waldeckers were inspired by none of these. Indeed, any unit might perform quite well in peace time, its fighting spirit, or lack of it, only becoming apparent on the battlefield, and the Waldeckers did not see combat until the climactic battle at the Blaauwberg – with disastrous consequences.

The 5th Waldeck was the latest in a long line of mercenary units to be hired out to other nations during the 18th and early 19th centuries by the princes of Waldeck-Pyrmont, one of the smallest, poorest and most thinly populated of the independent German states.[23] Its immediate predecessor, the 3rd Waldeck Regiment, of whose 1 225 soldiers only 470 were actually citizens of Waldeck-Pyrmont, was leased to the British in 1776 for service in the rebellious American colonies. The regiment saw hard campaigning before being captured *in toto* at Pensacola in 1781. By the time it was repatriated in 1783 it had shrunk by well over 50%, with 720 men dead, missing or posted as deserters.

These remnants were incorporated into the new 5th Waldeck Regiment, which was then hired out to the Dutch for service at the Cape. This transaction might have lined the Prince of Waldeck-Pyrmont's pockets, but the regiment's presence in the Cape forces was to prove disastrous for Janssens. Like its predecessor the 5th contained many non-citizens, mainly Austrians and Hungarians who, by one telling, had been more or less forced to enlist. The Waldeckers esteemed Janssens personally, but had no enthusiasm for defending the Cape, which they regarded as a place of exile and disliked it so much that a number were to commit suicide. Another negative factor was that although some Waldeckers' service contracts had expired in 1803, they had been unable to return to Europe because of the resumption of the war with Britain.

In addition, there was a certain disinclination – presumably mainly among the remaining veterans of the American campaign – to fight their recent allies, the British. It was even said that they had reached a secret agreement with the British to flee if battle were joined; this was later denied by the British, but it is on record that Janssens was aware of the rumour. It is also possible, according to DW Krynauw, that the Waldeckers' morale had been affected by the loss of their commanding officer when the *Vreede* sank on the way to Cape Town.[24]

Little is known about the 5th Artillery Battalion, except that, in a letter to De Mist, Janssens complained that his gunners were 'new', implying they were inexperienced or inadequately trained. But the Cape

Dragoons, all Batavian regulars, would seem to have been of good quality, and it is a fact that their light artillery troop under a Lieutenant Pellegrini would later acquit itself very well in battle.

Janssens' only real advantages over any potential invading force would be that he had enough horses for his dragoons, field artillery and 'field train' (logistics vehicles), whereas an invading force would have almost none; his expatriate soldiers would also be thoroughly acclimatised and physically fit, rather than lacking in condition as a result of months at sea on poor rations.[25]

There seems to be a widely-held belief that Janssens' actions before, during and after the Battle of Blaauwberg were mainly *ad hoc* responses to the British invasion, but nothing could be further from the truth. His objective and intelligent appreciation of the Cape's military capability and how best to defend it is to be found in the writings of his friend and confidant, the doctor and naturalist Heinrich Lichtenstein, and several others.

According to Lichtenstein, Janssens made the logical assumption that, sooner or later, the Cape would be invaded by a vastly superior force, and understood that any subsequent occupation of Cape Town by the invaders did not necessarily have to mean the automatic collapse of all Batavian resistance.

As to coastal defences, Krynauw quotes Janssens as saying that soldiers were better defenders than any number of coast batteries, which were worthless without enough troops to man them and protect them (it is to be remembered that with one exception, the great Amsterdam Battery west of the Castle, the coastal batteries were open at the rear and were thus vulnerable to any invading troops who might manage to reach dry land).

Janssens' logical option was therefore first to meet an enemy landing and give battle, then to withdraw out of range of the enemy fleet's guns to the natural defensive line offered by the daunting and almost impassable Hottentots Holland mountain range, which lay 90km southeast of Cape Town, and at the time had only one pass (today's Sir Lowry's Pass). From there he would be able to cut both passes which gave access to the interior, the one at Roodezand, near Tulbagh, and the Hottentots Holland *kloof* (ravine/pass) itself. In this way he could not only prevent the British troops from moving inland but also cut off Cape Town's sources of meat and grain. In so doing, Cape Town would actually become a burden for the invaders rather than an asset. The inland stronghold would also serve as an all-purpose supply depot, provide an alternative seat of military and civil government after the fall of Cape Town, and pose a constant threat to the invaders.

It might be wondered why Janssens saw any purpose in continuing to resist in the face of what would surely be overwhelming odds, but there was still the possibility of a French force being sent to the Cape. If that happened, the British invasion forces would find themselves fighting the French on the one hand and Batavian guerrillas attacking from the Hottentots Holland stronghold on the other.

Janssens set immediately to work, making maximum use of whatever breathing space that might exist – as a result of a French invasion of Britain, for example – to prepare for an assault. He despatched officers to reconnoitre all locations which could reasonably be defended and pinpoint places suitable for establishing supply depots inside the line, and made several personal visits himself to the Hottentots Holland mountains.

It was a sound conception, and if it had been carried through the story of the 1806 British invasion might have been considerably different. But, as with everything else, Janssens simply did not have the means to implement his plan. Bowing to his circumstances, he decided to ignore the Roodezand pass and concentrate instead on setting up a single stronghold in the Hottentots Holland *kloof* – although even this could not be brought to full fruition.

The task of setting up supply depots inland from Cape Town was given to Paravicini di Capelli in August 1804, and by mid-September there was a string of grain stores and magazines stretching out all the way to Swellendam. The supply depots were never properly established, however, because of a prolonged drought which caused a serious drop in the availability of wheat.

Janssens nevertheless continued to implement the rest of his planning for the withdrawal, interdiction and mobile-warfare phases which would follow an invasion, and also addressed the subject of his resident 'fifth column': the 70 or 80 British subjects at the Cape who had arrived after the first invasion and had stayed on; no doubt he was perfectly aware of the role some resident Britons – particularly two British East India Company officials named Owen and Cust – had played in facilitating the 1795 invasion by assisting in the collection of intelligence.

British nationals were already subject to a number of restrictions and actions dating back to September 1803, when De Mist had confiscated the salted food supplies and funds. Trade of any kind with Britons or British organisations had been forbidden; British nationals had been required to take an oath of submission and restrictions had been placed on their movements to prevent sabotage to government property. Later, all British nationals were ordered to leave the Cape unless they had special permission to stay, and in September 1804 those remaining were told to travel to Stellenbosch within three days in the case of an alarm, on pain of arrest. There they would have to report twice a day to the local military commission.

The following month all persons, but especially those at military installations, were ordered to see that deserters and strangers were arrested; strangers could only stay at the Cape with Janssens' permission, and were not allowed to travel beyond Cape Town, the exceptions being French nationals known to the government.

Janssens also forbade the hoisting of flags anywhere along the coast except over government buildings, the aim being to prevent passing ships from gaining any information about the settlement's preparations, and restrictions were placed on small craft. Each boat had to be registered, none was allowed at sea after sunset and no contact with ships was allowed except by special permission.

Janssens was acutely aware of the potential military value of St Helena Bay and more particularly Saldanha Bay, in the event of an invasion, and in May 1804 inspected both places in the company of Paravicini di Capelli, who later paid the west coast another visit. The result was that Janssens could report back to the Political Council that a detachment of soldiers had been stationed at Saldanha Bay and instructions had been given to the post holder and local field-cornets about measures they were to take if the British appeared on the scene.

Erasmus provides an interesting quotation from the recollections of

Lieutenant-Colonel Robert Wilson[26] of the 20th Light Dragoons, written several years later, to the effect that Saldanha Bay was regarded as being of such importance, especially because its harbour was so safe and Table Bay so difficult to defend in the face of an attack in force, that 'proposals were even made at one time about shifting the capital from Cape Town to Saldanha Bay.'[27]

CHAPTER 11

LOCAL FORCES AND DISTANT THREATS

Janssens was well aware of the fact that the only force multiplier at his disposal consisted of whatever locally enlisted full-time and part-time soldiers he could lay hands on. In practical terms this manpower pool consisted of just two sources. Firstly there were the trained and experienced former light dragoons, foot infantry and gunners of the defunct pre-1795 Burgher Militia, disbanded by the British after their first invasion. Secondly there were the 300 or so soldiers of the former Cape Corps, both full-blooded Khoina and Bastaard-Hottentotten, who now lived in official limbo at their base at Rietvallei, near Cape Town, with about 500 of their women and children plus various camp followers.

Initially the Cape Corps represented a major potential problem. Thanks to General Craig's policy of using them to intimidate the free burghers along the eastern border, the latter were antagonistic towards the Pandoeren, who in turn quite naturally feared for their future. The permanently hot-headed John Barrow even claimed, on what evidence is not known, that some of the burghers had threatened to put the Cape Corps soldiers in irons and distribute all of them as slaves.

In fact, the matter was already in hand. In late 1802 the outgoing British governor, General Dundas, and the unit's commanding officer, Major Donald Campbell, took steps to pre-empt any problems during

194

the transition. Batavian concerns about a possible breakdown in discipline were not realised because Campbell had managed the unit well, but he and Dundas were concerned about the Khoina soldiers who had been recruited in the eastern interior: if they were summarily discharged, lacking any other source of income, they would simply head back to the interior and make use of their military skills for criminal purposes – a common occurrence after wars in Europe – either by themselves or in alliance with the Xhosas. In point of fact, Dundas and Campbell were too late, as some had deserted already.

Attempts were made to reassure the troops about the transfer of power to the Batavian Republic, and Dundas and Campbell came up with an eminently sensible proposal to the British Government, namely that it suggest to the Dutch that the 'Hottentot Corps', as they called it, be reformed under Batavian officers. Horse Guards in London agreed, and this request was transmitted to Amsterdam by way of the British diplomatic representative in Paris.

The Batavian Government also agreed, and in September 1802 decided to maintain the unit *pro tem*, at least until a thorough investigation into its circumstances and potential had taken place. Dundas personally explained the problem of the Hottentot Corps to De Mist within days of the latter's arrival at the Cape, and, accompanied by Janssens, De Mist went out to Rietvallei on 11 January 1803 to see them for himself.

De Mist was not impressed, and gave it as his opinion that a mere 25 Batavian dragoons could easily put them all to precipitate flight. To Janssens' trained eye, however, it must have been clear that the remains of the Cape Corps could be worked up into a very useful unit once more; so, on 24 February 1803 De Mist recommended to the Batavian Government that the corps should be retained, although he still had doubts (some of which Janssens shared) about the quality of some of its members.

Janssens immediately set about re-establishing the local troops as a coherent force. In addition to getting the Hottentot Corps back to fighting condition, he began to resuscitate the pre-1795 Burgher Militia, one of his aims being to raise rural companies of light dragoons once again – men who could be summoned in good time to help defend Cape Town, and would be able to stay in uniform for the duration of the emergency.

He also launched an energetic personal campaign to re-energise the burghers' martial spirit, which was at a low ebb after most of a decade under British rule, and in August 1803 published a general mobilisation plan which applied not only to burghers but also to all men who had formerly served as soldiers and sailors of the VOC. The plan was, as one would say today, user-friendly. To allay the part-timers' traditional concern about leaving their homes and farms unattended for long periods, only every sixth man would be called up, in principle, although Janssens reserved the right to mobilise additional men if the circumstances demanded; volunteers would be welcome, all members would enjoy the same conditions of service as the regulars while in uniform and would serve in their own corps under their own officers.

By this time Janssens' regular manpower had shrunk even more, because in February that year the 23rd Batavia, by far his most fully manned unit, had been abruptly ordered away to the East Indies. To De Mist he remarked bitterly:

> Our resources here are limited, and in many ways even more limited than when this distant part was attacked in 1795 ... One cannot conceive how difficult it is to provide the necessary here ... I am short of hands, especially in the artillery and workshops; a very large number of the soldiers cannot be regarded as reliable [he did not specify which]; the dragoons are moderately mounted for a small portion, and the artillery is new. A large number of the troops do not understand any of the languages known to their officers [most likely a reference to the Waldeckers, a great many of whom were Hungarians].[1]

The number of 'combat effectives' was to be reduced even further as a result of desertions, ordinary deaths and uncommonly severe losses from a typhoid epidemic in November and December 1804, which seemed to hit the regulars much harder than the locally born.

A less visible but equally important factor was the quality of Janssens' staff officers and higher-ranking commanders, who often left much to be desired. His senior field commander was a Frenchman named

Colonel PJ Henrij, whose only means of communication was a mixture of French, Dutch and German. Language aside, Henrij was indecisive, inconsistent and weak; according to Janssens himself, he 'lacks all the qualities a military commander-in-chief should possess ... he is not feared or heeded, and his pronouncements are ignored.'[2] More often than not, Janssens found himself sorting out problems resulting from Henrij's actions.

Lieutenant-Colonel Christiaan Jan Queysa of the Bataafsche Jagers was 'the most unsuitable creature ever to have filled such an appointment', and his 'whims, brutalities and lack of understanding were common and revolting.'[3] The 5th Artillery's commander was the 'repulsive' (to use Janssens' word) Lieutenant-Colonel J ter Horst, who was capable enough but so insubordinate that he was eventually posted on to the East Indies. By that time the 5th Artillery was so demoralised that it stayed on an even keel only through the efforts of a wise old veteran named Captain Steffens.

Most officers of the 22nd Batavia did not engender much confidence in Janssens either, although there were various exceptions of whom he made good use. This is not to say that he did not have some very sound leaders in the group: officers like the Frenchman Captain J Madlener, Captain Frans Sebastiaan Valentijn le Seuer of the 22nd Batavia, and Ritmeester (Cavalry Captain) Verkouteren, the regular dragoons' commander and Janssens' aide-de-camp, all proved to be worthy of their salt. So did the valiant Lieutenant Pellegrini of the regular dragoons' horse artillery and (until he was recalled to the Netherlands in 1805) Captain WBE Paravicini di Capelli.

Little is known about the quality of the Waldeckers' officers, but at least one of them, Major C von Glisten, must have been competent, because Janssens placed him in command of Fort Frederick at Algoa Bay, a sensitive post. Janssens also had a number of first-class burgher light dragoon officers like Ritmeester Jacobus Linde of Swellendam, who were later to justify his faith in them.

Things seem not to have been much better in the case of Janssens' civilian staff. De Mist had tended to be lax about getting rid of malcontents and incompetents, and after his departure Janssens did some house-cleaning, sacking the attorney-general for inappropriate legal behaviour and Cape Town's harbourmaster for incompetence – but his ability to effect enough change was limited. However, he also had officials like his military administrator, a civil servant named Deel, who was very efficient and remained loyal to the end.

In June 1803 Janssens laid out the precise responsibilities for six different categories of men of military age: free burghers (and other Dutch nationals who were not technically 'free burghers'), regular soldiers, former VOC soldiers, British subjects who had received permission to stay on at the Cape (they were required only to obey the government), and foreigners residing at the Cape without permission to do so.

The Cape was divided into a number of districts, each consisting of six wards, with a field-cornet in each ward (the old ranks of militia corporal and *veldwachtmeester* now faded away, as would the field cornets in favour of captains). The field cornets would be nominated by their local landdrost and confirmed by Janssens. Their primary tasks would be to mobilise the burghers and then lead them under the overall district commander, a *veldcommandant*.

The burghers themselves were divided into three age categories: 16–30, 30–45 and 45–60. If all members of a specific age group were not needed, bachelors and the unemployed would be mobilised first, while the unmobilised burghers could be called on to assist with providing supplies, horses, food and transport. Essentially the plan meant that the entire population of the Cape, barring the Bastaard-Hottentotten, would be slotted into a comprehensive reservist defence plan made up of several layers.

Janssens had other plans for the Bastaard-Hottentotten and the remnants of the Cape Corps, which was now temporarily called the Oude Corps Hottentotten, or 'Old Hottentot Corps'. He had given the matter careful thought, and it is clear that his intention from the start was to create a well-trained, well-equipped, motivated, loyal and well-led light infantry battalion, which would not only be tailor-made for local conditions but would also remedy a long-standing problem – the mobilisation of farmers for long periods of 'away' commando service, a source of justifiable grievance and a negative economic factor at harvest times.

Such a unit would be economical for the Batavian Government, since no European-style enlistment bounties would be needed, and it would not be necessary to spend money on getting the soldiers to the Cape from Europe, possibly losing some of them on the way.

From an operational viewpoint they would be entirely better suited to local conditions than a Batavian battalion sent out from Europe. In Janssens' opinion the Bastaard-Hottentotten soldiers, if properly selected, would be able to march longer distances and experience less fatigue, while they were usually more observant and many of them were adept at the use of firearms.

Janssens was of the opinion that the old corps must be totally disbanded in favour of a new unit that incorporated the best of the veterans. To this end he took several steps to create the right climate for the transition. He ordered that they continue to receive the same pay and terms of service as before, presented a gold coin to each of the eight Khoina clan chiefs the British had accommodated at Rietvallei, and hand-picked a commanding officer in the shape of Captain Frans le Seuer of the 22nd Batavia, whom he had identified (correctly, as it transpired) as the best possible candidate.

Le Seuer was an old Africa hand. A well-qualified military engineer by profession, he had arrived at the Cape in 1792 as a second-lieutenant on the way to Ceylon. As it turned out the resident engineer officer, Lieutenant Louis-Michel Thibault, needed urgent assistance with the upgrading of the defensive works, and on his warm recommendation Le Seuer stayed behind as a full lieutenant. Le Seuer served under Thibault until the end of the VOC's rule in 1795, and with the handover to Janssens and De Mist, had been commissioned into the 22nd Batavia.

Le Seuer's would be no easy task, as his first detailed report showed. In addition to the large number of women at Rietvallei – the consequence of the soldiers having been allowed to practise their traditional polygamy during the British period – there were also scores of *bijlopers* (hangers-on, or camp followers), consisting of full-blooded Khoina from the eastern frontier who had been allowed to attach themselves to the unit by the British to prevent them from possibly joining marauding bands in the interior.

No doubt the *bijlopers* were a source of manual and domestic labour of the type any army encampment needed, but in military terms they were so many useless mouths to feed out of the scantily filled Batavian coffers, because the majority were unfit to be soldiers as a result of age, infirmity or other factors. De Mist therefore applied his mind to formulating an exit strategy which would benefit both the camp followers themselves and the Cape's economy.

His plan, which was approved by the Political Council in April 1803, decreed that farmers were to be encouraged to take on such men as labourers, with each signing an official printed contract in the presence of a landdrost, senior military officer or other designated person. The Political Council also ordered that in future all Khoina were to be given such a contract when taking employment on a farm. By May 1803 the various measures had reduced the total number of Rietvallei inhabitants who needed feeding from 977 to 599.

Inevitably Le Seuer also found that there was a degree of confused loyalties among the remaining ex-Cape Corps rank and file, and in many cases there was mutual bad blood between them and the free burghers – thanks not only to Craig's use of the corps as a weapon of intimidation, but also because the British had bought their loyalty by paying them at a higher rate than comparable European troops.

Le Seuer's report was answered by a set of very specific instructions from Janssens, whose intention was to establish a hard core of founder members which could then be expanded as more recruits enlisted, leaving experienced wagon drivers available for service in other arms, for example as transport personnel for the artillery.

The new unit was to receive the same pay and allowances as the Batavian soldiers; unmarried men were to be preferred, and the period of enlistment was to be one year, with a provision that this could be extended if the circumstances dictated. The terms of service were to be carefully explained to each recruit before he signed on. Former Cape Corps members were to be enlisted only if they had good records, were loyal to the Batavian Republic and were satisfied with the new terms of service.

At the same time Le Seuer was to cultivate the support of the farmers, particularly the ones on the eastern frontier. He was to convince them of the need to expand the Cape's defensive capability, and allay their fears that recruiting would rob them of labour – which was scarce[4] – by enticing their workers to join up.

Janssens also instructed Le Seuer to visit the Baviaanskloof[5] mission and obtain the cooperation of the missionaries there so that they would encourage suitable congregants to join the new unit. De Villiers notes that 'Janssens had great confidence in the honesty and loyalty of the Hottentots of Baviaanskloof [and] that was why he wanted as many of them as possible in the new Hottentot corps. Most of the recruits from the mission station would be appointed as corporals and sergeants.'[6] De Mist (who had now given his whole-hearted support to the new unit in spite of his original misgivings) also approved a suggestion by Le Seuer that the families of the Baviaanskloof men, most of whom were married, be given a weekly grain subsidy of about 17lb (7.7kg) for each woman and 8lb (3.6kg) for each child; he believed that it would encourage recruiting, and this proved to be correct.

Janssens instructed Le Seuer to make sure that his soldiers underwent constant training and were subject to firm discipline, but that they were to be treated well, with sympathy and restraint. Medical services would be provided, and Le Seuer was to take steps against the drunkenness and loose living that had apparently become common in the old British days of the regiment.

Near the end of August 1803 the Corps Vrije Hottentotten, or 'Free Hottentots Corps', officially came into being at the Rietvallei camp. On the 23rd its very first recruit signed up: one Lammert Lammertes who, as Amraal Lamberts, was later to become a well-known 'captain' or clan chief in Great Namaqualand, later South West Africa, and now Namibia.

By 30 November the new corps had 103 privates and 28 corporals and was still growing, with recruiting now in full swing. Janssens was so satisfied with the results of his initial effort that he decided to bring the corps to full strength as soon as possible. This caused some problems in the agricultural districts, but the recruiting drive was successful

Meanwhile, Janssens busied himself with the broader defence network as well. He appointed a military court and established an officers' training course; appeals to the free burghers to donate materials and labour for repairing and refurbishing the coastal gun batteries elicited a good response and even a spirit of competitiveness.

He also created a type of skeleton depot system, for which free burghers, for compensation or through outright requisitioning, would supply a total of 300 wagons, 800 horses and 2 000 oxen at various places in time of emergency. To provide for his plan of withdrawing into the hinterland and fighting on in the case of an invasion, he ordered the construction of a powder magazine at Swellendam and a grain store at the old VOC outpost of Soetmelksvlei on the Sonderend River.

In addition Janssens ordered a naval officer named Lieutenant Pheil to carry out a comprehensive survey of all possible places along the coast where an enemy could land, and personally inspected the string of signal posts dotted along the coast. Discovering that some signal-men did not have a good grasp of their duties, he re-organised the entire system, so that there was one unbroken line of communication right around the Cape Peninsula.

He reactivated or upgraded other outposts at St Helena Bay and Saldanha Bay, and set up a series of 'correspondence posts' that ran from St Helena Bay's Soldatenpost to Cape Town. Each of these posts was to have a small contingent of soldiers, and he established a company of paid full-time despatch riders to man each post, carry messages and provide escorts as required – a chain of similar posts was set up leading into the hinterland up to Fort Frederick in Algoa Bay. Janssens revamped the existing signal-gun system, by locating the guns nearer one another.

By now De Mist had returned from a fact-finding tour of his own. On 9 October 1803 he had set off on a lengthy trip which first took him northwards to Saldanha Bay and St Helena Bay, then turned inland, passed over Pikenierskloof, between today's towns of Piketberg and Citrusdal, and thereafter struck out for the Hantam, the westernmost edge of the Karoo. From there he travelled through the Roggeveld and Bokkeveld and arrived at the Land van Waveren in today's Tulbagh basin, rested a few days, then carried on down the Breede River Valley, passing the future site of the town of Worcester before turning southwards towards Baviaanskloof.

Baviaanskloof was then the largest mission station in the Batavian territory, with nearly 1 100 inhabitants, of whom some were Khoina but most Bastaard-Hottentotten. The historian George McCall Theal gives a vivid description of the mission station as De Mist found it:

[The inhabitants] occupied about two hundred wattle-and-daub cottages, small and scantily furnished, but a great advance upon Hottentot huts. Each little cottage stood in a garden, in which vegetables and fruit trees of various kinds were growing. There was an air of order and neatness over the whole place, and marks of industry were apparent on all sides.

The most thriving of the residents were naturally the half-breeds, many of whom had really comfortable homes; but even the pure Hottentots had made advances towards civilisation. Some of the men belonging to the station were away in service with farmers, but at stated intervals they returned to their families with their earnings.

There were five missionaries, two – Rose and (Johann Philip) Korhammer by name – having come from Europe in 1799 to assist the three who founded the station. They were living in plain, but comfortable houses. They and their wives were all engaged during stated hours of the day in teaching industrial occupations, and in the evening the whole community assembled in a large and neat building to join in the worship of God.[7]

According to Theal the missionaries maintained strict discipline and had the power to expel unruly elements, but it was discipline of the parental type, 'tempered by love and interest in their welfare. Nothing more admirable than this excellent institution could be imagined, and Mr De Mist and the officers of his train had a difficulty in finding words to express their pleasure and satisfaction with what they saw.'[8]

From Baviaanskloof De Mist and his entourage headed eastwards via Swellendam to Algoa Bay, where he conferred with Major von Gilten at Fort Frederick. Here De Mist was visited by the eccentric missionary Dr Johannes van der Kemp, whom he had known in the Netherlands 35 years before and who was now in charge of the London Mission Society's new Bethelsdorp station.

Van der Kemp presented a strange sight. He was 'dressed in coat, trousers, and sandals,' Theal records, 'but was without shirt, neck-cloth, socks, or hat. In a burning sun he travelled about bareheaded and thus strangely attired. Yet his conversation was rational, and his memory was perfectly sound.'[9]

Van der Kemp's attire resulted partly from his theory that 'to convert the Hottentots to Christianity it was necessary to descend in style of living nearly to their level, to be their companion as well as their teacher and being thoroughly in earnest he was putting his views into practice.'[10]

So far Van der Kemp and his colleague, a missionary named Read, had clearly not yet succeeded, and there was 'no indication of industry of any kind, no garden – though it was then the planting season – nothing but a number of wretched huts on a bare plain, with people lying about in filth and indolence.'[11]

De Mist was evidently well aware that a comparison with Baviaanskloof would be invidious, because Bethelsdorp's inhabitants had barely emerged from their traditional nomadic lifestyle, whereas most of Baviaanskloof's residents were people who had been born into Cape society and could

> ... appreciate the advantage of a fixed residence, and who were accustomed to the use of such food as could be derived from gardens and orchards. It was not therefore the absence of improvement that gave Mr De Mist and those who were with him an unfavourable impression of Bethelsdorp but the absence of any effort to induce the Hottentots to adopt industrious habits, and the profession of principles that tended to degrade one race without raising the other. The missionaries themselves were living in the same manner as the Hottentots, and were so much occupied with teaching religious truths that they entirely neglected temporal matters.[12]

Van der Kemp complained loudly that local free burghers did not contribute to Bethelsdorp's maintenance, which he believed was their duty, and often tried to lure his school-going congregants away to work for them.[13]

Before leaving, De Mist made a small grant of money towards the mission's funds, 'more with a view of keeping the Hottentots out of mischief than with any expectation of this institution becoming useful', adding 'some sensible advice.'[14]

North-east of Bethelsdorp,[15] De Mist 'found parties of Kosas [*sic*] wandering about the country begging and making themselves a nuisance to such colonists as had returned to the devastated farms, but not committing any open hostilities.'[16] He invited Ndlambe and his fellow chiefs Cungwa, and Jalusa to confer with him at the Bushmans River, but they did not turn up for the gathering. A meeting he arranged with Ngqika also failed; one of Ngqika's councillors arrived and invited De Mist to travel further into the interior because 'the chief was anxious to see the great captain of the white people', but could not leave his kraal just then because he was preparing to attack Ndlambe. De Mist declined, and the party turned homeward. He spent a few days at Graaff-Reinet on administrative matters and on 23 March 1804 was back in Cape Town.

De Mist's arduous journey achieved little in concrete results, but no doubt it gave him much food for thought by bringing home to him how complex the situation on the eastern frontier really was, and the effect this could have on the Batavian Republic's ability to administer and defend the Cape.

One can imagine that De Mist's descriptions of his experiences gave further impetus to Janssens' efforts to build up the Free Hottentots Corps into a viable fighting unit of between 350 and 400 men, in anticipation of receiving permission from the Netherlands for a permanent battalion. The unit would be divided into three companies each consisting of seven officers and NCOs drawn from the Batavian establishment, and 112 enlisted men, ranging in rank from musketeers to corporals.

It is certain that he was already making sure that they were well fed and clothed, providing consignments of bread and mutton, sheepskins and oxhides.[17] Janssens also addressed the matter of a new regimental headquarters. The Rietvallei camp was not really suitable, and in any case the accommodation needed large-scale repairs and additions, since the unit was now growing almost by the day. Early in 1804, therefore, he authorised the construction of a new regimental base at

Wynberg, while decreeing that Rietvallei be retained for the accommodation of the troops' wives and children, who would be allowed to plant barley and raise livestock there.

It was an innovative solution, and certainly as early a manifestation as anywhere in the world of separate married quarters for other ranks. At one blow it solved a problem that had existed since the raising of the Corps Pandoeren in 1793 – the soldiers' concern that their families would suffer in their absence. Now the troops themselves would be near Cape Town in a purpose-built regimental base, but at the same time their dependants would be secure and self-sufficient, within reasonable reach.

The new base was built with all possible speed, because in April 1804 another tranche of 100 recruits was authorised for the unit, which was already about 300 strong, and Janssens also ordered that additional officers be appointed (in time of war the unit's soldiers could best be utilised as small, mobile groups of light infantry and sharpshooters). A total of 22 new thatched barrack huts were erected, and existing structures were converted to new use – a government building was taken over as the administrative headquarters and magazine, and one wing of the existing government hospital was turned into a ward for the exclusive use of the Free Hottentots Corps.

The corps acquired a chaplain, the Rev Johann Kohrhammer from Baviaanskloof, who was given free accommodation, a batman and the same pay and allowances as the chaplain of the Regiment Waldeck. Considerable amounts were also spent during this time on uniforms and equipping the corps in spite of its uncertain future – another indication of just how important Janssens saw its role, and also an indication that it was by now a well-found unit which was worth the drain on the tight Batavian budget.

On 8 June 1804 the Batavian Government authorised the establishment of the unit, and on 13 October 1804, within a few days of the news arriving at the Cape, Janssens officially converted the Corps Vrije Hottentotten into the Battaillon Hottentotsche Lichte Infanterie (Hottentot Light Infantry Battalion). Commanding it was Le Seuer, who was now immediately promoted to lieutenant-colonel. Its 448 men were divided into four companies, each commanded by an experienced captain.[18] Its headquarters establishment included a surgeon-major and medical orderlies, an armourer and a drum major. No less than six new second lieutenants were also appointed to the corps.[19]

The battalion had already had a taste of active service, when in August 1804, some detachments had joined mounted free burghers in a sweep of parts of the Cape Peninsula to round up the deserters, run-away slaves and habitual criminals who infested parts of the mountains and committed constant thefts.

In the meantime another attempt at stabilising the eastern frontier was made, although the garrison at Fort Frederick was reduced to half of its authorised strength. Captain Lodewijk Alberti, who was due to take over from Major von Gilten, was told to continue urging the Xhosas in the Zuurveld to cross the Fish River without delay.

In August 1804 Alberti duly set off, but – presumably to no-one's great surprise – it was a complicated and largely fruitless task he had embarked upon, because of the constantly shifting alliances inside the Xhosa confederation and Ndlambe's recalcitrance. His followers were cultivating the west bank of the Bushman's River in spite of his prom-ise not to do so, while parties of his supporters, in between fighting Ngqika, were stealing cattle in the area whenever the opportunity pre-sented itself.

Alberti made no impression at all on either Ndlambe or his follow-ers. The following month Chief Cungwa came to terms with Ngqika, and promised Alberti that he would leave the Batavian area as soon as the crops his people had planted had been harvested. But soon afterwards Chief Jalusa also joined forces with Ngqika, and the new alliance then attacked Ndlambe with the intention of rousting him out of the Zuurveld once and for all. They failed, and the land east of the Bushman's River remained in a state of turmoil that made it impossible for the free burghers to return to what remained of their farms.

The rest of the Graaff-Reinet district stayed reasonably tranquil, but, given the eastern frontier's history, this was obviously no guarantee of anything, and the reduction of Fort Frederick's garrison naturally did not reassure anyone either.

In late 1804, with the Hottentot Light Infantry well on the way to becoming a useful unit, Janssens tapped into other hitherto unused sources of local manpower. In October De Mist announced that a certain number of slaves were liable to be called up in time of need, with their owners being duly compensated, and that same month he raised a fifth company of the Burgher Militia, consisting of local Khoina and various people of mixed race who had not had a military obligation up to that time.

Little is known about the 5th Company, also called the 'Free Corps', except that according to Erasmus,[20] its members were given the same pay as regulars. It seems likely that the 5th Company was a support or logistics unit with more or less the same duties as the Corps der Vrijswartzen (Corps of Free Blacks) of the early 18th century, and it is assumed that it would also have accommodated the slaves De Mist had earmarked for service.

In November Janssens drew on yet another group – the substantial and, by now, economically important population of free Malays, most of whom were manumitted slaves or the descendants of manumitted slaves. From them he recruited a volunteer unit called the Javaansche Artillerie Corps (Javanese Artillery Corps). At its head he placed the experienced Captain Madlener, and appointed a prominent Malay religious personality, Imam Frans van Bengalen, as its *veldpriester* ('field priest').[21]

The Javanese Artillery Corps was primarily a garrison artillery unit whose members were trained to man the coastal guns at the Castle and elsewhere, but they were later to gain fame as the only 'foot artillery' unit ever to take to the field in South Africa's history (foot artillery gunners marched with their guns instead of riding on the ammunition limbers or gun horses) – all because of a last-minute change in role.

The new unit was a striking illustration of the sweeping changes that the Batavian Republic was bringing to the Cape. A record of their oath of loyalty survives to this day:

> I promise and swear, by the One and Only God and his great Prophet Mohamet, [sic] loyalty to the Batavian Republic, this land in which we live, to defend the Batavian Republic against all enemies.[22]

This oath shows two things: firstly, the fact that the Muslim gunners were able to take their oath in the name of Allah showed that the granting of religious freedom had not been a mere token act of political expediency but a genuine right to be exercised. Secondly, it proved the sincerity of Janssens' conviction that the members of the Malay community were loyal citizens.

There seems to have been widespread community support for the corps – one cannot imagine that a person of Frans van Bengalen's stature would have allowed himself to be involved otherwise – and it is a fact that it soon earned the reputation of being an efficient unit. Both its loyalty and its efficiency were to be tested in the near future, and not found wanting.

The Batavian era brought other benefits to the Malay community. Prayer rooms had been made available at five different sites after 1800, the moment when 'Islam actually took root in the Western Cape', as Mahida says in his *History of Muslims in South Africa*,[23] but Janssens promised the community a site for a mosque, although this was only actually erected after 1806.[24]

Then trouble between the trekboers, Xhosas and Bushmen on the exasperating eastern frontier boiled over yet again, forcing Janssens to rob the thin protective blanket of troops spread out over the Cape Peninsula, and send contingents to trouble spots like the Gamtoos River. A measure of his desperation is to be found in his appeal to the frontier farmers, as Erasmus notes, 'to put aside their internal quarrels and try not to clash with the Xhosas.'[25]

Another major problem, however, and possibly one of the causes of this new eruption, was the fact that the 1803–1804 wheat harvest had been very poor. Apart from its impact on the civilian population, it meant that Janssens would have great difficulty in accumulating a large enough stock of provisions to feed his troops in the event of a full mobilisation – not only in Cape Town, which was likely to end up under siege, but also in the countryside to which the Batavian forces could withdraw and cut off supplies to the British.

Janssens was aware of the burgher soldiers' difficulties, but as Krynauw points out, he 'thought highly of the citizen forces and cherished great expectations',[26] in spite of their one great weakness, their

lack of availability at harvest times. Trouble on the border and murmurings among the militia was the last thing he needed. As a result he
went to considerable lengths to heighten the citizenry's martial spirit
and patriotism. Many parades were held, and Janssens 'frequently addressed the troops and urged them to stand fast at the Cape for the
liberty and honour of the motherland'.[27] On 23 October 1803, for example, the anniversary of a Batavian victory of 1799,[28] the coastal batteries and ships at anchor in Table Bay fired salutes, and he inspected
the burgher troops at a parade in Strand Street.

Janssens clearly understood the value of the media, in the shape
of a lone weekly newspaper called the *Kaapsche Courant*, which the
Batavians had inherited from the British occupation. No week should
go by, he told the Council of Policy in January 1805, without an appropriate article which would inspire the local population and prepare
them for 'durable sacrifices'.

De Mist's and Janssens' journeys had substantially altered their attitude towards the Cape and all its various ethnic groups. What distinguished them from many other reformers, however, was that they were
willing to modify their views to conform to reality as they saw it – and the
reality was that the Cape, particularly on its eastern outskirts, was a typical frontier society which had not yet developed to the point where the
Batavian Republic's liberal-humanitarian principles could simply be applied without consideration for local circumstances. Thus, although De
Mist was an implacable foe of slavery and in addition was duty-bound
to abolish it, he devised a way to do so that would not wreck the local
economy, and would avoid creating popular ill-will that would encourage
general resistance to the Batavian reforms. They were also both agreed
that the only way to ensure some sort of peace on the eastern frontier
was to reduce or eliminate the main cause of friction by persuading the
Xhosas to move back across the Fish River of their own free will.

In this they failed, however, like all their predecessors, and for the
same reason. The treaties they signed with Ngqika and other chiefs,
aimed at keeping the peace and respecting defined borders, did not
hold much water among the leaders who had not been involved. In
any case their co-signatories just did not believe that signed pieces of
paper were really binding. Consequently, the position on the frontier

remained confused, and liable to descend into war at any moment, while Batavian authority had to be enforced over the Khoina and Xhosas living on the western side of the Fish River as well as over the free burghers there – with all that that implied for the defence of the Cape of Good Hope.

Janssens' hearts-and-minds programme, as it would be called today, seems to have worked, so that by 1805 he could eventually report back to the Council of Policy that a broad, positive, military spirit now existed at all levels. But he still had to resolve crucial shortcomings without significant help from the Batavian Government.

Foremost among them was his shortage of trained manpower and a lack of basic equipment. Janssens could deal with the latter to a certain extent – for example, by having footwear made locally instead of importing it – but no troops were forthcoming from either the Netherlands or the Far East. The Batavian Government's general attitude was that the Cape must not become a burden to it.

By late 1805 the Hottentot Light Infantry numbered about 600, and under Le Seuer's expert leadership was giving early proof of its worth. Contingents served on the eastern frontier with Janssens' other troops, and although generally very small physically (the average height was about 1.5m, or five feet), they often proved more useful than the white regulars, being generally good shots and trackers, and possessed of great endurance. Like their predecessors they needed careful handling at times. They disliked leaving their livestock and women behind when they went on campaign, and had a tendency to desert when they felt disgruntled. But their virtues far outweighed their defects.

By now they had also been equipped with the uniforms that, presumably, they wore at the Battle of Blaauwberg. No uniform of the Hottentot Light Infantry is known to survive, but from the facts available it appears it is possible to paint a reasonably accurate picture: a tailless blue jacket or sleeved hip-length waistcoat with red facings on the collars and cuffs; a round-brimmed hat (possibly the same tall-crowned black headdress with upturned right brim used by the Cape Corps in the earlier British era) and a *mus* or brimless bonnet, presumably as a forage cap; and finally *velskoene*, either normal low shoes or slightly higher ankle boots.[29]

The overall picture that emerges of the Hottentot Light Infantry in late 1805, on the eve of the Battle of Blaauwberg, is thus of a well-trained light infantry unit, adequately officered, housed, shod and fed, and even possessed of its own band. The final proof of its worth was to come when it fired its first shots in anger.

De Mist departed in February 1805, taking with him a heartfelt but fruitless plea for assistance from Janssens. Gone, too, was the indefatigable Paravicini di Capelli. Janssens was on his own in all senses of the word, with the likelihood of a British invasion overshadowing his every thought. As well it might, because as the year passed there were continual reports that things were astir in England and Europe.

To add to his problems, a persistent drought had ensured that the 1804–1805 harvest was even poorer than the previous year's, and resulted in many livestock deaths; the situation was so bad that at one stage bread had had to be rationed. Once more Janssens was unable to stock up on the provisions that would be needed in case of a full mobilisation.

Instead he took such steps as were within his powers to conserve what there was and augment it where he could. Large quantities of rice were imported, the feeding of wheat to horses was forbidden, as was the export of food, and a commission was set up to determine the current and likely future state of food stocks. Plans were also made to buy up quantities of grain in places where a reasonable 1805–1806 harvest was expected, but that would not happen until January 1806, and by then he was facing a far greater disaster.

CHAPTER 12

CRISIS IN EUROPE –
AND A FATEFUL DECISION

In 1805 the struggle for mastery in Europe, and therefore in a great portion of the known world, had reached crisis point. it was to be a year of titanic battles on land and sea between the British and the French and their respective allies; in time the conflict would spill over onto the distant shores of the Cape of Good Hope and change its future forever.

It was a time of acute anxiety in Britain. Unrest in Ireland had been rumbling on since 1803 and was ripe for another eruption, and the fragile Peace of Amiens was finally broken in December 1804, with Spain realigning with France once again.[1] Worst of all was the fact that Napoleon, the greatest general of his time and the conqueror of huge swathes of Europe, was now waiting for the right moment to storm the shores of Britain herself.

Napoleon knew very well that if he could neutralise Britain he would snap the backbone of the resistance to his greater plans. To achieve this he had spent years assembling an enormous invasion force which he called the Armée d'Angleterre (the Army of England[2]) at Boulogne, a mere 54km east of Dover. Originally he had collected 70 000 veteran infantrymen, 16 000 cavalry and 9 000 artillerymen with more than 400 guns; by now his force had grown to at least 150 000 (some sources say 180 000). Standing by to transport this battle-hardened horde across the Straits of Dover were more than 2 200 landing barges and other vessels.

To many people it must have seemed as if all Europe were holding its collective breath. Britain's all-volunteer army was small in comparison to Napoleon's huge number of well-trained, well-equipped regulars and conscripts, and many of its regiments were serving elsewhere in the world; its only support consisted of stalwart but often sketchily trained and armed yeomanry and militiamen. If his torrent of horse, foot and artillery ever flowed ashore at Dover there was a very distinct possibility that they would soon end up marching triumphantly through the streets of London – the first successful invasion of England since that of William, Duke of Normandy, in 1066, almost 800 years earlier.

All that was holding Napoleon back was Britain's incomparable navy, then the best maritime fighting force in the world. Under the guiding hand of the wise old First Lord of the Admiralty, Lord Barham,[3] the Royal Navy had long maintained a grimly determined blockade of French and allied coasts in both fair weather and foul, ready to fight at the drop of a hat. Napoleon calculated he needed only a 24-hour break in that unsleeping vigil to cross the Straits of Dover and gain a substantial foothold on British soil. This might well have been a trifle over-optimistic: although Napoleon was a genius at fighting on land, his grasp of naval warfare left much to be desired[4] – but a few days would certainly have been enough, given reasonable weather conditions in the notoriously treacherous English Channel.

Napoleon and his admirals conceived a bold deception plan aimed at making the invasion possible. Vice-Admiral Pierre-Charles de Villeneuve[5] was to break out of Toulon and collect Spanish reinforcements at Cadiz, from which they were to head for the French-held Caribbean island of Martinique. Here he would be joined by 20 more fighting ships from Brest under Vice-Admiral Honoré Joseph Ganteaume.[6]

The aim of all this was to draw the British blockade force after Villeneuve's and Ganteaume's 40 ships, away from the Mediterranean and the Channel. The combined force would then double back to Europe, drop off some troops in Ireland to ignite an open insurrection, and then sail on to the English Channel. There it would join hands with a smaller but nevertheless potent force from Rochefort under Commodore Zacharie Allemand.[7] This massive combined fleet would fall on the weakened British blockade and clear the way for the invasion.

The blockade of Toulon was commanded by Villeneuve's old adversary from the Egyptian days of 1798, Admiral Horatio Nelson. Nelson believed in a 'loose' blockade, with his fast frigates watching from close quarters while his main force stayed out of sight, the aim being to lure the French out from under Toulon's guns into open waters. In this case Nelson's approach backfired when a gale blew him badly out of position, the result being that on 29 March 1805, Villeneuve managed to break out of Toulon with 11 ships of the line, six frigates and two brigs, and sailed unhindered to Cadiz. By the time Nelson established Villeneuve's route and gave chase through Gibraltar on 7 May, it was too late: Villeneuve was already within five days of his rendezvous with the Brest fleet at Martinique.

In Britain all these developments caused great public concern. As one Member of Parliament put it, 'a great portion of the Royal Navy [is] tied down blockading the French coast, but [France] has equipped armaments that have escaped our vigilance, committing depredations highly prejudicial to our interest, and disgraceful to the nation.'[8]

In addition to the anxiety about the invasion an ever-louder chorus arose, both in the press and in Parliament, for something concrete to be done about protecting British interests abroad, particularly at the Cape of Good Hope. As Erasmus points out, the strategic importance of the Cape had been downplayed during the Amiens negotiations, but 'by 1805 it was clear that the handing back had been a great mistake', because all at once the Cape was now useful for three purposes:

> Firstly, the French would be able to send a fleet there to plague British trade; secondly, [a] French fleet on passage to conquer India could take on supplies at the Cape; thirdly, the French would be able to use

the Cape as an assembly-point for the fleets attempting an attack on India.[9]

There was no lack of scare journalism and alarming reports in Britain. As early as April 1804 a British merchant named SE Greene wrote to a friend (who duly passed on the letter to Lord Castlereagh, the Minister of War) that Janssens had

> … about two thousand men but the other voluntary corps might increase it to three thousand. Two men of war and a sloop is the marine force.
>
> A new battery has been erected at Rogge Bay and the Imhoff and other fortifications put into excellent repair. The Castle is in fine condition, the government having spared no expense to put everything into the best possible state for defence. They have established a train of flying artillery, a cart gun with six horses and riders which they manage with dexterity.
>
> They are constantly employed at shooting at a mark and have cottages erected between the Cape Town and Green Point for the firing of red hot shot. In short general Jansen [*sic*] is indefatigable, neglecting no part of the duty of a good officer for the protection of the place he governs.[10]

In June 1805 one newspaper report quoted a passenger in an American ship that had called in at the Cape as saying that the garrison was lying in wait just outside the town, and that a camp was being prepared for a large French force Janssens was expecting – possibly an outdated misinterpretation of the new Hottentot Light Infantry camp at Wynberg.

The following month another newspaper report had it that Cape farmers had been ordered to bring all their grain to Cape Town, obviously for the French troops which were believed to be on the way, while a report from Texel, a principal Dutch port of embarkation, claimed that a large expeditionary force had been assembled there in secret, its destination unknown, and that a naval squadron to support it, commanded by a veteran French admiral, was already at sea after breaking through the blockade. Reports like these would have been a source of wry amusement to Janssens as he struggled to work up a credible defence plan for the Cape in spite of his serious lack of money, equipment and reinforcements.

No doubt British intelligence was well aware of the fact that at least some of these hair-raising reports were the result of the French disinformation campaign aimed at luring the Royal Navy out of the English Channel. But they could not all be ignored, and the public clamour fell on receptive ears in Westminster, where the Prime Minister's office was once again occupied by William Pitt the Younger – the same man who had launched the 1795 invasion and later, while in opposition, had strongly opposed the return of the Cape to the Batavian Republic.

It was, of course, an extremely inappropriate time to consider assaulting the Cape. The prospect of a French invasion was a grim reality, and the Royal Navy was heavily committed to the Channel blockade, a task made more onerous by the fact that Spain's coast had been hostile since 1796 and its warships were at the disposal of the French.

Although Britain had formed the 'Third Coalition' with Austria, Sweden and Russia by mid-1805, this was no great consolation. If Napoleon could find a way to neutralise the Channel blockade for those few days he needed, he would be on British soil. In addition, the need for naval intervention in Latin America – where more and more Spanish colonies were raising their voices in favour of independence, and British interests might have to be protected or fostered – could not be ruled out.

However, Britain's possessions, and at all costs her interests in the East Indies, had also to be protected, which meant securing the sea route there and back. Pitt decided to send an expedition to the Cape – partly, it would appear, on the strength of highly secret information about the weakness of the Cape defences which had been passed on to him by a respected and politically well-connected British naval officer, Captain Sir Home Popham.[11] Popham's information about the state of the Cape defences, Erasmus remarks, might well have been the final factor that persuaded Pitt to take action.

As Krynauw points out, 'England's main purpose regarding the conquest of the Cape was therefore a military and not a colonial one – not the expansion of the Empire but safeguarding the Empire.'[12] The fact that in the event the conquest of the Cape eventually led to the large-scale colonisation of southern and central Africa is a classic example of the old military axiom that a plan rarely remains unchanged once the first few shots have been fired.

❦

At Martinique Villeneuve waited in vain for Admiral Ganteaume to join him, but Ganteaume did not arrive. When Villeneuve then got word on 7 June that Nelson had finally made landfall at the British colony of Antigua, he believed the deception plan was blown and, contrary to Napoleon's orders, returned home.

On 16 July, as Villeneuve was nearing Europe, the irascible but extremely competent Commodore Allemand dodged past the Royal Navy's Rochefort blockade with a small but powerful force consisting of his 120-gun flagship *Majestueux*,[13] three other ships of the line and several frigates and brigs – his orders: join up with Villeneuve for operations in the English Channel.

On 21 July Villeneuve's Franco-Spanish fleet was nearing Cape Finisterre on the French coast, and Britain's Vice-Admiral Sir Robert Calder was ordered onto the attack. The squadrons sighted one another around 11am on 22 July. With 15 ships of the line, Calder bore down on the 14 French and six Spanish vessels. Allemand, who could have tipped the scales, had no idea the two opposing fleets had met off Finisterre. In the end it was an indecisive engagement in failing light, in which Calder captured two of the Spaniards before breaking off the action. He also decided against renewing the attack the next day. It would later cost him a court martial.

Villeneuve made a disastrous decision as well: instead of attacking Calder the next morning he too broke off and sailed southwards to the Spanish base of La Coruña. The intricate invasion plan had gone disastrously wrong.

❦

By this stage the British plans to invade the Cape of Good Hope were already in progress. On 25 July Lord Castlereagh notified the Admiralty that the government had decided to invade the Cape, and that the necessary naval preparations must be undertaken. He also informed the veteran Major-General Sir David Baird[14] that he would command the expedition, with the naval component being commanded by Captain Sir Home Popham in the appointment-rank of commodore. Castlereagh gave Baird some very explicit guidelines for the invasion.

First of all, he must try to negotiate a peaceful capitulation by offering advantageous terms, such as undertakings to respect local inhabitants' religious practices, property and customs. If Janssens was not willing to capitulate without a fight, however, Baird must attack immediately in maximum strength. He must also try to suborn the Waldeckers.

If he succeeded in taking the Cape, he was to send on any troops he did not need for its occupation to India. If he could not (rather ominously, Castlereagh warned him not to rely too much on the Batavian force strength mentioned in the instructions) he must fall back on St Helena and await further orders. To conceal the purpose and destination of the expedition it had been arranged that the ships involved in the expedition would not leave the same harbour at the same time, but would rendezvous off Madeira.

For the British it was a neat solution to several problems. The invasion of the Cape would be carried out by soldiers who were needed in India in any case, and thanks to the French naval forces' return to Europe they would not be needed as reinforcements for the West Indies. This meant that Britain's sparse military assets would not be unnecessarily weakened.

The recipient of Castlereagh's instructions was a man to be reckoned with. A veteran of battle in India as a captain Baird made full colonel by 1797. His thorough personal knowledge of the Cape and its defences was also a factor in his selection. On his way back to Britain from India in 1797 the then governor, Lord Macartney – an acquaintance from his India days – prevailed upon him to stay behind and help train the British garrison. Promoted brigadier-general, Baird was placed in command of a 2 000-man brigade.

According to Krynauw this was a ticklish task because 'a large pro-portion of the British garrison was not well-disposed' towards Major-General Francis Dundas.[15] Baird stayed for almost a year, and by all accounts made a superb job of bringing both officers and men to a high state of efficiency and morale. The result was that when he was recalled to India in 1798 because of a renewed military threat, this time at the hands of the legendary Tipu Sultan,[16] he was well ac-quainted with the Cape, its terrain and its fortifications.

Baird avenged his captivity in a most satisfactory manner by leading the assault that captured Seringapatam in May 1799, assisted, among others, by the future Duke of Wellington, Colonel Arthur Wellesley of the 33rd Regiment. Baird later went on to serve in Egypt, where he landed his sepoys on the Red Sea coast and marched on both Cairo and Alexandria.

While in Egypt Baird had made the acquaintance of Captain Popham, and from his writings it is clear that the two men liked and respected one another: 'I can only add,' Baird wrote to Popham on one occasion, 'that it will be a source of real satisfaction, again to cooperate with you.'[17] – which would, of course, happen in the not-too-distant future.

Popham was a 'dashing daredevil of an Englishman', as Ian D Colvin described him in later years[18] (actually he was Irish), and as good a fighting man as Baird and, like him, had considerable know-ledge of southern Africa. His speciality was maritime cartography, and as a lieutenant he was involved in an intensive survey of the southern African coast.[19]

Baird's and Popham's qualities were also to be seen in various of their subordinates, who included Brigadier-General William Carr Beresford, an efficient soldier with a talent for logistics; Brigadier-General Ronald Craufurd Ferguson, a distinguished veteran of the first invasion and various battles in Europe and India; and Lieutenant-Colonel Robert Thomas Wilson, commanding the 20th Light Dragoons, who at only 28 had already had an adventurous ca-reer and had won a reputation as a writer of incisive military books.[20]

There were interesting minor characters in Baird's and Popham's entourage, two of whose names would later be writ large on South

African history. One was American-born Captain Jacob Glenn Cuyler, who was attached to Baird's staff because he could speak Dutch, and a Scottish major named John Graham of the 93rd Regiment, whose name was also to feature in the Cape's history books at a later date and whose surviving letters provide a famous eyewitness account of the Battle of Blaauwberg. Not counting Royal Marines and sailors, with them on the task force went some 6 700 formidable officers and men.[21]

The very discreetly assembled British invasion fleet consisted of 65 vessels: three ships of the line and six smaller fighting craft, 17 East India Company merchantmen and a variety of transports and troopships, including a hospital ship and one outfitted to carry horses and fodder.

In July 1805, the 59th Regiment of Foot, the 20th Light Dragoons and some 300 artillerymen and recruits were gathered at Falmouth, ostensibly to head for the East Indies under escort by the brig-sloop HMS *Espoir* (18 guns) and the 14-gun brigs HMS *Encounter* and *Protector*. Soon afterwards, the 24th, 38th, 59th, 71st, 72nd, 83rd and 93rd infantry regiments were massed at Cork, together with the *Diadem* (64 guns), *Raisonable* (64), *Belliqueux* (64), *Diomede* (50) and Popham's 32-gun frigates, the *Narcissus* and *Leda,* all supposedly bound for the Mediterranean theatre.

Between them Popham's warships mounted more than 350 guns, not counting the armament on the support ships, but, as was the case during the first invasion, they would only be useful if land actions took place within their effective ranges. Baird himself had only eight field pieces – two howitzers and six 6-pounders – and no animals to draw them. In addition he did not have enough mounts for Wilson's 320 dragoons, a matter of great concern because of the possibility of meeting up with Janssens' seasoned light horsemen. The only solution was to try to acquire suitable extra livestock along the way.

Despite the intelligence they received, Baird and Popham were by no means certain of what sort of resistance they were likely to encounter. Janssens could not prevent passing ships from observing conditions at the Cape (all neutrals subsequently calling at St Helena were being routinely debriefed for information) and the small Fifth Column of British and pro-British residents constantly passed on information about the state of the defences as best they could.

But such information was not always accurate and took a long time to reach Britain, leaving a potentially fatal time gap during which drastic changes in force strength could take place – for example, through an infusion of troops from France or even the Batavian possessions in the Far East.

There was also a large question mark about the possible presence of French warships at the Cape. As late as 21 July Baird still believed not only that Janssens disposed over 3 000 readily available infantry, light horsemen and gunners but also that 1 000 French troops were on the way to the Cape, and that there might be two French warships stationed nearby.

In the meantime Baird collected as much recent information about the Cape as he could; among other things he consulted General Francis Dundas and also a Captain Jones of the 20th Light Dragoons, who had just arrived in England via the Cape. The greater threat, however, lay out to sea.

Popham's preparations were complete when his East Indiamen arrived at Cork from Falmouth on 14 August, but he was told to stand by because of a report that a number of French warships, those of Allemand, it would seem, had broken out from Rochefort and were posing a distinct danger. In view of the events taking place at sea, Popham wisely decided to wait.

Now a dispirited Villeneuve, having sat in La Coruña since 1 August, received orders from Napoleon to sail north to Brest, link up with Ganteaume's 21 ships of the line and, with Allemand's squadron, head for the Channel to disrupt the thinly stretched British blockade. But unable to locate Allemand's squadron, and possibly influenced by a false report that a large British fleet was operating in the Bay of Biscay, he made a second disastrous decision. Overruling the Spanish Admiral Gravina's objections, he turned and headed back to Cadiz on 14 August. Villeneuve sailed past the Spanish port of Vigo without stopping; when Allemand called in there two days later no instructions awaited him. Thus at one stroke he not only permanently doomed Napoleon's invasion plan but set in motion a train of events which would end in the effective destruction of French naval power and ultimately Napoleon's overthrow. Napoleon wrote in 1815 after his final defeat at British hands:

> If Admiral Villeneuve … had contented himself with rallying with the Spanish squadron, and had sailed for Brest to join Admiral Ganteaume, my army would have landed; it would have been all over with England.

Once Villeneuve's fleet was spotted returning to Cadiz on 21 August, Lord Barham informed William Pitt that 'I think this is the proper time for the expedition and India ships to sail from Cork. The sea is now free.' The Minister of War then gave Popham the go-ahead. For safety's sake a naval squadron was sent to patrol the coasts around Ferrol to protect the Cape expedition, and on 1 September, Popham quietly put to sea with the bulk of his force, the general distraction with greater events making his departure from British waters every bit as discreet as the mustering of his force had been. Twenty-eight days later, on 28 September, he made rendezvous with the Falmouth fleet off Madeira.

It is a strange irony that by the time Popham left Cork the strategic situation already had begun to change so radically that within two months of his departure – and long before he made landfall at the Cape – the war between the British and the French had undergone a drastic re-orientation: deciding that Villeneuve was no longer coming to Brest as ordered, Napoleon summarily scrapped his invasion plans for the second time since 1798. Learning of a new threat by an army of 72 000 Austrians who had marched prematurely ahead of their Russian allies who were still advancing through Poland, Napoleon broke camp with astonishing speed and in a matter of days had his Armée d'Angleterre, now renamed the Grande Armée, marching off to Germany. The immediate threat to Britain was over.

While Napoleon was getting to grips with the Austrians and Nelson was prowling around the approaches to Toulon, trying to lure Villeneuve into open battle, Popham anchored his fleet at Madeira to take on water and buy additional horses. He had had the good fortune to miss running into Admiral Allemand's homeward-bound force by a matter of days, thereby avoiding a possible disruption of his plans and damage to his ships.

On 29 October Popham detached Captain Ross Donelly's frigate, the *Narcissus,* and sent him off south-westwards into the Atlantic to scout out the situation at the Cape: Baird and Popham, it will be remembered, still had no clarity about the size of the Batavian force and, just as important, its will to resist. John Barrow had claimed that the Cape district would not be able to yield more than about 1 000 fighting men, who would be too afraid to fight in any case and would be unwilling to leave their farms at the mercy of marauders, and that Janssens' coloured soldiers were dissatisfied and would desert at the first opportunity. But Baird and Popham were too experienced to take these unsubstantiated (and by this time quite outdated) assertions to heart, and subsequent events proved them right

Donelly's orders were to call in at St Helena and glean the latest information about the Cape's defences, the arrival of any reinforcements since April 1805 (the date of the last accurate reports Baird and Popham possessed), and the general political feeling there. After leaving St Helena he was to head westwards and reconnoitre the Cape waters in person to confirm what he had been told at St Helena, even if that meant entering Table Bay under French colours.

Thereafter he was to round the Cape and stop passing ships, not only to interrogate their captains but also to spread a false report that Britain and France had made peace, under the terms of which the Cape had to be handed over to Britain. Finally he would rendezvous with Popham off the Cape coast to pass on what he had found out.

The next day, Popham set off from Madeira, heading for South America. This course he chose was partly to camouflage his real intentions, but by steering considerably further westwards than usual yet then diverting southwards back out to sea again, he avoided the South American coastal climate, hoping not only to spare his sailors and soldiers from as much tropical heat and rain as possible, but also to have good winds for the last leg of his journey.[22]

By now the Admiralty in Britain was aware that Napoleon's invasion had been aborted, but Popham's tasking remained valid because there remained the possibility of an attack on their Indian possessions, a much more important asset than the Cape. Baird's soldiers thus provided an available reserve on which the East India Company could call if necessary, even if it meant evacuating the Cape altogether after capturing it.

In mid-October Villeneuve learnt that Napoleon intended to replace him with Admiral François Etienne de Rosily-Mesros, and recall him to Paris to account for his actions. This impending disgrace proved too much for Villeneuve to stomach, and on the 18th he sailed forth to give battle.

The following day, 19 October, Napoleon finished off the Austrians at Ulm, but whatever satisfaction he derived would prove to be very short-lived. On 21 October 1805, Villeneuve learnt of the size of Nelson's fleet and turned back into Cadiz once more. But it was too late. Nelson intercepted him off Cape Trafalgar, and flung his 27 ships of the line at Villeneuve's 33.[23] The result was the greatest naval defeat – and certainly the bloodiest – ever inflicted upon the French. More than 6 000 men died, and the British sank one French ship and captured 21 others (including the French flagship, *Bucentaure*, with Villeneuve on board[24]) without losing any of their own. However, it came at the terrible cost to Britain of Nelson himself, shot in the back in the heat of the battle. Admiral Gravina managed to escape with what was left, although he was so badly wounded that he died some months later.

It was a defeat of such devastating proportions that the French permanently lost any hope they might still have had of gaining even a partial control of the high seas, although it was not the end of the

French navy, as is often supposed. Napoleon would go on to win his greatest victory in December, when he smashed the Austrians and Russians at Austerlitz (in the present-day Czech Republic) and their coalition with Britain fell apart, but by then the emperor had lost his last chance to dominate the known world.

For practical purposes Trafalgar had confined him to Europe and handed control of the East India sea route – not to mention the world's oceans in general – to the Royal Navy. Nelson's great victory had been a turning-point, and Britain would not face another significant invasion threat for one and a half centuries.

At Trafalgar, as the historian George McCall Theal later commented, 'issues were decided in comparison with which the fate of the Cape Colony dwindled into insignificance.'[25] But Popham's expedition carried on, unaware as yet of what a seminal event had taken place off the Spanish coast.

Popham's original intention had been to put in at Rio de Janeiro and wait for favourable winds, but he changed his mind and opted for the Brazilian port of San Salvador instead, with Ross Donelly well on the way to St Helena. On 10 November Popham put in at San Salvador after a long, rough and costly trip. At times his ships had been becalmed, and at others beset by storms. Two of his East Indiamen, the *King George* and the *Britannia*, had run aground on reefs and gone down, while another transport had been so badly damaged that it could go no further. Only three men had been lost in the wrecks – although one was a brigadier-general – but the soldiers' pay went to the bottom and the survivors added to the existing over-crowding on the support ships.

An unusual feature of the expedition was that some of those involved in the journey were male and female civilian passengers travelling to India in one of the East Indiamen, the *Union*. Among them was a newly ordained clergyman called Henry Martyn. The tight discipline and general orderliness of the Royal Navy did not apply in a civilian ship like the *Union*, and his first contact with the rough-hewn

226

sailors and soldiers in the *Union* was a considerable shock for the gently reared and rather naïve young clergyman. His letters are now a primary reference source on the second invasion:

> The evening is a time of great idleness and noise on board, 'All are talking and laughing, the soldiers doing nothing but jeering one another and swearing. My ears are constantly assailed and shocked by the most horrid oaths, and I see no method of putting a stop to it, except by perseverence [*sic*] and preaching the gospel to them. Outward restrictions would help a little, but as the captain and officers on board sanction it by their own example no attempt can be made that way.[26]

Popham's squadron spent 20 days of comparative leisure at San Salvador, reprovisioning and holding regular musketry practice for the troops while Lieutenant-Colonel Robert Wilson scoured the surrounding area for troop horses and mules for drawing the artillery pieces. By dint of considerable ingenuity he managed to buy 30 horses – he actually needed 100 – but mules were scarce, and he could lay hands on only four.

On 28 November the fleet departed San Salvador on the last leg of the journey to the Cape. Baird was travelling with Popham in the *Diadem*, where they studied John Barrow's book about his travels in the Cape in 1797 and 1798, which contained much information of military value. One of the most valuable items, ironically, was a map Governor van de Graaff had had specially drawn in 1786, which not only detailed the Cape fortifications and gave soundings in Table Bay, but also indicated the best places for ships to anchor and troops to land.

Drawing on his extensive knowledge of the Cape, Baird had favoured the Blaauwberg coast even before leaving Britain: it was out of range of the heavy batteries defending the opposite shore of Table Bay, and at several points offered the attributes needed for landing a large force – an open bay with a beach, with water deep enough for Popham's ships to anchor reasonably close to shore.[27] However, they considered other spots as well.

By early December they had settled on the best possible landing place: Losperd's Bay, the site of today's hamlet of Melkbosstrand.[28] It provided a much safer close-in anchorage for ships than the coastline actually opposite the Blaauwberg mountain range, and 'the land suddenly trenches towards the eastward there,' as Popham wrote in a pre-planning memorandum, 'and forms a point to the southward to defend it from the natural surge or roll of the sea in that direction, owing to the prevailing winds from that quarter.'[29]

In essence their final plan called for Popham to anchor the main body of ships between Robben Island and Losperd's Bay. At least one of the two brigades into which Baird had divided the invasion force would land at Losperd's Bay; depending on circumstances the second brigade could land there as well – if so, he could later land his stores, heavy artillery and baggage at Rietvallei, which was nearer to Cape Town but still out of range of the Batavian guns. The Batavians had long ago identified Losperd's Bay as a good landing place, but had never had the resources to fortify it.

But Blaauwberg would come in useful as well. Baird's lack of horses remained a concern, because Col. Wilson had not been able to obtain many at San Salvador, and some of his purchases had died en route; he ordered Wilson to make a separate landing near Blaauwberg, probably at the site of today's Big Bay, as soon as possible and visit three farms in the vicinity in the hope of acquiring more mounts.

Having finalised their attack plan, Popham and Baird then made sure that all the ships' captains as well as the landing force's leader group were thoroughly briefed about what was to happen and the roles they were to play.

In the meantime tension mounted steadily at the Cape. Passing ships brought reports of Britain's intention to attack, and Janssens' last hopes of reinforcement were fading fast. In early November, too, his only potential naval asset vanished with the loss of the 44-gun *Atalante*, one of a new generation of heavily armed frigates the French were building.[30]

Under command of Captain Gaudin-Beauchêne,[31] *Atalante* had arrived at the Cape after a successful Indian Ocean cruise in consort with the *Belle Poule*, but on 3 November she was blown ashore while at anchor off the Cape. Although only one member of the ship's company drowned, the *Atalante* was so badly damaged that after being refloated she was written off as a total loss. Her guns, stores and some of her complement were loaded into the French privateer *Napoléon* for transport to Mauritius, and most of her officers and men were re-constituted as an infantry unit several hundred strong, a small but welcome addition to Janssens' forces.

This left Janssens – theoretically, at least – with just one combat ship at his disposal, the Batavian Republic's 74-gun *Bato*, which now lay anchored at Simon's Town. But the *Bato* was strictly a paper asset, because due to a total lack of essential stores she could not put to sea and thus was nothing more than a floating battery.

Later that month, too, Janssens' hopes of speedy reinforcement were finally extinguished when a request he had sent to Batavia in the Far East for troops and supplies elicited the reply that supplies could be sent, but it would be too expensive to send troops, and in any case the Batavian Republic's indigenous Asian soldiers were unwilling to serve so far from home.

He had also sent a personal representative, one R Dozij, direct to the Netherlands, but apart from a promise of more supplies the government could offer nothing more; the Cape must not be a burden on the homeland. And Popham was only a few weeks away.[32]

What neither Popham nor Janssens knew was that that very month, December 1805, a substantial French force of six ships of the line and two frigates under Contre-Amiral (Vice-Admiral) Jean-Baptiste Philibert Willaumez[33] – enough to inflict serious damage on the British expedition, or even defeat it altogether – had managed to break out from Brest and had sailed southwards to patrol the waters around the Cape and St Helena, although whether it would arrive on time was in the lap of the gods.

Christmas Day produced more disheartening news for Janssens: Donelly in the *Narcissus* had jumped the *Napoléon* at Olifantsbos, near Hout Bay, and driven her ashore (another story has it that the captain beached her rather than strike his flag to a British ship). Whatever the case, the ship was a wreck and a significant number of her company were lost; the survivors were incorporated into the *Atalante* unit.

Next day an American ship, the *Swanwick*, arrived and its captain reported that at Madeira he had heard that a British fleet had passed through with 8 000 men, probably bound for the Far East. Janssens knew better: the British ships' eventual destination might be India, but first they would force their unwelcome attentions on the Cape.

Given these tidings, Janssens made the logical assumption that the *Narcissus* must have support in the vicinity, and the Cape defences went on a high state of readiness. On 28 December a warning appeared in the *Kaapsche Courant*, warning military personnel, coast watchers, field cornets and landdrosts to be on the alert, and Janssens met with the Council of Policy to lay plans. A sense of foreboding gripped Cape Town – particularly at the Castle, where Janssens and his staff were gathered, as the first days of 1806 approached and then arrived.

On board Popham's ships Christmas was marred by the fact that Ross Donelly and the *Narcissus* had not effected the planned rendezvous. Still wary of unpleasant surprises, Popham sent Capt John King and the *Espoir* ahead to make a hasty reconnaissance of all the contemplated landing places. The *Espoir* headed off a neutral ship outside Table Bay and King obtained a valuable item of information, namely that although the Cape was on the alert and being prepared for an invasion it had not received any reinforcements.

On 3 January Popham sent *Leda* under Captain Robert Honeyman, to sail openly into Table Bay to reconnoitre, discover the strength of the non-existent Batavian naval force and then retire without wasting any time. In due course the *Leda* returned, to report that there was no sign of any naval activity around the Cape.

The winds remained favourable, and Popham pushed on. At 8am on 4 January, Janssens' western lookouts on Lion's Head and Vlaeberg (today's Signal Hill, previously known as the Lion's Haunch) reported that a large fleet was in sight. An hour later the lookout on Lion's Head confirmed the sighting. By 1.30pm the ships' royal-blue ensigns were clearly visible.

The arrival of Popham's fleet, Krynauw says, 'must have been an alarming and impressive spectacle for the Capetonians ... In Cape Town there was turmoil.'[34] One Capetonian later provided a graphic description of the scene:

> Officials and citizens gathered in the squares discussing the news. Those who were young and active at once scrambled up the height of Lion's Hill, and some of the more aged followed, blowing and dragging their stout corpuses up the steep acclivities. The spectacle which met their gaze was novel and astounding.
>
> The day was a warm summer one, and the air was as clear as those only who know our South African climate can conceive. Westward, whither all eyes were directed, the expanse of unruffled ocean was at intervals streaked with dazzling sunbeams, beyond which the strained vision of the observers descried a number of vessels, aided by a gentle but favourable breeze, standing in towards them.
>
> In a short time the nearest of the vessels was distinctly seen. They were large heavy ships with threatening broadsides, and their decks crowded with men, and the Union Jack floating from them told their nationality and their character. They were English warships.
>
> They approached the port perceptibly every minute, and gradually their number was seen to increase, as another and another came up on the horizon until a fleet of some sixty sail was in sight and could be plainly counted.

The balloon had now well and truly gone up.

CHAPTER 13

PRELUDE TO BATTLE

Janssens' innermost thoughts when the news reached him can only be guessed at. Krynauw speculates that 'the arrival of the English fleet must have been a form of relief, because it broke the tension in which he had been living for three years.'[1] Be that as it may, his carefully calculated defence plan kicked in without delay.

The orange-white-and-blue Prinsevlag, the Dutch battle flag since the days of the liberation war against the Spanish, was hoisted over the Castle, and the deep thudding of the signal guns began to march inland, raising the countryside to the furthest reaches of Batavian influence.

Despatch-riders set out in all directions, and Janssens sent reinforcements to coastal posts at Simon's Bay, Muizenberg and elsewhere. The two Dutch merchantmen at anchor in Table Bay were warned of the British approach, but they were trapped without hope of escape.[2] The local Burgher Militia commanders were summoned for immediate orders, and command of Cape Town was handed over to Janssens' subordinate, Lieutenant-Colonel CH von Prophalow. Militiamen – including the Javaansche Artillerie Corps – manned the Castle and other fortifications to free Janssens' army for mobile operations. By 5pm Popham's fleet was clearly visible, and by evening it was swinging at

anchor between Robben Island and Blaauwberg, out of range of the
coastal batteries, opposite the little farm of 10 *morgen* in extent (about
eight hectares) which had recently been granted to one Daniël Brink.

The bustling seaside town of Bloubergstrand covers the bones of
Brink's farm now, but in those days it consisted of little more than a few
fishermen's huts, Brink's modest home and a small permanent spring
with an overflow dam. The grant had been made with the specific aim
of promoting the fishing industry, but Capetonians also came visiting
to obtain firewood and seashells for their lime kilns. Nearby, on the
sandy plain, were two other farms, Blaauwbergsvlei, owned by Justinus
Keer, and François Duminy's Compagniesdam.

In the meantime the signal guns had reached out as far afield as
Swellendam and the burgher dragoons were mobilising, while scouts
were sent out to watch the British movements. 'The troops [were] im-
patient to land,' a Royal Marine officer named Richard Fernyhough
recalled later. 'We made our preparations for debarkation, fired guns
and hoisted English colours – a broad hint to the enemy of our errand
which was quickly taken, for the town appeared to be in great confusion. We saw a party of cavalry [Janssens' despatch-riders] riding in
various directions.'[3]

By 5 January, when Popham sent his sloops out to sniff round sundry
places along the coast, most of Janssens' army was in place and ready
at its assembly points, although many burgher light dragoons were still
on the way from the outmost reaches of the signal guns, about 240km
from Cape Town. But it was even thinner on the ground than it should
have been, for three main reasons. First, the alert system left little time
for mobilisation, and second, for the Burgher Militia it was, moreover,
the worst possible time of year for a call-up: they had just begun taking
in the harvest. Third, to make matters even worse, it was so devastat-
ingly hot that the burgher dragoons hurrying in from Swellendam and
beyond in response to the signal guns could only travel at night for fear
of killing their horses with exhaustion.

As yet, Janssens could not afford to put all his eggs in one basket, as
Baird's and Popham's plans were still unclear, and thanks to their ships
they had a range of tactics and landing places to choose from. As a
result he had to leave a substantial portion of his forces behind in Cape

Town under Von Prophalow's command. This meant that Janssens had just under 2 000 men to lead into battle.

These 2 000 included Dutchmen, Germans, Austrians, Hungarians, Frenchmen and local inhabitants of all races. There were 358 officers and men of the 22nd Batavia; the Waldeckers with 312 line fusiliers and an 82-man light company; the Hottentot Light Infantry, numbering 181 all ranks; 240 French sailors; 202 members of the Bataafsche Jagers; the 5th Artillery Battalion, 141 strong; 54 foot-gunners of the Javanese Artillery Corps; 138 regular Batavian dragoons; and Lieutenant Pellegrini with his 19 horse gunners. There were also 104 non-combatant auxiliaries such as drivers for the artillery ammunition wagons. Exactly how many burgher light dragoons had managed to reach Cape Town in time remains uncertain. There were certainly 224 from Swellendam, and a contingent from Stellenbosch.

His sole advantage over Baird's invasion force was that he had slightly more artillery, even after leaving some of his guns behind for Von Prophalow – two high-angle howitzers, six 6-pounders, two 3-pounders, and six 1-pounder field guns. He also had 13 ammunition wagons, at least some of which were presumably armoured mobile magazines like the one deployed at Muizenberg a decade earlier, so that he would have a better ammunition supply than Baird. In addition he had 530 horses, enough for all his purposes, while Baird, of course, had none except for his officers' chargers.

The 1-pounders listed might, though probably do not, refer to the unusual guns served by the 54 men of the Javanese Artillery Corps who had been redeployed from the coast batteries, where the bulk of their unit was stationed. In the absence of enough field pieces the Malay gunners were armed with a number of the light bronze swivel guns they called *lantakas* which were traditional boat weapons in Indonesia.[4]

Where the *lantakas* came from seems to have been long forgotten, since as far as is known they were not on the Batavian artillery inventory. A last-minute improvisation, they were mounted on big-wheeled field carriages which had been designed to retain their swivel capability, a great advantage on a fast-moving battlefield. It is possible that the JAC men ended up doing much of the pulling themselves; Krynauw says the corps had 106 auxiliary helpers, consisting (as one contemporary description had it) mainly of 'Moors, Malabarans and Bengalis' who had been commandeered from a captured British ship, and displayed so little stomach for the coming fight that when the first shots were fired they fled precipitately in all directions.[5]

Under Von Prophalow's command was a substantial portion of the Batavian forces, nominally 1 232 officers and men (in reality somewhat less, however, since this figure included those who were in hospital, in detention or stationed so far away that they were beyond immediate reach). These consisted of 380 Burgher Militia under a Captain Gie who were stationed at various fortifications; 68 auxiliary gunners under Captain CL Kendler at Camps Bay; 107 Kaapsche Jagers, or Cape light infantry, of the Burgher Militia, who were also helping to man the fortifications; another 309 auxiliary gunners; and 92 men who formed the bulk of the Javanese Artillery Corps in the batteries around Cape Town, Hout Bay, Simon's Town, Muizenberg and Steenberg.

Some of the French sailors from the *Atalante* were posted to the defences on the left flank of the Castle, namely the big stone-built Amsterdam and Chavonnes Batteries and the smaller earthworks at Three Anchor Bay and Camps Bay. The survivors of the *Napoléon* were also posted into the coastal defences – this kept the direct seaward approaches to Cape Town and the immediate flanking coastline down the Cape peninsula utterly impregnable.

A patrol of Swellendam light dragoons under the capable Ritmeester Jacobus Linde was sent off to Blaauwberg to keep an eye on the British, while another element of light dragoons from Stellenbosch was held at the ready at the foot of the Tijgerberg, (later 'Tygerberg') 15km from Cape Town. Linde's orders were specific – to observe enemy strengths and actions, then come back to report – and Janssens had no doubts that the dragoons would do just that.

Linde was a prosperous farmer then aged 46, and by far the best of the dragoon commanders. Small in body but strong in personality and fiery in spirit, he was not averse to laying his sjambok whip over the backs of his troops if they did not carry out their orders properly. He had already served with gallantry in three minor military campaigns and had been on good terms with Janssens since accompanying him on his visit to the frontier in 1803. He had been involved in Janssens' inland preparations and by now was the *veldcommandant* for the Swellendam area.[6]

Feverish preparations were set in motion. Extra musket balls were cast, and vehicles and draught animals were assembled; in the batteries Von Prophalow's gunners readied their artillery pieces and started stoking the shot-ovens.

❧

In the British ships, where the Batavians' likely reaction to their arrival was still uncertain, similar preparations were made to land and, if necessary, go immediately on the offensive. Baird was keen to get ashore as soon as possible, because he was still concerned about an intervention by the French warships, reported so many weeks earlier. Although he and Popham had agreed on Losperd's Bay, at two o'clock next morning most of Brigadier-General Beresford's 1st Brigade – the 38th, 83rd and 59th Regiments – was despatched to hit what is now Blaauwberg's Big Bay beach with HMS *Espoir* in support. Meanwhile his 24th Regiment with HMS *Lydia* set off to make feint landings at Hout Bay and Camps Bay, to draw Janssens' forces away.

The reasons why Baird and Popham changed their minds and picked Big Bay are easy to identify if one looks at the topography and considers the British priorities. At that stage Baird still believed that Janssens had 5 000 men available, most of them mounted, with 23 pieces of horse artillery (which meant that he was about as wrong as he could be). But the burning question was whether the Batavians had ensconced themselves on the Blaauwberg heights.

As mountains go, the Blaauwberg[7] did not compare with others at the Cape, but it was the only high terrain in the area, and did not lend itself to an assault; the slopes of both Grootberg and Kleinberg, which make up the Blaauwberg, were steep and strewn with loose stones, the last thing an assault force needed when attacking uphill. Traversing the *nek* or pass between the low *kopje* peaks would not be difficult in itself, but if occupied by the Batavian artillery or infantry or both, a storm of close-range fire could be brought down on the British troops. Taking the Blaauwberg by storm might therefore turn out to be an expensive exercise, in both blood and time. But a landing at Big Bay would out-flank the Blaauwberg altogether. In addition, the beach was the only place in the vicinity that was fairly free of reefs, which would make it easier for assault boats to land and would allow the warships to anchor close to shore.

However, the beach had disadvantages: it was long and open, so that the surf tended to come up with such force that landing boats there was difficult even when the sea was calm, and positively dangerous when it was not. In addition it was backed by rows of loose white dunes which presented a formidable natural obstacle for soldiers in full equipment. But Blaauwberg it was, and the 1st Brigade took to its boats that night, and made for the beaches.

Table Bay, whose treacherous weather and waters had brought so many ships to grief, decided at this moment to make its presence felt. A south-easter came up and the calm seas of the previous days turned angry; the surf crashed down so furiously on the beach that Beresford gave up all hope of landing at Big Bay and instead sent his boatloads of soldiers – no doubt well-soaked by now – through the moonlight a few kilometres up the coast to Losperd's Bay, the original target settled upon by Baird and Popham, with the *Espoir* going on ahead to recon-noitre.[8]

Although it afforded some protection from the south-easter, and Popham's ships could anchor close enough to shore to provide ad-equate covering fire for the landings, it was so small and littered with reefs and banks of seaweed that only two boats would be able to enter at a time. HMS *Espoir* anchored just over a kilometre from the beach, acting as a floating assembly point for the boats. But here, too, the surf was so rough that an immediate landing was patently out of the ques-tion.

Watched with interest by Linde's dragoons from a dune barely a musket-shot away, the British gave up and spent what remained of the day reconnoitring the Table Bay coast almost within range of the out-lying batteries. A spot near Rietvallei, today's Witsand, was considered, but this was also discarded – the surf was just as bad, and the bottom shallowed so rapidly near the shore that the ships would have had to keep their distance or run aground.

That evening Baird and Popham considered their options and concluded that landing anywhere in Table Bay would be impossible *pro tem*; this being the case, they decided that next day, 6 January, Brigadier-General Beresford must take the 38th Regiment and elements of the 20th Light Dragoons to Saldanha Bay in nine support ships under the protection of HMS *Diomede* and HMS *Espoir*. They would capture the Batavian outpost there and try to acquire cattle and more horses. If the sea in Table Bay did not abate, the rest of the task force would follow on 7 January.

Saldanha Bay was anything but an ideal alternative. It had a wonderfully safe natural harbour, with a lagoon which was well suited for unloading both troops and horses, but it lay a long, dry 90km trek from Cape Town, during which time the invaders would be unable to communicate with the *Diomede*, and all chances of stealing a march on Janssens would be lost.

But the need for urgency outweighed these disadvantages, and Baird knew that about 30km from Saldanha was the outpost of Theefontein (in the present-day Hopefield district), owned by Oloff Bergh and Jan van Reenen, a magnificent farm which was known to have ample water, grain, horses and cattle. Furthermore, it would make a good resupply point for Beresford on his trek to Cape Town, and its capture would threaten the Roodezand Pass near Tulbagh, which gave access to the interior.

After Beresford's departure on 6 January, however, the ever-fickle Cape weather changed once again, this time to the advantage of the task force. The wind abated and the sea calmed. Baird, Popham and their staff decided to risk a landing at Losperd's Bay after all, to be spearheaded by Brigadier-General Ferguson's 2nd Brigade, consisting of three Scots regiments, the 71st, 72nd and 93rd.

Ferguson personally reconnoitred the bay in HMS *Diadem* and designated a narrow landing corridor, which was then marked with beacons. Popham also ordered that one of his smaller support vessels – a little brig that drew only six feet of water – be beached to act as a breakwater for the boats when they reached land. The 38th Regiment's infantrymen swarmed into the support ships' boats while the *Diadem, Leda, Encounter* and later the *Protector* stood close in, rolling and tittupping in the rough seas, to provide covering fire if needed.

At 12.30pm Ferguson was satisfied with the preparations and signalled from HMS *Encounter* that the landing could commence. By now the British soldiers' and sailors' blood was well and truly up, and their eagerness to get ashore first resulted in a grievous loss before so much as a single shot had been fired: 'The joy that was manifest in the countenance of every officer,' Popham later said in his report to the Admiralty, 'heightened the characteristic ardour of the troops, and under an anxiety probably to be the first on shore, induced them to urge the boats to extend their line of beach further than was prudent, and occasioned the loss of one boat of the 93rd Regiment.'[9]

Major John Graham of the 93rd later provided his own description:

> We had unfortunately to make a turn to the right in order to evade a sunken rock, then from the swell of the wind, the boats unavoidably got into such a crowd that many of the turning boats could make no use of their oars. We were not then half a common shot from the beach or sand hills. Had the enemy had a couple of guns, we must have lost a vast number of men – every shot must have told.
>
> As the leading boats got within half musket shot, about 100 yagers threw themselves into the bushes and kept popping away until the 71st Light Company landed. They very soon made them scamper away from the first ridge of sand hills to the second ... one of the boats from the Charlotte had been unable to push to windward of the rock abovementioned, she touched it, instantly turned bottom up, and down went 36 of our brave fellows [of the 93rd] cheering as they sank.[10]

The '100 yagers' were, of course, Linde's burgher dragoons.[11] The dragoons wounded three men of the 71st, one of them mortally, and then hastily retreated in accordance with their orders, pursued by elements of the 72nd Regiment as well as the light companies[12] of the 71st and the 93rd, which according to Major Graham, in a boat by himself, had 'contrived ... to get ashore,'[13] in an apparent contravention of the order of landing.

Whether the dragoons were under fire from the ships as well as the Highlanders' muskets is unclear, but whatever the case they reportedly suffered two dead, three wounded and three missing in action. They had achieved their primary aim, however, and Linde sent them back to Rietvallei to report to Janssens, while he and a Lieutenant Albertus of the Burgher Militia light troops stayed behind to keep the British under observation.

The three missing dragoons were captured by the British and according to Robert Fernyhough 'informed us that their main body consisting of about five thousand men including Hottentots, were encamped behind the mountains six or seven miles off and intended to give us battle next morning.'[14] Whether this exaggerated claim about the Batavian strength resulted from ignorance or was a deliberate attempt at disinformation will never be known, but it cannot have done anything for Baird's peace of mind.

The light Batavian resistance at this stage has often been remarked upon, but as Krynauw points out, the rough weather actually benefitted the British, in that they themselves had not known where to land until the last moment, and Erasmus comments that 'the [Batavians] did not expect another attempted landing here [Losperd's Bay] because the first attempts had failed, and also because the group that departed to Saldanha Bay had been clearly seen by them.'[15]

Janssens did not fool himself about his chances of victory, although the full burden of his hopeless situation he shared only with two of his most trusted staff officers. The threat of naval bombardment loomed over every possible scenario. In addition, Erasmus says, Janssens was still not positive as to Baird's and Popham's intentions, the Blaauwberg landing notwithstanding. This, too, is understandable when one considers his circumstances. He did not know how many troops the British had brought in the massive fleet, now riding at anchor between Robben Island and the later Big Bay; for all he knew, Baird had enough men at his disposal – and he certainly had the vessels to carry them – for a simultaneous landing elsewhere in Table Bay.

By now Janssens himself was well on the way to the Blaauwberg. He had already appointed RA de Salis of the Political Council as acting governor, and within an hour of receiving confirmation that the British were indeed landing at Losperd's Bay his little army was on the march from its assembly area at Papendorp (today's Woodstock). It passed Paarden Island, forded the drift at Jan Biesjeskraal, where the Diep River (then called the Great Salt River) ran into the sea, and finally stopped at Rietvallei, where he set up camp for the night. There Linde's dragoons briefed him on what was happening at Losperd's Bay.

Baird's men spent all of 7 January battling with the rough seas and crashing surf to ferry ashore the rest of his troops, artillery pieces, stores, equipment and ammunition, as well as some Royal Marines and about 500 seamen who had volunteered to drag the guns. It was not only arduous but personally perilous; Popham nearly lost his life in the process, and Baird later remarked that the circumstances were so difficult that only British seamen could have made the landing possible.

Perhaps Popham was a 'lucky man', as Napoleon had mistakenly considered Villeneuve to be; as Erasmus notes: 'The British had picked the moment of landing very fortunately and advantageously, because the weather in this season had previously been regarded as a safety measure for the colony against similar enterprises in this regard. For various days after this a landing on this coast, from Saldanha to Cape Town, would normally have been impossible.'[16]

Landing operations continued into the midsummer twilight until an increase in the surf's ferocity led to Baird calling a halt at 8pm. There was a small spring close by the house, but apart from yielding brackish water which was anything but pleasant to drink, it was not enough to satisfy the needs of the large number of troops already on land, and wells were sunk all along the shoreline; these supplied some water at a depth of three or four feet, but still not enough of it, and digging parties fanned out inland.

To supplement their supplies of food the British, as Krynauw comments drily, 'went over to the proven military usage of confiscation and plundering at the farms in the vicinity'[17] – in spite of the fact that before their arrival Baird, mindful of the importance of gaining the cooperation of the Cape's inhabitants, had forbidden any looting and required that receipts were to be given if any inhabitants' possessions needed to be confiscated. 'But,' as Krynauw notes, 'to enforce these orders against plundering was not so easy.'[18]

The first victim was Christiaan Brand, who had fled when the landing commenced, leaving everything behind. At De Melkbosch a small group of soldiers – 'exuberant after spending many months cooped up on the ships at sea … virtually ran amok,' Krynauw notes, 'engaging in an orgy of destruction that left the aged farmer destitute and homeless.'[19] Krynauw quotes from the claim for damages that Brand later lodged (and which was paid out after Janssens himself interceded with Baird):

That on the 6th of last month January, when the English troops had been landing at Blue Mounts, a great many of them overwhelming his habitation, destroyed all his goods, they broke open his press and carried away all his raiments, crushed his precious clock, violently opened his desk, dashed in pieces four chests and carried away all his books and written papers, amongst which was a valuable Bible with copperplates, they broke open his storehouse and burnt his corn loft, the plough, the harrow, the readymade door and window casements, the beams, the caskets and the oxen wagon, they dashed to pieces two new bedsteads made of yali wood.

They destroyed all the kitchen tackling as well as a chest of carpenter's tools and a hundred sacks of lime. They then burnt eight hundred sheaves of corn, they furiously ran to the fish house and either took away or cut to pieces all the caskes [sic] of salted fish, as well as a large saine of 85 fathoms long. Besides yet, they carried off two boats and even the cutter called *Netherland-Africa*, which lays now here in Table Bay.[20]

Jan Mostert, whose farm 'Blaauwberg' (originally 'De Rustplaats') was only a short distance from Losperd's Bay on the slopes of the Blaauwberg, was the next to suffer. He possessed a dam at which the desperate redcoats could slake their thirst, but that did not stop them from running amok as well in spite of their officers' best efforts to keep them under control, and as Mostert later testified, they 'nevertheless ruined and partly carried away the greatest part of his furniture, utensils, poultry etc. to the amount of 685 rixds. at the most moderate calculation ...'[21]

At Olifantskop, a little further on, farmer Jan Munnik tried to avoid being plundered by doing his best to be cooperative and supply the soldiers' wants, but 'to his sorrow they did not only destroy the greatest part of his stock of provisions but even ruined and took away most of his furniture to the amount of 250 rixds. at the most reasonable and conservative calculation.'[22] From there the soldiers went on to one D Verwey's farm Brakkekuil, where they wrought more devastation, as well as at several other places.

The only positive aspect of these depredations – at least from the British point of view – is that, as Krynauw points out, 'these visits helped the invaders over their first obstacles and [so] they did not suffer from lack of food at Losperd's Bay.'[23]

In Cape Town, meanwhile, Colonel von Prophalow found himself faced with a desertion problem of a most unusual kind. The French *Atalante* crewmen, deployed in the batteries facing the roadstead, were full of fight and not happy about being left out of the coming battle, the result being that a number of them deserted their posts, not to run away but to join their shipmates in Janssens' army. In contrast, the survivors of the privateer *Napoléon* were happy to stay put; they had got their hands on liquor and were soon so drunk that they were nothing more than another burden on Von Prophalow's heavily laden shoulders.

His larger burden, though, was the desertion of the *Atalante* men, laudable though their intentions might have been. Thanks to Baird's feint attacks there appeared to be a very real possibility of a landing at Camps Bay or Hout Bay, so Von Prophalow was forced to rob the fortifications west of the Castle to replace the Frenchmen with some of his burgher militia.

Next morning the British landings continued, while at the same time Janssens began to advance cautiously but determinedly towards the Blaauwberg, leaving his wagons and ambulance behind at Rietvallei under Ritmeester Jan van Reenen of the burgher dragoons. Linde's dragoons were sent forward again to observe the enemy, and that afternoon the main body followed in extended line.

His left flank was made up of two companies of the Hottentot Light Infantry in the dunes near the sea, then the Bataafsche Jagers to their right, then more burgher light dragoons under Commandant Willem Wium. His centre comprised the 22nd Batavia, the French sailors under Captain Gaudin-Beauchêne and his massed artillery, while the right wing consisted of his Batavian Dragoons squadron, the dragoons' horse artillery troop, the Waldeck Regiment's light company and a detachment of burgher dragoons under Commandant Human. Where the Waldeck line infantry were at this stage, as Erasmus points out, is obscure, but presumably they were somewhere in the centre. The fact that Janssens advanced in extended line – essentially a battle formation – rather than in column indicates that he was prepared to fight at short notice.

At 9am Janssens took his senior staff officers on a personal reconnaissance, and estimated that so far 600 invading troops had already landed and were setting up under the protection of the ships' guns. On his return he received word from Lieutenant Klapp at Saldanha Bay that Beresford had landed there. He sent a message back that Klapp was to retire, if necessary all the way to Stellenbosch, but to keep the enemy under observation.

At this stage the British did not know that Janssens was advancing on them, and that night the warships laid down an intense bombardment on Rietvallei. But of course their bird had flown, and Ritmeester van Reenen managed to move the wagon park and ambulance out of harm's way (the bombardment continued into the next day, and its intensity can be judged from the fact that it could be heard as far away as Tulbagh, 125km from Cape Town).

At Justinus Keer's farm, Blaauwbergsvlei, Janssens called a halt for the night and held a final order group. Here it was decided to go into the attack the following morning before Beresford arrived back from

Saldanha Bay with the remainder of his force. Janssens sent a despatch to Von Prophalow at the Castle, informing him of the impending attack and confirming that if forced to he would fall back over the Hottentots Holland mountains to Swellendam; if this happened, Von Prophalow must send him all available horses and wagons.

Janssens was confident that his outlying piquets would provide ample warning of any British movements, and he was proved correct, although at midnight there was an outburst of musket fire from one of the foremost positions occupied by the Hottentot Light Infantry in the dunes; this generated an immediate rumour that the British were attacking. Janssens sent out Ritmeester Linde with a small party of dragoons, and they returned to report that it was a false alarm, the culprit being a Batavian sergeant stationed with the light infantry who had got drunk and succumbed to pre-battle nerves.

Beresford did not pose any immediate threat. Earlier that day, while Baird's main force had been battling the surf at Losperd's Bay, strong winds had propelled Beresford into Saldanha Bay, whose resident garrison consisted of no more than Lieutenant Klapp, 15 soldiers and a solitary artillery piece. The British had no idea of how many or how few defenders there were, so Captain King and an engineer officer went ashore with a view to discovering the strength of the defence element and possibly also to negotiate with the post-holder, JC Stofberg (in accordance with Baird's original instructions to talk first and only fight if that failed).

This proved a futile enterprise, because Stofberg and Klapp were in no mood simply to surrender. From the signal station on the Postberg opposite Langebaan (today's Oude Post), Klapp opened fire with his gun and scored a direct hit on the boat. King sensibly abandoned his mission and beat a hasty retreat. So did Klapp and Stofberg, but in the opposite direction.

Since negotiations were obviously not an option, Beresford now prepared to land Lieutenant-Colonel Wilson with 300 infantrymen and 50 light dragoons for a rapid advance on Theefontein. But the wind had strengthened to gale force in the interim, and the ships could not proceed into the lagoon. Instead – having been informed (correctly) by an officer from an American ship which happened to be in the bay that Klapp had retreated along with Stofberg and all other local inhabitants and their livestock – Beresford ordered Wilson to get ashore by boat along the open bay.

It proved to be a difficult and exasperating task. The infantry waded ashore, up to their waists in the water, but the boats carrying Wilson's precious San Salvadorian horses could not get close in. The only ex-pedient was to bring the boats as near to the shore as possible, secure them with grapnels and push the horses overboard to swim ashore. This worked, but in the process three were lost. A relatively small force of Batavian dragoons with a couple of light guns would have done seri-ous damage to Wilson's men at this moment of maximum weakness, but Janssens' cupboard was bare, and Wilson was able to get his entire force onto dry land unhindered by late afternoon.

There was no question of a breathing space, however, and at 5pm they set out for Theefontein under the guidance of a dragoon sergeant who had been stationed in the area during the first British occupation. It was hard going, and 'the ground being covered with thick and high brushwood, the infantry suffered much,'[24] Wilson later recorded, so that by midnight most of the foot-soldiers had clearly reached the end of their tether. Wilson told them to bed down for a few hours while he went ahead with his dragoons and about 80 infantrymen who still retained some energy.

Wilson's dragoons and remaining infantrymen slogged on through the first two hours of 8 January and then reached some dwellings, where 'a Hottentot came out, who, upon my asking him where the cattle and horses were, undertook to guide me to his master. I went on with twenty dragoons a league and came to a large farm; here I found a team of noble bullocks,' he reported later. 'Fourteen, but only one horse. The farmer hid himself as I learnt afterwards in a wheat stack, but his wife, a delicate, pleasing woman, remained: I did my best to calm her fears, giving a receipt for the wagon, oxen and Hottentots.'[25]

That was the good news. The bad news, as Wilson found to his dis-may, was that his less-than-expert guide had taken him on the wrong road, and that he would have to backtrack for 21km. Grimly he set off to retrace his footsteps, consumed with the urgency of his mission, not knowing that his effort was already irrelevant because the final act in the great drama was about to commence at Blaauwberg.

CHAPTER 14

'A MOST TREMENDOUS FIRE'

All this activity, spread over an area covering hundreds of square kilometres, began moving rapidly to a conclusion on the morning of 8 January – a day that would see the only full-scale battle to be fought in the European style in the history of sub-Saharan Africa.

By 3am, as Wilson was busy confiscating the oxen and wagon near Saldanha Bay, the Batavian troops at Blaauwberg were up and ready to advance. Janssens ordered his regimental commanders forward to the spot where he had made his observations the previous day. From there they could acquaint themselves with the latest British dispositions and the general lie of the land. With them would go a French naval officer named Captain Richard, who had voluntarily attached himself to Janssens' staff, to assess the bombardment capabilities of the British warships.

But before they could set off, one of Ritmeester Linde's dragoons galloped up to report that the British were already advancing. This was no less than the truth. Baird had got off to an even earlier start and was well on his way to the Blaauwberg. Janssens knew that there would be no more movement forward: the time had come to stand and fight. He reshuffled his force into the battle formation he had concluded would work best with what he had at his disposal.

His reading of the enemy's most likely course of action was that they would not want to stray far from the protection of the ships' guns, and would therefore be concentrated in the area between the coast and the western aspect of Grootberg's north-eastern feature. Somehow he would have to cover this entire front to prevent Baird from launching an attack on either the left or right flank – a particular danger in those days of relatively inflexible linear battlefield formations. The only way to do this would be to deploy his troops in a line, stretching from Justinus Keer's farmyard to Kleinberg. This would give Baird the impression that the entire British front was covered; and, all going well, Janssens' left flank would be able to delay the British right long enough to allow his right flank to swing around and attack Baird's left.

It was a great deal of territory to cover with the inadequate manpower available from his under-strength units.[1] On the extreme right of his line he posted his 138-man Batavian Dragoon squadron with its troop of horse gunners under Lieutenant Pellegrini. Next were the fast-moving and specially-equipped light infantry, the Bataafsche Jagers,[2] with two howitzers and three 6-pounders manned by the field gunners of the 5th Artillery Battalion. These elements had one thing in common: mobility, exactly what was needed to loop swiftly around the British left and attack its flank, its most vulnerable point.

The all-important centre of Janssens' line, the component which would take the main shock of a frontal attack, was made up of the 22nd Batavia, followed by the French naval contingent, and then the Regiment Waldeck's three fusilier companies. Janssens' left consisted of sharp-shooting mobile horse and foot troops: the Hottentot Light Infantry, the Javanese Artillery Corps, with its *lantakas*, the Waldecker light company, and finally the burgher dragoon companies of Ritmeesters Linde, Human and Wium.

It was customary for the infantry to go into battle in close order, not only to maintain cohesion amid the smoke and confusion of the battlefield, but also to repel cavalry; similarly, regiments were grouped in close proximity to one another because of the danger that a unit's flank could be turned by a sudden cavalry charge. But on this day, Janssens could not afford such luxuries.

The individual infantry in his single line were in open rather than the customary close order, and the regiments were separated by gaps that were, in his own words, 'sorely large', which Janssens considered an acceptable risk because the British had no mounted troops to speak of. But there was no way of filling the yawning gulf between Kleinberg and the dragoon companies.

Janssens addressed this problem by despatching Linde and Human with some of their burgher dragoons to occupy Kleinberg (the number is not known, but the presence of two ritmeesters implies the same number of companies), and deployed two field-pieces of the 5th Artillery on its lower inland slopes; this would provide maximum flexibility in covering the gap between Kleinberg and the rest of the Batavian army. On the seaward side of Kleinberg he deployed 50 sharpshooters – 20 Bataafsche Jagers and 30 men of the Hottentot Light Infantry – to provide early warning in case of a flanking movement by the British and skirmish if it took place.

Baird had, however, considered the nature of the terrain, accurately deduced Janssens' limited options and deployed his forces accordingly. His right was the 1st Brigade, consisting of the 24th, 59th and 83rd Regiments and commanded in Beresford's absence by his brother, Lieutenant-Colonel Joseph Baird. His left was Brigadier-General Ferguson's 2nd or 'Highland Brigade' with its three regiments of veteran Scots, the 71st, 72nd and 93rd, and all his sailor-drawn guns. The plan was to advance more or less side by side up the Blaauwberg, the 1st Brigade crossing over the *nek* east (or inland) of Grootberg and the Highland Brigade further east across Jan Mostert's Blaauwberg farm. Once they had come over the crest they would spread out in an extended line stretching from Mostert's land all the way to Grootberg's eastern slope.

It was a classic battle plan, a straightforward advance to contact along a single axis, which made it easier to move in good order and yet – since at this stage Baird did not yet know exactly where and how the Batavians were deployed – still allowed for flexibility when contact was made. In all Baird disposed over 4 000 troops, not including 500 Royal Marines drawn from the various warships and about 500 sailors armed with boarding pikes to haul the eight guns. In reserve on Popham's ships were more marines, for whom another task awaited.

Actually advancing was easier said than done, particularly for troops who were out of condition after several months at sea. Major John Graham of the 93rd Regiment later graphically recorded: 'It is impossible to give an idea of the difficulty of march on the ground over which we had to go, the great irregularity of the surface, the deepest sand I ever saw, and the whole covered with almost impenetrable brushwood.'[3] This was still in the cool of the early morning; they had yet to suffer the brutal January heat.

The British evidently moved faster than Janssens had expected, so that at 4am he was astonished to see the 1st Brigade coming over the inland shoulder of Grootberg. The soldiers and sailors of the 1st Brigade, no doubt breathless after 6km of desperate effort, were equally surprised on cresting the Blaauwberg to find the Batavian army not only drawn up in battle formation on the plain below them but actually cheering.

What they did not know was that the cheering was not an example of the customary pre-battle braggadocio of those days but the response of Janssens' troops as he rode down his line, urging his soldiers to make their best effort. He was aware of the fact that the three Waldecker fusilier companies' cheering was noticeably less enthusiastic than the others, but being preoccupied with his other concerns, the significance did not sink in, and, Erasmus says, he 'still cherished the highest of hopes for them.'[4] It was now almost 5am, and light enough for the battle which would shape the future not only of the Cape of Good Hope, but all of what later became South Africa.

The field artillery of both sides, placed out in front of the troops, opened fire long before the infantry were within effective musket-range of each other. Who fired first is not certain. Some say it was Baird, but it must have been the Batavians, whose guns were already in place and cleared for action. One of the eyewitness accounts, from Captain Dugald Carmichael of the Highland Brigade, is quite specific on this point:

> When we arrived on the crest of the hill we perceived the enemy drawn up on the other side. Our disposition was soon made. We formed in echelons of brigades; the left or the Highland brigade being about 200 yards in advance of the other.

> In this relative position we advanced sometimes in line, at others
> in file from the heads of companies, according to the nature of the
> ground. We no sooner arrived within range of the enemy's artillery
> than he opened fire on us from 22 field pieces.[5]

Whatever the case, the battlefield was soon wreathed in clouds of gunsmoke as the artillerymen on both sides fired repeatedly.[6] The gunners
were now working like automatons, sponging the barrels, ramming,
loading, firing – and soon the cannons' thunderous barking expanded
into an almost continuous roar in the face of which men's voices became puny things. On board the East Indiaman *Union* an awestruck
Rev Henry Martyn could hear 'a most tremendous fire of artillery ...
behind a mountain abreast of the ships. It seemed as if the mountain
itself was torn by intestine convulsions.'[7]

Down on the plain the thin blue-coated line of Batavian infantry,
gunners and sailors braced themselves as the round shot began to land
around them, while opposite the two British brigades poured like a
remorseless red tide down the southern slope of the Blaauwberg, the
men forcing their way through the *fynbos* scrub, directed by officers on
their chargers with swords drawn, and all the while the bagpipes of the
Highland Brigade screamed the ancient war songs of faraway Scotland.

Standing fast in the face of a cannonade, upright and vulnerable
while the enemy's round shot dismembers the man next to you, was
probably the greatest test of discipline in Napoleonic-era armies with
their linear battle formations and almost ritualistic tactics. But the
Batavian line held, although early signs of trouble became visible when
some of the first British artillery rounds landed among the Waldecker
fusiliers and caused 'more sensation' in their ranks, as Janssens later
reported, than he had expected.

It is tempting to speculate about whether the Waldeckers were deliberately targeted because Baird knew about their poor state of morale – it is certainly the case that they could easily be identified by
the distinctive yellow facings on their uniforms – although this seems
unlikely; the centre of the Batavian line would be likely to receive the
most attention in any case. Be that as it may, it had a serious effect on
the Waldeckers' already flagging enthusiasm.

Baird's first move was to detach the 24th Regiment's flank companies and throw them at Kleinberg with its small garrison of Swellendam
dragoons. The dragoons were ready for them. Part-time soldiers they
might have been, these farmers, hunters, artisans and shopkeepers, but
they were led by first-class officers – particularly Linde – and they were
well trained, many had seen action of some kind before and most tended to be above-average shots with the long-barrelled muskets which
were so vastly superior in range and accuracy to the stubby little car-
bines customarily issued to mounted troops.

The results were soon to be seen. The 24th companies advanced
stolidly towards Kleinberg, bayonets fixed, and the dragoons fired, re-
loaded and fired again, the British ranks simply closing in as men were
bowled over by the burgher dragoons' big round lead bullets. But the
end was inevitable, especially after the 24th Regiment's flank companies were reinforced. Major Graham of the 93rd Regiment wrote later:

Sir David ... ordered me to advance down the hill a little to cover the
formation of our line. The Light Battalion was about 1/4 of a mile in
front of them ... I observed 20 or 30 of the enemy's mounted riflemen gallop out from their left towards [Kleinberg].

I was well aware what the consequence of such fellows being opposed to anything but light troops would be, and immediately ordered
the Light Company of the 24th to go as fast as possible, and throw
themselves into the bushes, without firing, thinking to cut them off.
As soon as the 24th Light Company began to fire to their right, from
the hiding place they had been in, the enemy began with his cannon
upon them. By this time, the sharpshooters on top were bringing
down the 24th Grenadiers with every shot.

I then saw some more of the mounted riflemen apparently inclined to go and support their friends, on which I took the 71st Light
Company also towards the ground between the hill and the enemy's
left.

Here they had fine cracking at us with their guns, and these guns
were so much in advance that I was determined to try and take them,
and so made a signal for the rest of the battalion to follow, thinking
to draw them up and give them a little breath at the bottom of the hill

and have a dash at the two guns: during my manoeuvre the line was advancing at an astonishing rate down upon the enemy.

The whole of the enemy's artillery now opened upon our line, and immediately afterwards ours returned the compliment. One of the 24th Light Company shot a rifleman, who seeing the different mode of fighting from that which the Grenadiers adopted were now making the best of their way off, they hardly waited to fire a shot at us. As soon as the order was given to charge, how Mynheer did run to be sure![8]

But 'Mynheer' ran for a reason. The dragoons were now grossly outnumbered, and in any case the 'last man, last round' concept had no place in either Janssens' philosophy or his overall battle plan. Linde withdrew his men,[9] according to one Swellendam local historian, LL Tomlinson: 'Commandant Linde ordered his men to stop when they came across a herd of cattle in the dunes [and] from this cover the charging soldiers were stopped one last time,'[10] and they rejoined the seaward end of the Batavian line, having suffered some losses of their own and in return inflicted a number of casualties on the 24th Regiment.[11]

So far the Batavian line had not fired a shot, and for a very good reason. Several hundred metres still separated the antagonists, and Janssens knew perfectly well that the smoothbore muskets of those days were not to be trusted for effective fire over 100m. What he intended to do was wait until the British had approached well within effective musket range and then, as he later described it, 'loose a murderous general discharge from our side.'

But all this time Baird had the Highland Brigade bearing down on the Batavian line. At 250 yards the Batavians fired a hopelessly premature volley (supposedly because of a misunderstood order) and another at about 150 yards. Neither achieved anything. But soon the Highlanders were within effective range, and clouds of white gunsmoke bloomed out in front of the Batavian line as its soldiers started firing.[12]

On board the East Indiaman *Union*, Henry Martyn saw how 'the smoke arose from a lesser eminence on the right of the hill and on top of it troops were seen marching down its further declivity. Then came such a long drawn fire of musketry that I could not conceive anything like it. We all shuddered at considering what a multitude of souls must be passing into eternity.'[13]

If Martyn had been on the battlefield itself he would have done more than shudder. The once-peaceful plain had erupted in an orgy of controlled violence on a scale never before seen at the toe of Africa. Artillery pieces boomed, muskets rattled off individual shots or roared in volleys. Wounded men and horses screamed as they wallowed in their own blood, officers and sergeants shouted orders in voices hoarse with thirst, torrents of sweat turning their powder-stained faces into devils' masks. Drums rattled, Highland bagpipes screeched eerily, overlaying frenzied cries in Dutch, English, French, Gaelic, German, Hungarian and the local dialect that would later be called Afrikaans. Everywhere lay the dead and wounded, some in the red coats of Imperial Britain, others in the dark blue of the Batavian Republic.

Janssens was no armchair general, and as the fighting started in all earnest he was in the thick of it out in front of the Batavian line, a position of the utmost peril. Around him clustered his staff officers; his orders were calmly received ('as if on parade', Lourens Erasmus notes[14]) and rapidly and clearly passed on to the regiments. Janssens was concerned that they were placing themselves unnecessarily at risk, but 'no-one was willing to stand away and thus give the impression that he wished to diminish the danger to himself,'[15] Erasmus says. Miraculously, none of them suffered injury, although Captain Richard's horse was killed under him.

At 60 metres Ferguson ordered the Highlanders to fix bayonets, and they moved unflinchingly forward in spite of everything that was now being thrown at them by the Batavians. 'The Highland brigade ... advanced with the steadiest step under a very heavy fire of round-shot, grape and musketry,' Baird reported afterwards.

> Nothing could surpass or resist the determined bravery of the troops, headed by their gallant leader, Brigadier-General Ferguson; and the

number of the enemy, who swarmed the plain, served only to augment their ardour, and confirm their discipline.

The enemy received our fire and maintained his position obstinately; but in the moment of charging, the valour of British troops bore down all opposition, and forced him to a precipitate retreat.[16]

The primary cause of the retreat, however, was the sudden collapse of the Waldeckers' three fusilier companies, a key component of Janssens' centre. They had been badly shaken when some of the first shots fired by the British howitzers had landed among them; now more arrived among them, and what was left of their fighting spirit abruptly evaporated – especially with the oncoming forest of Highlander bayonets twinkling in the morning sun. Janssens was just about to give the order for his carefully calculated 'murderous general discharge' when these troops, in which he had vested so much trust, turned around and ran.

Janssens threw himself in among them, reminding them of the fame of their regiment and the honour of Germany and the Prince of Waldeck, calling on their honour as soldiers (according to Wilson, he also beat the commanding officer with the flat of his sword and dropped one of the soldiers with a pistol bullet in the head). But it was all in vain: in spite of the efforts of their officers to stem their flight the Waldecker fusiliers 'fled shamefully', as Janssens later said.

Fearing that he would be borne away by the sheer pressure of the fleeing mob, Janssens abandoned the Waldeckers and galloped over to the French contingent, which was standing fast. While there he noticed to his dismay that the 22nd Batavia's left flank was also beginning to show signs of wavering.

He hastened over to them, and at first the waverers responded to his exhortations. But it was only a temporary respite for Janssens. The integrity of the Batavian line had been destroyed beyond repair, and uncertainty is the soldier's greatest enemy; confused and unsure of what to do amid the swiftly escalating chaos, not to mention the ever-nearing lines of bayonets wielded by the Highlanders, the 22nd Batavia started giving way as well.

With the 22nd Batavia trickling away, Janssens rode up the line to what remained of his right flank, the Batavian Dragoons and the 9th Bataafsche Jagers. With the departure of the 22nd Batavia the left flank of the Jagers was now threatened as well, and inevitably they too had begun to pull back, although in good order rather than in an undisciplined rush. With them, naturally, went the 5th Artillery's guns.

All that remained now of the Batavian right and centre was the Batavian Dragoons near Blauuwbergsvlei, still awaiting Janssens' orders, and the staunch French sailors under Captain Gaudin-Beauchêne and an officer named Lieutenant Du Belloij, the latter badly wounded.

To their left the Hottentot Light Infantry, the Waldeck light company, the burgher dragoons and the Javanese Artillery Corps were also standing fast and firing continuously. But Janssens knew that it was all over. He ordered the Batavian Dragoons to withdraw and then the left wing as well, before the Highlanders got to them and wiped them out.

By now Ritmeester Verkouteren, his aide, had taken a bullet in the side and Captain Steffens of the 5th Artillery had also been wounded, although less seriously, while Captain Richard had had yet another horse shot dead under him. Janssens himself had been hit in the side, but the bullet had been deflected by something in his pocket; his officers implored him not to expose himself further, because his presence was essential to the Batavian soldiers' morale.

Before long the entire Batavian force was withdrawing, except for one gun under a 2nd Lieutenant Dibbetz of the 5th Artillery, which had lost six gun-horses and several of its detachment killed or wounded. Dibbetz made sure to spike the gun and then left with his remaining men.

Soon all of the Batavian right was gone – except for Lieutenant Pellgrini with his horse-gunners, who were still firing at the approaching Highlanders from a low sand hill at the extremity of the line in spite of their comrades' departure. Janssens rode over and found them calmly serving their guns. He ordered Pellegrini to withdraw immediately. Pellegrini chose to interpret this as advice rather than an order and carried on firing.

Janssens was so impressed by the young man's cool daring, especially after the disgraceful example set by the Waldeckers, that he promoted him to captain on the spot and then ordered him once again

– in completely unambiguous terms now – to withdraw and cover the Batavian retreat. This time Pellegrini obeyed.

It was now, as can best be calculated, about 10am. It had taken just five hours for Cape history to swing around into a radically different direction. Janssens sent his adjutant-general, HC Rancke, and later Colonel Henrij, back to Rietvallei to start reorganising the Batavian troops, then joined the rearguard in spite of his staff's concern for his safety.

In all truth there does not seem to have been much that he could have done, or done differently. After the battle Lieutenant-Colonel Wilson commented that Janssens should have thrown all his dragoons into a flanking attack, because:

> … if the three hundred burgher cavalry and a hundred and fifty regular Dutch cavalry moving with the guns had seized the moment when the British line was charging, to wheel upon its exposed flank, the issue of the day would probably have not, at all events, been so decisive and any check to the infantry in their state might have been fatal … Even after the infantry had retired, the cavalry might have disputed some of the laurels of the victors.[17]

Coming from a superb cavalry tactician who was well acquainted with the British capabilities, this must be seen as a valid criticism. However, it should be remembered that Janssens did not intend to make an all-or-nothing last stand at Blaauwberg; the battle was merely the first phase of his larger plan to withdraw to the Hottentots Holland mountains and interdict the flow of supplies to Cape Town. This being the case, he could not risk losing too many of his regular dragoons, the most valuable form of fighting soldier at his disposal because of the distances involved.

Riding back to Rietvallei, Janssens knew that his plans for mounting significant further resistance beyond the Hottentots Holland mountains were now in doubt, given his losses. Retiring to Cape Town would serve no purpose. The town had no defenders except the small number he had left with Von Prophalow, and had, as far as he could calculate, no more than two days' supply of bread left. The chances of being either rapidly starved into submission or overrun in a British attack were high, and would result in needless destruction to the lives and property of the burghers who had supported him so faithfully. In either case the result would be a winner-takes-all unconditional surrender.

There was now no hope of mounting a workable defence of the Cape. To adhere to his original plan was impossible because he did not have the resources to defend both the Hottentots Holland and Roodezand passes. This meant that although he could interdict the route to the eastern frontier he would not be able to prevent the British from seizing the wheat- and wine-producing districts of the Boland and reaching the interior by way of the Roodezand pass.

Logically, all he could do was retreat beyond the Hottentots Holland range, after which one of two things could happen: he could hold out in the hope that a French relief force would turn up; or he could use his army as a bargaining-chip in negotiations – though mauled by the British it still posed a threat – and guarantee a capitulation agreement embodying the best possible terms, not only for his soldiers but also for the civilian population.

On arrival at Rietvallei he set about reorganising his shattered army, starting by contemptuously ordering the Waldecker fusilier companies back to Cape Town, but not the regiment's more spirited light company, which had stood fast to the end and now volunteered to a man to stay with him.

He would have liked also to retain the remnants of Captain Gaudin-Beauchêne's 240 valiant French seamen, who had fought to the end and paid heavily for it (110 out of 240 did not answer to their names when the roll was called), but their commander felt that they would be of little value inland, so far out of their element. Because their losses had already been so great Janssens reluctantly ordered them back to Cape Town by a roundabout route to man the batteries, a task for which they were more suited in any case. It is likely that he now also told the remaining 44 men of the Javanese Artillery Corps to go home, since foot artillery would have too much difficulty keeping up with the rest of the Batavian forces in the retreat to the Hottentots Holland.

This done, he despatched his naval staff officer, Lieutenant Pfeil, to hasten to Major von Horn, the commander of the Hottentot Light Infantry companies stationed at Muizenberg and Simon's Town, with new orders. Horn and his men must make haste to the Hottentots Holland as soon as he had helped himself to whatever he needed of the battleship *Bato*'s ammunition, dumped the rest into the sea, and set her alight.

To Von Prophalow in Cape Town went a message to send some of his troops, horses and wagons to the Hottentots Holland without delay, and to the Political Council a directive to grant farms to Linde, Human, Wium, Theunissen and a number of other burgher dragoons for their gallant service on the battlefield.[18]

His most doleful task was counting the cost of the action, made more difficult because he was naturally unable to police the battlefield, so that even though some hospital returns were later added, the exact toll will never be known. When the rolls were called at Rietvallei, however, a total of 337 men did not answer to their names.

The official British casualty figure is given as one officer and 14 other ranks killed, nine officers and 180 other ranks wounded, and nine other ranks missing, a total of 213, which seems low when one considers the circumstances and some of the eyewitness testimony.[19]

Janssens was still busy with his reorganisation when at 11am the Batavian rearguard still at Rietvallei faced yet another attack. Popham brought the *Diadem* and *Leda* as close inshore as possible and bombarded the old government farm to cover the landing of a party of Royal Marines and two light artillery pieces. The marine officer Robert Fernyhough later wrote a detailed description of this little-known aspect of the Battle of Blaauwberg:

> It is astonishing to me how we did land through such a tremendous surf … The nearest point we could get to the shore, was forty or fifty yards, so that we were obliged to wade that distance, up to the middle, before we could reach it.

I was completely ducked, for in getting out of the boat, a sea came and dashed me overhead, and I thought I would have been obliged to swim for it, but another wave set me on my legs again. I then took to my heels and ran until I got safely beyond the reach of the sea.

To my great annoyance I found an excellent pistol spoiled, which I had swung in my belt, and all my ammunition rendered useless. Several of our men experienced the same, which was an unpleasant circumstance in the face of the enemy. The *Diadem* and *Leda* covered our landing and just as we were leaving the boats, some of the enemy advanced down the hill towards us, but the gun-brig opened a fire of grape-shot among them, killed two and the rest retreated. Another part of the enemy during our debarkation attempted to get a piece of cannon upon an eminence but a well directed fire from our ships completely baffled the attempt, so effectively had the squadron covered our landing.

As soon as we had formed and our piece of artillery was properly manned, drawn by our sailors, we advanced up the hill expecting the enemy there, but to our disappointment they had retreated. We now observed a part of the Dutch army at some distance to our right, but could not make out if it was advancing or retreating; however, we commenced firing with our artillery upon a large building, which was situated at some distance in our front, and where we supposed some of the enemy cavalry to be concealed, as we saw them galloping in that direction.

After we had advanced some distance, some of our own army appeared upon a hill to the left of it. We immediately halted, and sir David Baird came riding up to us, apparently in high spirits, saying, 'The day will soon be our own.' He then ordered us to join the brigade in sight which proved to be the second consisting of the 24th and 83rd regiments, till further orders.

The Dutch force, that we saw on our right proved to be the part of the army commanded by the governor, General Jansens, [*sic*] which had just been defeated by our second brigade, but was beginning to rally again, till he saw our force appear on the hill before mentioned: this caused him to pause a little, as he perceived we had recently landed. He was eventually determined to retreat, by a discharge of grape-shot from the ships which had protected our landing, and which threw him into some confusion, so that he faced about and retreated up the country ...[20]

Caught unawares, the Batavians were incapable of anything more than skirmishing, and Janssens knew that if he remained at Rietvallei he was in danger of being surrounded, since Baird was closing in from the direction of the Blaauwberg. There was nothing for it but to withdraw even further, and as soon as possible.

And so the weary and battered Batavians set off again, this time on an orderly retreat to the farm Roozeboom, on the road to what is now Durbanville, with Fernyhough's marines and the Highlanders in hot pursuit.

Weary though Janssens and his men were, he did not realise that Baird's oncoming redcoats and bluejackets – ill-conditioned to start with, exhausted by their exertions, wracked by thirst and fried by the blazing summer sun – were in infinitely worse shape. As Baird later reported to Castlereagh:

> It is utterly impossible to convey to your lordship an adequate idea of the obstacles which opposed the advance and retarded the success of our army, but it is my duty to inform your lordship that the nature of the country, a deep arid sand, covered with shrubs scarcely pervious to light bodies of infantry, and above all the total privation of water under the effect of a burning sun, had nearly exhausted our gallant fellows in the moment of victory and with the utmost difficulty were we able to reach Riet Valley where we took our position for the night.
>
> A considerable portion of the provisions and necessaries with which we started had been lost during the action and we occupied our ground under an apprehension that even the great exertions of Sir Home Popham and the navy could not relieve us from starvation.[21]

So desperate was their plight, Krynauw says, that 'when a small water-dam was found somewhere on the plain – probably on the farm Compagniesdam – and later also at Rietvallei, where the little spring only flowed slowly, Baird was forced personally to supervise the doling out of water to his thirsty men ... everyone who has made the acquaintance of the sands of Melkbosstrand and Bloubergstrand in the hot sun will know what Baird and his troops had to suffer through.'[22]

Theoretically Janssens could have taken advantage of the British troops' condition if he had realised how enfeebled they were, because (as Captain Dugald Carmichael later wrote):

> To tell you the truth, we were in no condition to molest him. Fresh from the cool bracing climate of Ireland, then cooped up for five months on board of crowded transports, a march of six hours over the scorching sands of Africa, exhausted us to such a degree that even the exhilarating sight of a flying enemy could not prevent immense numbers from escaping to the rear.[23]

Robert Wilson, too, wrote feelingly of the British suffering after he had gathered eyewitness accounts of the halting pursuit of the Batavians:

> The enemy were no sooner routed than great anxiety was occasioned by the want of water. The heat of the sun, its reflection on a white soil, the depth of the sand, the exertion of the onset and the very apprehension of the inability to slake thirst occasioned great distress. The soldiers dropped fast and several sailors died at the guns they had been dragging through a soil over which it was not supposed by the enemy cannon could be brought by men.[24]

In spite of all this the 72nd Highlanders remained in surprisingly good spirits. According to Lieutenant Ronald Campbell 'the soldiers suffered excessively from the heat of the sun, which was as intense as I ever felt it in India; though our fatigue was extreme, yet, for the momentary halt we made, the grenadier company requested the pipers might play them their regimental quick step, "*Capper Fiedth*",[25] to which they danced a Highland reel, to the utter astonishment of the fifty-ninth regiment which was close to our rear.'[26]

This diversion seems to have exemplified the general mood of the 72nd – as Baird noted in his report to Castlereagh, the regiment's commanding officer was wounded during the Highland Brigade's charge, but remained at the head of his troops to the end.

Was Janssens lax in not counter-attacking, either near Rietvallei or later at the Tijgerberg?[27] The answer must be 'no'. He knew nothing of the enemy weaknesses and his over-riding priority remained getting to the Hottentots Holland area. Inflicting a few more casualties on the overwhelmingly larger British force would have served no real purpose and might well have caused further losses that he could ill afford.

By now Von Prophalow in Cape Town knew of the defeat, by way of a letter from Rancke to De Salis which had arrived in mid-morning. A little while later groups of the disgraced Waldecker fusiliers came straggling in, now little more than a leaderless rabble, and gave themselves over to such lawless behaviour that Von Prophalow disarmed them. As time passed more Waldeck stragglers came in and were also disarmed.

Von Prophalow did not give in upon receiving the news. Pending further instructions from Janssens, he sent off additional patrols to the Salt River area, and ordered all coastal batteries to fire at will on any British ship which might approach the shoreline. The coast gunners kept their shot-ovens stoked up.

At Blaauwbergsvlei Justinus Keer had unexpectedly emerged as a Good Samaritan. Of his own volition he turned his home and its outbuildings into a makeshift hospital, impartially nursing the wounded of both sides as they were brought in by British search parties which scoured the battlefield.

Keer was visited by the Rev Henry Martyn, who had come up from Losperd's Bay by way of Kleinberg with one of the search parties; at Kleinberg he saw the corpse of Captain Foster lying where he had fallen, his face and neck covered in blood and his limbs contorted, as if, Martyn wrote later, he had died 'in the greatest anxiety'.[28]

Having picked up several wounded British soldiers, the party found its way down the slopes to Blaauwbergsvlei, where Martyn – already deeply moved after passing over the battlefield with its gory remains – was shocked and saddened by the sight of more than 200 soldiers lying in and outside Keer's home, covered in blood.

Later he went out into the veld with a British doctor and found several of Janssens' wounded; while trying to calm a member of the Hottentot Light Infantry who was in his death throes, Martyn came close to being bayoneted by a drunken Highlander who had mistaken him for a Frenchman.

Keer was to perform his mission of mercy for the next 10 days, for which he was duly thanked by the British and awarded a sum of money for damage his farm had suffered in the process.

While Keer tended the wounded at Blaauwbergsvlei, Robert Wilson was still persevering far to the north-west with his unwitting wild-goose chase. Kilometre after kilometre he and his men trudged through the thick sand, suffering terribly from heat and thirst, until the infantry were so fatigued that Wilson had to stop and let them rest.

Eventually they reached a farmstead where there was water, but it tasted so bad that Wilson had to restrain his men from drinking more than the bare minimum. Wilson sent the owner off to Saldanha Bay with a message for Beresford, ordered three hours of rest and then set off again with his dragoons and 25 volunteers from among the infantrymen.

This leg of his journey proved no less arduous than the first, and 'Job never showed more patience than I did in these vexatious and cruel circumstances,' he wrote later.[29] To help the infantry Wilson and his dragoons carried their coats and eventually also some men's muskets – 'after marching two miles in sand and heat more oppressive than I had ever experienced, the light infantry spirit began to droop. One man became sick. I put him on my own horse, and taking his musket marched six miles in great pain, for my boots galled me severely.'[30]

Around 5pm they crested a hill from which their guide showed them the distant buildings of Theefontein. Taking no chances on revealing himself, he called another rest period until dusk had fallen, 'and we all slept in luxurious forgetfulness of care.' At 8pm they set off again, struggled through four miles of sand which was thicker than ever, so that Wilson was hard put to it to keep his foot soldiers together, and finally reached the houses.

There they found a kraal full of oxen; 'the sight rewarded me for some of our vexations, and was a compensation for the injury that our non-occupation of Tea Fonteyn earlier might have done the army.' But then 'our joy ... was somewhat damped by finding that the place was called Elands Fonteyn, and that Tea Fonteyn was still ten miles distant.' It might as well have been 100 miles; Wilson's little force had reached the limit of its endurance: 'the men and horses could not stir, and the cattle required a guard and convoy to Saldanha in the morning. We therefore lay down and slept in the sand: it was very cold.'[31]

Wilson and his men were not the only British soldiers to find an uncomfortable bed that night of 8 January. After resting, Baird's force set off again on their tramp to Rietvallei, but it was no pleasant haven. Its springs could not supply enough water, and the redcoats were hungry, because most of their provisions had been lost during the battle (one assumes as a result of the Batavian artillery fire).

Baird arranged for rations and water to be brought ashore, and after they had eaten the soldiers and sailors bedded down on the cold sand, a chilly south-easter ensuring that their sleep was none too restful. By contrast, the marines and Highlanders apparently spent a more comfortable night after they halted, completely exhausted, at the foot of the Tijgerberg, but their sleep, too, was interrupted.

Very conscious of the possibility of a Batavian counter-attack during the night, Brigadier-General Ferguson took all possible precautions, even making sure the guns were ready to go into action at a moment's notice. As it turned out there *was* a night attack of sorts, but it seems to have been an impromptu affair, consisting of no more than small-arms fire which did no damage apart from unsettling the worn-out redcoats' nerves.

Only the Batavians did not bed down for the night. Roozeboom was still too close to the British for comfort, so Janssens allowed his troops to rest while he dealt with preparations for the next phase and sent off messengers in various directions; among other things he requested the landdrost of Stellenbosch to gather large quantities of provisions and fodder, as well as transport, and Ritmeester Wium was dispatched to the Hottentots Holland to make sure that the communication system was functioning.

Then he roused his men. At 11pm they set off again, heading this time for Meerlust, the Myburgh family's farm at the Eersterivier. The Cape resistance was about to begin.

CHAPTER 15

LONG LIVE KING GEORGE!

The morning of 9 January saw all the forces on the move. Janssens' men were marching at their best pace towards Meerlust, fagged out but still holding together. At Rietvallei, Baird's soldiers and sailors shook the kinks out of their muscles and set off for Salt River by way of Jan Biesjeskraal. At Elandsfontein Wilson got his foot-weary and saddle-sore soldiers woken up and ordered that two oxen be slaughtered for breakfast.

> After a brief repose one hundred and twenty oxen, under an escort of three dragoons, were sent to Saldanha, and eighteen were left in the pen for the troops that were expected to follow ... The remaining dragoons, having received a share of raw meat to cook at their journey's end, marched immediately with me towards Tea Fonteyn ...
>
> When we approached Tea Fonteyn our horses were nearly exhausted; but although they lay down at the shortest halt, they rose and moved again when the march was ordered with a courage that entitles this race to noble consideration.[1]

Bergh and Van Reenen, the owners, were absent, but they had not evacuated the farm's cattle or emptied it of useful items, and had told the foreman to cooperate fully with the British. This order seems to have been disobeyed in part, because when Wilson eventually arrived at Theefontein he and his men saw that 'armed boors [*sic*] were engaged in taking away [livestock], but they fled upon our advancing.' They found, however, 'a house with very large premises. A steward who proved most friendly to us was left in charge. There was abundance of corn, some wine, horses chiefly wild or unbroken, but no cattle, as the greater part had been removed the day before.'

Nevertheless, the cooperative spirit at Theefontein, 'was a striking contrast to the conduct of anyone else on that route, the cattle from every other place having been drove off and whatever could have been useful to the troops removed, and I can state that without the assistance received at the Tea Fonteyn it would have been difficult if not altogether impracticable to have brought the troops by that route.'[2]

Thanks to the goodwill thus generated, the British authorities later paid Bergh and Van Reenen 8 575 *rix*-dollars' compensation for three out-buildings which had accidentally caught fire and been destroyed, along with large quantities of oats.[3]

Wilson did not tarry long at Theefontein. Later Beresford and his remaining troops arrived, bearing the unwelcome (as far as Wilson was concerned) and by now slightly outdated news that Baird had already landed at Losperd's Bay.

Beresford was not noticeably upset at having missed the fighting, but the eager young cavalryman was keenly disappointed and briefly wondered whether Baird had not deliberately sent them off to Saldanha to deny them participation in the invasion, although he later admitted to himself that there were no grounds for his suspicion.

At daybreak on 10 January Beresford and Wilson pressed on southwards with all speed, and reached Groenekloof in the evening. Early next morning they surprised a burgher travelling towards them and extracted the news that the fighting was over. They hurried on to the farm Brakkefontein, just north of Losperd's Bay.

❦

By now Major von Horn, having carried out his orders to sabotage the *Bato*, was force-marching towards the Hottentots Holland pass with his two Hottentot Light Infantry companies as well as 50 artillerymen.

Janssens, meanwhile, had arrived at Meerlust at 9pm the previous night, of 9 January, and immediately set about refining his plans, working out his losses and reorganising. According to legend, he was also overcome with rage when the commanding officer of the Waldeckers came to apologise for his troops' appalling failure the day before. The story goes that the exasperated Janssens was moved to act completely contrary to his normal gentlemanly manner and kicked him down the steps of the back stoep with such force that he tumbled into the little garden below.

That night loyal burghers arrived from Cape Town to tell him that the red flag proclaiming martial law had been struck, and a white one hoisted in its place. Although Janssens had no independent confirmation of a surrender, it was clear that the sooner he set out for the Hottentots Holland pass, the better. To this end he sent ahead his baggage train with its slow-moving wagons, and arranged for the wounded to be taken to Stellenbosch and placed in the care of the burghers there.

The burghers' tidings were essentially correct. While Janssens and Von Horn had been heading for the Eersterivier and the Hottentots Holland respectively, the inhabitants of Cape Town had faced up to the fact that for the second time in just over a decade they were about to be conquered, and that there was absolutely nothing they could do about it with only 1 285 officers and men. Not only this but the disgraced Waldecker line companies had now degenerated into complete lawlessness. Consequently, some of the remaining troops had to be deployed on internal-security duties, the remainder to be stationed at outlying places.

To make matters worse, Cape Town was in imminent danger of famine. As Janssens had estimated, enough food remained for it to feed itself for just two days, and although wheat was being harvested in the outlying districts, Baird's presence at Salt River meant it would not be able to reach consumers if he did not want it to.

There was also the naïve general belief that the Cape might one day be returned to the Batavian Republic after peace with France had been made, so there seemed little sense in taking a course of action which would lead only to suffering and devastation.

It was decided that the best approach, therefore, would be to send all the remaining field artillery to Janssens and then negotiate a provisional agreement with the British. Von Prophalow despatched the last of the guns and a batch of stragglers to the Hottentots Holland rendezvous, and two delegates named Cambier and a Captain Schoester ventured forth under a white flag to parley with Baird.

Near Craig's Tower – ironically, a relic of the first British invasion – they met up with Baird, who not unnaturally welcomed this heaven-sent opportunity to take control of Cape Town without another shot being fired. He responded with a carefully calculated mixture of velvet glove and iron fist. On his behalf Brigadier-General Ferguson demanded that Cape Town's outer defences, including the Fort Knokke battery, be surrendered within six hours or there would be a full-scale assault on the town that night – but he would be willing to stay his hand for 36 hours to allow provisional peace terms to be worked out.

At 3.30pm on 10 January, Janssens' troops reached the foot of the Hottentots Holland pass and found Major von Horn there with his gunners and infantry. They joined hands and the long, arduous and frequently dangerous business of getting the Batavian troops, guns, ammunition and stores over the rudimentary road through the pass began.

By now the terms of the provisional capitulation had been hammered out by Brigadier-General Ferguson, representing Baird, and the secretary to the Batavian administration, Janssens' friend JA Truter. True to his instructions to dictate lenient terms in order to facilitate a peaceful transition, Baird's provisions were generous, to burghers, farmers, and troops alike.

At Brakkefontein, Beresford and Wilson managed to obtain some fresh horses, and with a small escort of Wilson's dragoons made all speed to Cape Town, leaving their troops to catch up. But they were just too late to be in at the kill.

At 4pm on 10 January victors and vanquished gathered at Papendorp on Cape Town's outskirts. There, under a large milkwood tree next to a small thatch-roofed cottage, Baird, Popham and Von Prophalow put their signatures to the provisional agreement.[4]

A salvo of cannon-fire marked the capitulation, but there seems to have been no vainglorious display on the part of the victors. 'There is a pleasant story which I am inclined to believe,' according to Ian D Colvin, 'that when Baird and Von Prophalow ... signed the capitulation the British band outside [the cottage] struck up the national anthem and were immediately stopped by Baird out of consideration for the feelings of the other side.'[5]

Certainly Baird had his soldiers march into Cape Town without excessive display, which they did under the eyes of crowds of Capetonians; Beresford and the somewhat disappointed Wilson arrived just in time to watch the British troops occupy the nearest coast batteries. The terms of the provisional agreement were read out from the Kat Balcony in the Castle, and so ended the Batavian sway at the Cape – although a permanent treaty had yet to be signed, it would clearly be a mere formality. The Batavian Republic was dead, at least at the Cape; long live King George!

Baird knew perfectly well that he was not out of the woods yet by any means. In fact his responsibilities had increased, because he was now the new Lieutenant-Governor of the Cape as well as the military commander-in-chief until Horse Guards in London decided otherwise. This left him with two distinct sets of responsibilities.

First of all, he needed to ensure a swift, smooth transition to British rule by a population which at best was peaceful, if not exactly enthusiastic about its new masters. Second, as the military commander he had to achieve a substantive peace. This meant neutralising Janssens, who commanded an intact combat force in the interior which might not be strong enough for a direct confrontation but could be used to prolong hostilities, if necessary by recruiting sympathisers from the rural population.

Baird was also convinced that Janssens was playing a delaying game because he was expecting a French or combined Franco-Dutch relief force, and obviously was painfully aware of the fact that he would be at his most vulnerable if such a relief force arrived out of the blue while his troops and warships were spread out all over the Cape and its coasts during the take-over phase.

Baird therefore took a number of urgent steps to prepare for a possible Franco-Dutch attack and simultaneously isolate Janssens in his mountain stronghold as a preliminary to final capitulation negotiations. The Highland Brigade settled in at Wynberg Camp, but the 59th Regiment and an additional element marched to Stellenbosch as the first step towards taking control of the vital Roodezand pass, so that communications with the interior would not be cut off. Other troops occupied Paarl, while HMS *Raisonable*, the *Belligerent* and the *Protector*, with the 83rd Regiment secured False Bay. Yet other troops were despatched to Algoa Bay to make sure that Janssens did not retreat to the eastern frontier. All horses were requisitioned for military use.

On 11 January he issued three proclamations that laid the foundations for all these purposes. The first assured inhabitants of the rural districts of British protection, but warned them to stay at home and refrain from joining Janssens' forces or helping him in any way; inhabitants of Cape Town and its environs who continued actively to support Janssens would have their property confiscated. The second proclamation required that civil servants and leading citizens of Cape Town take an oath of loyalty to the British crown, while the third appointed WS van Ryneveld as the new chief magistrate.

Van Ryneveld was adept at trimming his sails according to the prevailing political winds. After the 1795 invasion he had swiftly made himself extremely useful to the British – this had left him in some disgrace after the Batavian takeover, but he had gradually worked his way back to a position of some influence in time to turn his coat again with equal celerity. His appointment was an astute move on Baird's part. However ambiguous he might be politically, Van Ryneveld was an exceptionally capable and hard-working administrator who immediately set about serving his new masters energetically, doing everything he could to calm the local population and advise Baird on how to expedite Janssens' capitulation.

His was not the only such appointment: Baird did not make the common mistake of purging the former enemy administrative leadership, and requested a number of officials to stay on, at least for the time being, to ensure a smooth transition. This worked very well over the next while.

That same day Baird made his first overtures to Janssens by sending him copies of the three proclamations and a graciously worded letter, which he requested Brigadier-General Beresford at Stellenbosch to pass on. He complimented Janssens on having done his duty at the head of his 'gallant tho' feeble' army (which in those days does not have today's pejorative overtone but meant 'weakened'), but pointed out that the British had taken over the seat of government and had an army of occupation of such size that further resistance would serve no purpose and only cause needless destruction, which he did not believe Janssens would like to inflict on the territory he had so lately governed.

Beresford added a letter of his own to the effect that he was authorised to open negotiations, and then sent everything off to the Hottentots Holland in the hands of one of his officers, a Major Deane.

Cape Town meanwhile began to resume its day-to-day activities, and Baird made it an early order of business to send ships to St Helena and even India for supplies of rice and wheat to tide the town over until normality returned to the flow of food from the interior. In the days to come he also repealed grain taxes and proclaimed a new law providing for the government to store wheat purchased at fixed rates. This encouraged many farmers to bring out undeclared supplies of wheat, so that prices fell – a boon for the population.

On the afternoon of 13 January Janssens met with Major Deane, at the foot of the Hottentots Holland pass. To ensure that the British would have no idea of his assets and deployments, Janssens informed Deane that he did not believe that he would be justified in ending hostilities while the Batavian army was capable of fighting a destructive war, because it was still possible that France or the Netherlands might send reinforcements.

This being the case, he would like to be briefed about events in Cape Town, and suggested that a member of the defunct Batavian administration be sent to enlighten him and also assist him in his deliberations. Deane delivered the message and Baird agreed to this, sending Janssens' trusted friend, Secretary to the Government JA Truter, to the Hottentots Holland with a copy of the provisional capitulation. In the meantime Deane reiterated to Janssens the strength of the British forces deployed against him.

Janssens was well aware of the fact that Baird's proclamations might have an adverse effect on his own plans, and issued a counter-proclamation of his own. The seat of government had been captured, he pointed out, but the British would not be masters of the situation until they controlled all parts of the Batavian territory. Citizens in areas already controlled by the British could not be protected by him and he did not expect them to remain obedient to Batavian authority, but those in areas not yet captured were still under his authority.

But Janssens clearly knew that he had reached the end of the line. His army was now down to just over 1 000 men: 343 of the Hottentot Light Infantry, 180 of the 22nd Batavia, 104 of the Bataafsche Jagers, 52 men of the Waldeck light company, 146 dragoons and 177 artillery-men – too few even to defend the Hottentots Holland pass. He had lost some troops through desertion and knew he would lose more.

For the time being he had enough food for his men, although most of them were almost in rags by now, but he was short of fodder, and word of Baird's requisitioning of horses had come to him. That could signify only one thing: Baird was building up a strong mounted force with which to attack him. In the meantime British forces were already closing in on him. They had already reached Mossel Bay and occupied the Roodezand pass to Tulbagh, which meant that they could now attack him from the rear.

Theoretically he could form a small dedicated guerrilla force and retreat further into the interior to resist the British for as long as possible, but he must have known that in practical terms it would not be viable, and that the families of his local soldiers would be at the mercy of the British.

General Craig's stratagem of using the Cape Corps as a weapon of intimidation had not been forgotten, and Janssens was concerned about a reprise, with murder and plundering by criminal and outlaw elements as a potential result. His burgher soldiers, while remaining steadfast, were clearly becoming worried about what was happening to their families, and Janssens knew that the support of the population in the interior – racked by uncertainty as it was – was beginning to fade.

On 15 January Truter arrived and confirmed what Baird had said in his initial letter. Janssens thought things over and called a conference of his staff at which he laid out the situation. Colonel Henrij proposed 'an honourable capitulation', failing which they would follow Janssens wherever he might go, and his brother officers agreed.

Lieutenant Dibbetz said that Janssens had done everything in his power to obtain an honourable capitulation, and that since it was possible that the Cape might be returned to the Batavian Republic after a European peace, military manpower should not be wasted to no purpose. No doubt the contribution by Deel, Janssens' capable Commissioner for War, carried considerable weight: the Batavians, he pointed out, had provisions for just one month more.

Janssens, an experienced soldier and nothing if not a realist, agreed with these views and said he would open negotiations forthwith. He would propose that his officers retain their personal weapons and property, and that they not be made prisoners of war but receive free passage to the Netherlands; he would consult with them before giving any undertaking.

He also sent home all of his burgher troops whose properties were in the British-occupied areas, including the dragoon companies of *Ritmeesters* Linde, Wium and Morkel. In spite of their personal concerns they were unwilling to leave him, but he insisted, and after a moving farewell they rode reluctantly away.

❦

Truter arranged a meeting with Beresford. At 7am next day, 16 January, the two generals and their senior staff faced one another at a farm at the intersection of the Hottentots Holland, Stellenbosch and Cape Town roads, which was appropriately named *Goedverwachting*, (Good Expectation).

Negotiations were conducted in a courteous fashion, albeit with an underlying sense of urgency by both men – Beresford because of the need to complete pacification as soon as possible, Janssens because he did not want to give the British the opportunity of encroaching too much on his attenuated army, his only bargaining tool.

Agreement was reached on most conditions but not on others – one main sticking-point was the Batavian officers' extreme reluctance to give up their personal weapons. Beresford proposed that out of respect for the Batavian troops' meritorious service they would not be made prisoner but would be transported back to the Netherlands, provided they promised not to take up arms against Britain or her allies before arriving there.

But there was no question of the Batavians marching out under arms, Beresford said; the British soldiers' honour was also involved. Janssens' troops must assemble at Simon's Town for departure home, but the Hottentot Light Infantry must be allowed to enlist in the British service if they so desired (something Janssens agreed with, to the point of asking for special treatment for them because of their staunchness in battle).

Time was running out fast now. On 17 January a British column appeared and set up camp within view of the Hottentots Holland mountains, while Janssens received word that Baird had sent another column to Franschhoek and warships to the Breede River mouth. Baird continued to pile on the pressure to speed up the negotiations. Two regiments were despatched to Tulbagh to get behind Janssens by way of the Roodezand pass, while the 93rd Regiment headed straight for the Hottentots Holland.

Janssens addressed his remaining troops to tell them about the possibility of a capitulation agreement being signed, adding that much would still depend on them. They assured him of their loyalty, but (as he later reported) he could feel that they believed that the peace terms should be accepted. It was clear now that he had exhausted all realistic options. On 18 January he and Beresford met again to sign the articles of capitulation. Next day Baird and Popham refined and confirmed them.[6]

Thanks to Janssens' persistence and Baird's sense of urgency, as well as his instructions to treat the Cape people gently, the terms were very favourable to the Batavians – it was even agreed that the Dutch officers and soldiers would be maintained and paid by the British until their departure. Erasmus notes that, in 1816, the treaty was severely criticised in a book published in London for being far more generous than would normally have been the case.[7]

The very next day, 20 January, the Batavian army began to wind down. Janssens' men emerged from their stronghold in the Hottentots Holland and under escort by Wilson's dragoons set off on the long, thirsty march to Rondebosch, where they handed over their horses and weapons; Janssens was reunited with his family at Government House (today's Tuynhuys), and his officers were lodged in the town, while British soldiers were quartered on the local population in the surrounding rural areas, where no barrack facilities existed.

Janssens spent the next few days dealing with various remaining matters of civil governance. Among other things, the Political Council had secretly paid out large sums to certain officials as compensation for the looming loss of their posts, on the understanding that in the event of a Batavian restoration they would have to repay the money. Baird was tipped off by one of JA Truter's female slaves, however, and he insisted that the payments be recalled. After much effort Janssens succeeded in getting back almost all of the money.

Another major problem concerned the raising of the two richly laden Dutch East Indiamen which had been scuttled in Table Bay on the arrival of the British. Other problems plagued him as well. One was a dispute about the status of the wounded Batavian officers. Baird had intended to keep them at the Cape as prisoners of war but eventually allowed them to accompany Janssens; they were simply extra mouths to feed at a time when there was a threat of food shortages. Then there were the French sailors of the *Atalante* and *Napoléon*, who were classed as prisoners of war but in many cases hid themselves among the Dutch soldiers. At times Baird and Janssens exchanged hard words, but without ever abandoning their mutual courtesy.

❦

Months passed under the new governorship of the Cape. But just before Janssens' departure, Baird fortuitously received advance warning, possibly by a neutral ship, of Admiral Willaumez's long-anticipated arrival. Willaumez was to rendezvous with the 44-gun frigate *Volontaire*, which had left Brest on 13 December 1805. But off Gibraltar she scored an unexpected victory by capturing a British troopship with one company each of the 2nd and 54th Regiments on board. No doubt unwilling to delay his chase after Willaumez, the *Volontaire*'s captain transferred the British soldiers to his decks and for some reason let the troopship carry on. After an uneventful voyage, having missed the rendezvous with Willaumez, the *Volontaire* made landfall at Cape Town on 4 March, saw that the Batavian flag was still flying over the batteries and proceeded into Table Bay, confident of a warm welcome.

The welcome turned out to be warm but hardly friendly. Baird and Popham had laid a neat ambush. The *Narcissus* and *Leda* frigates cut off the *Volontaire*'s escape, while the Chavonnes Battery fired a shot across her bows and then ran up the Union Jack. Caught flat-footed, the *Volontaire* had no option but to strike her colours or be blown out of the water by the battery's 36-pounders. Apart from liberating the two companies of prisoners, a search of the *Volontaire*'s papers confirmed that Willaumez was on his way to the Cape with his six ships of the line and two frigates.

This was bad news indeed. Some of Popham's fighting ships had already left to escort the East Indiamen, which had accompanied the invasion fleet, on the next leg of their journey to the Orient; all he had left were his flagship, HMS *Diadem*, the *Diomede*, which mounted only 50 guns, the 32-gun frigates *Leda* and *Narcissus*, and two or three brigs – not nearly a match for Willaumez's squadron.

Without the protection and support of the Royal Navy things could become very difficult for Baird. Willaumez could land anywhere – he might call in at Saldanha Bay, for example, to refit and replenish his water, or go elsewhere along the coast and make mischief to his heart's content – and any reinforcements for Baird would take many months to reach the Cape. The French arrival might even sabotage all of Baird's efforts for a smooth and peaceful transition to British rule by inciting the more rebellious elements of the local population, such as the Graaff-Reinetters, to fresh resistance and making use of his freedom of movement to supply them.

Baird and Popham did not panic, but immediately set to work on a defensive plan which made the best use of what assets they had, starting with an embargo on the departure of all civilian vessels in Table Bay.

On 6 March, two days after the capture of the *Volontaire*, Janssens, his family and hundreds of Batavians – 94 officers, 573 other ranks, 31 civil servants, and 53 women and children – finally embarked on the *Bellona* and several other ships for the voyage to the Netherlands.

The last words on the short-lived Batavian repossession of the Cape must come from Janssens himself. Before he left he wrote Baird a final letter that speaks volumes both for his innate generosity and also his fondness for the people he was leaving behind:

> Allow me, Sir, to recommend to your protection the inhabitants of this colony, whose happiness and welfare ever since I have been here were the chief objects of my care, and who conducted themselves during that period to my highest satisfaction.
>
> Give no credit in this respect to Mr Barrow nor to the enemies of the inhabitants. They have their faults, but these are more than compensated for by good qualities. Through lenity, through marks of affection, and benevolence, they may be conducted to any good.[8]

Nor did he forget his trusted friend JA Truter, who had stayed loyal to him while WS van Ryneveld and others were turning their coats with indecent haste. He asked Baird to grant his

> ... benevolence and protection to my able and virtuous friend ... Mr JA Truter – he is worthy of being the friend of all honest men ... His readiness to be useful to the colony, consistent with the feelings of a

delicate and honest man, shall whenever required by Your Excellency answer your highest expectations.[9]

The ever-modest Janssens had wished to depart quietly, but Baird and Popham came on board to say their farewells and the *Bellona* and her companions sailed out of Table Bay with full military honours.[10]

🌸

Meanwhile, Baird and Popham finalised their plan for dealing with Willaumez. It involved enticing him into a larger and more elaborate ambush of the kind that had so adroitly trapped the *Volontaire*.

Popham's ships, all flying the Batavian flag, would be carefully positioned on either side of the heavily armed Chavonnes and Amsterdam batteries. Hundreds of veteran sailors were drafted in to ensure that the batteries were fully and expertly manned, and Popham's remaining Royal Marines were reinforced by the 71st Regiment's light company, presumably to be used for boarding parties.

Willaumez would sail into the bay and anchor his squadron 'in the centre of this pleasant ambush', as Ian D Colvin puts it, 'before they discovered their mistake.'[11] At the appropriate moment the French ships would then be raked by a devastating cross-fire, with broadsides from the British ships combining with a storm of red-hot round-shot, chain-shot and grape-shot fired by the batteries. No doubt Popham found it reminiscent of the Battle of the Nile, where Nelson had trapped a French fleet in the shallows of Aboukir Bay and virtually annihilated it.

Then they sat and waited for Willaumez to arrive, filled with keen anticipation, because one of his captains was truly a prize of the first water, none other than Napoleon's younger brother, Jérôme.[12] If ever there was a French force that needed to be captured or destroyed, it was this one. It must have left a bitter taste in Janssens' mouth to sail out of Table Bay in the knowledge of what might have been, and knowing, too, that the British were lying in wait for the man who might have helped to keep the Batavian flag flying over the Cape of Good Hope.

But Baird's and Popham's grand plan to lay Willaumez by the heels came to nothing. He got word that the Cape had been well and truly captured, and altered course for San Salvador, where he watered and refitted before heading for the West Indies. What if Willaumez had left Brest a little earlier and arrived while Janssens was still holed up in the Hottentots Holland mountains?

Janssens called in briefly at St Helena and then headed for home. Almost exactly three months later he sailed into Dutch waters once more and made landfall at Vlissengen. By the time he arrived the Batavian Republic, for which he had worked so hard, was dead after just 11 years of existence. While he was still at sea Napoleon had strengthened his grip on the Dutch national throat, not to mention its purse-strings, by abolishing the republic and setting up a puppet state.

Napoleon proclaimed the new state the Kingdom of Holland, and on the throne he installed his younger brother Louis, whose name was suitably indigenised to 'Lodewijk' as a sop to Dutch sensibilities. Many Dutchmen welcomed the new dispensation because they saw it as preferable to being incorporated into the French Empire. Lodewijk wisely made it his business to see to his new subjects' interests instead of simply reigning as an autocratic Napoleonic puppet. Indeed, he did this to such an extent that in 1810 Napoleon abruptly forced his brother to abdicate, dissolved the Kingdom of Holland and annexed its territory to France.

Sir David Baird's tenure as Governor of the Cape was brief, cut short by a failure of judgment which seems extraordinary in a man of his calibre and experience. Baird received little thanks for his capture of the Cape beyond the customary expressions of approbation: the Tory government had fallen after William Pitt's premature death in 1806, and the knives were out for him. As Krynauw says, 'it appears as if there was dissatisfaction because the Cape was not conquered completely without casualties.'[13]

His public enemies' spite seems to have known no bounds; when it was proposed that he receive a vote of thanks from Parliament – a gratifying but by no means exceptional honour – the government's response was that 'it did not appear that the capture of the Cape was a military exploit of that splendid nature that called for such a distinguished mark of approbation as the thanks of the House which should not be made cheap by being too frequently conferred.'[14]

The writing on the wall seemed clear: his conquest of the Cape of Good Hope, a model of good planning and implementation, was to be sneered at by the Whig government. No doubt this evoked bitter memories of how he had been denied full credit for his successes in India in favour of the later Duke of Wellington because of his lack of political patronage, which had left him so disgusted that he had taken premature retirement.

Whether this second rejection motivated him is unknown, but it might have played a part in his decision to authorise a madcap scheme thought up by Sir Home Popham which not only terminated his governorship but came close to destroying his military career as well.

Popham had been champing at the bit since Admiral Willaumez had declined to take his bait; when he could bear his frustration no longer he resurrected his old mission to attack Spanish possessions in Latin America, from which he had been diverted shortly before Pitt decided to capture the Cape. Now Popham proposed to Baird that he sail off with part of the invasion force and carry out his original plan for (as he undoubtedly saw it) liberating Buenos Aires from its Spanish oppressors.

Before his departure for Britain in June 1806 the astute Lieutenant-Colonel Robert Wilson strongly advised against the planned attack, and one can see why. Buenos Aires' thirst for rebellion, or the lack of it, was neither here nor there. Popham had no authority to undertake such an expedition, and except in extreme circumstances Baird was not empowered to use his troops for tasks other than the ones he had been given, unless he obtained express permission to do so. It was also a fact that Latin America was a highly volatile region, and without recent information Baird and Popham could not know of any British political actions or intentions there which might be derailed by an unscheduled military intervention.

Baird nevertheless allowed himself to be persuaded by Popham, and sent him off to South America with 1 400 troops under Brigadier-General Beresford. The quixotic quest started well, only to turn almost immediately into a full-scale fiasco. Beresford captured Buenos Aires without too much difficulty, but the Spanish colonists were in no mood to take this lying down.

They rose – but not, as Popham had believed, in support of the British – and not only recaptured the city but took the entire landing force prisoner, Beresford included. Beresford's force had to be liberated by an expeditionary force sent out from Britain, and the whole episode was an embarrassment of the first order which caused an almighty fuss.

Needless to say, both Popham and Baird soon felt the weight of official disapproval. First Popham was recalled and court martialled for leaving his station. Officers had been beached or cashiered for less, but Popham got away with being severely censured – a mere slap on the wrist in the circumstances – no doubt because he was well connected politically (he was a sitting Member of Parliament between 1804 and 1812).

The verdict evoked 'the great joy of both his colleagues and the public', as Krynauw notes. The City of London, then a very important politico-economic entity in its own right, presented him with a sword of honour for (of all things) helping to 'open new markets', and later that same year he was given the honorary but prestigious appointment of groom of the bedchamber to the Duke of Gloucester.

For Baird, however, the Buenos Aires expedition was an unmitigated disaster. In his short time as lieutenant-governor he had proved a wise and sensitive ruler who had gained the goodwill and cooperation of King George's reluctant subjects, but now all that was forgotten. He was severely reprimanded and told that he was to hand over the governorship and return to Britain as soon as either the new governor, Lord Caledon, or the new lieutenant-governor, General Henry George Grey, arrived. Baird spent the rest of 1806 under sentence of dismissal and on 17 January 1807 relinquished control of the Cape to General Grey.

Two days later, exactly one year after accepting Janssens' capitulation, he sailed for Britain, and 'his humiliation had been so well-organised in England,' Krynauw says, 'that to the general dismay of his troops and the Cape inhabitants he had to depart in a simple troopship, the *Paragon*.'[15] Perhaps the humiliation was somewhat softened by the torrent of letters and verbal expressions of regret from the local community.

❦

The defunct Napoleonic Kingdom of Holland was resurrected after just four years. Napoleon was finally defeated in 1814 and imprisoned on the island of Elba. William, the long-exiled Prince of Orange, returned, this time as a fully-fledged king rather than merely the *stadhouder* of the pre-1795 days. Many at the Cape hoped that their homeland would be returned to the new Dutch kingdom, since the new monarch was a British ally. But they hoped in vain.

When the victors convened the Congress of Vienna in 1814 to divide up the spoils and seek reparations, the British hold on the Cape did not relax. In August that year the Netherlands, lacking allies (and lacking a bargaining chip now that Napoleon had been caged up on Elba), was compelled to cede the Cape to Britain under the terms of the Treaty of London.

However, Napoleon was, of course, not as impotent as his late victors had supposed. In 1815 he escaped from Elba, suborned virtually the entire French army at one stroke and launched his brief new bid for power in what became known as the 'Hundred Days'. There followed a series of savage battles which culminated with Waterloo, at which the reconstituted Kingdom of the Netherlands fielded a contingent (nominally led by the Prince of Orange himself) of the British-led Seventh Coalition.[16]

But Waterloo was merely a footnote to the story of the Cape. The Union Jack continued to fly in solitary splendour over Isbrand Goske's grim old Castle, and would do so until it was joined in 1926 by the Union of South Africa's national flag – an embellished version of the orange-white-blue Prinsevlag Janssens had hoisted when Sir Home Popham's fleet sailed into Table Bay. The 'Union Flag', as it was known, was replaced by the present national flag in 1994.

WHAT IF ... ?

It is always intriguing, at the end of any story about things past, to look back over what has emerged in the telling of it and ask: 'What if this or that had happened instead?' Sometimes a few startling conclusions leap out of such a venture into what is called 'alternative history'.

So it is with this book. To the British, the 1806 invasion which marked the end of the Cape's early military history was no more than the tying up of yet another loose end in their long, hard war against Napoleon. By the nature of things neither they nor their unenthusiastic new subjects at the Cape had any inkling of the consequences that were to result from their conquest of the toe of Africa. But Baird's victory at Blaauwberg set in motion a train of far greater events – some deliberately launched, some incidental – that swung the history of the entire southern portion of the African continent around into a radically new direction.

This having been said, is there a positive message emanating from the Battle of Blaauwberg? It depends on one's outlook. It could rightly be said that in its wake the battle brought immense suffering and troubles which have still not run their course. On the other hand, it could also be said with equal correctness that in a very real sense it changed world history for the ultimate good.

What no-one can dispute is that when the first redcoat planted his boot on the sands of Losperd's Bay, and the first burgher dragoon took a pot-shot at him from the dunes, the future of southern Africa, and the world, took a turn that not one of the men who were soon to be frantically reloading and firing their muskets at one another amid the roiling clouds of powder-smoke at Blaauwberg could have anticipated.

History does not play favourites. It simply happens in response to an ever-changing set of circumstances, and all that any generation of humankind can do is study it in an attempt to avoid repeating the mistakes of the past.

THE VOC AND SLAVERY

The VOC's involvement in the world-wide slave trade was basically that of a consumer rather than a producer. Initially the Lords Seventeen harboured distinct Calvinist qualms about trafficking in human flesh, although the GWC, the Dutch West India Company, seems not to have had similar inhibitions.

But, as CR Boxer says, this unease was subsequently undermined by the realities and brought about a change of mind, if not necessarily of heart: 'If the Dutch entered the slave-trade, whether East or West, with some hesitation in the early 17th century, they soon stifled their scruples ... the search for slave-markets took their East Indiamen as far afield as Madagascar and Mindanao.' That lingering unease might well be the reason why slaves at the Cape were generally treated better than those in places like the future United States of America, or the West Indies.

The most prominent dealers along the west coast, for example, were the Portuguese, and on the east coast the Arabs ran a huge operation that dated back several centuries. Where the dealers themselves obtained their merchandise varied from location to location; in many cases, certainly along the West African coast, it was customary for the victors in an inter-tribal war to combine business with pleasure by selling their captives into slavery, or even to undertake deliberate slaving raids on their weaker neighbours.

In the modern era the embarrassing fact that the wretched cargoes of 'black ivory' which arrived at such destinations as America and the West Indies were often first introduced to bondage by their fellow Africans and merely sold on by Arabs and others tends to be buried under layers of political correctness. As a matter of interest, it is now also largely forgotten that slaves of that general era were not all people of colour. It appears that the Portuguese and Spanish sold hundreds of thousands of captured European protestants to Arab potentates along the Mediterranean coasts, mainly for galley slaves, a virtual guarantee of a brutally cruel existence whose only merciful aspect was that it was usually quite short.

The common image of a slave is that of a harried creature, frequently in chains and subject to endless cruelties and assaults. There is no doubt this certainly happened, but the available evidence indicates it was not the general rule at the Cape, particularly in the urban areas.

Boxer writes that in 1772 the renowned Captain James Cook RN, 'who had seen more of the world than most of his contemporaries, and whose opinions are always deserving of respect,' wrote that Cape slaves 'are in general treated with great lenity, and sometimes become favourites with their masters, who give them very good clothing,' although they were not allowed to wear shoes. Boxer adds that 'of course there were exceptions, and cruel masters may have been relatively more numerous' up-country than in Cape Town, but 'the evidence on this point is conflicting.'

OF Mentzel, that renowned chronicler of the early Cape, says that the Company gave its slaves generous issues of food, clothing and tobacco, and supplied each with a full set of clothing once a year which included veils or head-cloths for the women, while 'privately owned slaves in Cape Town were usually very well looked after, providing help in every branch of housekeeping ... Female slaves from Bengal or the coast of Coromandel, or from Surat, were much in demand, as they had a good reputation for needlework ... tailors, too, were valued, and prominent officials kept their own tailor as part of the household. It was said that there were more tailors in Cape Town than any other town of its size.'

In her book *Fashion in South Africa 1652–1900*, Daphne H Strutt notes that privately owned slaves' clothes and circumstances depended on those of their owners. In more status-conscious households they might be dressed in anything from elaborate livery to clothes they had made themselves or received from their owners, but, sartorially speaking, things went considerably less well in the rural areas. Rural owners sometimes fulfilled their clothing obligation 'by purchasing second-hand clothes from hostelry-keepers whose guests had been unable to settle the bill and were forced to leave their clothing behind in lieu of payment. Thus the less important farm slaves went about in a motley array of cast-off clothing.'

Boxer says that Cape slaves, unlike their contemporaries in other parts of the world, 'were not entirely without legal means of redress, and they were entitled to petition for relief if they were atrociously handled or inadequately fed' (as in an early successful petition dating from 1672), while 'private owners who made themselves notorious through the ill-treatment of their slaves were usually, although not invariably, punished; in a few extreme cases slaves were removed from the control of sadistic owners.'

He mentions a VOC-run elementary school where some slave children were taught arithmetic and to read and write Dutch, while 'private owners sometimes had their slaves' children educated alongside their own, either at an elementary school or in their houses.' Daphne Strutt adds that 'there were instances of European lads being apprenticed to skilled slave craftsmen ... who were thereupon responsible for housing and feeding and clothing these apprentices ... a strange situation.'

All this is an indication of just how important a place slaves, whether owned by the VOC or private individuals, occupied in the skilled and semi-skilled labour force. Boxer writes: 'The Company ... employed them as stevedores, bricklayers, builders, millers, potters, dairymen, grooms, hospital nurses, bookbinders, gardeners, thatchers etc ...

'Many [Cape Town] residents depended for their livelihood to a large extent on those of their slaves, who were trained in various callings and hired out by the day or by the month. Indonesian male slaves made excellent masons, house-painters, confectioners, cooks and fishermen, and many of the women were skilled sempstresses.'

It was also an accepted practice for an owner to allow a skilled slave to ply his or her trade for personal gain, as long as the owner's work received first priority and the slave paid over what amounted to a royalty on all outside work done. As a result, some slaves were able to accumulate a little capital and improve their personal circumstances, which could include buying their freedom.

However, in a phenomenon not unique to the Cape, Boxer comments that 'it was inevitable in any slave-owning society that slaves would normally be more severely punished than freemen for identical offences – occasional instances to the contrary notwithstanding.'

In the earlier years, when most of what is now the Western Cape was not under Company control, escaping slaves could easily survive as outlaws (an interesting point made by Nigel Penn in his book *Rogues, Rebels and Runaways,* is that in those years the resident Khoina did not welcome runaways because many were armed and dangerous, and the Khoina frequently betrayed or turned them in to the VOC).

Slaves were not the only runaways to lose themselves in the wilderness in the 17th and 18th centuries. Various military deserters, indentured servants, outright criminals and others also fled into the interior, sometimes forming alliances and sometimes not, to the detriment of the Company and often the local inhabitants as well.

Extracts from:

Boxer, CR, *The Dutch Seaborne Empire 1600–1800,* London: Pelican Books, 1973.

Mentzel, OF, *A Geographical and Topographical Description of the Cape of Good Hope,* Part 1, ed. HJ Mandelbrote, Cape Town: Van Riebeeck Society, 1921.

Strutt, Daphne J, *Fashion in South Africa 1652–1900,* Cape Town: AA Balkema, 1975.

APPENDIX TWO

NAMING THE KHOINA AND BUSHMEN: THE CONTROVERSY

What the original inhabitants of the Cape actually called themselves is a subject about which many historians and anthropologists argue to this day. The generic term 'Hottentot' (or even 'Hotnot') is now generally eschewed for being racist and colonialist, the preferred alternative being 'Khoi' or 'Khoikhoi' without regard to singulars or plurals. 'Bushmen' is similarly regarded as politically incorrect in some circles and is often replaced by 'San' – an incorrectly spelt singular form that now serves as a plural as well.

Professor Richard Elphick wrote in the 1980s that the southern Cape pastoralists did not use the word 'Hottentot' to refer to themselves, but 'Kwena' (men) or perhaps 'Kwekwena' (men of men); 'Khoikhoi' was used by the Namaqua, living hundreds of kilometres to the north, in what is now called Namaqualand. Throughout Elphick uses 'Khoikhoi' only for clarity, adhering to an incorrect usage which has been sanctified by decades of unjustified misuse.

Elphick's work on the pronunciation of the name received some indirect and unwitting support from archaeologist Michael Wilson, writing in the quarterly bulletin of the National Library of South Africa in 2007; he established the etymology of the pronunciation of 'Khoikhoi' should instead be 'Khoekhoe' – but subsequent examination proves that this is best expressed phonetically as 'Kwehkweh' in English and 'Kwêkwê' in Afrikaans.

Both Elphick and Wilson also have doubts about 'San'. Elphick calls it a 'quasi-ethnic' term, and not adequate to describe the complex relationship between the Khoina and the !Kung, Wilson adding that 'if "Khoekhoe" is accepted into the lexicon of South African English, for consistency the Nama spelling "Saan" should replace "San".'

Another who disagrees with the conventional academic wisdom is Dr Cyril Hromnik, an American researcher-historian resident in Cape Town whose doggedly held contrary views on various matters have enraged the mainstream community for decades.

The ever-simmering Hromnik-versus-academia debate boiled over in 2007, when the academic Kobus Faasen hit the newspaper headlines with his stated intention of taking the use of the word 'boesman', or bushman, to the Equality Court because of its allegedly racist overtones; one of his supporters in this endeavour being none other than the then Minister of Arts and Culture, Dr Pallo Jordan.

Dr Hromnik not only publicly admonished Faasen in South Africa's *Sunday Times* newspaper but also took on various academics who advocated the use of 'Khoikhoi', saying:

> The Dutch called them Hottentots; 300 years later we're still getting it wrong. I wonder why Kobus Faasen ... is fussing over the historical and non-abusive name Boesman or Bushman, when he is happy to call himself by the recently concocted and grossly abusive name 'Khoisan'?
>
> If he takes seriously [the] interpretation of the name San as meaning 'robber', while Khoi means 'a man', then by calling himself a 'Khoisan', Faasen seems to be happier to be called 'a robber man' than a bushman, a man of the bush or forest. He should know better, and should not allow himself to be pulled by the nose by manipulative ideologues and politicians who masquerade as would-be professors ...
>
> Numerous other professors [have] spent the last 30 and more years brainwashing themselves and trying to brainwash their 'coloured' compatriots into believing that calling themselves 'Khoisan'

was better than calling themselves by the historically attested and commonly used name Otentottu, mispronounced by the Dutch as 'Hottentot'.

They did so even though they knew that the name 'Khoisan' had been invented only in 1928 by the German Professor Leonhard Schultze. They never understood the name Otentottu and never even tried to understand it. It was easier to attribute to it the pejorative meaning of the nickname Hotnot and blame it on apartheid, colonialism and other nasty forces of the misunderstood past.

To repair the historical, cultural and even psychological damage and to heal the wounded self-esteem of the Quena, 'coloured' and Bushman inhabitants of South Africa, we have to look afresh at the names Bushman, Kwena, and Otentottu, as well as at the terms khoi, khoikhoi and khoisan.

The latter three words should never be written with capital letters. The word khoi, properly khoe, is not a name but a word meaning 'man'. Khoekhoe with the small initial letter k means 'man-man', which is neither a plural nor a sensible singular and, therefore, totally useless.

Neither did 'San' mean 'robber', as some commentators averred, added Hromnik:

In reality, San is a Quena nickname for the Bushmen, which describes them as 'naked' ... when compared with the kaross-clad or dressed-up [in textiles] Quena, the Bushmen were indeed naked. However, applying this nickname to the Quena ... is totally nonsensical and our school textbooks should get rid of it, the sooner the better ...

But what about the 'Khoisan' pollution that litters the textbooks, the so-called scholarly works, our museums and even some of our churches? How long will it take to clean them of this soul-destroying miscreant misnomer?

It is high time to return to the sensible and historically justified nomenclature. The only name that is applicable to most of the surviving groups of the aboriginal hunters of southern Africa is Kung. The real Kung can be seen today only in Angola, northern Namibia and, perhaps, a few in Botswana.

The colonial Dutch never encountered any real Kung. The hunting people encountered by the early trekboers and other early Dutch in the territory of modern South Africa, who they called Boesman, were not the real Kung. They were a mixed stock that resulted from the mixing of the Quena (Otentottu) men with the Kung women, but their language was more Quena-like than Kung-like.

They were employed frequently by the Quena as shepherds. The Quena masters had a special name for them, calling them Sonqua (in the south) and Soaqua (in the northern parts of the Colony). One of their groups, which was called Ubiqua, lived relatively close to Camissa (the Quena name for Table Valley, where Cape Town grew up) ... Their name, Ubiqua, translated into Dutch as Boesman – and there is the source of the name Boesman and Bushman, which was misapplied broadly to all hunting and gathering people of southern Africa.

Who are the Quena and Otentottu? They are one and the same people, and both names were used and transferred to the early Dutch by the very same people. The Dutch definitely did not invent these names. They only corrupted the original name Otentottu. The Quena and Sonqua people urgently need a second liberation, this time not from colonialism but from artificial and deliberately false academic imperialism.

See Elphick, Richard, *Khoikhoi and the Founding of White South Africa*. Johannesburg: Ravan Press, 1985.

CASTLE ROUTINE IN THE 1720s

The routine at the Castle of Good Hope has been a matter of some curiosity over the years and sheds valuable light on an aspect of daily life in Cape Town in the early 1700s. The following has been gleaned from the work of 18th-century author OF Mentzel.

A little before four o'clock every morning the corporal of the night-guard, having formed up his men outside the guardroom, collected the two duty *rondegangers* (lit. 'round-walkers') and set out on his last round of inspection, which also involved kick-starting the day's activities.

He woke the garrison adjutant, the company sergeants, the duty drummer for the day, the duty fifer and the six other designated *rondegangers*, sending a man to the Governor's Guard section of the barracks to rouse the guard's drummers and grenadiers. These worthies were required to get up and put on their underclothes, so that they could turn out fully dressed and equipped at short notice in case the governor had decided during the night to make an unscheduled early departure.

The inspection was timed to bring the inspection party past the tower at precisely 4am, one of the *rondegangers* tolling the bell. Outside the guardroom the night-guard formally challenged their corporal and gave out the password, then dismissed them. This was the signal for the duty trumpeters to sound the morning call and 'some other pieces' (Mentzel does not specify, but one imagines that this was the equivalent of the more modern 'quarter-call', the prelude to an executive call). Then the fifer and two drummers (the night duty man and his replacement) sounded the reveille.

At this stage the adjutant, the sergeants and the other *rondegangers* appeared out of the early-morning gloom and marched to the guardroom, where the night-guard was now standing to arms again. The adjutant then headed for the Governor's Quarters to fetch the keys to the Van der Stel Gate, escorted by six *rondegangers* armed with long pikes and a seventh who was the designated keyman.

Having taken receipt of the keys, the adjutant's party crossed the Voorplein and marched into the Van der Stel Gate's arched flagstone tunnel with its two great spike-studded doors. The keyman unlocked the small *klincket* or wicket, scarcely a man's width in extent, which pierced the right-hand door, and the corporal and two of his men stepped outside.

Having satisfied himself that no enemy lurked without, the corporal marched his men down to the *barrière*, about 50m away from the Castle. The exact description and location of the *barrière* has been lost; it could have been either a barred gate or a large turnstile, and logic dictates that it was situated on the inner side of the moat, approximately where the Lion Gate of later years stands to this day.

The corporal unlocked the *barrière*, posted one of his men to guard it and marched back with the other soldier to report to the adjutant that no enemy awaited outside the Castle. The night-guard then presented arms, the keyman unlocked the main doors of the Van der Stel Gate and the drummers beat a flourish, the signal for the outside sentry to open the *barrière*.

The remaining *rondeganger*, who had climbed into the bell tower in the meantime, now rang the bell, and the adjutant and his escort marched back to the Governor's Quarters to return the keys. The last act of the opening ritual consisted of the various sergeants reporting to the adjutant, after which all concerned returned to their quarters.

The 6am bell was the signal for the slaves and craftsmen to start work, and for recruits to be drilled by a sergeant in front of the guardroom, but the daily mounting of the guard did not take place for nearly an hour.

A little before 7am the new guard formed up – probably in the Wapenplaats, just below the barracks – and the old guard in the Voorplein, while the duty fifer and two drummers took up position. At the last stroke of the bell the bandsmen sounded the 'fall in', and the corporals of the new guard marched their men to the armoury below the Nassau bastion in the far corner of the Wapenplaats. There the adjutant announced the duties of the day. This done, he might have drilled them before dismissal.

Towards 8am the lieutenant of the guard made his appearance with the garrison's six hautboyists, and on the stroke of the hour marched the new guard through the Kat archway, to the sound of drums and the high-pitched hautboys. The new guard halted in front of the Governor's Quarters, presented arms, then shouldered their muskets again.

While the officers and sergeants of the two guards waited, their corporals marched off to relieve the night-sentries inside and outside the Castle, the hautboys playing all the while. When the corporals returned to report that all the new sentries had been posted, the bandsmen fell silent, the old guard marched off to barracks, and the new guard took over the guardroom. Now the stage was set for the daily round of military and civilian activities, all of it strictly regulated by the duty *ronde-gangers'* hourly bell-tolling.

The 8am bell brought a stream of senior and junior merchants, book-keepers and clerical workers to attend to the Company's business, while townspeople desiring a personal audience with the governor headed for his quarters. At 9am the bell announced that the Council of Policy was now in session to deliberate the Company's affairs or interview petitioners or other persons it had summoned to appear. On Saturdays, however, the Council transformed itself into the Matrimonial Court, to quiz couples wishing to marry 'about possible hindrances, such as nearness of kin,' as Mentzel puts it, and 'if there are none their names are entered in a book and the marriage licence is given to them.'

The 11am bell signalled the start of an apparently leisurely lunch break for the officials, craftsmen and slaves, but not for the garrison.

At 12 noon by the sundial in the Voorplein, the sergeant of the guard, halberd in hand, marched into the governor's office to hand in a written report, while the lieutenant of the guard went off duty for lunch, either in his quarters or at the governor's table.

At 1pm the craftsmen and slaves returned to work, but the officials and clerks did not go back until an hour later and couched their quill pens again at 4pm, unless circumstances such as the impending departure of a return-fleet required them to stay longer.

At 6pm the civilian working day finally ended with the departure of the slaves and craftsmen, and preparations for closing the Castle could begin. The hautboyists formed up outside the barracks to play an evensong and other pieces, while the duty drummer climbed up onto the Leerdam Bastion. At 6.30pm the hautboyists fell silent, and for the next 30 minutes the duty drummer beat the retreat – intended to warn off-duty soldiers to hasten back to quarters before the roll-call on the dot of 7pm (Mentzel records that the barracks corporal stood by at roll call, equipped with a long cane so that he could chastise any latecomers).

Roll call over, the corporals marched their men off to the hall of the Governor's Quarters for evening prayers; by now the adjutant had fetched the keys and made for the Van der Stel Gate with his keyman and six pike-armed *rondegangers*. While the guard stood to attention the great iron-bound doors were closed, although they were not yet locked, the little wicket remaining open under the watchful eye of a *rondeganger*, so that the corporal of the guard and two of his men could go out to close the *barrière* and post a sentry.

As soon as the corporal returned to the guardroom the bell was rung and divine service began – 'a verse and a prayer are sung,' Mentzel says, 'then comes a short prayer; and then after another verse the ceremony is over. The corporals go out to the guard and the soldiers return to their barracks.'

The captain of the garrison then gave the adjutant the two passwords for the night – one for the Castle sentries and the other for the Burgher Guard, the offshoot of the Burgher Militia which patrolled the streets after dark with rattles and cudgels – and passed on any orders which were to be communicated to the night-guard. Thus equipped, the sergeant of the Burgher Guard went off to brief his officers and the governor's civilian counsellors.

Now peace reigned in the Castle, but not for long. At 9.30pm the bell began to toll, an incessant clangour that lasted for half an hour and was the signal for all military occupants to turn out for the final roll call just before 10pm, and 'woe betide any man,' Mentzel says, 'who is absent overnight without leave.'

At this stage, too, a surgeon from the military hospital would arrive 'with certain medicines and instruments for blood-letting' to spend the night in case of unexpected illness; if the sick person needed more attention than the surgeon could administer on the spot, he would be 'at once taken to the hospital and ... well looked after there.'

Now the Castle could finally be closed for the night. The fifer and two drummers sounded a tattoo; the corporal of the guard retrieved his outside sentry and locked the *barrière*, the Van der Stel Gate's doors and the *klincket*, and the adjutant went with the two duty *rondegangers* to return the keys to the Governor's Quarters.

The adjutant then made his final rounds, visiting the barrack-rooms and taking roll call reports from the corporals. Having dropped the *rondegangers* off at the guardroom, he was free to return to his own quarters.

The Castle did not sleep, however. At 11pm the sergeant of the guard went on his rounds, and on his return to the guardroom was met by the orderly officer, to whom he gave the night's password. Just before midnight, however, the *rondegangers* would start making their hourly rounds, each one timed so that they visited the sentry posts before the striking of each hour, 'their object being to catch any sentry who might happen to have gone to sleep on duty and who would probably be awakened by the sound of the bell,' Mentzel says. According to Mentzel the drill for such occasions was somewhat peculiar. When the *rondegangers* were about 20 paces away the sentry challenged them with a cry of '*Werda?*' (who goes there), and on being given the password, sent them on their way. But then the same drill had to be gone through when they had gone another 20 paces.

'I do not know the reason for this double challenge and answer,' Mentzel says, 'unless it be to make strangers believe that the Castle is guarded by twice as many sentries as are really there' – a not unreasonable conclusion; foreigners often passed through Cape Town, and the VOC would have had no option but to assume that at least some of these birds of passage were spies for the other East India companies. An even more elaborate stratagem was employed at Batavia, the VOC's Far East headquarters, where 'the adjutants, when they make the rounds, usually let the sentries challenge them two or even three times before they answer' – the result in one case being that a soldier just arrived from Europe shot and killed an adjutant who had failed to respond immediately.

Extracts from:

Mentzel, OF, *A Geographical and Topographical Description of the Cape of Good Hope*, Part 1, ed. HJ Mandelbrote, Cape Town: Van Riebeeck Society, 1921.

THE BATTLE OF BLAAUWBERG
AN ANALYSIS

COMMANDERS

Given the limited coverage of this most important battle in any modern histories, it is worthwhile looking at the planning and actions of the two commanders at Blaauwberg, and examining how they reacted to their circumstances.

Lourens Erasmus concedes that although Baird carried out his mission correctly, certain comments are worth making. Firstly, if Baird had diverted Beresford's force to the Roodezand pass as soon as it was clear that an advance from Saldanha Bay would not be needed, he would have been able to interdict the pass, which might have led to an earlier capitulation, foiling Janssens' Hottentots Holland plan. Secondly, Baird relied too much on his escort ships' firepower, as a result of which he failed to occupy the heights of the Blaauwberg as soon as possible and thus can be blamed for the water shortage after the battle. What Erasmus does not mention is that if Baird had not sent Wilson and his Light Dragoons to Saldanha Bay and if it had been possible to mount all or most of them, the proceedings at Blaauwberg might have looked very different.

Erasmus acknowledges that Janssens handled himself well on the battlefield and, unlike Sluysken in 1795, did his utmost to defend the

Cape. But 'nevertheless ... his consistent doubt about his own competence and the Cape's defence possibilities ... must eventually have filtered through to his officers and soldiers ...' According to Erasmus Janssens did not make full use of his burgher soldiers; 'the British were very vulnerable during their landing, and seeing that Ritmeester Linde's scouts had achieved a measure of success, a larger force could have stopped the British.'

At the same time, though, Erasmus admits that the British landing took place very soon after Popham's arrival; that Janssens initially had to keep his troops near Cape Town because of the threat posed by the British warships, enabling Baird to concentrate his troops in one place – whereas Janssens had to keep the defence of the entire colony in mind; and that it would have been rash to attack the British troops while they were landing under protection of the ships' guns. But if Janssens had not made such a 'hesitant' advance on 7 January, 'after having already reached [Rietvallei] during the evening of 6 January', he could 'very easily have already occupied the heights of [Blaauwberg] on 7 January and thus would not have been too late to do so on the 8th.

> From the heights of Blaauwberg Janssens could have caused great confusion among the British with his artillery while the latter were mounting the steep slopes ... while he would still have been able to beat a safe retreat ... A commander must be able to anticipate the enemy's intentions and then gamble sensibly. Janssens did not gamble when the British could fruitfully have been attacked at the shoreline during and after their landing ...

While Janssens' conduct during the battle was 'faultless', Erasmus says:

> ... it must definitely be seen as a mistake that he decided to tackle the great British preponderance with his motley army on the open plain. He certainly had an advantage in artillery and cavalry that he could have used on the plain. Even after the Cape infantry retreated the Cape cavalry could still have inflicted damage on the British. What an effect could such an attack not have had on the British while they were experiencing the problem of a shortage of water!

After arriving at the Hottentots Holland Janssens made no effort to call up more burghers to help him further, although Baird was so convinced of his strong situation that he offered Janssens very favourable peace terms, just to end the resistance.

Erasmus also says that Janssens was too 'complacent about the quality of his Cape soldiers', particularly the Waldeckers: 'Janssens himself claims that he was acquainted with all sorts of stories that they would commit treason on the battlefield, yet he still was forced to trust them and rely on them.'

There is a considerable amount of truth in what Erasmus says, but although a good commander certainly takes risks at times, an expert gambler rarely does so unless he knows he has an edge of some kind. Janssens had little or no edge; given Baird's ability to strike elsewhere at short notice, he decided that denuding Von Prophalow of troops to bolster his own army would have been too great a gamble.

If there is one aspect on which Janssens can be faulted it is that he could have caused the British great difficulty during the landing phase and later if he had formed his regular and burgher dragoons, with Pellegrini's horse gunners included, into a sort of flying column which could have harassed the British to great effect, probably without suffering great losses from the ships' guns.

All this having been said, one can only agree with Erasmus's final conclusion on the quality of the two commanders:

> Under the circumstances Janssens made the best preparations to defend the Cape, but his lack of a greater number of reliable troops made his task almost impossible. ... the fact that Baird knew the Cape and had a strong army of veterans with him, together with inventiveness and determination, swung the balance in favour of the British to much too great an extent, from the start.

What does emerge clearly is that Janssens deserves a place among South Africa's pantheon of military leaders. For two centuries he has been denigrated, vilified or simply written off as a poor general. Yet if this book has proved anything it is that all these depictions of him are incorrect – and he deserves to be judged by his actions, rather than by the words of a disapproving chorus of armchair warriors. He was not only a capable fighting general of great personal courage, but a first-class planner who prepared a sound defensive strategy in spite of a truly horrifying lack of resources. And finally, he should be classed as a humane man, whose first concern was for his troops and the innocent civilians under his overall command.

Baird, too, emerges as one of Britain's best fighting generals of the time. But he was more than merely a warrior. His planning and implementation of the invasion plan was impeccable, and his ability to think on his feet, even to the point of Janssens' capitulation, was proven beyond doubt.

What lifts both of them even further above the common ruck is their record as civil governors. Janssens' achievements stand to his credit. He and De Mist did not succeed in their endeavours to turn the Cape from a mere replenishment station into a possession governed by a liberal-democratic constitution – once again because they lacked almost everything needed to do so – but they managed to leave behind them a footprint whose traces endure to this day.

Baird, too, proved to be a wise and sensitive civil administrator during his regrettably short tenure, so that the Cape's transition to British rule was a relatively painless one that earned him the respect of the inhabitants. If he had not allowed himself to be talked into the Buenos Aires fiasco by Popham, he might well have laid the foundation of a far better dispensation in the Cape, with all that that would have implied for the later South Africa.

MYTHS AND MISINFORMATION

The Battle of Blaauwberg was not just a military victory for the British but a propaganda triumph as well. In the years that followed, a substantial body of myths arose – or was allowed to arise – in the British Army about what had actually happened: the chief of which was that Baird had won an almost bloodless victory against a far superior enemy force better supplied with artillery. This seems to have become firmly embedded in British military folklore.

As late as 1892, almost a century after the battle, the compilers of a history of the 24th Regiment could still state confidently that the Batavian army consisted of 'five thousand men with twenty-three guns', and that Baird's force of only 4 066 men with six artillery pieces 'drove [them] off with a loss of seven hundred men and three guns' – at a cost of just one officer and 14 other ranks killed, and nine officers and 180 other ranks wounded.

This version of events, evidently an accepted one, with no eye-witness still alive to object, is demonstrably incorrect. As we have seen, Baird was definitely not outnumbered. The verified Batavian combat strength at Blaauwberg was 1 951 infantry and dragoons, and 94 artillerymen, a total of 2 045. Baird's verified strength (the figures vary slightly but not significantly from source to source) was about 4 000 infantry and gunners, about 500 marines, and 500 sailors for dragging his guns: a total of at least 4 500 bayonets, or 5 000 overall. In combat effectives he outnumbered Janssens two to one. Janssens' only real advantage was that he had some mounted troops available at Blaauwberg while Baird had none.

As for artillery, Janssens might have had more than 20 guns in total, but only a few of them were at Blaauwberg and some of these were short-range weapons. In point of fact he and Baird were fairly evenly matched when it came to heavier guns: two howitzers and six 6-pounders each, with a maximum range of c1 200m when firing round-shot. Janssens' 3-pounders, firing round-shot, would most likely have had a maximum 'reach' of about 1 000m, again with a much shorter effective range. The small 1-pounders and *lantakas* would have fired grape-shot only, to about the same range as a musket. These figures tell the story. If Janssens' guns had all been 6-pounders, Baird would have suffered very much heavier casualties before getting within effective musket range. The short-range gunners could not therefore come into action as soon as the 6-pounders – although when they did they were, of course, deadly to infantry because of their spread of shot.

What all this says is that Baird and others were not exaggerating when they talked about the intense artillery fire brought down on the British troops. Furthermore, Janssens did not, as far as can be determined, lose three guns to the British, but just one. It had been spiked and left behind because the gun-horses had been killed. There was some loose talk immediately after the battle about his loss of guns, but no concrete figure seems to have emerged.

The exact number and type of Batavian guns – whether taken to Blaauwberg or left behind with Von Prophalow – appears to be a mystery, and a Royal Artillery survey of 1809 sheds very little light on the subject. Only four Dutch 6-pounders are listed in the artillery park, although a number of 3-pounders, 8-pounders and the like were located at various batteries. It is possible that some of the Batavian field pieces were shipped to England after the battle as trophies – a common military practice to this day – and some of the 'make do' converted light guns were transferred from their improvised field carriages and returned to the batteries to resume their original role as signal guns.

The matter of casualties is a considerable enigma. Whatever the Batavian battlefield casualties were, they certainly did not total 700, or anything near it. When the Batavian units' rolls were called after the battle, all except those of the disgraced Waldecker line companies, who were already straggling back to Cape Town after being chased away by a disgusted Janssens, a total of 337 soldiers did not answer to their names: 110 men of the 240-strong French contingent; 103 of the 22nd Batavia; 17 of the Hottentot Light Infantry; 43 of the 9th Bataafsche Jagers; 18 of the Waldeck light company; 18 of the 5th Artillery; 10 of the Javanese Artillery Corps; four burgher dragoons, six Batavian Dragoons, and eight of the artillery support troops.

A final overall total of the surviving Batavian wounded, including those in hospital, came to 13 officers and 121 other ranks: 32 French, 25 of the 22nd Batavia, 11 of the Hottentot Light Infantry, 13 of the 9th Bataafsche Jagers, 37 of the Waldeck Regiment; eight of the 5th Artillery, five of the Javanese Artillery Corps and three Batavian Dragoons. It is very probable, though, that a proportion (high by today's standards) subsequently died either of their wounds or because of the rudimentary medical care then available.

The number of Waldecker fusilier dead is uncertain because of their instant descent into rabbledom and subsequent expulsion from Rietvallei before their roll was called. Krynauw believes seven of them were killed, but Janssens does not mention whether the 37 wounded in his report consisted of men from the line companies or the steadfast light company, or both.

Krynauw also notes that one AC Snouckaert, in a book entitled *De Kaapkolonie in 1806*, later made the unsubstantiated claim that one entire Waldecker line company was captured on the battlefield, but there is no evidence of this and it is highly unlikely in any case, given the fact that they were already well on the way back to Rietvallei before the British got anywhere near them.

It is to be noted that at the time of the capitulation Janssens still had just over 1 000 men left, although not all had taken part in the battle: he had released the French sailors at Rietvallei, but had gained Major von Horn's two Hottentot Light Infantry companies from False Bay and Simon's Town. (We also know that along with the last of the field artillery, Von Prophalow despatched to Janssens an unknown number of stragglers who had somehow reached Cape Town after the battle, and would obviously have been among those who had not answered to their names when the rolls were called.)

As to the British casualties – if all the verifiable facts and eyewitness accounts are taken together, the official figures of British losses at Blaauwberg exhibit a strange contradiction that, with one exception, seems to have gone unnoticed, even by the generally excellent Lourens Erasmus. The only person who has noticed something wrong about the British figures is DW Krynauw.

On the British side, from Baird on downwards, it was consistently reported that the British force came under sustained and intense small-arms and artillery fire during the battle, and it is a fact not only that the Batavians were firing the notoriously lethal grape-shot and explosive howitzer shells but that three of their units were known for sharpshooting, and remained on the battlefield until the last moments.

Yet Baird's casualty figures – which later became generally accepted – give British losses as only 15 dead, 189 wounded and eight missing. This cannot be accurate. On top of that, Baird's official figure deliberately leaves out the 35 men who drowned when their boat capsized in Losperd's Bay, and did not include those men who died on the march, nor those witnessed by Capt Dugald Carmichael during the advance on Rietvallei, where 'the soldiers dropped fast and several sailors died at the guns they had been dragging.' Subsequent commentators have followed this example. Ignoring the uncounted casualties on the march, at the very least Baird should have put the minimum known British death toll at 50, not 15.

Secondly, there is expert and unbiased eyewitness evidence from Major John Graham of the 93rd that the assault on Kleinberg was very far from the usual portrayal of a swift and almost bloodless charge that effortlessly swept away the handful of burgher dragoons holding the *kopje*. It is clear that the 24th Regiment's flank companies, and later the 24th and 71st light companies, came under sustained fire from marksmen and artillery, the latter firing at close range. From Graham's account we know that when the 24th flank companies advanced in the early stages, 'the sharpshooters on top were bringing down the 24th Grenadiers with every shot.'

Even allowing for exaggeration, it has the feel of credibility, as the Swellendammers were undoubtedly the Batavians' best and coolest shots. Many were veterans of previous campaigns, skirmishes, cattle-retrieving expeditions and the like, not to mention seasoned hunters, since Swellendam was renowned for the quantity of its game; men who did not simply loose to-whom-it-may-concern volleys into massed bodies of enemy troops, but picked their targets and aimed carefully before firing.

If one assumes that there were 100 dragoons (a not unreasonable estimate, and very possibly a conservative one) on Kleinberg, and that each fired 10 shots (also a conservative estimate, since any trained shot could get off at least two rounds a minute), it means that at least 1 000 bullets were sent off at the British. Even if Graham's statement that they were bringing them down 'with every shot' is reduced by half in order to err on the conservative side, it means that at least 500 shots would have hit their targets.

Graham also mentions that while the flank companies were being raked by the dragoons' fire, 'the enemy began with his cannon on them'. Then, when he took the 71st light company towards the gap between Kleinberg and Janssens' left flank, 'they had fine cracking at us with their guns, and these guns were so much in advance that

I was determined to try and take them.' In addition to this the 24th Regiment's flank companies were under fire from the Batavian artillery, while Graham also makes it clear that the 24th Regiment's light company was under continuous close-range artillery fire – this would most likely have been lethal grape-shot, swarms of small-calibre balls able to scythe down groups of soldiers at a time.

Yet the result, if the official figures are to be believed, is that all this thunder and lightning against the 24th resulted in just four killed and 15 wounded.

As a footnote, it is worth mentioning that in the 1892 history of the 24th Regiment quoted earlier the Kleinberg wounded are given as *16*, rather than 15, to include one drummer. If this means that the flank companies were marching in formation (hence the drummer) it would have made them even easier targets for the dragoons, although such an assumption cannot be made without some supporting evidence.

There is also ample expert anecdotal evidence that the heavy line infantry of the Highland Brigade came under intense small-arms and artillery fire when it advanced on the Batavian line. Baird himself reported that the Highlanders had advanced under 'a very heavy fire of round-shot, grape and musketry', at a range that at the end was considerably less than 100m.

Once again, three of the Batavian units faced by the brigade contained marksmen: the Hottentot Light Infantry, the burgher dragoons, and the 9th Bataafsche Jagers, who did not use muskets, but rifles, which had a greater effective range and accuracy. There were well over 500 Jagers and HLI, and they stayed on the field until the bitter end. If one assumes only five shots were fired per man (who, again, could fire at least two rounds per minute) this amounts to a staggering 2 500 shots, fired by expert riflemen and hunters, mostly at a range of 100m or less, into the close-packed ranks of Highlanders.

There is a unit-by-unit breakdown of casualty figures in the 24th Regiment history quoted above which provides much food for thought. According to this document the 71st suffered a total of just five dead, 67 wounded and one missing; the 93rd suffered only two dead and 58 wounded. The 72nd, which did not take part in the Kleinberg fighting, lost two dead, 38 wounded and one missing.

In other words, the closely packed Highland Brigade, subjected to intense rifle, musket and artillery fire at close range of more than 2 500 rounds (which could have been fired in a conservatively generous period of only some five minutes' action) – suffered only a total of nine dead, 163 wounded and two missing. A tacit betrayal of this account is the fact that the brigade's wounded included three senior field officers (two majors and a lieutenant-colonel), five lieutenants and five sergeants. If one bears in mind that sharpshooters always target the leaders of a group, and that in those days units had fewer officers than now, a case could be made that the Batavian marksmen were, in fact, aiming selectively rather than simply 'browning the mob'.

Another strange feature is that although the 59th and 83rd Regiments suffered virtually no dead or wounded because they saw little close-in action, they had three soldiers missing, whereas the entire Highland Brigade lost only two, despite the heavy action in battle. This gives rise to another question: what happened to the total of eight men listed as missing? Surely they did not desert in a hostile environment. They were not simply wounded and abandoned, because we know that afterwards the battlefield was policed and the wounded taken to Justinus Keer's makeshift hospital; the Blaauwberg battlefield was quite a small area. That being the case, it is possible that they were among those Keer buried after they had died of their wounds. But if that were so, why was no record made of their identities so that they could be struck off the regimental rolls?

The ratio of dead to wounded in the official British figures also appears strangely skewed. By Baird's reckoning there were almost 14 wounded for every fatality, and there is no category in the published breakdown to list how many of the official 189 wounded died thereafter. This is relevant because in those days a high percentage of battlefield wounded did not survive owing to infection and primitive medical treatment.

Krynauw quotes Col Wilson as writing to a friend in England, following discussions with brother officers soon after his late arrival from Saldanha, that 'in the action the English lost about two hundred men', and comments: 'Precisely what Wilson meant is not clear … it is unlikely that he would have described wounded as "lost".'

Krynauw's point is clear: Wilson was an established military writer and highly intelligent career soldier who, although he was dealing with second-hand information, would surely have taken pains to establish reasonably accurate figures. Among others of his works, his history of the 1801 Egypt campaign stands out for its meticulous attention to detail.

There is a case to be made, therefore, that British losses at Blaauwberg were actually much greater than the accepted official figures have it. Or, as Krynauw puts it: 'It appears strange that in an action in which there were no less than 189 wounded, there were only 15 dead. It arouses the suspicion that the figures were tampered with.'

A possible clue is to be found in Krynauw's statement that British officers later gave Janssens precise details about the size of the expeditionary force, but not about the extent or even the number of its casualties, except to say that they had been considerable. Krynauw asks, quite rightly: 'Did the English officers hide their losses from him?'

If this was, in fact, the case, why did it happen? The easy way out is simply to ascribe it to official British duplicity. But there is a less biased explanation to examine if one considers the circumstances. The Battle of Blaauwberg took place halfway through what was a life-and-death struggle between Britain and France in which no clear outcome was in sight for either side. The Royal Navy had earned a fearsome reputation, but at that stage the British Army had made only one major success, in the reconquest of French Egypt, which shattered the myth of French invincibility in battle for the first time.

But this might not have been enough for the British Government. Psychological warfare was as valuable then as it has been in later conflicts, and it could very well be that Baird's men were reluctant to disclose any information to an enemy, information which could later have been used in the European press as anti-British propaganda. What better than a virtually bloodless victory in a pitched battle, leading to generous terms of capitulation? That Baird's troops were too exhausted for a swift follow-up, and that Baird himself was under orders to facilitate a transition by granting such terms, and wanted to settle the matter as soon as possible, are the sort of uncomfortable facts that any French propagandist worth his salt would not have hesitated to ignore.

Ideally, the message to the world would be that Britain was willing to attack any French or French-allied territory, no matter where it was or how strongly it was defended – as they did later in Java – and that the British soldier was unbeatable on the battlefield, even when the odds were against him.

Whatever the case, it is a mystery that will never be solved. There is no mass cemetery for the Blaauwberg dead, so that today the location of most of their graves is unknown. In the 1950s DW Krynauw spent many hours combing the battlefield area for identifiable gravesites and drew a blank. Were there exhumations and reburials in later years? Once again, no record of this seems to exist, if it ever happened.

There is another aspect to this matter. The Battle of Blaauwberg is nowhere commemorated in Cape Town, although it took place virtually on the city's doorstep, and one has the impression (admittedly subjective) that in the years after 1806 there was a largely successful attempt by the victors to de-emphasise and then bury memories not just of the Batavian defence but the entire period of Batavian republicanism enjoyed at the Cape between 1803 and 1806.

Indeed, it might well have been felt wisest to defuse the substantial sympathy for the Batavian Republic (and by extension for the French) that still existed at the Cape. By the time the 'Great French War' ended in 1815, the damage had been done, so much so that even South African histories barely mention the battle, or its tremendous significance to Southern and Central Africa. It is, perhaps, a classic illustration of that aged truism, 'history is written by the winners'.

The overall result is that except for a few historians and military-history enthusiasts, Capetonians have very little or no collective memory of their city's greatest and most important battle. It is a crying shame and, one could say a disgrace, for a city that allegedly is very conscious of its history – although one promising development is that the battlefield area has been preserved unscathed by including it in a conservation area, and that there are plans to develop it into an appropriate tourist attraction.

Extracts from:

Erasmus, Lourens J, *Die Tweede Britse Verowering van die Kaap, 1806* [The Second British Conquest of the Cape, 1806], (unpublished MA thesis, University of Potcheftroom), 1972.

Krynauw, DW, *Beslissing by Blouberg – Triomf en Tragedie van die Stryd om die Kaap* [Decision at Blouberg: The Triumph and Tragedy of the Battle for the Cape], Cape Town: Tafelberg-Uitgewers Beperk, 1999.

APPENDIX FIVE

UNITS AND UNIFORMS
AT MUIZENBERG AND BLAAUWBERG

THE CORPS PANDOEREN

In recent times certain commentators have attempted to portray the Corps Pandoeren as unwilling conscripts, badly treated by the rest of the VOC military – miserable press-ganged victims of oppression, an ill-paid, ill-armed, ill-clothed and bare-footed Khoina rabble, thrown together as a last-minute act of desperation.

Yet no commentator has asked the fundamental question of why such allegedly put-upon creatures exhibited such technical competence and courage when the balloon went up in 1795. There were no significant numbers of deserters, then or later, despite performing full-time military service and being paid slightly less than the other low-paid VOC troops. Indeed, in his meticulously sourced dissertation, entitled '*Hottentot-Regimente aan die Kaap, 1781–1806*' [Hottentot Regiments at the Cape], in the 1970 edition of the *Archives Year Book for South African History*, Johannes de Villiers has gathered sufficient information to suggest to any keen observer that the Pandoeren were not generally unhappy with their lot.

Firstly, describing the Pandoer rank and file as Khoina, as is often done (doubtless because of the politically correct disinclination to use the term 'Hottentot') is an over-simplification. By that stage, thanks

316

largely to the great smallpox epidemic of 1713 and another in 1755, few Khoina had survived, particularly in the general vicinity of Cape Town. Consequently the greater number of Pandoeren were most likely the so-called Bastaard-Hottentotten, namely, people of mixed ethnic origin.

Far from being a last-minute improvisation, the unit had been systematically built up for two years by the time the British invaded in 1795 – as a European-style light infantry regiment, designed and equipped to fight at the Cape. The heavy line infantryman of the day was used in close formation for volley-firing and bayonet charges. The light infantryman, on the other hand, was primarily a sharpshooter, scout and skirmisher, lightly equipped, hardy, self-sufficient and extremely mobile (this was why the British rifle regiments became known as the 'foot cavalry').

It had been axiomatic from Simon van der Stel's time that the best method of defending the Cape was by means of small and highly mobile forces, which was why such emphasis was laid on forming mounted dragoon companies, and the establishment of a light infantry regiment fitted this concept like a glove.

Some serious misrepresentations exist about the Corps Pandoeren's uniform, weapons and equipment. An almost universal faux pas is mislabelling pictures of the red-coated Cape Corps members of the post-1795 British occupation as Pandoeren. The only attempt to portray a Pandoer is in one reputable museum, where there is a figure wearing a short grey leather jacket and trousers and a round grey leather cap, minus any sort of footwear or personal equipment (originally the figure carried a blunderbuss, although this was later changed to a musket). But Johannes de Villiers' dissertation makes it clear that this laudable attempt at resurrecting the Corps Pandoeren uniform and equipment is not quite correct.

The light infantry uniform in Europe tended to be dark, more camouflaged at a time when military clothing usually blared out its wearer's nationality; the rifle regiments in particular often wore very dark green uniforms in the Prussian 'Jager' style (known consequently to this day in Britain as 'rifle green') and many adopted the hunting bugle as their trademark, from the Prussian 'Jager' huntsmen. Owing to the number of Poles and Germans in the British 60th Rifles in the 18th century, the standard-issue green breeches became known even into the 20th century as 'Jagers'.

Like most military uniforms of the era, the Pandoer uniform was adapted from the civilian clothes its men were accustomed to wearing. Thus the Pandoer private wore a black linen shirt, a hard-wearing short leather jacket and leather trousers. The colour of these outer garments is now lost, but was probably a dark or reddish brown, the normal shades of tanned leather in those days. The headdress was a round leather '*mus*', or brimless bonnet, again, not unlike some European rifle regiments.

No specific mention is made of shoes, so commentators have simply assumed that the Pandoeren had none, defying all military logic. Most Pandoer recruits came from Genadendal and would have been used to wearing shoes in civilian life; and the condition of a light infantryman's feet was as important to him as a correctly functioning musket.

De Villiers supplies a convincing answer: 'It is likely that they made their own *velskoene*, as was the case during the [first] British rule over the Cape (1795–1803). A quantity of cattle hides was provided to the corps ... these hides could be used for many purposes – for *velskoene*, trousers and even for the skins of the corps's drums.'

Quite apart from the VOC's desperate lack of money for things like orthodox military footwear, the light, flat-soled or low-heeled *velskoen* as made and worn at the Cape by generations of frontiersmen, hunters, farmers and labourers of all races, was infinitely more suitable for mobile foot warfare than the standard infantry boot, and could easily be made or repaired *in situ*.

The weapons and equipment issued to the Pandoeren have also been misrepresented. The blunderbuss (from the Dutch '*donderbus*': lit. 'thunder-box') formerly carried by the museum figure mentioned above was a close-range weapon with a short barrel which sprayed out a load of large slugs when fired, but precisely the opposite of what a sharp-shooting light infantryman needed.

De Villiers makes it clear that the standard personal weapon was the long-barrelled flintlock musket, either of military issue or a civilian weapon which had been reconditioned in the VOC armouries. De Villiers confirms that a small number of blunderbusses were, in fact, issued, but possibly to officers or, as some have suggested, to guards and sentries.

The Pandoeren were not issued with bayonets, for very good reasons: fast reloading was difficult if not impossible with a fixed bayonet, and De Villiers remarks that 'because of the short stature of the Hottentot soldiers, bayonets on the long weapons were always more of a nuisance than an advantage for them.' This last would certainly have been a valid consideration, since the troops seem to have varied between 1.37m (about 4'8") and 1.61m (about 5'6") in height. Half a dozen officers were also issued with *boslemmers* – long knives with pointed blades, equally suitable for slashing and stabbing – that were worn in a sheath on the belt like a dirk, and another half dozen with French sabres, the latter more as a symbol of rank than anything else.

It would appear that the Pandoeren underwent considerable training, particularly in marksmanship, and had the necessary personal equipment for servicing their firearms: flints, ready-made paper cartridges and bar lead for casting bullets, powder horns and priming wires for clearing the muskets' touch-holes, and sailcloth for the making of bullet pouches.

The Pandoeren ate well, probably better than many of them did in civilian life. De Villiers says the authorities gave them regular supplies of food and a spirits ration, a common practice in most armies of the time, as well as a generous allowance of tobacco, to which they were apparently very partial.

By 1795, the Corps Pandoeren, though still small in numbers, had achieved the status of a fully-fledged combat unit. The corps had its own regimental colours, a fife, drum and bugle band, and, De Villiers says, it was 'fully slotted into the Cape's defence force. They were ready to defend the Cape in battle against a possible foreign aggressor.'

They were the right type of men for a light infantry regiment – hardy, often good marksmen and, like typical countrymen of the time, versed in tracking and other aspects of veldcraft; in a way they were the dismounted equivalent of the dragoons. They were well fed, well-trained, suitably equipped for their task and, it would appear, led by experienced officers and senior non-commissioned officers who spoke the same language and understood how to handle their men

This was certainly the case at Muizenberg. The commanding officer there was Captain Johan Gerhard Cloete, formerly a first lieutenant in the Stellenbosch Dragoons, and another officer was a former *wacht-meester* from the same company named Joël Daniël Herold, who was promoted to the brevet rank of cornet. De Villiers adds that 'two other burghers, the brothers Linde, would later be praised for the manner in which they led the Pandoere.'

On the eve of the final British advance on Cape Town in 1795 there was a bloodless minor mutiny in the ranks of the Pandoeren after Captain Cloete fell ill and was replaced by an officer of the Nationale Battaillon. The affair was soon resolved and they returned to the line. Nevertheless, De Villiers comments in another article, 'the Pandours were regarded by both Dutch and British eyewitnesses as good soldiers when commanded by efficient officers such as Jan Cloete and the Linde brothers. Although the Pandours did not play a major role in preventing the final British occupation of the Cape, they rendered valuable military service to the Dutch regime of the Colony.'

The unit's name is unique in South African military terminology. Pandoer was the Dutch spelling of *pandûr*, a name first given to a highly mobile, notoriously fierce body of infantrymen – 'a savage host', as De Villiers describes them – which was raised in Hungary in 1741 by one Baron Trenck from an enclave of Serbo-Croatians for the purpose of fighting the invading Turks. Later, as part of the Austro-Hungarian army, the unit fought against Prussia.

How the name surfaced at the Cape is a mystery. In his 1970 dissertation De Villiers notes that in certain parts of the Netherlands '*pan-doer*' had become a type of generic colloquial nickname for all foot soldiers (something like the British 'Tommy' of a century later), adding that 'it could have been [conferred by] one of the local officials or even the founders Nederburgh and Frijkenius themselves.' It is worth mentioning that for generations after the unit's disappearance following the first British occupation '*pandoer*' was the generic popular name for any coloured soldier of mixed race.

BATAVIAN UNIFORMS AT BLAAUWBERG

In some cases Dutch uniforms at the Cape differed from those of the continental Batavian army and, contrary to popular belief, the soldiers of yore usually did not go into battle dressed in the colourful but rather impractical formal uniforms which are almost always depicted in illustrations or films. Field uniforms did not carry much finery and tended to be simpler and more practical, particularly on occasions when European troops were serving in hot climates.

As a general rule the official uniform of a soldier of the Dutch continental line infantry at the time of Blaauwberg was a dark blue coat with collar, lapel facings and cuffs in a specific regimental colour or combination of colours; white belts and pouches; a white waistcoat; tight white breeches with black spatterdashes (leggings buttoned at the side and extending over the knee), and black buckled or laced shoes. Officers wore roughly the same colour of coat, but with long tails, and usually with riding breeches and boots because they tended to be mounted – a uniform usually tailored at private expense.

Headdress varied, but by 1806 officers had an elaborate side-to-side bicorne, a wide-brimmed black hat cocked up at back and front (senior officers wore fore-and-aft bicornes). Other ranks mostly wore the stovepipe-like peaked shako, fixed with a plain or brass-scaled chinstrap and hackles, cockades or other distinctions

All available evidence indicates, however, that the uniforms worn by the full-time Batavian forces at Blaauwberg differed considerably from what has generally been depicted. Two obvious reasons for this can be detected: Janssens could not depend on the home government for supplies of uniforms and footwear, and by that time the trend towards simpler, more comfortable hot-weather field uniforms had taken firm root in the British, French and Dutch armies because of their experiences in India, America, the Caribbean and the Far East. Among other things, soldiers now tended to wear looser-fitting long trousers over short calf-high spatterdashes.

One of the few accurate sources of information, apart from some paintings of uncertain provenance, is to be found in Dr FG de Wilde's exhaustively researched book *De uniformen van het Nederlandse Leger ten tijde van die Bataafse Republiek en het Koninkrijk Holland, 1795–1810* [The Uniforms of the Dutch Army at the Time of the Batavian Republic and the Kingdom of Holland 1795–1810].

According to De Wilde the rank and file of the 9th Bataafsche Jagers wore a black stovepipe shako with a tall dark-green plume or hackle on the left side; a dark blue short-skirted jacket with facings and plastron of dark green, white cotton patches and flat white metal buttons. Trousers were similarly dark blue, tucked into short black spatterdashes reaching to just under the calf of the leg.

The 22nd Batavia's other ranks, De Wilde says, wore much the same as their continental equivalents – a black shako with cockade, blue short-tailed coat with plastron and cuffs in red, a black cravat and a high white standing collar piped in red and a white waistcoat – but instead of breeches and thigh-high spatterdashes, had long white trousers tucked into black spatterdashes reaching to just below the calf. It can be assumed that the Waldeckers wore a similar uniform, but with yellow facings and plastron.

However, by 1806 the original issue of clothing would have been pretty well worn out, and in April 1804 the Political Council had authorised the purchase of 4 000 ells of coarse serge for trousers for the entire full-time garrison; 2 000 ells were bought locally, and quantities of blue and black cloth were obtained from the merchantman Minerva which had arrived at the Cape – providing 2 750 running metres of cloth for about 1 800 pairs of trousers. roughly enough to provide the 22nd Batavia, the Waldeckers and the Bataafsche Jagers with two pairs of dark blue or black trousers per man. If the issue was one pair per man, this would have been enough for the entire full-time garrison.

There is also an intriguing (though remote) possibility that at least some of the Batavian soldiers might have been wearing white linen trousers of material with thin blue or red vertical stripes, similar to ticking. This had become common in French uniforms, closely resembled by the Batavian in many ways.

The Hottentot Light Infantry's other ranks therefore would have sported a wide-brimmed black round hat, presumably with the right side cocked up, a hip-length blue jacket, blue or black trousers and high-sided *velskoen* ankle-boots of dark or reddish-brown leather. Yet another possibility is that the HLI went into the field clothed in the hard-wearing leather trousers of which the government had ordered 440 pairs in April 1804.

According to De Wilde, the 5th Dragoons' uniform closely resembled that of the British light dragoons: a 'Tarleton helmet' of shiny black leather with a black-and-white piebald fur 'roach' over the top and a red 'turban' around the lower edge of the helmet. With this was worn a short-tailed dark blue jacket with red collar and facings, a yellow waistcoat, half-boots and blue trousers.

To judge by contemporary illustrations, the last were probably what De Wilde calls 'riding trousers', or 'overalls' in British usage – that is to say, not breeches but fairly tight-fitting long trousers which were buttoned up the outside leg, reinforced with leather on the inside leg and worn over the boots. De Wilde's facts do not jibe completely with the Blaauwberg painting, which shows the 5th Dragoons wearing pale-coloured breeches and boots instead of blue 'riding trousers', but this might be merely artistic licence.

In this same painting the Batavian artillerymen are shown wearing dark blue, top and bottom, possibly with black spatterdashes. The French sailors were probably dressed according to the 1804 dress regulations – round black cockaded hats, blue jackets (although these might have been discarded because of the heat), black cravats, red waistcoats and navy blue or white linen trousers.

The uniform of the Javanese Artillery Corps is totally unknown, but presumably consisted of the same short blue jacket as that of the HLI, and possibly white linen trousers. What the gunners wore on their heads is also a matter for speculation – it might have been a turban or the 'toering', the pagoda-shaped woven hat of Malaysian origin which was popular around Cape Town (and was, in fact, an ideal hot-weather headdress), both of which were in wide use.

What the burgher light dragoons probably wore can be deduced from the few existing illustrations. In the Drostdy Museum in Swellendam is a portrait of Captain Jan Zacharias Moolman, one of the heroes of Blaauwberg (see Chapter 14). Moolman is wearing a short-tailed green jacket with a great deal of silver lace on the chest and collar, buff-coloured breeches and knee-high riding-boots. He has a tricolour waist sash and a curved light cavalry sabre, and on his head is the older style of light cavalry headdress, a low black topper with a fur roach over the top and a peculiar cockade on the left side.

This order of dress is obviously a parade uniform, but it is basically quite practical for the climate, although a plain laceless jacket was likely worn by other ranks – and probably by officers as well when in the field – his sword probably reinforced or perhaps replaced by a musket and pistols, carried on his mount in saddle holsters. If Jan Zacharias Moolman did, in fact, shoot Captain Andrew Foster out of his saddle, it could well have been with his musket.

The British infantry and marines wore much the same style of dress as they had in the 1795 invasion (see Chapter 8), chiefly red coats and white breeches, although their white trousers were later replaced by grey as the war with France dragged on. The Highlanders wore kilts or tartan trousers in varying circumstances – but whether they wore kilts in the Battle of Blaauwberg is a moot point, though not unlikely: the Scots kilt marked them out in the field easily, and their reputation was a fearsome weapon, contemporary illustrations to the contrary.

APPENDIX SIX

LATER CAREERS OF KEY FIGURES

GENERAL JAN WILLEM JANSSENS GCMWO
(1762–1838)

Upon his arrival in the Netherlands in June 1806 Janssens met his new king, Lodewijk, who asked him for a detailed report on what had happened at the Cape. Later that month Janssens delivered it, along with a letter in which, characteristically, he requested that his conduct there be thoroughly investigated, adding that he hoped the outcome would be of such a nature that he would be given further employment.

Evidently it was, because almost immediately he was made a councillor extraordinary and Secretary-General of the Ministry of War and the Navy. During the next five years he occupied several other high posts, culminating in his appointment as Director-General of War in December 1807, which he occupied until he was honourably retired at his own request in May 1809. However, in early 1811 Napoleon yanked him out of retirement to sort out the problems in the Dutch possessions in the Far East.

On arrival in Java Janssens found himself saddled with a chaotic state of affairs: a population which was deeply discontented, thanks to the unwise conduct of his immediate predecessors, and an army – mainly of local recruits – which was in a state of virtual mutiny. He was still trying to bring some order to this mess when the British invaded Java in early August, less than four months after his arrival.

Janssens did what he could, including launching an attempt to withdraw inland and negotiate, as he had done at the Cape, but this time he achieved little and was compelled to surrender on 17 September. He and his staff were sent to Britain as prisoners of war, and stayed there until November 1812 before being paroled to the Netherlands. On arrival he requested once again that his actions and conduct in Java be examined, this time by a court martial, but Napoleon replied that he had looked at the whole affair himself and found that Janssens' conduct had been completely justified.

Napoleon not only exonerated Janssens but made him a baron of the French Empire, and placed him in command of a division in Groningen and later another division in France. He occupied this post until April 1814, when he retired from the French army at his own request and returned to the Netherlands at the rank of lieutenant-general with the special task of reorganising the infantry and cavalry. In 1815 he was appointed Commissioner-General of War, but once more was retired at his own request.

He was then installed in the prestigious post of Chancellor of the Willemsorde (Military Order of William), a Dutch order of chivalry, and raised to the Dutch nobility. He spent the next 23 years in retirement and died in 1838 at the age of 76, having spent his entire working life serving honourably the government of the day, without fear or favour.

SIR HOME POPHAM, KCB (1762–1820)

Although Popham survived his court-martial after the Buenos Aires debacle almost unscathed, the verdict could still have left him high and dry, but any professional disgrace which might have clung to him was soon washed away by the need for his services. In 1807 he was made captain of the squadron sent to attack Copenhagen – perhaps, it is thought, because of his knowledge of the area gained during his previous service there in 1800.

He acquitted himself well, and in 1809 was given the warship HMS *Venerable* (a 74-gun ship of the line), which he commanded with success against the French during the Peninsular War, helping Spanish guerrillas in 1812 and 1813, and attacking French coastal fortresses in support of Wellington's advance. He was promoted rear-admiral in 1814, and admitted as a Knight Commander to the Order of the Bath the following year. He died in Cheltenham, in Gloucestershire, on 20 September 1820.

SIR DAVID BAIRD, BT, GCB (1757–1829)

After his involvement in the Buenos Aires attack, Baird was saved by a twist of politics. By the time he arrived back in England the post-Pitt Whig government had fallen again, and his old associate Lord Castlereagh was back as Minister of War. 'I confidently trust that His Majesty's present ministers will consider that I have not deserved the harsh and mortifying treatment I have experienced,' he wrote to Castlereagh, 'but that, as my degradation has been as public as unmerited, so ought it to be as publicly done away.'

Which it was. When the Copenhagen expedition was put together in 1807 he was given a division. As usual Baird was in the thick of the action and was wounded during the city's bombardment (carried out, among others, by his old friend-cum-nemesis, Home Popham). A little later he was sent out to the grim Peninsular War under another old acquaintance, Arthur Wellesley, then the Viscount Wellington.

Here he served as second-in-command to the renowned General Sir John Moore, regarded as one of the greatest Scottish soldiers of all time, and leader of the famed fighting withdrawal to the port of La Coruña. Baird took command when Moore was killed just outside the city in a heroic action, when he turned the army on the pursuing French and gave them a thorough mauling. But soon afterwards his left arm was shattered and amputated, and he was invalided home.

This time Baird was thanked by Parliament and made a Knight Grand Cross of the Order of the Bath. But his personal and political enemies did not cease to badger him, and he was never again given a field command. They triumphed once again in 1813 when the governorship of the Cape fell vacant with the departure of Sir John Cradock and Baird immediately applied for the position.

Although he was eminently qualified for the appointment it went to the arrogant and dictatorial Lord Charles Somerset, 'and the Cape got a governor,' Krynauw remarks, 'who would do incalculable damage to the name of the English in South Africa.'

But some honours still came to him. In 1814 he was belatedly promoted to full general, while in 1820 he became Governor of Kinsale, appointed Commander-in-Chief in Ireland and made a Privy Counsellor for Ireland. As he had at the Cape, Krynauw notes, 'he also earned the popularity of the (Irish) population.' But the command was soon reduced, and he resigned in 1822.

In 1829 he was recalled to take up the appointment of Governor of Fort George in India, but this last opportunity for service was denied him at the eleventh hour: soon after returning from a visit to London to thank the King for appointing him, Baird fell seriously ill and died.

CAPTAIN JACOB GLENN CUYLER

In a sense Captain Jacob Glenn Cuyler was also a 'child of the Company' – and this was why he landed at the Cape with Baird. He was born in the state of New York into an old Dutch family which stayed loyal to the British crown after the American War of Independence – and eventually joined the British Army. A fluent Dutch speaker, he was attached to Baird's staff for the invasion.

Cuyler never left South Africa again. Baird appointed him as landdrost of Uitenhage and Commandant of Fort Frederick at Algoa Bay. He fought as a major in the Fourth Frontier War of 1811–12, and in 1815 earned equal portions of fame and notoriety for his role in quashing the Slagter's Nek Rebellion and presiding over the execution of the surviving rebels.

In 1820, by now a colonel, he helped to place the 1820 Settlers on their new farms in a new district called Albany after his birthplace in upstate New York. He went on to serve in the Sixth Frontier War of 1835 and died at 78 at the rank of lieutenant-general.

MAJOR JOHN GRAHAM (1778–1821)

Scots-born John Graham became another of Baird's officers who settled in South Africa. After fighting at Blaauwberg he was appointed Commanding Officer of the Cape Corps, the new regiment which was to be raised from the bones of the Hottentot Light Infantry, and during the Fourth Frontier War of 1811–1812 he played a major role in the fight against Ndlambe in the Zuurveld.

After the war Graham, now the permanent military and civil commissioner for the area, founded Graham's Town and erected a number of small frontier forts. Later he saw service abroad while on overseas leave and in 1814 was promoted to full colonel; on his return to the Cape in 1815 he became Commandant of Simon's Town and served there until his death in 1821.

CHIEFS OF THE AMAXHOSA, NGQIKA AND NDLAMBE

Ndlambe did not achieve either of his two ambitions, and his feud with Ngqika was to last for another two decades. The enmity between the two chiefs escalated drastically in 1817, when the then Governor of the Cape, Lord Charles Somerset, recognised Ngqika as the paramount chief of the Ngqikas and made an agreement with him that in the event of livestock thefts the kraal to which the cattle's spoor led would be held responsible.

Blocked in his attempts to achieve his main ambitions – to become chief of the Ngqikas and then paramount chief of all the Xhosas – Ndlambe went on the warpath, and at the great Battle of Amalinde in 1818 he defeated Ngqika with the help of the Gcalekas under his ally, Chief Hintsa.

Somerset then took Ngqika under his protection, to which an enraged Ndlambe – on the advice of his sangoma (traditional tribal healer) and spiritual adviser, Makana – responded by invading the Cape Colony and attacking King William's Town, thereby igniting the Fifth Frontier War. The attack on King William's Town was beaten off, however, thanks mainly to superior British firepower (Makana reputedly assured the Xhosa warriors that he could turn the white men's bullets to water), and Ndlambe was decisively defeated.

He and his followers were then driven back across the Keiskamma River, after which Somerset proclaimed the area between the Keiskamma and the Fish River a *cordon sanitaire* in which neither whites nor blacks would be allowed to live (how well this was obeyed by either side is a matter of conjecture).

Thus ended Nlambe's involvement in affairs of state, as it were, and he died at Mount Coke in 1828, having reached the ripe old age of 80 in spite of more than three decades of warfare. His adviser Makana was less fortunate; imprisoned on Robben Island, he remained as defiant as ever and drowned while trying to escape in a makeshift boat.

Ngqika's fate was a more tranquil one. With Ndlambe pushed back beyond the Keiskamma, his paramount chieftainship was confirmed by Somerset and he established his capital along the Tyume River, where he too died in 1828 at the untimely age of 53. He was succeeded by his son Maqoma, acting as regent for Sandile. In due course Sandile, Hintsa's son Kreli (more correctly 'Sarili'), Maqoma and some of their other contemporaries became famous people in the Xhosa folk memory.

During the 'armed struggle' of the 1970s and 1980s some propagandists condemned Ngqika for being a collaborator with the whites. But little was said about the undeniable fact that Ndlambe was a usurper and, in pursuance of his personal ambitions, betrayed the trust of the tribal elders who appointed him as regent while Ngqika was growing to manhood; or that to get what he wanted did not hesitate to enlist the support of notorious white outlaws like Coenraad Buys against his fellow Xhosas.

NOTES

CHAPTER 1

1   In Dutch: Vereenigde Oost-Indische Compagnie, 'United East-India Company',
    founded 1602. Although not in its title, the VOC also habitually used the
    term 'Honourable' to refer to itself, as did the English 'Honourable East India
    Company'; old VOC documents are studded with the mark 'Ed. Comp', i.e. *Edele
    Compagnie* or 'Honourable Company'. In histories of the East Indies, however, the
    English company is usually referred to by the acronym 'HEIC' and the Dutch by
    'VOC'.

2   See Sleigh, Dan, *Die Buiteposte VOC-buiteposte onder Kaapse bestuur 1652–1795*
    ['VOC Outposts Under Cape Administration 1652–1795'], Pretoria: HAUM,
    1993.

3   See Grobbelaar, Paul, *Die Ontstaan van 'n Westerse Militêre Tradisie aan die Kaap
    tot 1795* ['The Origins of a Western Military Tradition at the Cape'], (unpublished
    MA thesis, University of Stellenbosch), 1993.

4   Gelfand, Dr Michael, & PW Laidler, *South Africa: Its Medical History*, Cape Town:
    C Struik, 1971.

5   Eng: William I, Prince of Orange, 'William the Silent'; Du.: Willem van Oranje,
    Willem de Zwijger, (1533–1584).

6   'Aelianus Tacticus', also 'Aelian', a Greek writer of Rome whose *Taktike Theoria*,

331

c.106 AD, became a blueprint for Renaissance infantry combat tactics, studied all over Europe and the Middle East, but perfected by the Dutch.

7   The Greeks and Romans made use of mounted troops as well, but cavalry did not begin to evolve into a major combat arm, as the world was later to know it, until the 6th century AD, when armies in Europe and the Middle East adopted a vitally important technological innovation: the solid-tree saddle with cantle and stirrups.

8   Also, more fully, Vereenigde Nederlantische Geoctroyeerde Oost-Indische Compagnie.

9   Also 'Maluka'.

10 Fluyt: Du, pr. 'flight'; a broad-beamed, heavy cargo ship of the 17th century.

11 The Harrison chronometer, used for accurate determination of longitude, was not available until the 1780s.

12 Table Bay was a dangerous harbour when the north-wester gales raged, and countless ships were driven ashore during the winter. Eventually VOC ships wintered in False Bay, men bringing cargo and stores over the rough mountain roads. Saldanha Bay possessed a much safer natural harbour, but it did not have enough fresh water, timber, or a large, free indigenous pastoral population with which to barter for livestock. In the end Cape Town's advantages outweighed its disadvantages.

13 Also Wollebrant Geleyns de Jongh, or Jonge (1594–1674).

14 Jan van Riebeeck (1619–1677), Dutch founding father of Cape Town, and thereby the nation of South Africa.

15 Geoctroyeerde Westindisches Compagnie, 'Chartered West Indian Company'; or 'GWC', founded 1621.

16 Founded 1600, known as the Honourable East India Company, later the 'HEIC', 'EIC', the 'Honourable Company or even 'John Company'.

17 La Compagne française des Indes orientales, formed in 1664 from the union of three other Indies companies covering Madagascar, China and India.

18 Boxer, CR, *The Dutch Seaborne Empire 1600–1800*, London: Pelican Books, 1973.

19 Gelfand, Dr Michael, & Laidler, PW, op cit.

CHAPTER 2

1   Elphick, Richard, *Khoikhoi and the Founding of White South Africa*, Johannesburg: Ravan Press, 1985.

2   The Mardijker people were the descendants of freed slaves, originally in Batavia
    (Jakarta). A remnant of the Portuguese penetration into the Far East, they were
    the mulatto descendants of soldiers or colonists who had opted to stay behind
    after the Dutch had taken over the spice islands. Their mother tongue was
    Portuguese; some were Muslims but the majority appear to have been Christians,
    many converting from Catholicism to the Protestant faith; given that the VOC
    later exempted free Muslims from compulsory military service because they were
    not Christians, Van Riebeeck's contingent was probably drawn from the former
    Catholic section. 'Mardijker' is also said to be a corrupted version of the word
    'merdeka', meaning 'freedom' and lingered on into the 19th century.

3   Sleigh, Dr Dan, *Die Buiteposte*, op cit.

4   Ibid.

5   Ibid.

6   Ibid.

7   Ibid.

8   Anglicised into 'snaphaunce' or 'snaphance'; a forerunner of the flintlock
    mechanism which was to become the standard for the next two hundred years.

9   Included in Bouch, Captain RJ, *Infantry in South Africa*, Pretoria: SADF
    Documentation Service, 1977.

10 Grobbelaar, Paul, op cit.

11 In later years 'commando' came to have such a renowned meaning that at the
    start of World War II Britain's Prime Minister Winston Churchill, a veteran of the
    Second Anglo-Boer War, personally conferred it on his newly established special
    raiding forces, because he considered them to have the same fighting ethos as the
    Boer commandos.

12 This would explain two rather puzzling aspects about these expeditions – their
    perilously small recorded size and their ability to track down the veld-wise raiders.
    There is indisputable evidence that the Cape clans shared a broad cultural
    identity but not a national one, and that therefore men of one clan did not
    hesitate to join forces with the VOC in acting against another. In addition, all were
    opposed to the 'wild' Bushmen – ie, the ones who had not become virtual serfs of
    the clans, and made free with any Khoina livestock they could lay their hands on.

CHAPTER 3

1 Heese, Hans, *Groep Sonder Grense* ['Group Without Borders'], Cape Town: Western Cape Institute for Historical Research, 1984.

2 Achmat Davids moots the possibility that some of the handful of servants Van Riebeeck brought along with him were Muslims, although he has no certainty about this. The 12 slaves present at the Cape in 1658 might well have been Muslims, and it is certain that from 1654 onwards the VOC began using the Cape as a place of exile for political prisoners from the Far East, with some free Muslim artisans and tradesmen also arriving from that time on. Quoted in Mahida, Ebrahim Mahomed, *A Muslim History of South Africa: A Chronology*, Dept of Islamic Studies: University of Durban-Westville, 1993.

3 Elphick, R, & Giliomee, H, (eds/contribs), *The Shaping of South African Society, 1652–1840*, Cape Town: Longman Ltd, 1985.

4 Hoge, JH, '*Personalia* of the Germans at the Cape', *Archives Year Book for South African History 1946*, Pretoria: 1946.

5 Heese, op cit.

6 Like the VOC, although the British HEIC was not directly involved in the slave trade, it doubtless traded with merchants who were.

7 Elphick, op cit.

8 Ibid.

9 Ibid.

10 Elphick R, and Malherbe VC, (contribs): *The Shaping of South African Society, 1652–1840*, Cape Town: Longman Ltd, 1985.

11 Laband, John, University of KwaZulu-Natal.

12 De Villiers, Johannes, 'Hottentot-regimente aan die Kaap' ['Hottentot Regiments of the Cape'], *Archives Year Book for South African History 1970*, Pretoria: 1970.

13 Taylor, Stephen, *The Caliban Shore – The Fate of the Grosvenor Castaways*, London: Faber & Faber, 2004.

14 Elphick R, and Malherbe VC, op cit.

15 Sheikh Yusuf, also known as Abadin Tadia Tjoessoep (1626–1699). Indonesian nobleman, warrior and holy man. Exiled to the Cape in 1693, where he was instrumental in putting the Islamic faith on a sound footing.

16 Worden, Nigel; Van Heyningen, Elizabeth; & Bickford-Smith, Vivian, *Cape Town – The Making of a City*, Cape Town: David Philip Publishers, 1998.

17 Any armed force has a 'tail' or support echelon to undertake the various skilled

and unskilled duties needed to keep the combat element in operational shape. Most male slaves were probably past the prime combat age by the time they were manumitted, but very valuable, however, for dealing with logistical, support, transport and construction tasks or as cobblers, leather-workers and carpenters.

18 Heese, op cit.

19 Ibid.

20 Ibid.

21 Ibid.

22 Biebouw and his companions were thrown in jail and flogged in public a month later. He then became a sailor, and in 1716 departed to Batavia, where he died in 1719, at the age of 29.

23 Giliomee, H, *The Afrikaners: Biography of a People*, Cape Town: Tafelberg Publishers, 2003.

CHAPTER 4

1 First Anglo-Dutch War, also known in England as the 'First Dutch War' 1652–1654, fought in the midst of England's revolutionary Commonwealth which was instituted by Oliver Cromwell after the English Civil War.

2 The origins of the word 'Kat' have caused some confusion and controversy. Well-known academic, Prof Jan Visagie, points out that the term 'kat' was coined in the Low Countries in the Middle Ages to describe one of two things: a type of siege engine designed for filling the moat of a besieged fortress or undermining its walls, preparatory to storming it – or 'an elevated firing position with battlements and firing apertures in a bastion or in the middle behind a curtain (wall) of a fortress to fire on attackers from above.'

3 '4-pounder' refers to the weight of the solid cast-iron round-shot or cannon ball fired by the gun eg, 6-pounder, 18-pounder, 24-pounder etc.

4 The German contribution to the Cape's military and civilian gene-pool during the VOC's time was much larger than most people realise; thousands of people from German-speaking areas either spent time at the Cape or put down roots there. *The Archives Year Book for South African History* for 1946 published a nominal roll compiled by JH Hoge which listed about 4 000 Germans, including those from Austro-Hungary, German-speaking Swiss cantons and Baltic states. Of these 'only a very limited number – about 100, as far as we have been able to

ascertain – left the Cape again.' By the mid-18th century 'nearly all the members of the garrison and the majority of the artisans, wagon-drivers and stable-boys of the Company were German.' Of the 422 rank and file serving in 1761 in the 'Nationale Battaillon', or National Battalion, the permanent garrison's infantry regiment, 'there were only 24 Dutchmen, and only one in the higher ranks ... In the (1780s) even the Governor's life guard consisted exclusively of Germans.' – Hoge, JH, '*Personalia* of the Germans at the Cape', *Archives Year Book for South African History 1946*, Pretoria: 1946.

5 Elphick, R, *Khoikhoi and the Founding of White South Africa*, op cit.

6 Mentzel, OF, *A Geographical and Topographical Description of the Cape of Good Hope*, Part 1, ed. H Mandelbrote, Cape Town: Van Riebeeck Society, 1921.

7 Governor Simon van der Stel can probably be regarded as the father of South African military bands. A great believer in pomp and ceremony, he expanded the number of bandsmen in the garrison and introduced the first hautboys; when he met an important personage he would be accompanied by drummers and trumpeters. See Imrie, Cdr John, *The Military Band in South Africa*, Pretoria: SADF Documentation Service, 1976.

8 The later Witwatersrand was not the Land of Ophir, however, but much further to its north of the Witwatersrand-to-be there *was* a genuine ancient gold field, and there *had* been a tribal king named Monomotapa in more recent times, both of which had excited learned men's expectations long before Van Riebeeck's arrival at the Cape and would continue to do so long after his departure. See Steenkamp, Willem: *Land of the Thirst King*, Cape Town: Howard Timmins, 1977.

9 Elphick R: *Khoikhoi and the Founding of White South Africa*, op cit.

10 Zacharias Wagenaer (also spelt Wagner, Wagener and Wagenaar), 1614–1668, Governor of the Cape 1662–1666. Saxony born, he was the only German ever to become Cape Governor.

11 From the Cape he and his family sailed first to Batavia and then to Malacca, where he was installed as governor on 24 October 1662. There he stayed till late 1665, when he suffered a double bereavement on the deaths of his wife, Maria de la Quellerie, and daughter Johanna within months of each other. Leaving Malacca for Batavia, he became Secretary to the Council of India, marrying Maria Scipio, widow of Admiral Jacob Gruys; he was bedridden for the last five months of his life, but stayed at his post until the day he finally died, on 18 January 1677 at the age of 58.

12 It was a consequence of this humiliation that the Royal Navy redesigned its ships,

retrained its crews, and built what was to become the deadliest navy on earth.

13 Sole Bay and Ostend (1672) and Kijkduin and the Texel (1673).

14 This was the last war between the English and the Dutch for more than a century. Charles II died in 1685 and was succeeded by the Duke of York, who was crowned James II. Being openly Catholic and overtly friendly with the King of France, he did not last long in predominantly (and fiercely) Protestant England. Overtures were made to the Netherlands, that other Protestant bastion, and in 1688 came the 'Glorious Revolution', when James's nephew-in-law, Prince William III of Orange, acceded to pleas that he become King of England as well.

15 Johan Bax van Herenthals served as Governor of the Cape 1676–1678.

16 Today the name 'Wapenpleyn' is almost forgotten, and the modern Grand Parade has shrunk to about half its original size, the victim of thoughtless – and heedless – urban sprawl and the encroachment of the railway lines; but it remains one of the early military's greatest legacies to future generations.

17 Simon van der Stel (1639–1712) was the last Commander and first Governor of the Cape of Good Hope (1679–1699). He retired at the Cape and died there. The town of Stellenbosch and the seaport of Simon's Town are named after him, as was a destroyer of the South African Navy in 1952.

18 Hendrik Adriaan van Reede tot Drakenstein (1636–1691), nobleman and colonial administrator in Dutch East Indies, served as Governor of Colombo 1670–1677.

19 When the first burgher infantry company was raised from volunteers among the scanty population of the *Caabse Vlek* in 1658 it had an orthodox structure identical to that of the regular garrison. The most basic structural principle – that the militia was not a mere appendage of the regular forces but a distinct component in its own right, commanded by its own officers, although under the ultimate authority of the full-time commander – endures to this day. But the true formalisation of the Burgher Militia can be dated to 1670, when Commissioner Mattheus van den Brouck wrote a report in which he called for its expansion, the appointment of proficient officers and four annual drill and skill-at-arms sessions at the fort. It took a while for the instruction to filter back to the Cape, but on 13 July 1672 the first 94 members of the Burgher Militia began their non-continuous training.

20 The term 'dragoon' was later to be applied to light cavalrymen, but in its original concept in the 17th and 18th centuries a dragoon was first and foremost a mounted infantryman, albeit one trained and equipped for conventional foot-warfare. Like the commando burgher, the dragoon was well-suited to local

conditions, and the classic type did not disappear from the Cape until the beginning of the 19th century.

21 'It can be accepted that the laid-down drill and musketry practice was definitely that of the drill-code used by the garrison.' Grobbelaar, Lt Col. Paul M, op cit.

22 Ibid.

23 Ibid.

24 The European dragoon of the time relied heavily on his pistols, a typical battlefield tactic being to swoop in, fire at close range and then withdraw to reload and repeat the process. The Cape dragoon, on the other hand, could also fight on foot and at longer range, thanks to his musket. Given his mobility, the rough terrain and his local knowledge and marksmanship, he would be a formidable opponent for any European-style soldier.

25 The Dutch Staatse Leger was the first modern state army of its kind in Europe, well organised, well equipped, drilled and disciplined. Its professional style was copied throughout the continent.

26 It should be noted that the Commando Force of modern times annually performed thousands of hours of part-time crime-prevention service in support of the police before finally being disbanded in 2003.

CHAPTER 5

1 Grobbelaar, op cit.

2 Grobbelaar, op cit.

3 De Vries, Cdr Gerry, & Hall, Jonathan, *The Muzzle-Loading Cannon of South Africa*, Cape Town: Cannon Research Projects, 2001.

4 Ibid.

5 Grobbelaar, op cit.

6 On the eve of the feast of Bartholomew the Apostle in 1572, six days after the marriage of King Charles IX's sister Margaret to the Protestant Henry III of Navarre (the future Henry IV of France) a series of assassinations and mob violence by Roman Catholics against Protestants started. Estimates of deaths vary from 5 000 to 30 000, and resulted in an exodus of many survivors to the Netherlands and other Protestant countries.

7 Mentzel, OF, op cit.

8 Gorgets were long obsolete even in the 18th century, except as badges of office.

They vanished almost entirely during the early 19th century, but their vestigial remnants are still in daily use in all Commonwealth armies: the red lapel patches worn by officers of the rank of colonel and above are elaborations of the buttons by which the gorgets were secured to the collar in their later days.

9   Mentzel, op cit.

10 Mentzel, op cit.

11 A Dutch musket of the 1720s had a 1.152m (47") barrel, in very large .75 calibre. Few VOC muskets survive, however, because almost the entire VOC arms inventory was removed to Britain at some stage and thereafter vanished completely. None of its items has ever appeared for sale anywhere.

12 In 1720, 212 pairs of hose arrived at the Cape, half of them blue, and half yellow. Historian Dr Dan Sleigh deduces that the yellow hose were issued to the grenadier company on a scale of two pairs per man, seeing that it was only enough to outfit one company and the grenadiers already had a distinctive uniform. Later, the Cape garrison received 8lb of blue camel hair, possibly for hackles or plumes for the officers or their horses, and then a large consignment of hose in a colour variously spelt 'ponse' and 'ponzon' – possibly a corruption of the French ponceaux, meaning poppy-coloured. The deduction from this is that from 1722 the grenadiers lost their distinctive yellow hose and all soldiers wore bright red. Along with the 'ponse' hose came 226 scarlet canvas capes that, as Sleigh puts it, 'gave the regiment its special dash of colour' when they paraded on a cold or wet winter's day.

13 Van Loon, Agnes, *Mannen met een missie naar Kaap de Goede Hoop/Men on a mission to the Cape of Good Hope*, Alphen a.d. Rijn: Canaletto/Repro-Holland, 2007.

14 One trick in naval gunnery was to fire when an enemy ship was heeling or listing away to leeward – her hull thus partly exposed, she could be hit below the waterline, the hole then submerged when she rocked back.

15 The shortcomings of the battery chain became evident when the British first invaded in 1795; instead of approaching the dread guns they approached overland. Thereafter, during the three short years of the Batavian Republic's sway the batteries held off any approach, but when the British came for the second time in 1806, once again they steered well clear of the batteries and came ashore on the other side of Table Bay. De Chavonnes would doubtless have rectified this chink in the Cape's armour, but clearly no one in the hierarchy was as far-sighted as the great man himself.

16 It is possible that this latter statement is not quite accurate, however. Any sailors who had served in the Dutch or VOC navies before arriving at the Cape would have been trained as gun-crews as a matter of course, and the sailors probably received some periodical training by way of the Burgher Militia.

17 Mentzel, op cit.

18 Hendrik Swellengrebel (1700–1763) was the first VOC governor to be born at the Cape. He held this office between 1739 and 1750, the town of Swellendam is named after him.

19 A drostdy was a magistracy, presided over by a landdrost who was also the head of civil administration. To this day, the Afrikaans equivalent of the title of 'magistrate' is *landdros*.

CHAPTER 6

1 Often referred to as the Fourth Anglo-Dutch War (1780–84), many historians believe it should not be part of this 'series' of conflicts from a century earlier, brought on as it was by entirely different pressures.

2 Boxer, CR: *The Dutch Seaborne Empire 1600–1800*, London: Pelican Books, 1973.

3 Tanap Research Project (online) 2010.

4 Knight, Ian, *Queen Victoria's Enemies (I): Southern Africa*, London: Osprey Publishing, 1989.

5 Also knobkerrie.

6 Marais, JS, *Standard Encyclopaedia of Southern Africa*, Cape Town: Nasou Limited, 1972.

7 Pieter, Baron van Reede van Outshoorn, Lord of Oudsthoorn Gnephoek, Ridderbuurt and Drakenburg (1714–1773), Governor of the Cape. He joined the VOC in 1741 and served at the Cape as a 'senior merchant' ie, a high official, and also as the 'fiscal', the rough equivalent of an attorney-general who reported directly to the Lords Seventeen, then as *secunde*, or second in charge. After a return to the Netherlands, he was appointed Governor of the Cape in 1772, but died at sea en route in January 1773.

8 In front marched the Burgher Militia, horse and foot, then three horse-drawn artillery pieces and the Castle garrison. Behind them were two trumpeters in heavy mourning and servants leading Van Oudtshoorn's charger and riding horse, men and animals draped in black. Officers carried his escutcheon, helmet, cuirass,

spurs and gauntlets, and his two swords, one sheathed and the other drawn and reversed. Twelve Company servants and minor officials bore his coffin, followed by four pallbearers and his official bodyguard. After his interment the horse gunners fired three salvoes, the Imhoff Battery and the ships in the bay replying. The musketeers fired three volleys; the Groote Kerk's bell and the Castle's minute-guns fell silent, and all flags were lowered in tribute.

9   One of several ancestors of the author involved in these commando actions.

10   Moodie, Donald, *The Record, or a series of official papers relative to the condition and treatment of the native tribes of South Africa*, Cape Town: AS Robertson, 1838.

11   Ibid.

12   Ibid.

13   Ibid.

14   Baron Joachim Ammena van Plettenberg (1739–1793) was acting Governor of the Cape from 1771, and then became substantive Governor in 1774. He served until 1785. The town of Plettenberg Bay was named after him in 1779.

15   Adriaan van Jaarsveld (1745–1801) was a frontiersman who moved to the Bruintjieshoogte area in 1776. He was a renowned field commander and rebelled both against the VOC and the British after the 1795 invasion. Arrested by the British in 1799, he died in captivity in 1801.

16   Charles Johannes Marais (1738–1782). Field-cornet for Beaufort West and later farmed in the Camdeboo district (Graaff-Reinet area).

17   Amiral le Comte Pierre André de Suffren de Saint Tropez, bailli de Suffren (1729–1788), was a renowned, much-decorated French naval officer who fought successfully in many pitched sea battles against the British, particularly in the Indian Ocean. A first-class tactician, he held that in overseas wars the first priority was to disable the enemy's fleet.

18   Commodore George Johnstone RN (1730–1787) saw service in the War of the Austrian Succession, the Seven Years' War and the American War of Independence, rising to the rank of post-captain. At various times he was also a member of Parliament, a director of the East India Company and first Governor of West Florida (1763–1767).

19   Privateers were officially sanctioned pirates used by most nations, permitted to seize enemy goods on behalf of their government, and were a vital adjunct to naval operations.

20   It was remarkable that Johnstone did not press matters – Jervis, Duckworth, Nelson or Sydney Smith would almost certainly have taken the offensive.

Johnstone's conduct hereafter became the matter of a long and bitter court martial.

21 For a full description see Couzens, Tim, *Battles of South Africa*, Cape Town: David Philip Publishers, 2004.

22 Grobbelaar, op cit.

23 Picard, Hymen WJ, *Masters of the Castle*, Cape Town: C Struik Ltd, 1972.

24 Robert Jacob Gordon (1743–1795) was a Scottish-descended Dutch soldier, explorer, naturalist and linguist. He undertook six long journeys of exploration and diplomacy north and east of Cape Town, going as far afield as the Orange River and the eastern frontier and introduced Merino sheep to the Cape. He spoke fluent French, Dutch and English, and reportedly some Khoina and Xhosa as well.

25 The re-naming is a key to Gordon's loyalties, which were to play such a significant role in his actions during the 1795 invasion. He was pro-British in principle, but he was first and foremost a staunch supporter of the House of Orange. This was ultimately to bring him to an untimely end.

26 Colonel Cornelis van de Graaff (?–1812), Governor of the Cape from 1784 to 1791. In 1794 he was appointed Major-General in the Dutch military engineers, but after the overthrow of the Prince of Orange in 1795 he fled to Germany, where he remained until his death.

27 Picard, Hymen WJ, *Masters of the Castle*, op cit.

28 Louis-Michel Thibault (1750–1815), a trained French architect, cartographer and surveyor, came to Cape Town with the Swiss mercenary unit, the *Régiment De Mueron*, but in 1785 transferred to the Dutch East India Company. Thereafter he performed various tasks under the VOC, British and Batavian administrations, both as a soldier and a civilian. His remaining buildings and survey work are regarded as national treasures.

29 The Vlaggemanskloof batteries which guarded Cape Town's back door have not vanished altogether. Two 18-pounders are still emplaced on the seaward verge of the road which descends to Camps Bay from today's Kloof Nek, and in front of the forestry station on the slopes of Table Mountain on the other side of the road is another gun, approximately where the second battery's 18-pounders once grinned a warning to intruders.

30 More than two centuries later, the Zoutman Battery built by Governor van de Graaff is almost forgotten by all except history enthusiasts, but it survives and is still an active installation. Now known as the Lower North Battery, it is part of

the South African Navy's gunnery school and is said to be one of the oldest gun batteries in continuous service anywhere in the world.

31 It was a constant danger and often happened when their chambers became too seriously eroded or an undetected casting fault succumbed to the pressure generated by the exploding gunpowder.

32 Further improvements to both the coastal defences and the Cape garrison were to go on right up to the first British invasion of 1795, when precisely this scenario took place.

33 Grobbelaar, op cit.

34 See *The Standard Encyclopaedia of Southern Africa*, op cit.

35 The Württembergers' sojourn at the Cape had introduced another concept to the South African military, that of the consciously elite infantry unit whose carefully selected officers and men could set a standard in discipline, drill and fighting efficiency by which all regiments could be measured and to which they were expected to aspire.

CHAPTER 7

1 Advocate Sebastian Cornelius Nederburgh (1762–1811) joined the VOC as a lawyer in 1787. He was later posted to Batavia and in 1791 was appointed Governor-General. Later he played a leading role in the formulation of the Charter of 1801, also known as 'Nederburgh's Charter', which laid down Dutch colonial policy after the government took over the VOC.

2 Captain Simon Hendrik Frijkenius (?–1797). Captain in the VOC's navy, died at Batavia.

3 Tanap Research Project (online) 2010.

4 With the proclamation of the revolutionary Batavian Republic, the four members of the 'Hollands-Zeeuwse Staatscommissie' representing the province of Holland were replaced by regents drawn from the ranks of the Patriotten. On 1 March 1796, the Lords Seventeen were forced to resign, in favour of a 'Comité tot Zaken van de Oost-Indische Handel en Bezittingen' (Committee for East Indian Trade and Possessions). The VOC continued to exist and its charter was renewed, first to the end of 1798 and then to 31 December 1800 but it was a shadow of its former self; there were widespread employee lay-offs and premises were dismantled and eventually the Dutch flag flew only over Java and the outposts

at Canton in China and Deshima in Japan. By 1803, bankrupt and crippled, the VOC's debts and possessions were taken over by the States-General and two centuries of history went on to the scrap-heap. In its place was born the Dutch East Indian Empire. But in 1811 the British also took Java, the heart of the once-omnipotent Company's business. It had once been the greatest commercial venture in the history of the world.

5 Honoratus Christiaan David Maynier (1760–c.1831).

6 Moritz Hermann Otto Woeke (1743–1815). Appointed first landdrost of Graaff-Reinet in 1785, chose the site for the drostdy offices and established his court there in 1786.

7 Heemraad: A member of a rural district council, appointed to assist the landdrost.

8 Second Frontier War: 1789–93.

9 27 August 1791, when Austria's Leopold II threatened vague action in concert with other European nations should any harm come to Louis XVI or his queen, Marie Antoinette.

10 The French force consisted of veterans of pre-Revolution days, particularly the artillery, its use in this battle later renowned for its incomparable accuracy and efficiency.

11 Consisting of several phases, it became known as the Great French War, 1792–1815, ending with the Battle of Waterloo.

12 Willem Ferdinand, Baron van Reede van Outshoorn, Lord of Oudsthoorn, Gnephoek, Ridderbuurt and Drakenburg, son of Baron Pieter (1755–1822), member of the Council of Policy and commander of the Pennisten Corps during the 1795 invasion. He was the only council member who wanted to fight on, and afterwards refused to take the oath of allegiance to the British crown.

13 Coenraad Buys or De Buys (1761?–1823?), frontiersman, farmer, rebel outlaw, cattle rustler and freebooter. Reputedly seven feet tall, very intelligent and enormously strong, he was a sometime adviser to Ngqika of the Xhosas and fathered a large number of children by Xhosa women, the 'Buysvolk', who were later granted their own tract of land by President Paul Kruger.

14 Formerly Napoleone di Buonaparte, of Italian blood, b. Ajaccio, Corsica, 1765, d. St Helena, 1821. A Francophile, he changed his name to Napoléon Bonaparte, rose in the officer ranks of the French Revolutionary Army, and conquered Italy, the Rhineland, Malta, Egypt and the Holy Land by the age of 29. He was later formally styled Napoléon I, Emperor of the French, King of Italy, and Protector of the Confederation of the Rhine.

15 Commissioner Abraham Josias Sluysken (1736–1799), last VOC ruler of the Cape (served 1793–1795). He took service in the VOC in 1765 and became Governor of Surat before returning to the Netherlands in 1793, only to be intercepted at the Cape and made acting governor.

16 Potgieter, Cdr TD, *The First British Occupation of the Cape*, Cape Town: Castle Military Museum, 1997.

17 Ibid.

18 The Nationale Battaillon, 'National Battalion' was the standing garrison of the Cape, c.1795) consisting of regular infantry and artillery.

19 Eng 'sepoy', Fr '*sipoy*' – from the Persian '*siparhi*', for 'soldier', a term applied by the East India Companies to native troops from India.

20 The *rijksdaalder* or 'national dollar' was a unit of currency in coins of various denominations, first issued by the United Netherlands government in the late 16th century during the revolt against Spanish occupation.

21 General Jean-Charles Pichegru (1761–1804). In later years he became a royalist supporter and was found dead in prison – either murdered or dead by his own hand – after being arrested for leading a failed attempt to restore the monarchy in 1803.

22 The French Revolutionary Army promoted men through combat experience, thus a sergeant could theoretically rise to senior officer rank, though this was undoubtedly rare. This occasionally created senior officers who had insufficient command experience of large numbers of men on a battlefield.

23 Friedrich Carl David Gerotz (?–1836).

24 Horse Guards' Parade, off Whitehall in London, known often as simply 'Horse Guards', was the headquarters of the British Army in the 18th and 19th centuries and is still the office of the GOC London District.

25 Henry Dundas (1742–1811), first Viscount Melville and Baron Dunira. Scottish lawyer and politician, later involved in political scandal.

26 Pogieter op cit, quoting CJ de Villiers: *Die Britse Vloot aan die Kaap 1795–1803*.

27 Sir Frances Baring (Chairman of British HEIC) to Dundas. 12 January 1795.

28 Letter to Dundas from his Under-Secretary, 25 February 1795.

29 Some observers believe the British exerted pressure on the prince to take the action he did, but evidence to that effect is scanty. It is interesting to note, though, that it would seem the VOC administration at Batavia had little regard for the Prince of Orange's letter; if one can judge by Potgieter's reference to HF Nel, in is book *Die Britse Verowering van die Kaap in 1795/The British Conquest of the Cape*

in 1795, that when Captain Dekker brought the *Medenblik* frigate into Batavia on 9 August 1795 after Elphinstone had allowed him to leave False Bay, he 'handed the letter of the Prince of Orange to the authorities there, but they did not regard a letter from a renegade prince as of any value.'

30 Sir John Jervis, 1735–1823, later the 1st Earl St Vincent after his victory against a Franco-Spanish invasion fleet at the Battle of Cape St Vincent in 1797 – in which Horatio Nelson famously disobeyed orders and cut off the enemy line of battle, boarding several ships in quick succession.

31 Admiral George Keith Elphinstone, first Viscount Keith (1746–1823).

32 Major-General (later Sir) James Henry Craig (1748–1812). Also see footnote 10, Chapter 9.

33 The 78th Highland Regiment of Foot, also named the Seaforth Highlanders.

34 Major-General (later Sir) Alured Clarke (1745–1832) fought in the American War of Independence and later became Lieutenant-Governor of Jamaica and was promoted major-general while serving in Canada in 1791. He left for India with Admiral Elphinstone after the VOC capitulation, and became commander-in-chief of the British forces in Bengal.

35 Potgieter, op cit.

36 Ibid.

37 Ibid.

38 Mackenzie to Craig (no date). See GM Theal, *Records of the Cape Colony.*

39 Gordon to Elphinstone 14 June 1795. See GM Theal, *Records of the Cape Colony.*

40 Potgieter op cit.

41 Ibid.

42 Ibid.

43 Ibid.

44 Ibid.

CHAPTER 8

1 This was one of the causes of Johnstone's defeat at Porto Praya by De Suffren, and De Brueys' defeat at the Battle of the Nile: a significant portion of their fleet crews were ashore revictualling when the enemy descended upon them.

2 The Kijk-in-de-Pot ('Look in the Pot') Battery was built in 1795 – just before the British invasion – at the personal insistence of Colonel Robert Jacob Gordon;

its whimsical name, deriving from the blubber-pots of the whaling station at today's Granger Bay directly in front of it, is thought to have been bestowed on it by Gordon himself. After 1795 it was kept in service by the British until the Cape's hand-over to the Batavian government in 1803. It was dismantled in 1827, but it was too well-situated to be disposed of, and the military authorities retained the site. The little battery lay derelict and gunless until the early 1860s, when apprehensions about the American Civil War brought about the decision to resurrect it. Under the supervision of military engineers, 100 hard-labour convicts from the nearby Breakwater Prison turned the old earth ramparts into a substantial stone construction, armed with massive 68-pounder guns and named after Lieutenant-General RH Wynyard, commander of Cape forces and Lieutenant-Governor of the Cape Colony. Fort Wynyard guarded the approaches to Table Bay through two world wars and various smaller conflicts. Later it became a coast artillery museum under the aegis of the South African Navy, and today it is the headquarters of the Cape Garrison Artillery, once a coast artillery regiment but now an anti-aircraft unit.

3   Located about 3 000 km (1 945 miles) north-west of Cape Town, the island of St Helena was remote and small, measuring only about 128km^2, but was strategically important as a replenishment-point for ships sailing to and from Europe from Asia and Africa. It was particularly important for the British at that time, since they had no foothold anywhere along the southern African coast.

4   Potgieter, op cit.

5   Ibid.

6   Bar and chain-shot was used to dismast a ship, one of the few ways to disable a vessel of those days, short of sinking it. See De Vries & Hall, op cit.

7   PW Marnitz (1751–1821). He later wrote a book about his experiences entitled *Verhaal van de Oorgawe van de Kaap de Goede Hoop aan de Engelschen* ['The Story of the Surrender of the Cape of Good Hope to the English'].

8   It is worth noting that in 1795 there was a somewhat similar state of confusion when the British made a disastrous landing on the Brittany coast in support of exiled French royalists who were involved in the counter-revolutionary movement in the Vendée region.

9   Details vary, some saying the barrage lasted some thirty minutes, and in that time some 800 rounds were fired.

10 Percival's eyewitness report *An Account of the Cape of Good Hope*, quoted by Potgieter from HF Nel, *Die Britse Verowering van die Kaap in 1795*, in the *Archives*

Year Book for South African History, 1965, Pretoria: 1955.

11 To some later historians there is an eerie resemblance to the Battle of Blaauwberg during the second British invasion in 1806, when the Batavian mercenaries also fled and the field was held for a considerable time by Dutch horse gunners, the burgher dragoons, the *Hottentotsche Lichte Infanterie* – the successors to the *Pandoeren* – and a handful of Malay light artillerymen. The difference between the two battles is that, in the latter, the Batavian resistance was not rotten at the top.

12 Potgieter, op cit.

13 Quoted by Patrick Cullinan in *Robert Jacob Gordon, 1743–1795*, Cape Town: C Struik 1992.

14 Potgieter, op cit.

15 Oberholster, quoting C J Barnard's *Robert Jacob Gordon se Loopbaan aan die Kaap/ Robert Jacob Gordon's Career at the Cape*, op cit.

16 Potgieter, op cit, quoting HF Nel.

17 Ibid, quoting Cullinan.

18 Ibid.

19 Sluysken returned to the Netherlands a pathetic figure who had ended his long and faithful service to the Company as, in the words of Johan de Villiers, 'a victim of circumstances for which he could not be blamed.' *Archives Year Book for South African History, 1970*, Part II. Pretoria: 1970.

20 Today's Union Jack, minus the red Irish cross of St Patrick.

21 Louis-Michel Thibault stayed on at the Cape and became the foremost early architect of Cape Town, leaving a legacy of beautiful buildings of which many endure to this day.

22 Admiral Elphinstone went on to play a prominent role in the suppression of the Royal Navy's mutiny at the Nore in 1797, and later served in important posts in the Atlantic and Mediterranean, negotiating the surrender of the French in Egypt in 1801. He was created a baron in 1797 and a viscount in 1814, taking the title Lord Keith.

23 However, the VOC's original charter provided for the Company's army and navy to be embodied in the national forces in time of emergency, and the Netherlands had always been under the ultimate control of its parliament, not the Prince of Orange. It cannot be denied that on 28 June 1795 the American ship *Columbia* had arrived with a newspaper which contained a notice that the States-General had absolved all Dutch subjects of their allegiance to the House of Orange. Therefore, Elphinstone and Craig with their letter from the Prince of Orange, had

officially become belligerents instead of allies, and Gordon knew it.

24 Lieutenant-Colonel CMW de Lille turned his coat with indecent haste and promptly took service with the British as a barrack-master, but his later career is veiled in well-deserved obscurity. Possibly he stayed on at the Cape, since he was a long-time resident (he had arrived from the VOC's Bengal garrison in 1771) and his name survives there to the present day.

25 Potgieter, op cit.

CHAPTER 9

1 Giliomee, Hermann, *Die Kaap Tydens die Eerste Britse Bewind 1795–1803* ['The Cape During the First British Occupation'], Cape Town: HAUM, 1975.

2 Ibid.

3 The Martello Tower is still a fixture in England, where they dot the southeast coast, built specifically to withstand Napoleonic invasion.

4 Lieutenant (later Captain) John Campbell. Succeeded by Major (later Lieutenant-Colonel) Fielder King.

5 Did Craig's Cape Corps soldiers go bare-footed? This is another oft-repeated assertion based on only one painting depicting two off-duty Cape Corps soldiers in full uniform but *sans* any sort of footwear. Much as with the *Corps Pandoeren*, in this author's opinion it is a fallacy – 18th-century military paintings were not always accurate, and this might well have been a bit of artistic licence to emphasise that these were 'native' soldiers. In the opinion of De Villiers, they made their own *velskoene* for footwear. It is comforting, therefore, to see that the large depiction of a Cape Corps soldier in the Castle Military Museum in Cape Town shows him wearing boots and calf-high spatterdashes.

6 The Rev John Barrow (1764–1848), later a baronet, was a traveller, amateur botanist, geographer and cartographer who first came to the Cape as Lord Macartney's private secretary and became deeply embroiled in the turbulence on the eastern frontier. In 1804 Lord Melville made him Second Secretary of the Admiralty, and he stayed in this post for almost 40 years.

7 Giliomee H, op cit.

8 Ibid.

9 Craig went on to higher office after his work securing the Cape. On his return to England in 1797 General Craig was created a Knight of the Bath and posted

to India, where he remained until 1802. In 1805 he commanded a division of the British Army in Italy, but after a year was invalided home through ill-health. In 1807, however, he was made Governor-General of Canada, which post he occupied until 1811.

10 Giliomee H, op cit.

11 Ibid.

12 Ibid.

13 Ibid.

14 Ibid.

15 Jan Pieter van Woyer was Graaff-Reinet's district medical officer in early 1796. A fiery republican, he stirred up the Dutch inhabitants against the British with a number of wild untruths, among other things that Craig had no more than 800 soldiers, that he (Van Woyer) had more than 900 pounds of gunpowder and intended to drive the British from the Cape with the cooperation of the Xhosas. Craig's offered reward was merely a token gesture. A hundred *rijksdaalders* was an inconsiderable sum, even for those days, and in any case (as Craig quite likely knew perfectly well) Van Woyer was long gone; he had travelled to Algoa Bay during the mid-year period and taken passage to Batavia, the old VOC head office, which was now the Dutch Government's Far Eastern headquarters.

16 Giliomee H, op cit.

17 George Macartney, first Earl Macartney KB (1737–1806) and Governor of the Cape 1796–1798. Irish-born of Scottish descent, he was a leading statesman and diplomat of his time who played an important role in the expansion of British imperial holdings and apparently coined the phrase that Britain had acquired 'a vast Empire, on which the sun never sets'. Raised to the peerage in 1795, he resigned prematurely as Governor of the Cape due to ill-health.

18 Giliomee H, op cit.

19 Ibid.

20 Ibid. Lady Anne Barnard (1750–1825), née Anne Lindsay, eldest daughter of James Lindsay, 5th Earl of Balcarres was born at Balcarres House, Fife, Scotland. A beautiful and talented artist and travel writer, she spent five years at the Cape (1797–1802) as the wife of the Colonial Secretary, Andrew Barnard. During this time she went to great effort to promote reconciliation, and produced paintings and sketches which are still regarded, along with her writings, as primary sources of information about the Cape in the early years. She also wrote the lyrics to the well-known Scottish ballad 'Auld Robin Grey'. Several places are still named after

including the Lady Anne Barnard ballroom at the Castle of Good Hope.

21 Giliomee, op cit.

22 Ibid.

23 Ibid.

CHAPTER 10

1   Battle of the Nile, 1–2 August 1798. Admiral Horatio Nelson (1758–1805) fell upon the French battle-fleet in Aboukir Bay, near Alexandria. The French were arrayed in line in the shallows of the bay, but the British ships passed between them and the shoreline, while others held back, to pin the French in a point-blank crossfire. One of the Royal navy's greatest victories, only three French ships escaped destruction or capture, owing to a wind change.

2   This was the first major defeat of French land forces and resulted in the capture of over 25 000 men. Not only this but the French occupation had rediscovered the antiquities of ancient Egypt, making extensive records which served as a blueprint for later archaeological expeditions.

3   The republic was on shaky legs, and considered almost a vassal state by the French – to the extent that a French General, Pierre Augereau, had become premier of the nation after a rigged election which amounted virtually to a coup.

4   Pitt (1759–1806) knew the war with France was coming and taxed Britain to its utmost to pay for her vast ship-building programme.

5   Erasmus, Lourens J, *Die Tweede Britse Verowering van die Kaap, 1806* ['The Second British Conquest of the Cape, 1806'] (unpublished MA thesis, University of Potcheftroom), 1972.

6   See article re Janssens in Vol. 6 of the *Standard Encyclopaedia of Southern Africa*.

7   See article re De Mist in Vol. 3 of Ibid.

8   Krynauw, DW, *Beslissing by Blouberg – Triomf en Tragedie van die Stryd om die Kaap,* ['*Decision at Blouberg: The Triumph and Tragedy of the Battle for the Cape*'], Cape Town: Tafelberg-Uitgewers Beperk, 1999.

9   Rutger Jan Schimmelpenninck (1761–1825, Lord of Nyenhuis, Peckedam and Gellicum, statesman, jurist, ambassador and leader of the Patriot Party. During his rule (1805–1806) he introduced wide-ranging fiscal and educational reforms.

10 Erasmus, op cit.

11 See article re De Mist in Vol. 3 of SESA, op cit.

12 See article re Batavian regime in Vol. 2, ibid.

13 It was Bonaparte himself who first freed slaves and wrote slavery out of a constitution during his occupation of Malta in 1798. When emperor however, he later reinstituted it in the West Indies.

14 Mahida, Ebrahim Mahomed: *A History of Muslims in South Africa: A Chronology*, Department of Islamic Studies, University of Durban-Westville, 1993.

15 Jean-Jacques Rousseau (1712–1778), writer, composer and political philosopher, who influenced the French Revolution and the Romantic movement through his works such as *Emile, Julie* and others.

16 At that time there were three types of farm occupation: freehold, with a registered title and deed; quitrent or '*huurpacht*', which involved 15-year renewable leases of government land; and '*leeningsplaatse*' (loan farms), which stock farmers could lease for grazing livestock for six or 12 months at a time. Later, under British rule, the second was changed to 'perpetual quitrent', in terms of which a farm could become freehold after the rent had been capitalised for 20 years.

17 After the destruction of Tipu Sultan and the Marathas in 1799, Britain was set to become the only major commercial power in India in the vacuum left by the collapsing Mughal Empire.

18 Willem Bartholomé Eduard Paravicini di Capelli (1778–1848). Dutch soldier, traveller and diarist. Ended his military career as a major-general and artillery chief of staff, a Knight of the Legion of Honour and a Knight of the Netherlands Lion.

19 Dirk Gijsbert van Reenen (1754–1828) wealthy and widely-read businessman, farmer, brewer and horse- and sheep-breeder, who travelled extensively in southern Africa and was General Janssens' confidant and adviser. Great-grandfather of President W F W Reitz of the Republic of the Orange Free State.

20 Van Reenen, Dirk Gijsbert: *Die Joernaal van Dirk Gysbert van Reenen, 1803* ['The Diary of Dirk Gysbert van Reenen'], (ed. W Blommaert & J A Wiid), Cape Town: Van Riebeeck Society, 1937.

21 De Kock, WJ. Article 'Janssens, Jan Willem', *Standard Encyclopaedia of Southern Africa*, Vol. 6, Cape Town: NASOU Ltd, 1972.

22 Much as the British rifle regiments like the 95th and 60th carried special weapons, such as the equally famous Baker rifle.

23 Waldeck-Pyrmont was an ancient sovereign principality which later became part of the German Empire and, in 1929, a constituent state of the Weimar Republic. Its former territories are now part of present-day Hesse and Lower Saxony,

but its flag became the flag first of the Weimar Republic and then the Federal Republic of Germany.

24 There is some confusion as to this officer's identity. Krynauw names him as a Colonel Wilmowsky, whereas a Janssens biographer, Geert van Uythoven, says that the Waldeckers' commander until the end of 1802 was Colonel Gerhard Heinrich von Heldring, who was then replaced in January 1803 by Lieutenant-Colonel C Muller.

25 As it happened, a lack of fitness was not a major factor at the later Battle of Blaauwberg, so much as a fell combination of ferocious heat, lack of water, rough terrain and the absence of draught animals for the guns and wagons.

26 Robert Thomas Wilson, (1777–1849), soldier, spy, statesman, also known for his meticulous histories, including the *History of the British Expedition to Egypt*. Although most sources cite him at several points as commanding the 19th Light Dragoons, Krynauw quotes a copy of General Baird's instructions, which puts Wilson not with the 19th, but the 20th Light Dragoons; Lourens Erasmus quotes Wilson's own account of the invasion which corroborates this.

27 Erasmus, op cit.

CHAPTER 11

1 Krynauw, op cit.

2 Ibid.

3 Ibid.

4 Probably as a long-term result of the second smallpox epidemic in 1755, that had brought about further devastation to the remnants of the indigenous population

5 Better known today as Genadendal – the 'Vale of Mercy'. The missionaries approached Janssens in 1805 to change the name, and his approval was one of his last acts as Governor of the Cape.

6 Theal, GM, *History of South Africa 1795–1834*, London: Swann, Schonnenstein & Co, 1891.

7 Theal, ibid.

8 Ibid.

9 Ibid.

10 Ibid.

11 Ibid.

12 Ibid.

13 Ibid.

14 Ibid.

15 Ibid.

16 Van der Kemp outlived the Batavian Republic and spent all the years remaining to him after De Mist's visit happily pursuing his eccentric lifestyle, a considerable part of which was devoted to shocking the frontier farmers (eg, by marrying the 17-year-old daughter of a Madagascan slave) and irritating them by making allegations about their conduct. Nor did he change his way of running Bethelsdorp, indolent and lawless as it was. But in 1811 the governor recalled him to Cape Town, where he died that same year at the age of 64 – presumably without regretting anything he had done at Graaff-Reinet.

17 Theal, op cit.

18 In September 1803 alone the unit was provided with 3 248lb of bread and 4 942lb of mutton. In October 50 sheepskins were provided for the manufacture of *karosses,* or traditional skin-blankets, as well as the hides of two oxen for making *velskoene.* Later in the year another contractor supplied 100 leather bags, while the Waldeck regimental tailors made up 30 jackets and 60 pairs of long trousers.

19 Captains E August Egger, seconded from the Regiment Waldeck; Stephan Hendriks, an officer from the former Corps Vrije Hottentotten; Hubrecht Verschuuren, seconded from the Bataafsche Jagers; and Christiaan Eckhardt, seconded from the 22nd Batavia.

20 In February 1804 a local tailor named J Betram made items of clothing and also quarters flags. In April the Political Council authorised the purchase of 4 000 ells of coarse serge for trousers for the entire garrison, including the corps. Two thousand ells were bought locally and also quantities of blue and black cloth which had arrived at the Cape on the merchantman Minerva. In September 1804, administrator Deel informed Janssens that there were still about 3 400 ells of Flemish linen and *ravendoek* (a black material) in the government warehouses, and he intended to use it all to make two pairs of trousers for each soldier in the regiment. Later that year the tailor Betram was ordered to make 440 pairs of leather trousers for the corps, while another free burgher made leather ammunition pouches and yet another supplied 1 600 tanned sheep-skins for use as *karosses* as well as eight ox-hides, presumably for making shoes and other articles.

21 Erasmus, Lourens J, op cit.

22 There is a belief in some circles that there were actually two units called the

Javaansche Artillerie Corps, one commanded by Madlener and the other by Frans van Bengalen. This is a misunderstanding: Madlener was the unit's executive head, while Frans van Bengalen, as chaplain, was the spiritual leader. It appears that Van Bengalen, who was born somewhere along the eastern coastal belt of India, left the Cape for Batavia in 1811.

23 Krynauw, op cit.

24 Mahioda, Ebrahim Mahomed, op cit.

25 Another important milestone was reached in 1805, when the Cape local authority made a grant of land at the top of Longmarket Street, opposite a site where the Malay community had long been in the habit of burying its dead, for use as a cemetery. The Tana Baru, as it is called, is now full and disused, but it was the first official Muslim burial-ground in South Africa. and remains a place of enormous significance to adherents of Islam.

26 Erasmus, op cit.

27 Krynauw, op cit.

28 De Villiers, op cit.

29 During the War of the Second Coalition, a combined Anglo-Russian force under Prince Frederick, Duke of Albany, invaded the Netherlands in late August 1799 with the intention of neutralising the Batavian war-fleet and instigating a pro-Orange insurrection. After initial successes, the invaders suffered several defeats at the hands of a Franco-Dutch force, owing principally to supply problems, culminating with the Battle of Castricum. Frederick carried out a strategic retreat to the original landing place, and negotiated an agreement which allowed his force to evacuate unmolested on 19 November 1799.

30 Administrator Deel decided in September 1804 to use the government stocks of Flemish linen and black *ravendoek* cloth to make two pairs of trousers for each soldier in the regiment. Later that year he also ordered 440 pairs of leather trousers.

CHAPTER 12

1 Spain had been an ally of France since 1796, her war with Britain ending with the Treaty of Amiens in 1802. However, hostilities between the two resumed in 1804 and lasted until the French invasion of Spain in 1808, when Spain allied with Portugal and Britain.

2 In the habit of the French Revolutionary Army, invasion armies were named for the territories they were massed to conquer: Army of Italy, Army of the East, etc.

3 Admiral Charles Middleton, 1st Baron Barham PC (1726–1813) was a British naval officer and politician. As a vice-admiral he was made a Lord of the Admiralty in 1794 and in 1805 First Lord, in the rank of full admiral.

4 Napoleon did not trust his navy to fight, and hated being aboard ship, as he was usually seasick.

5 Pierre-Charles Jean-Baptist Silvestre de Villeneuve (1763–1806).

6 Honoré Joseph Antoine Ganteaume (1755–1818): Ganteaume had been ordered to rescue and reinforce Napoleon's men in Egypt before 1801, but had shilly-shallied to such an extent that the French wrote an insulting limerick about his timidity.

7 Zacharie Jacques Théodore Allemand (1762–1828). By the time Allemand returned to Rochefort on 23 December with his 'invisible squadron', so-called because of its elusiveness, he had captured no less than 43 merchantmen as well as the 50-gun warship HMS *Calcutta*, at no loss to himself, and had significantly disrupted British naval activities.

8 Turner, LCF, *The Cape of Good Hope and the Anglo-French conflict 1797–1806*, quoted by Krynauw, op cit.

9 Erasmus, op cit.

10 Letter from SE Hudson to John Greene (Cape Archives).

11 Home Riggs Popham (1762–1820): Royal Navy officer and politician. A fighting seaman and specialist in surveying and signals, he was promoted rear-admiral in 1814 and knighted in 1815. His signal-flag system was used by Lord Nelson to send his famous message at Trafalgar: 'England expects that every man will do his duty.'

12 Krynauw, op cit.

13 Some sources call her the *Républicain*, claiming she was renamed in 1797.

14 Sir David Baird (1757–1829): veteran commander of East India Company troops, and one of the victors over the French in Egypt in 1801.

15 He does not elaborate, but it is known that Dundas tended to be autocratic, and the British Army was still adapting itself – albeit with much reluctance on the part of some of its more diehard members – to recent drastic revisions to the drill-manual.

16 Son of Haidar Ali, Tipu Sultan was known as the 'Tiger of Mysore', and one of the few Indian rulers to inflict serious defeats upon British East India Company

forces. An ally of the French, and the key to their Egypt campaign, he was known in Paris affectionately as '*Citoyen Tipou*': 'Citizen Tipu'.

17 Hook, TE, *The Life of General sir David Baird*, Vol. 2, quoted by Krynauw, op cit.

18 Colvin, Ian D, *The Romance of Empire – South Africa*, London: Thomas Nelson & Sons, 1909.

19 Krynauw notes that when he visited Angra Pequena on the coast of what is now Namibia in 1786 he laid eyes on the 'padrao' or stone cross, erected there by Batholomeu Dias in 1486, not long before it was destroyed by persons unknown.

20 Wilson became one of Britain's finest and most resourceful cavalry field commanders, later leading a troop in Spain, harrying the French in guerrilla fashion, regardless of odds.

21 Numbers vary according to source.

22 This plan was so successful that Popham arrived at the Cape with all but a few score of his men fit to fight.

23 Nelson used a brilliantly unorthodox tactic known since as 'crossing the T', and split the Franco-Spanish line of battle.

24 Villeneuve did not long survive his defeat at Trafalgar. He was taken back to England, but was then released on parole and soon after repatriated to France. There he tried to resume his career, but the disgrace of Trafalgar (not to mention Napoleon's ire) was too great. On 22 April 1807 he was found dead in his hotel at Rennes with six stab-wounds in the chest. An inquest court brought in the improbable verdict of suicide, and the suspicion still remains that he was murdered, possibly by French government agents.

25 Theal, op cit.

26 Wilberforce, S, *Journals and letters of the Rev Henry Martyn*, London 1811, quoted by Krynauw, op cit.

27 This would facilitate the landing of troops and equipment, and give the men-o'-war the maximum opportunity for providing covering and harassing fire to support the landing parties.

28 'Losperd's Bay' was only one of several versions of the name given to the place where the British eventually landed. Since spelling in those days was not the precise science it is now, the bay became variously known as Loubsersbaai, Laubschersbaai, Lospersbaai and Losperdsbaai.

29 Popham's letter-book, see Library of Parliament, Cape Town, and Cape Archives; quoted by Krynauw, op cit.

30 Ironically, the Royal Navy's chief third-rate ship of the line was the '74', (74 guns)

also a French design, which became the mainstay of many world navies.

31 His specific rank was '*capitaine de frégate*', or frigate captain.

32 The negative reply came too late. By the time the Batavian Government's reply reached its destination the Cape was already in British hands.

33 Le Contre-Amiral Jean-Baptiste Philibert Willaumez (1763–1845) was a French sailor who saw considerable action during the Napoleonic Wars.

34 Anonymous article in the *Cape Times* newspaper's 1905 Christmas edition, entitled 'A hundred years ago: The capture of the Cape'. Quoted by Krynauw, op cit.

CHAPTER 13

1 Krynauw, DW, op cit.

2 These ships were later scuttled.

3 Krynauw, quoting Fernyhough, T, *Military memoirs of four brothers engaged in the service of their country*, London 1838.

4 Janssens' six 1-pounder guns are something of a mystery. Ordnance expert Gerry de Vries does not believe that they were the JAC *lantakas*, because it is believed there were only four *lantakas*, not six, and they were not one-pounders but of slightly smaller calibre. It is possible that the 1-pounders were *ad hoc* conversions, consisting of small signal guns or close-range ships' defensive weapons which had been temporarily mounted on field carriages.

5 Janssens' decision to detach part of the JAC's garrison gunners to serve as field artillery is the likeliest source for the long-held but erroneous belief that there were actually two JACs, one commanded by Madlener and the other by Van Bengale. We should assume that Madlener led the detached gunners, leaving Van Bengale, a man of great standing, to take general command of the remainder, under the operational control of the garrison commander.

6 There were many more men of Linde's stamp among the burgher dragoons – Marthinus Wilhelmus Theunissen, for example, who led a group of burghers from the Hottentots Holland mountains, was a veteran of peace interventions at Swellendam and Graaff-Reinet, and had served in the frontier wars.

7 The Blaauwberg (lit. 'Blue Mountain') is made up of three interlinked features: Grootberg ('Great Mountain') to the north, consisting of two large, relatively high *kopjes*, or hills, divided by a high *nek*, with a much lower one to the north-east,

separated from the others by a lower nek. South of Grootberg is Kleinberg ('Little Mountain'), which is much lower and blunter at its summit, and east of Kleinberg is a large open plain which was then covered in fynbos, or indigenous heathland.

8   Losperd's Bay was part of a modest farm called De Melkbosch, owned by one Christiaan Pieter Brand, one of its outbuildings being a *visschuur*, or 'fish barn', which probably doubled as a boathouse, since Brand had two small boats as well as a cutter for whale-catching called the *Nederland-Africa*, which was actually anchored in the bay.

9   See Sir Home Popham's Letter Book.

10 Letter to a friend.

11 According to Krynauw they were accompanied by members of 'the Cape Malay Corps', but this sounds unlikely, since the Javanese Artillery Corps's members were trained as gunners and in any case were not mounted – hardly the sort of soldiers likely to be sent out on a scouting task of this kind.

12 Line regiments in the British Army were usually accompanied by a 'light company' of skirmishing riflemen, derived from within their own ranks or more often seconded from the much larger crack sharpshooter rifle regiments(eg, 95th and 60th Rifles).

13 Letter to a friend.

14 Fernyhough, T, *Military memoirs of four brothers engaged in the service of their country*, London, 1838.

15 Erasmus, Lourens J, op cit.

16 Ibid.

17 Krynauw, DW, op cit.

18 Ibid.

19 Ibid.

20 Brand's petition to Baird, 5 February 1806.

21 Mostert's petition to Baird, 4 April 1806.

22 Munnik's petition to Baird, 24 April 1806.

23 Krynauw, DW, op cit.

24 Wilson, RT, *The Conquest of the Cape Colony in 1806*, London, 1806.

25 Ibid.

CHAPTER 14

1   There is a panoramic painting in the William Fehr Collection – reproduced many times because it seems to be the only actual depiction of the battle – illustrating both Janssens' problem and his solution. The painting shows the Batavians drawn up in only a single wide rank (making relay volley-firing by rank impossible) against the advancing British regiments on the slopes opposite in customary, and overwhelming, massed ranks. The painting seems to be accurate, showing how thinly Janssens had to stretch his forces.

2   The Bataafsche Jagers were on foot, of course, but they were light infantrymen who were trained and equipped to march and manoeuvre at much greater speed and be much more tactically flexible than the average fusilier, or line infantryman.

3   Atkinson, CT, *Supplementary report on the manuscripts of Robert Graham Esq of Fintry*, London 1940.

4   Erasmus, Lourens J, op cit.

5   Hildgard, HGT, *Historical record of the 72nd Highlanders*, Edinburgh, 1886. Alas, the Batavians were much less well-found for artillery than this.

6   The available literature on Blaauwberg is not very informative about the type of artillery ammunition used. At that stage of the battle the guns would have been firing solid round-shot, and, certainly in the case of the howitzers, what the British called 'common shell', a fused hollow round-shot containing a bursting charge (the advantage of common shell was that it had approximately the same range as round-shot, greater than the older grape-shot. This was confirmed when a fragment of a shell was found near Kleinberg, its location indicating it had been fired by a Batavian gun. We also know, from Baird's own testimony, that when the range closed the Batavian field guns switched to firing grape-shot, which sprayed clouds of small-calibre balls but could not be used at much more than musket range. In the opinion of cannon expert Commander Gerry de Vries it is unlikely that Baird's field pieces fired grape-shot, which was essentially a close-range defensive ammunition. It would have been in his interest to limit his ammunition types. For the Batavians with their 13 ammunition wagons and plentiful supply of horses this would not have been a problem.

7   Erasmus, Lourens J, op cit.

8   Wilberforce, S, *Journals and letters of the Rev. Henry Martyn*, London, 1837.

9   There is an apocryphal tale of this withdrawal which makes amusing reading. 'When the Swellendammers had to fall back in the dunes before the English,' LL

Tomlinson wrote in 1942 in *Geskiedkundige Swellendam*, '[Linde] ordered his men to ride back to front, with their back to the horse's head so that they were better able to fire at the enemy; and then the flintlocks' bullets, six to the pound, made it hot for the English.' Most horsemen and dragoon historians deny this tale, though it is a tenacious one, and persists to this day.

10 Tomlinson, LL, *Geskiedkundige Swellendam*, Cape Town: Nasionale Pers Bpk, 1945.

11 The actual extent of those casualties remains a matter of conjecture. The official British figure for Kleinberg states that one officer (Captain Andrew Foster) was killed and 15 of his men were killed or wounded, but testimony of at least one sober eyewitness – Major John Graham's – implies that the 24th suffered much more substantial losses (see appendices).

12 To modern eyes this might seem like a suicidal tactic, but it had been well-tested during the fighting in America. There the British had discovered that one or two volleys, followed by a bayonet charge, might bring early casualties but was more economical overall than a long exchange of musket-fire.

13 Wilberforce, S, op cit.

14 Erasmus, Lourens J, op cit.

15 Ibid.

16 Baird's report to Castlereagh, 12 January 1806 in Theal, GM, *History of South Africa 1795–1834*, op cit.

17 Wilson describes the classic big-battlefield cavalry tactic, used long before the days of Alexander.

18 The Political Council wasted no time in doing this, and by the time the British arrived in Cape Town the title deeds had been drawn up and duly registered.

19 See appendices for further details of inaccurate casualty figures.

20 Baird to Castlereagh, 12 January 1806 in Theal, GM, op cit.

21 Krynauw, DW, op cit.

22 Smith, C, 'The Biography of the late Captain Dugald Carmichael', *The Edinburgh New Philosophical Journal*, 1831.

23 Wilson, RT, *The Conquest of the Cape Colony in 1806* in H Randolph, *The Life of Sir Ronert Wilson*, London: 1862

24 Hildgard HGT, op cit.

25 Lt Ronald Campbell's description of this Highland reel has amused many students of the Battle of Blaauwberg. Alas, neither his facts nor his spelling are quite right. '*Cabar Feidh*' ('The Antlers of the Deer') was actually the regimental

motto, the quick step being 'Blue Bonnets Over the Border'. Not that the Sassenach English of the 59th, who were so amazed by this exotic display, would have known the difference.

26 Ibid.

27 As earlier in the text, this older spelling has since given way to 'Tygerberg'.

28 There is a story that when renowned Swellendammer dragoon Jan Zacharias Moolman saw Captain Andrew Foster leading the 24th Regiment's flank companies in the attack on Kleinberg, he not only promptly shot Foster out of his saddle but 'liberated' his horse, a fine pedigree charger. This story appears true, as there are later references to its being used as a stud stallion at Swellendam.

29 Wilson, RT, *The Conquest of the Cape Colony in 1806*, op cit.

30 Ibid.

31 Ibid.

CHAPTER 15

1 Wilson, RT, *Conquest of the Cape Colony*, op cit.

2 Ibid.

3 Local inhabitants' possessions had fared less well at Saldanha Bay, where foraging parties sent to nearby farms had indulged in systematic looting and destruction of property. They swooped first on JC Stofberg's nearby farm (today's Stofbergfontein) on the Saldanha Bay peninsula. Stofberg had taken his livestock with him as per Janssens' orders, but everything else in and around the house was intact when Beresford's troops arrived. When he returned later, however, all of his furniture was gone, together with his paintings and porcelain, and everything on the farmstead outside had been destroyed, including his fishing-nets and 100 chickens. It had been, he wrote later, 'totally plundered, robbed and finally reduced to a desert, so that presently I find myself with my wife and nine innocent children in the most lamentable state.' Janssens later interceded with Baird on Stofberg's behalf. At Dirk Slabber's farm Oostewal, near what is now Langebaan, the stable was burnt to the ground, and more than 4 000 sheaves of rye and oats were removed, as well as all his ropes and fishing-nets, leaving him destitute.

4 The 'Treaty Tree' under whose shade the Cape was surrendered still exists today in a side street off Albert Road, Woodstock, although its bronze commemorative plaque has been missing long since. The 'Treaty Cottage' is gone, however, torn

down in 1935 to make way for a factory, and the site no longer has a view of the sea, since land reclamation has barred it from the ocean with a wide strip of railway lines and buildings.

5   Colvin, Ian D, op cit. Strangely, however, the heroes of Blaauwberg and their great sacrifice against insuperable odds have been almost forgotten. No memorial perpetuates their deeds, no annual church parade reminds Capetonians of their bravery, and no-one now even knows where their dead are buried.

6   The terms of the provisional treaty were as follows:

- All hostilities to cease upon signing the agreement.
- The Castle and other fortifications must immediately be handed over.
- The Batavian troops were to march out, lay down their arms and become prisoners of war, although officers were to retain their personal weapons.
- Officers who were inhabitants of the colony, were married to local residents, or possessed enough land to be good inhabitants could remain. All other soldiers would be transported to the Netherlands at British expense.
- French troops were to be treated as the rest of the garrison, but all non-combatant French citizens were to leave the colony.
- Burghers who had taken part in the fighting were free to return to their farms or places of work.
- Private property was to be respected, but all government property was to be handed in immediately.
- The burghers were to retain all their rights and privileges, including that of religious practice.
- No-one was to be forced to undertake service with the British.
- The inhabitants of Cape Town were to be exempted from the quartering of soldiers in their houses.
- Paper money was to remain in circulation until the British Government decided otherwise.
- All other matters which might subsequently arise would be referred to the future colonial government.

7   Erasmus, Lourens J, op cit.

8   Alas, Janssens' plea for the Cape's inhabitants did not long survive Baird's departure. Insensitive and often arrogant treatment by some later British administrators, or their blatant disregard for the provisions of the treaty, resulted in unnecessary ill-feeling whose after-effects plague South Africa to this day.

9   Krynauw, DW, op cit.

10 Baird, as Erasmus says, 'must have heaved a sigh of relief when the Dutch were finally gone from the Cape', because the food situation had now become so critical that he had had to send more ships to Madras for rice and wheat.

11 Colvin, Ian D, op cit.

12 Jérôme-Napoléon Bonaparte (1784–1860) was the Emperor's youngest brother. He served in the French Navy, but was made ruler of the short-lived Kingdom of Westphalia (1807–1813). He briefly commanded an army corps in Napoleon's invasion of Russia and in 1813 unsuccessfully attempted to defend his kingdom. During the 'Hundred Days' he commanded a French division at Waterloo. After his nephew Louis Napoléon became President of the French Republic in 1848 (and later Emperor Napoléon III) he served in several official roles, being made a Marshal of France and President of the Senate.

13 Theal, GM, op cit.

14 Cobbet's Parliamentary Debates.

15 Krynauw, DW, op cit.

16 Perhaps unfairly, William Prince of Orange (later William II of the Netherlands) was considered one of the least intelligent men among his peers and known to many as 'Silly Billy'. The Dutch-Belgian troops he led at Waterloo, however, were some of the finest who took the field.

BIBLIOGRAPHY

SELECTION OF SOURCES CONSULTED

Ascoli, David, *A Companion to the British Army 1660–1983*, London: Harrap Limited, 1983.

Archives Year Book for South African History, 1965, Pretoria: Government Printer, 1965.

Atkinson CT, *Supplementary report on the manuscripts of Robert Graham Esq of Funtry*, London, 1940.

Barnard, CJ, 'Robert Jacob Gordon se loopbaan aan die Kaap' ['Robert Jacob Gordon's Career at the Cape'], *Archives Year Book for South African History, 1950*, Pretoria: Government Printer, 1950.

Barrow, J, *An Account of Travels Into the Interior of Southern Africa in the Years 1797 and 1798*, (2 vols), London: 1801–1804.

Becker, Dr Peter, *Path of Blood*, London: Longmans, Green and Co., 1962.

— *Rule of Fear*, London: Longmans, Green and Co., 1964.

Binns, CT, *The Last Zulu King*, London: Longmans, Green and Co., 1963.

Böeseken: AJ, *Die Nuusbode*, Cape Town: NASOU Ltd, 1966.

Bouch, Captain RJ, *Infantry in South Africa*, Pretoria: SADF Documentation Service, 1977.

Boxer, CR, *The Dutch Seaborne Empire 1600–1800, London: Pelican Books, 1973.*

Burrows, Edmund H, *Overberg Outspan: A Chronicle of People and Places in the South-Western Districts of the Cape*, Cape Town: Maskew Miller Ltd, 1952.

Changuion, Prof L, & Moolman, Janette, *So Much To Do – The Moolman Group of Companies: Their First 40 Years.*

Chant, Christopher, *Handbook of British Regiments,* London: Routledge, 1988.

Chartrand, R, & Back, F, *Napoleon's Sea Soldiers,* London: Osprey Publishing, 1990.

Colvin, Ian D, *The Romance of Empire – South Africa,* London: Thomas Nelson & Sons Ltd, 1909.

Cory, George E, *The Rise of South Africa,* Vol. 2, London: 1908.

Couzens, Tim, *Battles of South Africa,* Cape Town: David Philip Publishers, 2004.

Cullinan, Patrick, *Robert Jacob Gordon,* Cape Town: Struik, 1992.

De Kock, WJ. Article 'Janssens, Jan Willem', *Standard Encyclopaedia of Southern Africa,* Vol. 6, Cape Town: NASOIU Ltd, 1972.

De Villiers, Johannes, 'Hottentot-regimente aan die Kaap', *Archives Year Book for South African History, 1970,* Pretoria: Government Printers, 1970.

—'Die Britse Vloot aan die Kaap 1795–1803' ['The British Fleet at the Cape 1795–1803'], (unpublished MA thesis), University of Cape Town, 1967.

De Vries, Cdr Gerry, & Hall, Jonathan, *The Muzzle-Loading Cannon of South Africa,* Cape Town: Cannon Research Projects, 2001.

De Wilde, Dr FG, *De uniformen van het Nederlandse leger ten tijde van de Bataafse Republiek en het Koningrijk Holland 1795–1810,* ['The Uniforms of the Dutch Army at the Time of the Batavian Republic and the Kingdom of Holland'], Amsterdam: De Bataafsche Leeu, 1999.

Downs, Jonathan, *Discovery at Rosetta,* London: Constable, 2008.

Elphick, Richard, *Khoikhoi and the Founding of White South Africa,* Johannesburg: Ravan Press, 1985.

— & Giliomee, H, (eds/contribs), *The Shaping of South African Society, 1652–1840,* Cape Town: Longman Ltd, 1985.

Erasmus, Lourens J, 'Die Tweede Britse Verowering van die Kaap, 1806' ['The Second British Conquest of the Cape 1806'], (unpublished MA thesis, University of Potcheftroom), 1972.

Featherstone, D, *Weapons and Equipment of the Victorian Soldier,* Poole, UK:

Blandford Press, 1978.

Fernyhough, T, *Military memoirs of four brothers engaged in the service of their country*, London, 1838.

Gelfand, Dr Michael, & Laidler, PW, *South Africa: Its Medical History*, Cape Town: C Struik, 1971.

Gerard, Raoul, *Military Formations at the Cape, 1652–1806*, Pretoria: Raoul Gerard, 1953.

Giliomee, Hermann, *Die Kaap Tydens die Eerste Britse Bewind 1795–1803*, Cape Town: HAUM, 1975.

— *The Afrikaner: Biography of a People*, Cape Town: Tafelberg Publishers, 2003.

Grobbelaar, Lt Col, Dr Paul M, *Die Ontstaan van 'n Westerse Militêre Tradisie aan die Kaap tot 1795* ['The Origins of a Western Military Tradition at the Cape Until 1795'], (unpublished MA thesis), University of Stellenbosch, 1993.

Heese, Hans, *Groep Sonder Grense* ['Group Without Borders'], Cape Town: Western Cape Institute for Historical Research, 1984.

Hildgard, HGT, *Historical record of the 72nd Highlanders*, Edinburgh, 1886.

Hoge, JH, *Archives Year Book for South African History, 1946*, Pretoria: Government Printer, 1946.

Hook, Theodore Edward, *The Life of the Right Honourable Sir David Baird, Bart* (2 vols), London, 1832.

Imrie, Cdr John, *The Military Band in South Africa*, Pretoria: SADF Documentation Service, 1976.

Journal of the South African Military History Society (various issues).

Knight, Ian, *Queen Victoria's Enemies (I): Southern Africa*, London: Osprey Publishing, 1989.

— *Zulu 1816–1906*, London: Osprey Publishing, 1995.

Krynauw, DW, *Beslissing by Blouberg – Triomf en Tragedie van die Stryd om die Kaap* ['Decision at Blouberg: The Triumph and Tragedy of the Battle for the Cape'], Cape Town: Tafelberg-Uitgewers Beperk, 1999.

Lategan, Dr Felix, *Die Boer se Roer*, Cape Town: Tafelberg-Uitgewers Beperk, 1974.

Le Vaillant. F, *New Travels Into the Interior Parts of Africa, By Way of the Cape of Good Hope, in the Years 1783, '84 and '85* (3 vols), London, 1796.

Lichtenstein, H, *Travels in Southern Africa in the Years 1803–1806*, trans. Anne

Plumptre, (2 vols), Cape Town: Van Riebeeck Society, 1928–1930.

Mahida, Ebrahim Mahomed, *A Muslim History of South Africa: A Chronology,* Department of Islamic Studies, University of Durban-Westville, 1993.

Malherbe, Wilma, 'Die Eerste Theunissen van Vergelegen' (letter to author), 2005.

Mentzel, OF, *A Geographical and Topographical Description of the Cape of Good Hope,* Part 1, ed. HJ Mandelbrote, Cape Town: Van Riebeeck Society, 1921.

Nel, HF, 'Die Britse Verowering van die Kaap in 1795' ['The British Conquest of the Cape in 1795'], *Archives Year Book for South African History 1965,* Pretoria, 1965.

Oberholster, JJ, *Archives Year Book for South African History 1950,* Pretoria, 1950.

Paton, Col. George, (editor-in-chief), *Historical Records of the 24th Regiment, from its formation in 1689,* London: Simpkin, Hamilton, Kent & Co., 1892.

Penn, Nigel, *Rogues, Rebels and Runaways – Eighteenth-Century Cape Characters,* Cape Town: David Philip Publishers, 1999.

Paravicini di Capelli, WBE, *Reize in de Binnenlanden van Zuid-Afrika* ['Journey in the Interior of South Africa'], Cape Town: Van Riebeeck Society, 1965.

Picard, Hymen WJ, *Masters of the Castle,* Cape Town: C Struik Ltd, 1972.

Potgieter, Cdr TD, *The First British Occupation of the Cape,* Cape Town: Castle Military Museum, 1997.

Reid, S, & Hook, R, *The British Redcoat 1740–1793,* London: Osprey Publishing, 1996.

— & Turner, G, *The British Redcoat 1793–1815,* London: Osprey Publishing, 1997.

Sargent J: *Het lewen van den eerwaarden Henry Martyn, zendeling in Indië* (translated from the English, '*The Life of the Reverend Henry Martyn, Missionary to India'),* Amsterdam: G Jaspers, 1861.

Scholtz, Dr Leopold, *Beroemde Suid-Afrikaanse Krygsmanne* ['Famous South African Warriors'], Cape Town: Rubicom-Pers, 1984.

Schulten, Dr CM, & Smits, FJH Th., *Grenadiers en Jagers in Nederland* ['Grenadiers and Jagers in the Netherlands'], The Hague/'s-Gravenhage: Staatsuitgewerij, 1980.

Seemann, UA, *Fortifications of the Cape Peninsula 1647–1829,* Cape Town: Castle Military Museum, 1997.

Sleigh, Dr Dan, *Die Buiteposte: VOC-buiteposte onder Kaapse bestuur 1652–1795* ['The Outposts: VOC Outposts under Cape Administration 1652–1795'], Pretoria: HAUM, 1993.

Smith, C: 'The Biography of the late Captain Dugald Carmichael', *The Edinburgh New Philosophical Journal,* 1831.

South African Military History Society Journal, (various issues).

Standard Encyclopaedia of Southern Africa (various volumes), Johannesburg: NASOU, 1972.

Steenkamp, Willem, *Two Architects of SA's armies: King Shaka of the Zulus and Prince Maurice of Orange,* unpublished lecture to SA Military Academy, 2003.

— *Poor Man's Bioscope,* Cape Town: Howard Timmins, 1978.

— *Land of the Thirst King,* Cape Town: Howard Timmins, 1977.

Strutt, Daphne J, *Fashion in South Africa 1652–1900,* Cape Town: AA Balkema, 1975.

Tanap Research Project, online: www.tanap.net, 2010.

Taylor, Stephen, *The Caliban Shore – The Fate of the Grosvenor Castaways,* London: Faber & Faber, 2004.

Theal, George McCall, *History of South Africa 1795–1834,* London: Swann, Schonnenstein & Co., 1891.

— *Records of the Cape Colony.*

Tomlinson, LL, *Geskiedkundige Swellendam,* ['Historical Swellendam'], Cape Town: Nasionale Pers Bpk, 1945.

Tribe, Dr Geoffrey, Various published articles.

Tylden, Maj. G, *The Armed Forces of South Africa,* Johannesburg: Africana Museum, Frank Connock Publication, 1954.

Van Loon, Agnes, *Mannen met een missie naar Kaap de Goede Hoop/Men on a mission to the Cape of Good Hope,* Alphen a.d. Rijn: Canaletto/Repro-Holland, 2007.

Van der Merwe, Dr PJ, *Pioniers van die Dorsland* ['Pioneers of the Drylands'], Cape Town: Nasionale Pers Bpk, 1947.

Van Reenen, Dirk Gijsbert, 'Die Joernaal van Dirk Gysbert van Reenen 1803' ['The Diary of Dirk Gysbert van Reenen 1803'], eds W Blommaert & JA Wiid, Van Riebeeck Society, Cape Town 1937.

Van Uythoven, Geert, *The Batavian Army at the Cape of Good Hope (South Africa) in 1805* (online).

Van Wiechen, Pieter, *Vademecum van de Oost- en West-Indische Compagnie* ['Guide to the East- and West-India Company'], Utrecht: Antiquariaat Gert van Bestebreurtje, 2002.

Von Pivka, O, & Warner, C, *Dutch-Belgian Troops of the Napoleonic Wars*, London: Osprey Publishing, 2005.

Wilberforce, S, *Journals and letters of the Rev. Henry Martyn*, London 1837.

Wilson, RT, *The Conquest of the Cape Colony in 1806*, London, 1806.

Worden, Nigel, Van Heyningen, Elizabeth, & Bickford-Smith, Vivian, *Cape Town – The Making of a City*, Cape Town: David Philip Publishers, 1998.

INDEX